Student Study Guide
to accompany

Life-Span Development
sixth edition

John W. Santrock
University of Texas at Dallas

Blaine Peden
University of Wisconsin–Eau Claire

Allen Keniston
University of Wisconsin–Eau Claire

Brown & Benchmark
PUBLISHERS

Madison, WI   Dubuque   Guilford, CT   Chicago   Toronto   London
Mexico City   Caracas   Buenos Aires   Madrid   Bogotá   Sydney

ISBN 0-697-23585-8

Printed in the United States of America by Times Mirror Higher Education Group, Inc., 2460 Kerper Boulevard, Dubuque, Iowa, 52001

10 9 8 7 6 5 4 3 2 1

Contents

Preface

Using the *Student Study Guide* for *Life-Span Development* (6e)

You are about to undertake the challenging and, we hope, exciting task of learning about biological, cognitive, and sociocultural influences on life-span development. This *Student Study Guide* will assist you as you read *Life-Span Development* (sixth edition) by John W. Santrock. It will help you learn and test your understanding of key terms and persons, facts, and theories covered in the text; however, do remember that its use should supplement rather than substitute for a careful and thorough reading of the text. Each chapter of this *Student Study Guide* contains two sections (*Learning Objectives with Key Terms in Boldface*, and *Guided Review and Study*) designed to help you master the corresponding chapters in *Life-Span Development*. Two sections (Self Test A: Key Terms and Key Persons, and Self Test B: Multiple Choice) allow you to test your understanding of the chapter.

Learning Objectives

Each chapter of the *Student Study Guide* presents a detailed set of learning objectives in which key terms designated by the author appear in boldface. We have organized these objectives by major chapter headings, and subheadings, and numbered them accordingly. For example, the first section after the *Preview* in each chapter is numbered 1.0, and the associated objectives are numbered 1.1, 1.2, and so forth. These objectives cover all material in the chapter, including the chapter boxes. The learning objectives indicate as specifically as possible what you should be able to do after you have read and mastered the material.

The last section of the learning objectives always covers the *Chapter Boxes*. The objectives for this section of each chapter cover: (a) Sociocultural Worlds of Development, (b) Critical Thinking About Life-Span Development, and (c) Life-Span Health and Well-Being. Be sure to pay attention to these objectives as well as those for the main body of each chapter!

We have embedded the key terms in boldface in the learning objectives rather than listing them separately. We recommend that you prepare your own definitions for these key terms based on your understanding of the text's definitions. This is important because you will not know whether you really understand a term until you can define it in your own way. In addition, test items for the key terms often paraphrase rather than duplicate the textbook's definitions. You will have difficulty with test items about the key terms if you have only memorized a specific definition that you do not fully understand.

Finally, we recommend that you make extensive use of the learning objectives. For example, it is a good idea to review the key terms before and after you read each section, or subsection, of the textbook. In addition, you should review the learning objectives before you do the guided review and study for the section, or subsection. Finally, if you make any mistakes on the Key Terms and Key Persons Self Test, or the Multiple Choice Self-Test, you should review the appropriate learning objective while rereading that section of the textbook. We believe that consistent and extensive review of the learning objectives will help you better learn and remember the chapter content, and that in turn, will help you do your best on the examinations.

Guided Review and Study

The Guided Review and Study intermingles fill-in-the-blank and short answer questions to help you review and remember the material in the chapter. To benefit most from the Guided Review and Study, we recommend that you:

1. Review the learning objectives for the section, or subsection, of the chapter.
2. Reread the corresponding section, or subsection, of the chapter.
3. Answer the Guided Review and Study questions for the section, or subsection.
4. Review the learning objectives and textbook for questions that were difficult to answer.

Key Terms and Key Persons Self Test

The Key Terms and Key Persons Self Test in each *Student Study Guide* chapter are practice tests to help you assess your understanding of key terms and key persons in the chapter. To do these exercises, write the appropriate key term (or key person) in the space to the right of each definition (or description). This will test your knowledge of key terms and persons and provide a *partial* chapter glossary for study and review. Check your work with the Answer Key that appears at the end of each chapter; however, we urge you to try to figure out the answers before you consult the keys. This will give you the best indication of how well you know the terms and persons, or whether you need to spend more time studying them. We also encourage you to determine which learning objective goes with each key term and key person. Annotate each item with the number of the corresponding learning objective. This is another way to determine whether you understand the material or should do further studying of the chapter.

Please note that only *some* of the key terms and key persons in each chapter appear in Self Test A. This slightly enhances the challenge of this exercise and reduces the odds that you can guess at term definitions. Also, you will have to remember to study the terms and persons that we did not include in the exercise!

Multiple Choice Self-Test Questions

Because there is a good chance that you will take multiple-choice tests to measure your mastery of chapter material, we have provided an average of 32 multiple choice items for each chapter. Some chapters include as few a 21 questions, and some chapters include as many as 40 questions. The number of questions is roughly proportional the number of learning objectives for the chapter.

Please note the following features of Self Test B: (a) The items resemble the questions that will probably appear on tests given by your instructor. Notice that some items ask you to recall facts or persons, others test your understanding of concepts, and still others ask you to apply a concept. Items also vary in difficulty. Use your self-test performance to determine which types of items are especially difficult for you. This knowledge may help you to study more effectively, or may help you to ask your instructor specific questions about how to improve your test performance. (b) The items sample material throughout each chapter, but they do not cover every learning objective. This is very important for you to remember. Taking these tests will give you a general idea about how well you have mastered chapter material. Be sure to notice what material in a chapter the tests cover and what material they do not, and be sure to study the omitted material as well. A good idea is to annotate the numbers of the objectives relevant to each practice test item. This will help you to identify material that you have not reviewed by taking the tests, and possibly will suggest questions you can ask your instructor when you need help.

Some Final Thoughts . . .

. . . *about studying*: We designed this *Student Study Guide* to give you activities that we believe will enhance your ability to learn and remember knowledge about life-span development. However, effective studying involves more than the specific things you do to learn the material; it includes developing good general study habits, plans, and strategies. To help you develop these skills, we are including the following essay, "How to Be a Better Student," written by Michael G. Walraven for the third edition of a Student Study Guide that accompanied an earlier version of John Santrock's, *Life-Span Development*. Take time to read it, the investment will pay off!

. . . *about active learning*: We have included both learning and self-test sections because we firmly believe that you should be actively involved in your own learning. Indeed, research has shown that the other study aids we have provided do not really help unless you use them in a very active way (e.g., working through the guided review and study on your own, and checking the material you could not remember). If you agree with us, we hope that all of the activities in this *Student Study Guide* will be useful both as ready-made suggestions for study and as models for activities that you invent on your own to help you achieve your own course goals and objectives. In fact, we are interested to learn about your reactions to the materials in this *Student Study Guide*. Please relate both your experiences, both positive and negative, by writing us at the Department of Psychology, University of Wisconsin–Eau Claire, Eau Claire, Wisconsin 54702-4004, or by sending e–mail to either PEDENBF@UWEC.EDU or KENISTAH@UWEC.EDU. Also, send samples of additional activities, exercises, or assignments that have enhanced your learning, or that represent the kind of learning tools you like. We look forward to hearing from you!

Blaine F. Peden   Allen H. Keniston

Acknowledgment

We owe a special debt of gratitude to Barbara Liddell-Peden for her contributions to this *Student Study Guide*. Barbara painstakingly reviewed each chapter from the student's perspective, and provided many comments and insights about how to improve the various contents. We truly appreciate her efforts, which have helped us produce a manual that should minimize frustrations and maximize the opportunities for students to learn and assess their mastery of the material in *Life-Span Development* (sixth edition).

How to Be a Better Student

Everyone who goes to college wants to be a good student. As you chose your college or university, and perhaps even an area of major interest or concentration, you had certain goals in mind. I would be willing to bet that three of them were to do well in school, earn good grades, and graduate.

Unfortunately, many students find that they do not do as well in college as they had hoped and expected. There are several reasons for this disappointment, and in examining them it is possible to see how to avoid them. It is possible, in other words, to know how to be a good student, and to guide our behavior so we improve the chances of achieving our goals.

The oldest known definition of education is "how people learn stuff." For most of our history, educators have focused on the "stuff." Teachers were required to be masters of their respective academic fields. Even today, some states have requirements that speak only to the need to be qualified in the subject matter one teaches.

In the 1960s, we became more interested in the "people" part of the definition, a movement made manifest by fads like open classrooms and free universities. The idea was that people just naturally learn, and need only the opportunity to do so. These experiments were dismal failures, but they taught us something.

The key to the definition of education is the word *how*. Today, thanks to a wealth of research on the principles that guide the phenomenon of learning, and on the nature of learning and memory, we know a considerable amount about how learning occurs and how we can make it better. It is by the application of these principles that we can become better students.

Formulating the Plan

Anything worth having is worth planning for. Whether you hope to learn to teach, to fly, to write for profit, or to change diapers correctly, you have in mind a goal.

From the earliest days in elementary school, many students are asked what they want to be when they grow up. This usually means what they want to do as work when they reach adulthood. Although I have been teaching at the college level for almost 15 years, my father still asks me when I am going to get a steady job! The answer to these questions is one way of formulating a goal. Now that you are a college student, many people will expect that you know what you want to do for a profession or career. Yet you may not have the foggiest notion, or you might have an idea that is still slightly foggy. That is OK. What is clear, however, is that you want to succeed in your college courses. This is a relatively long-range goal, and as such can serve a purpose in keeping you on track.

But our day-to-day behavior is often hard to connect to our long-range goals. We need short-term goals to keep us organized, and to be sure that the flow of our activities is in the correct direction.

I suggest that as students, we need three types of short-term (relatively speaking) goals. First, we need goals for the semester or term; second, goals for the week; and third, goals for the day. Let's look at each of these separately.

Goals for the Semester

At the beginning of each semester, we find ourselves immersed suddenly in many new courses. Often, we are confronted by several new professors with whom we have not worked before. It is difficult to sort out the expectations and demands of these several courses. However, organizing this information is critical to effectively completing all these requirements, and to success.

If you can, obtain a large wall calendar, and mark on it all the dates of tests, exams, and term paper due dates. Be sure to write on the calendar for which course the date applies. Now, estimate how long it will take you to make final preparations for those exams, and mark those dates as warning or alert dates. Look over the dates on which papers are due, and see if they are bunched together. If your college is typical, they are. You can help yourself to avoid the last-minute all-nighters if you will simply determine a spread of due dates for yourself, and mark those on the calendar too. As you do this step, please be sure to avoid any days that have personal significance for you, such as birthdays, anniversaries, and the like. This calendar gives you an overview of major dates in your semester.

Goals for the Week

Students who are successful in college also schedule their time weekly. Sometime during the course of registration, you undoubtedly made up a schedule showing your classes arrayed over the week. If you also have a part-time or full-time job, you must allow time for that, too. And everyone needs some time for relaxing, eating, and sleeping, not to mention life's essentials: ice cream and love. With all these things in mind, it is no wonder we find very little time to study.

But good students do all these things, too, yet they study. Do they have more time? No, we all have the same amount of time. But successful students schedule their time carefully. So, make up a weekly schedule and block off time for all these necessary events: classes, work, relaxation, eating, sleeping, loving, ice cream, and studying. Is there any time left? If so, appoint a committee to decide what to do with it. If not, consider yourself a student.

As you make up your weekly schedule, you may find your study time in a large block. If this is true, please remember to take a short break every 20 to 30 minutes. This is called distributed practice and is far more efficient than studying for hours on end. After the first twenty or thirty minutes, most of us become much less efficient anyway.

Goals for Today

It is also helpful to keep a daily checklist, as a reminder of what must be done that day. Check off the things as you accomplish them. A pocket calendar is most helpful for this task.

If you have followed this carefully, you now have a large semester calendar plastered on your wall, a weekly schedule of major life events, classes, and study times taped over your desk, and a daily check list of must-do items in your pocket or purse. We have to hurry now; it's time to go to class!

Attending Classes

Many students believe that, since they are in college, they can decide whether to go to class at all. They are correct. Some students believe further that attendance in class is not important to their grade. They are misled! Some instructors even announce that they do not adjust grades based on attendance. But they do not have to! Students who do not attend class sessions almost always do more poorly on the tests and exams. Perhaps they were absent when a crucial item was discussed, or when the instructor lectured over the material this examination requires. Moreover, if you are not there, the instructor cannot get to know you (sorry, instructors are not telepathic), and therefore cannot give you the benefit of the doubt on your answers.

In study after research study, the data clearly show that those students who attend class regularly receive the highest grades and actually learn more, too! So, the first rule of effective studenthood is to attend classes. Besides, how else can you get your money's worth?

When you get to class, what do you do?

Benefiting from Lectures

Sometimes students attend lectures and just sit and pay attention. They reason that if they take notes, they will miss much of what the instructor says. But sitting and paying attention is difficult to do. For one thing, most people can think much faster than they can speak. While the instructor lectures at 80 words per minute, the student thinks at about 350 words per minute! If the student is using this extra "thinking capacity" to focus on what the instructor is saying, it is fine. This rarely lasts more than five minutes at a time, however. Most of the time, this extra "thinking capacity" is used in daydreaming!

Daydreaming can be helpful in resolving our emotional problems, planning the course of our lives, and avoiding work. Most of the time it is motivated by the desire to avoid work. For whatever motive, however, daydreaming is not compatible with attending a lecture. Human beings simply cannot attend to more than one stimulus at one time. And you have to admit, your daydreams can be ever so much more interesting than your professor's lectures.

Attending lectures is best done while taking notes. Use plenty of paper, and leave blank lines at regular intervals. You will use these lines later (they are not wasted!). If the instructor permits it, interrupt with questions if you do not understand what is being said. Lectures have a way of progressing. It is important to understand each point, or later points will be lost.

When you take notes, write out the major points, and try to just make simple notes on the supporting minor points. If you miss something, and you cannot ask a question about it, approach the instructor immediately afterward, when it is likely to still be fresh in both your minds.

Within one or two hours after the lecture, but for sure on the same day, go back over your notes, and do two things. First, fill in the rest of the minor points. This often amounts to completing the sentence or other element. Second, write brief summaries and any questions that you now have in the blank lines you left earlier (clever of you to leave those blank lines!). These few minutes spent reviewing and organizing your notes will pay off in greatly improved memory. The questions you have you can ask in class, or during the instructor's office hours, and reap two benefits. First, you will get the answers. Second, you will demonstrate that you are a serious student, and that will impress your instructor.

By the way, weren't we supposed to read something before the next class period? Oh yes, now where did I leave my textbook? I sure hope I can get through all those pages before I fall asleep!

Reading for Learning

We all know how to read. You are proving it by reading these words. Hopefully, you are also realizing some ideas as a result of reading. If you are only reading words, please WAKE UP! STOP DAYDREAMING!

We can read a variety of things: newspapers, movie reviews, novels, sleazy paperbacks, and textbooks. Textbooks are unlike all the others, and must be read with a strategy all their own.

There are a multitude of reading and studying strategies, and all of them work to an extent. Perhaps you learned one or more in the course of going to high school. Perhaps you even took a how-to-study course when you entered college. If so, you probably learned one or two of these systems. If you have one you like, that works for you, keep it. If you are interested in learning a new one, read on.

The SQ3R Method

One of the most successful and most widely used methods of studying written material is the SQ3R method, first developed at Ohio State University. Researchers had noted that students who were more successful were more active readers. This method teaches you the same skills that have made many thousands of students successful. If you use this method when you read and study, you will be more successful, too. If not, there's always snake oil.

The S stands for SURVEY. After you have read the overview or chapter outline, and the list of learning objectives, you should survey the chapter in the text. This is also called skimming. Look at the headings and subheadings, and get the gist of the major points in this chapter. If you have an outline of the chapter (some books provide them), check off each point as you pass it in the pages of the text.

The Q stands for QUESTIONS. Reading is greatly enhanced if you are searching for the answers to questions. For this text, the Student Study Guide provides learning objectives that can serve as questions. For other texts, make up questions for yourself, based on the chapter overview or on your own survey of the chapter. Be sure that you have at least one question for each major unit in the chapter; you will be less efficient at studying those units for which you do not have questions.

The first of the three Rs is for READ. As you read, look for the answers to the questions you posed, or to the study or learning objectives furnished for you. When you find material that answers these questions, put a mark (X) in the margin next to that material. This will help now, since you are actively involved, and later, when you review. It is a good idea to wait to underline or highlight lines of text until after you have read the entire chapter at least once, so you will know what is and what is not most important.

The second R is for RECITE. One of the oldest classroom techniques in the world (Aristotle used it) is recitation. In the classroom version, the teacher asks the questions and the students answer them. Unless you can get your teacher to study with you regularly, you'll have to play both roles. (Incidentally, if you do get your teacher to study with you regularly, please write and let me know how you accomplished it. Thanks.)

Stop periodically in your reading and say aloud (if possible) what the author is telling you. Try to put it in your own words, but be sure to use technical terms as you learn them. If you are not in a situation where you can recite out loud, do it in writing. Just thinking it is not enough.

People who do not use recitation usually forget half of what they read in one hour, and another half of the half they remembered by the end of the day. People who use recitation often remember from 75 to 90 percent of what they studied. This technique pays off. By the way, if anyone questions why you are talking to yourself, tell them that a psychologist recommended it.

When should you pause to recite? A good rule of thumb is that each time you come to the end of a major subheading, you should recite. I like to encourage my students to recite at least one sentence at the end of each paragraph, and two or three or more sentences at the end of each subunit (when you come to a new heading). Who ever said that students should be seen and not heard?

The third R (in SQ3R, remember?) is for REVIEW. You should review a chapter soon after you have studied it (using the SQ and first 2Rs). You should review it again the day or evening before a test. It is not usually helpful to cram the night before a test, and particularly not the day of the test! That type of study does not produce good memory, and is likely to make you more anxious during the test itself.

Taking Tests

One of the things students fear most is failure. Failure signifies that things are not going well, and alerts us to the possibility that we may not achieve our goals. Unfortunately, many students see tests and exams as opportunities to fail. They prepare by becoming anxious and fearful, and trying to cram as much as possible as near as possible to the exam itself. These students rarely do well on the exam. They often fail, thus accomplishing just what they feared. Perhaps they should learn to fear success?

Taking tests requires some strategy and planning. First, it is helpful to know what type of tests you will have. Your instructor probably told you during the first class meeting, or perhaps is waiting for you to ask. If you do not know, ask.

If you are going to be taking essay exams, the best way to prepare is by writing essays. Before you do this, it is a good idea to find out what types of questions the instructor asks, and what is expected in a response. Again, it is helpful to ask the instructor for this material. Perhaps you can even see some examples of essay questions from previous years. By finding out what is expected, you can formulate a model against which you can evaluate your answers.

Now, using the learning objectives, or some essay questions you wrote, actually sit down and write out the answers. HINT: If you usually feel more anxious during a test, it may help you to practice writing your essays in the room in which the test will be given. Simply find a time when the room is vacant, and make yourself at home.

If your instructor gives multiple-choice tests, then you should practice taking multiple-choice tests. For each chapter, either use questions provided in the Student Study Guide, or make up your own. You may find it helpful to work out an arrangement to pool questions with other students, thereby reducing the amount of work you have to do, and developing a network of friends. Good for you!

Whichever way you do it, the important thing is to prepare for tests and exams. Preparation is about 95 percent of the secret to getting a good grade. (Yes, there is some actual luck or chance involved in test scores, as even your instructor will admit!) Preparation is not only a good study and review technique, but also helps to reduce anxiety.

Dealing with Test Anxiety

Some students find that the prospect of a test or an examination produces a set of responses that leave them feeling helpless, very anxious, and certain of failure. They find it hard to read the questions, often leave the examination incomplete, have stomach pains and other somatic problems, and contemplate drastic measures, such as dropping out.

Other students are less severely affected. For some, a little anxiety gives them the "edge" they need to do well. In fact, anxiety can be a helpful drive, when it occurs in low levels. In 1908, Yerkes and Dodson showed that the amount of anxiety that could benefit performance was a function of the difficulty and complexity of the task. As the difficulty of the task rose, anxiety became less helpful and more likely to interfere with performance.

If you have ever been so anxious in a test situation that you were unable to do well, even though you knew the information, you have test anxiety. If you get your exams back, and are surprised that you marked wrong answers when you knew the correct answers, or if you can only remember the correct answers after you leave the examination room, you too may have test anxiety. Short of dropping out of college, or seeing a professional counselor, what can you do? In fact, you can do three things.

Strategy Number One: Effective Study

Using study habits that promote learning and make the best use of time is a sure help. Such study strategies as we discussed above, including scheduling your time and using the SQ3R system, reduce anxiety by increasing confidence. As you come to realize that you know the material, your confidence rises and anxiety retreats.

Strategy Number Two: Relaxation

Each of us develops a unique pattern of relaxation. Some people relax by going to a specific place, either in person or mentally. Others relax by playing music, by being with friends, by using autogenic relaxation phrases, or by meditating. Whatever you do, be aware of it, and try to practice relaxation techniques. If you are good at relaxing, try thinking about those situations that make you anxious, and relax while you think of them. To do this, allow yourself to think only briefly (15 to 30 seconds at a time) of the situation that makes you anxious, and then relax again. After a number of such pairings, you will find that thinking about that situation no longer makes you anxious. At this point, you may be surprised to find that the situation itself also no longer produces anxiety. You may find that it is helpful to think about these anxiety-provoking situations in a sequence from those that produce very little anxiety to those that are more anxiety-evoking. Such a list, from low to high anxiety, might look something like this:

1. Your instructor announces that there will be a test in four weeks.
2. Your instructor reminds you of the test next week.
3. As you study, you see on the course outline the word *test*, and remember next week's test.
4. One of your friends asks you if you want to study together for the test, which is the day after tomorrow.
5. You choose not to go out with your friends because of the test tomorrow.
6. As you get up in the morning, you remember that today is the day of the test.
7. You are walking down the hall toward the classroom, thinking about what questions might be on the test.
8. The instructor enters the classroom, carrying a sheaf of papers in hand.
9. The instructor distributes the papers, and you see the word *test* or *exam* at the top.
10. After reading the first five questions, you have not been able to think of the answer to any of them.

If you work at it gradually and consistently, pairing these types of thoughts (briefly) with relaxation and remembering to let go and relax after each one, this will dispel test anxiety and make test taking a more productive and successful experience.

Strategy Number Three: Thinking Clearly

Most students who have test anxiety think in unclear and unproductive ways. They say to themselves things like: "I can't get these answers correct . . . I don't know this stuff . . . I don't know anything at all . . . I'm going to fail this test . . . I'm probably going to flunk out of school . . . I'm just a dumb schmuck." These thoughts share two unfortunate characteristics: they are negative and they are absolute. They should be replaced.

When we tell ourselves absolute and negative thoughts, we find it impossible to focus on the test material. The result is that we miss questions even when we know the answers. Our thinking prevents us from doing well.

A good strategy for replacing these negative and absolute thoughts is to practice thinking positive and honest thoughts, such as: "I may not know all the answers, but I know some of them . . . I don't know the answer to that right now, so I will go on to the next one and come back to that . . . I don't have to get them all right . . . I studied hard and carefully, and I can get some of them correct . . . I am a serious student, and have some abilities . . . I am prepared for this test, and know many of the answers . . . This test is important, but it is not going to determine the course of my entire life."

By thinking clearly, honestly, and positively, we quiet the flood of anxiety and focus on the task at hand. Students who use this technique invariably do better on the tests. It takes practice to think clearly, but it is worth the effort. After a while, you will find that it becomes natural and does not take any noticeable effort. And as anxiety is reduced, more energy is available for studying and for doing well on examinations. The eventual outcome is more enjoyment with learning, better learning, more success in college, and the achievement of your goals.

Section I　　The Life-Span Developmental Perspective

Chapter 1　　Introduction

Learning Objectives with Key Terms in Boldface

1.0 The Life-Span Perspective

A. *Why Study Life-Span Development?*

1.1　Explain why it is important to study life-span development.

B. *The Historical Perspective*

1.2　Contrast historical accounts of child development during the Middle Ages, Renaissance, late nineteenth century, and contemporary times.

1.3　Explain how assumptions and philosophies of the **original sin** view, John Locke's **tabula rasa** view, and Jean Jacques Rousseau's **innate goodness** view apply to an understanding of child development.

1.4　Indicate when and how G. Stanley Hall began the scientific study of adolescence, and explain his **storm-and-stress view** of adolescence.

1.5　Evaluate the storm-and-stress view of adolescence in light of Daniel Offer's data.

1.6　Explain what it means to say that American society "inflicted" adolescence on its youth.

1.7　Compare and contrast the traditional view and the life-span perspective on development.

1.8　Describe changes in life expectancy over the past 100 years.

1.9　Explain why we are interested in adult development; list specific concerns.

C. *Characteristics of the Life-Span Perspective*

1.10　List and describe the seven basic contentions of the life-span perspective according to Paul Baltes, and explain the benefits of the life-span perspective to people.

1.11　List and describe the three interacting systems of contextualism (**normative age-graded influences, normative history-graded influences,** and **nonnormative life events**).

1.12　Indicate when age-graded, history-graded, and nonnormative life-events are each most likely to influence development during the human life span.

D. *Some Contemporary Concerns*

1.13　List three concerns that influence the study of life-span development.

1.14　List challenges to life-span health and well-being.

1.15　Outline how we can improve life-span health and well-being.

1.16　Identify characteristics of modern families that affect life-span development.

1.17　List criticisms of the American educational system, and explain how developmentalists may help devise reforms stimulated by those criticisms.

1.18　Describe trends in ethnic diversity in the United States.

1.19　Discuss how sociocultural contexts of development can affect life-span development.

1.20　Define and distinguish between **context** and **culture**.

1.21　Explain the purpose of **cross-cultural studies**.

1.22　Define and distinguish between **ethnicity** and **ethnic identity**.

1.23　Define and distinguish between sex and **gender**.

1.24　Define **social policy**, and explain why we need a social policy concerned with life-span development.

1.25　Explain how social policy influences life-span development.

1.26　Identify Marian Wright Edelman, and state her point about the importance of parenting and nurturing.

1.27　Define **generational inequity** and explain how it relates to family policy issues.

2.0 The Nature of Development

2.1　Define **development**.

A. *Biological, Cognitive, and Socioemotional Processes*

2.2　Define and distinguish among **biological processes, cognitive processes,** and **socioemotional processes**.

B. *Periods of Development*

2.3 Describe the major developmental periods from conception to death (**prenatal period, infancy, early childhood, middle and late childhood, adolescence, early adulthood, middle adulthood,** and **late adulthood**).

2.4 Compare and contrast the happiness and life satisfaction of different age groups.

C. *Conceptions of Age*

2.5 Explain what Bernice Neugarten means when she says we are becoming an age-irrelevant society.

2.6 Define and distinguish **chronological age, biological age, psychological age,** and **social age.**

2.7 Give an example of how developmentalists use the various conceptions of age.

D. *Developmental Issues*

2.8 Explain the **nature-nurture controversy** in terms of the concepts of **maturation** (nature) versus experience (nurture) explanations of development.

2.9 Define and distinguish between **continuity of development** and **discontinuity of development**.

2.10 Explain the **stability-change issue**.

2.11 Outline Klaus Riegel's **dialectical model**.

2.12 Outline the early-later experience issue.

2.13 Explain why developmentalists usually do not take extreme positions on developmental issues.

3.0 Thinking Critically About Life-Span Development

3.1 Explain the 10 ways you can think critically about life-span development in your own terms, and explain what you will learn by applying these 10 strategies while you are reading *Life-Span Development*.

4.0 Chapter Boxes

A. *Sociocultural Worlds of Development: Women's Struggle for Equality: An International Journey*

4.1 Summarize the political, economic, educational, and psychological conditions of women around the world.

B. *Critical Thinking About Life-Span Development: Imagining What Your Development Would Be Like in Other Cultural Contexts*

4.2 Give examples of perspective-taking and identification of sociohistorical and cultural forces that occur when you imagine what your development would be like in other cultural contexts.

C. *Critical Thinking About Life-Span Development: The Importance of Asking Questions—What is the Best Age to Be?*

4.3 Explain how asking questions is one way to think critically about life-span development.

D. *Critical Thinking About Life-Span Development: Some Critical Thinking Strategies*

4.4 Identify two strategies and explain how they would help you think critically about life-span development.

E. *Life-Span Health and Well-Being: Explorations in Health and Well-Being Across the Life-Span*

4.5 Compare the United States to other countries on a number of indices of health and well-being.

4.6 Discuss what you can do to feel better physically, mentally, and emotionally.

Guided Review and Study

1.0 The Life-Span Perspective

A. Why Study Life-Span Development

1. Indicate why you are studying life-span development, and compare and contrast your reasons for studying life-span development with those given by the author of your textbook.

2. Life-span development refers to human growth and change from conception to _____ .   *death*

B. *The Historical Perspective*

1. _____ work led Philippe Aries to say that childhood was not regarded as a distinct period,   *Art* and children were treated as miniature adults with no special status prior to _____ .   *1600*

2. Indicate why critics question the validity of Aries' conclusions, and what they say now about the way in which various societies viewed children.

3. The three philosophical views about the nature of children, and how to rear them, are original _____ , *tabula rasa*, and innate _____ .

sin
goodness

4. What does the original sin view say about the nature of children and the goal of child rearing?

5. John _____ proposed the *tabula rasa* view.

Locke

6. What does the *tabula rasa* view say about the nature of children and the goal of child rearing?

7. During the eighteenth century, Jean Jacques Rousseau proposed the innate _____ view.

goodness

8. What does the innate goodness view say about the nature of children and the goal of child rearing?

9. The contemporary conception of childhood is that it is a special time for development that provides a groundwork for the _____ years.

adult

10. The contemporary view also encourages special concerns for the care, _____ , and protection of children.

education

11. G. Stanley Hall wrote the first scientific book on _____ .

adolescence

12. According to _____ storm-and-stress view, an adolescent may be nasty one minute and kind the next minute.

Hall's

13. Daniel Offer and his colleagues indicate that most adolescents do not experience profound emotional turmoil, a finding _____ to Hall's view.

contrary

14. Cross-cultural research indicates that the self-esteem of adolescents is generally _____ throughout the world.

positive

15. Explain what it means to say that both biological and sociohistorical factors have contributed the emergence of adolescence.

16. The _____ approach to development assumes rapid growth from birth to adolescence, no change in adulthood, and decline in old age, whereas the _____ approach to development assumes that change occurs at all ages.

traditional
life-span

17. Improvements in medicine, nutrition, and sanitation have led to dramatic increases in life _____ .

expectancy

18. Longer life-expectancies have produced a large number of older adults, and generated a greater interest in developmental aspects of _____ .

aging

19. Characterize some of the concerns regarding adult development.

C. Characteristics of the Life-Span Perspective

1. According to Paul _____ , the life-span perspective on development entails seven fundamental contentions.

Baltes

2. To say that development is _____ implies researchers attend equally to experiences throughout the life cycle rather than focus on a single age period.

life-long

3. To say that development is multi_____ implies it consists of biological, cognitive, and social components.

dimensional

4. To say that development is multi_____ implies some components may increase while others decrease during a particular age period.

directional

5. To say that development is _____ implies it can follow many different paths.

plastic

6. To say that development is historically _____ implies it is profoundly influenced by the historical and social influences of a generation.

embedded

7. To say that development is multidisciplanary implies involvement on the part of experts from a number of _____ .

disciplines

8. To say that development is _____ implies individuals are best described as changing beings in a changing world.   *contextual*

9. Provide examples for each one of the seven basic contentions of the life-span perspective.

10. Explain how the life-span perspective can benefit individuals, families, and communities.

11. Contextualism, one characteristic of the _____ perspective, implies development results from the interaction of _____ distinct systems.   *life-span*
   three

12. Normative age-aged influences are _____ for individuals in a particular age group, whereas normative history-graded influences are _____ for a generation of individuals. In contrast, nonnormative life events are unique to _____ .   *similar*
   similar
   individuals

13. Explain why people going through puberty experience normative age-graded influences.

14. Explain why political upheaval and changing social norms illustrate normative history-graded influences on development.

15. Explain how unplanned pregnancies during the early stages of career development exemplify nonnormative life events.

16. Indicate when age-graded, history-graded, and nonnormative life events are most likely to influence the course of an individual's development.

D. Some Contemporary Concerns

1. Your textbook, *Life-Span Development*, explicitly addresses _____ contemporary concerns: health and well-being, parenting and education, and sociocultural contexts.   *three*

2. Explain what it means to say that the United States is a nation obsessed with health and well-being throughout the life cycle.

3. The current view regarding health and well-being is that the ultimate responsibility resides with the _____ .   *individual*

4. The increasing number of dual-career and single parent families raises concerns about aspects of _____ .   *parenting*

5. Many families struggle with the care of aging _____ .   *parents*

6. Indicate some of the criticisms of the American educational system, and explain the role of developmentalists in educational reform.

7. Demographic trends indicate an increasing _____ population in the United States.   *ethnic*

8. The third contemporary concern pertains to sociocultural _____ which encompass the four concepts of context, culture, ethnicity, and gender.   *contexts*

9. The setting in which development occurs is called the _____ .   *context*

10. Historical, economic, social, and _____ factors influence the context of individual development.   *cultural*

11. State the concept of culture in your own terms.

12. Performing _____ -cultural studies reveals whether aspects of human development are _____ , or culturally-specific.

13. Distinguish between the concepts of ethnicity and ethnic identity.

14. Sex is a _____ aspect of being male or female, whereas _____ refers to the sociocultural aspect of being female or male.

15. Sex and gender are important variables in the development of _____ and social relationships.

16. Social _____ refers to a government's actions intended to affect the welfare of its citizens.

17. Explain why research on life-span development should influence social policy.

18. Who is Marian Wright Edelman, and what are her views on parenting and nurturing?

19. Generational _____ refers to a condition in which older citizens receive inequitably larger allocations of resources than other age groups.

20. Explain why generational inequity is a social policy concern.

2.0 The Nature of Development

1. Express the concept of development in your own words.

2. Development is the _____ of biological, cognitive, and socioemotional processes.

A. Biological, Cognitive, and Socioemotional Processes

1. The _____ processes stem from the genetic composition of individuals.

2. The _____ processes involve intelligence, language, and thinking.

3. The socioemotional processes involve _____ feelings, personality, and interactions with others.

4. Although it is useful to study biological, social, and socioemotional processes independently, it is important to study ways in which they are _____ .

B. Periods of Development

1. Life-span developmentalists use age ranges to identify the major _____ of development.

2. Indicate the age ranges and characteristics of the eight major periods of life-span development:

prenatal period

infancy

early childhood

middle and late childhood

adolescence

early adulthood

middle adulthood

late adulthood

3. Individuals in the various stages of life-span development report _____ differences in their degree of happiness and satisfaction with life. *no*

C. Conceptions of Age

1. Although developmental periods represent theoretical conveniences and conventions, Bernice _____ now contends that ours is an increasingly age-_____ society. *Neugarten* *irrelevant*

2. An age-irrelevant society implies that developmental concerns and issues _____ the exclusive concerns of certain age groups. *are not*

3. Provide a definition, and explain how each of the following four ways of conceptualizing age contribute to an understanding of life-span development:

chronological age

biological age

psychological age

social age

4. Explain what it means to say that the life-span perspective indicates that an overall age-profile of an individual involves more than just chronological age.

D. Developmental Issues

1. Three developmental _____ concern maturation and experience, continuity and discontinuity, and stability and change. *issues*

2. _____ is the sequence of changes that result from the genetic blueprint, whereas _____ refers to the effects of the environment on development. *Maturation* *experience*

3. Express the nature-nurture controversy in your own terms.

4. Those who contend that development is a gradual process emphasize the _____ of development, whereas proponents of discontinuity assert that development entails a series of distinct _____ . *continuity* *stages*

5. The continuity view of development emphasizes _____ change, whereas the discontinuity view of development emphasizes _____ change. *quantitative* *qualitative*

6. Express the stability-change issue in your own words.

7. The stability-change issue raises a question about whether stability or change is the more _____ characteristic of human development.   *desirable*

8. Klaus _____ has argued that change is the key to understanding development.   *Riegel*

9. Riegel's _____ model emphasizes that actions and reactions to social and historical conditions produce ongoing change in personalities.   *dialectical*

10. The _____ experience issue is closely related to the stability-change issue.   *early-later*

11. The _____ experience doctrine argues that infant experience is the key determinant of development.   *early*

12. The _____ experience doctrine argues that later experience is as important as infant experiences in setting the course of development, and that individuals can change throughout their lifetimes.   *later*

13. Evaluate the claim that the majority of people in the world believe early experience is the key to understanding the development of an individual.

14. A key idea to understanding development is the concept of _____ .   *interaction*

15. Life-span developmentalists generally do not adopt _____ positions on these issues.   *extreme*

3.0 Thinking Critically About Life-Span Development

1. Your textbook author identifies _____ ways to think critically about life-span development.   *ten*

2. Create your own example for each of the 10 ways to think critically about life-span development.

4.0 Chapter Boxes

A. *Sociocultural Worlds of Development: Women's Struggle for Equality: An International Journey*

1. An international perspective on _____ for women reveals that they are disadvantaged in political, employment, educational, and psychosocial conditions.   *equality*

B. *Critical Thinking About Life-Span Development: Imagining What Your Development Would Be Like in Other Cultural Contexts*

1. Explain how imaging what it is like to grow up in a different culture would promote your ability to engage in perspective taking and identify the sociohistorical and cultural factors that influence life-span development.

C. *Critical Thinking About Life-Span Development: The Importance of Asking Questions—What Is the Best Age to Be?*

1. Explain how asking questions helps you to think critically about life-span development.

D. *Critical Thinking About Life-Span Development: Some Critical Thinking Strategies*

1. Identify two strategies and explain how they would help you think critically about life-span development.

E. *Life-Span Health and Well-Being: Explorations in Health and Well-Being Across the Life-Span*

1. Explorations of health and well-being across the life-span indicate that the United States rates _____ among the industrialized nations on measures of societal neglect.   *unfavorably*

2. Changes in one's _____ pave the way for better life-long health and well-being.   *life-style*

Self Test A: Key Terms and Key Persons

Write the appropriate key term or key person in the space to the right of the definition or description.

1. The nature of an individual's emotions, personality, and relationships with others.   _____

2. The term that refers to the expectations and social roles related to a person's age. _____

3. An advocate on the behalf of children and the person who authored *The Measure of Our Success*. _____

4. Unusual environmental events that profoundly affect an individual's life, but which do not fit a general or predictable course. _____

5. The view that individuals continually change as they act and react to various social and historical conditions in their lives. _____

6. The view that an aging society is unfair to its younger members because older adults receive an inequitably larger allocation of resources. _____

7. Changes in physical characteristics of an individual such as height and weight. _____

8. The individual who proposed an enlightened view of the nature of children and their rearing. _____

9. Biological and environmental influences that are similar for individuals in a particular age group. _____

10. Research that identifies similarities and differences between at least two different cultures. _____

11. A philosophical view that the child's mind is a blank slate at birth, and experience determines what kind of individual the child will become. _____

12. The developmental period that encompasses the late teens through the thirties. _____

13. The individual who contends that our society is increasingly becoming one that is age-irrelevant. _____

14. The degree to which early characteristics of an individual typify the same person at an older age. _____

15. The individual who initiated the scientific study of adolescence and who proposed the storm-and-stress view of adolescence. _____

16. The developmental period that encompasses the preschool years. _____

17. Mental activities such as attention, perception, language, memory, problem-solving, and thought. _____

18. The author of your textbook on *Life-Span Development*. _____

Self Test B: Multiple Choice

1. Philippe Aries' review of art and publications during the Middle Ages led him to conclude that
   a. infancy was not recognized by artists in the Middle Ages.
   b. childhood was not a distinctive period during much of history.
   c. adolescence was the focus of much early literature and art.
   d. early literature recognized several distinct developmental periods.

2. If parents believe that their children are basically good and need very little discipline, they have adopted the _____ philosophical view.
   a. original sin
   b. *tabula rasa*
   c. innate goodness
   d. storm-and-stress

3. From the viewpoint of the 1990s, the most representative description of childhood is that it is
   a. a period of preparing to become an adult.
   b. a period requiring much discipline to shape proper behavior.
   c. a period to be tolerated until adult behavior emerges.
   d. a time of growth and change requiring special care.

4. The study of adolescence first appeared
   a. at the beginning of the nineteenth century.
   b. in the middle of the nineteenth century.
   c. at the beginning of the twentieth century.
   d. in the middle of the twentieth century.

5. The life-span perspective emphasizes
   a. extreme change from birth to adolescence, little in adulthood.
   b. much change in childhood, stability in adolescence and adulthood.
   c. little change in adulthood, decline in older years.
   d. change during adulthood as well as childhood.

6. An investigator who has adopted a life-span approach to the study of honesty is most likely to be responsible for which of the following research projects?
   a. A study designed to determine the frequency of cheating on income tax returns for 30-year-olds.
   b. A study of what age group is most likely to return the change when a convenience store clerk gives the customer too much.
   c. A study of how frequently 8-year-olds versus 15-year-olds will agree to help deliver papers when one of their classmates asks.
   d. A study of how often 70-year-olds drive their nondriving friends to the store.

7. The average life expectancy for people born after 1980 is about _____ , and is expected to _____ .
   a. 65; increase
   b. 75; increase
   c. 65; level off
   d. 75; level off

8. Many older persons become wiser yet perform relatively poorly on cognitive speed tests. This supports the life-span perspective contention that development is
   a. plastic.
   b. multidimensional.
   c. contextual.
   d. multidirectional.

9. The death of a parent when a child is young is considered to be a(n)
   a. normative life event.
   b. history-graded influence.
   c. age-graded influence.
   d. nonnormative life event.

10. In recent decades, American adults have been more likely to be
    a. childless.
    b. unmarried.
    c. living alone.
    d. All of these answers are correct.

11. The most diverse and complex American ethnic group is that made up of
    a. African Americans.
    b. Hispanic Americans.
    c. Native Americans.
    d. Asian Americans.

12. The context of development is influenced by _____ factors.
    a. cultural
    b. economic
    c. historical
    d. All of the above answers are correct.

13. The goal of cross-cultural research is to determine
    a. how socioeconomic status affects life-span development.
    b. the universal aspects of life-span development.
    c. how a culture changes across time.
    d. how human beings grow and develop.

14. Ethnic identity is
    a. identical to one's racial identity.
    b. a powerful influence for every person.
    c. an unconsciously motivated, involuntary identity.
    d. a shared membership determined by factors such as cultural heritage.

15. _____ is to sociocultural dimension as _____ is to biological dimension.
    a. Sex; femininity/masculinity
    b. Femininity/masculinity; gender
    c. Gender; sex
    d. Sex; gender

16. A nation's course of action adopted by government to influence the welfare of its citizens is called
    a. social policy.
    b. social slate.
    c. propaganda.
    d. bill of rights.

17. The concept of generational inequity describes
    a. the situation in which older individuals receive more of the resources than younger individuals.
    b. differences in values, and is commonly called the "generation gap."
    c. differences in years of education between older and less educated individuals and younger and better educated individuals.
    d. family power patterns in which older individuals typically have more decision-making power.

18. Development is defined as a pattern of _____ across the life cycle.
    a. growth
    b. change
    c. decline
    d. stability

19. Which of the following would involve a cognitive process?
    a. compensating for the growth spurt during puberty
    b. learning a new language
    c. initiating a smile when a parent bends over the crib
    d. adjusting to the loss of a spouse

20. All but which of the following are characteristic of the early childhood period of development?
    a. emphasis on achievement
    b. ability to follow instructions
    c. development of school readiness skills
    d. development of personal hygiene abilities

21. People in the middle adulthood period of development would most likely spend their time in which of the following activities?
    a. developing a new career
    b. joining groups concerned about the environment
    c. going to the doctor
    d. writing an autobiography

22. Alex has just learned to say "da-de." Alex is most likely to be in the
    a. prenatal period.
    b. perinatal period.
    c. infant period.
    d. early childhood period.

23. Which one of the following is a characteristic of adolescence?
    a. coping with identity problems
    b. having positive relationships with family
    c. having feelings of competence
    d. All of these answers are correct.

24. Which of the following age groups reported being the most satisfied with their lives?
    a. 15 to 24 year olds
    b. 35 to 44 year olds
    c. people over 65
    d. there were no age differences in life satisfaction

25. Bernice Neugarten has emphasized reemerging life themes in development. Her observations have led her to conclude that
    a. life stages are important for understanding development.
    b. each person relives his or her childhood during later development.
    c. we must focus on the later developmental periods.
    d. age is becoming less important for understanding development.

26. Investigators who claim to be proponents of the nurture perspective would argue that
    a. genetics determines all behavior.
    b. the environment a person is raised in determines his or her longevity.
    c. how long an individual's parents lived is the best predictor of his or her longevity.
    d. genetics and the environment an individual is raised in combine to determine longevity.

27. Joe argues that children should be taught to read in nursery school. Joe probably believes that
    a. nurture, not nature, is the most important developmental influence.
    b. nature, not nurture, is the most important influence.
    c. nature and nurture are of equal influence.
    d. None of these answers is correct.

28. Theorists who emphasize maturation as an explanation for development are likely to emphasize
    a. distinct stages of development.
    b. gradual changes over the life-span.
    c. continuity of development.
    d. cumulative changes in development.

29. If the results of a study of cognitive development indicated that the change from concrete thinking to abstract thinking occur abruptly, which of the following views has been supported?
    a. continuity
    b. stability
    c. discontinuity
    d. dialectical

30. Most psychologists believe that development is due
    a. largely to nature.
    b. largely to nurture.
    c. to nature and nurture acting separately.
    d. to an interaction of nature and nurture.

Answers for Self Test A

1. socioemotional processes
2. social age
3. Marian Wright Edelman
4. nonnormative life events
5. dialectical model
6. generational inequity
7. biological processes
8. Jean Jacques Rousseau
9. normative age-graded influences
10. cross-cultural studies
11. *tabula rasa*
12. early adulthood
13. Bernice Neugarten
14. stability-change issue
15. G. Stanley Hall
16. early childhood
17. cognitive processes
18. John Santrock

Answers for Self Test B

1. b LO 1.2
2. c LO 1.3
3. d LO 1.3
4. c LO 1.4
5. d LO 1.7
6. b LO 1.7
7. b LO 1.8
8. d LO 1.10
9. d LO 1.11
10. d LO 1.16
11. c LO 1.18
12. d LO 1.20
13. b LO 1.21
14. d LO 1.22
15. c LO 1.23
16. a LO 1.24
17. a LO 1.27
18. b LO 2.1
19. b LO 2.2
20. a LO 2.3
21. b LO 2.3
22. c LO 2.3
23. d LO 2.3
24. d LO 2.4
25. d LO 2.5
26. b LO 2.8
27. a LO 2.8
28. a LO 2.9
29. c LO 2.9
30. d LO 2.13

Chapter 2   The Science of Life-Span Development

Learning Objectives with Key Terms and in Boldface

1.0 Theory and the Scientific Method

    1.1 Define and distinguish among **theory**, **hypotheses**, and **scientific method**.

    1.2 List and explain the purpose of each step in the scientific method.

2.0 Theories of Development

  A. Psychoanalytic Theories

    2.1 Identify basic assumptions of psychoanalytic theory.

    2.2 Define and distinguish among Sigmund Freud's personality structures (i.e., **id, ego**, and **superego**), and explain how they operate individually and collectively.

    2.3 Define **defense mechanism**, and illustrate it with the concept of **repression**.

    2.4 Define **erogenous zones** and explain the role they play in personality development.

    2.5 Describe Freud's five stages of psychosexual development (**oral stage, anal stage, phallic stage, latency stage**, and **genital stage**), and explain how a crisis at each stage contributes to adult personality.

    2.6 Explain the special role of the **Oedipus complex** in personality formation during the phallic stage.

    2.7 Explain why Erik Erikson formulated an alternative to Freud's theories.

    2.8 Compare and contrast Freud's and Erikson's theories.

    2.9 Define and distinguish among Erikson's eight stages of psychosocial development (**trust vs. mistrust, autonomy vs. shame and doubt, initiative vs. guilt, industry vs. inferiority, identity vs. identity confusion, intimacy vs. isolation, generativity vs. stagnation**, and **integrity vs. despair**), and explain how a crisis at each stage contributes to adult personality development.

  B. Cognitive Theories

    2.10 Identify basic assumptions of cognitive theory.

    2.11 Define and distinguish between organization and adaptation, and between **assimilation** and **accommodation**.

    2.12 Define and distinguish among Jean Piaget's four stages of cognitive development (**sensorimotor stage, preoperational stage, concrete operational stage**, and **formal operational stage**).

    2.13 Define the **information-processing approach** to cognitive development.

    2.14 Use Figure 2.3 to review the operations of a human mind according to the information processing approach.

  C. Behavioral and Social Learning Theories

    2.15 Identify basic assumptions of behavioral and social learning theories.

    2.16 Define **behaviorism** and explain how behaviorists view development.

    2.17 Explain why Albert Bandura and Walter Mischel developed **social learning theory**.

    2.18 Define and distinguish among concepts in Bandura and Mischel's social learning theory such as behavior, cognition, and environment, and apply them to a hypothetical college student's achievement behavior.

  D. Ethological Theories

    2.19 Identify basic assumptions of **ethology**.

    2.20 Define and distinguish ethological concepts such as **imprinting** and **critical period**.

  E. Ecological , Contextual Theories

    2.21 Identify basic assumptions of **ecological theory**.

    2.22 Define and distinguish the five systems in Urie Bronfenbrenner's ecological theory (**microsystem, mesosystem, exosystem, macrosystem**, and **chronosystem**).

    2.23 Sketch Glen Elder's **life-course theory**.

    2.24 Compare and contrast Glen Elder's, Urie Bronfenbrenner's, and Paul Baltes's views.

2.25 Explain how Elder understands human lives in terms of historical time and place, the timing of lives, linked lives, and human agency and social constraints.

F. Analogies for Development

2.26 Compare and contrast the staircase, seedling in a greenhouse, and strand of ivy in a forest analogies of life-span development, and indicate which theories they each characterize.

G. An Eclectic Theoretical Orientation

2.27 Identify basic assumptions of an **eclectic theoretical orientation**.

2.28 Explain why the author favors an eclectic approach to life-span development.

2.29 Use Table 2.2 to compare and contrast the five theories with regard to developmental issues and methods.

3.0 Methods

A. Measures

3.1 Define and give examples of systematic observation.

3.2 Compare and contrast research conducted in a **laboratory** with **naturalistic observation**.

3.3 Describe and evaluate alternative ways to collect data scientifically (observations; interviews and **questionnaires; case studies; standardized tests;** cross-cultural research; **life-history records;** and physiological research and research with animals).

3.4 Define and distinguish between **etic approach** and **emic approach** to cross-cultural research.

3.5 Define **ethnic gloss** and explain why the concept is important.

3.6 Describe the nature and purpose of the multimeasure, multisource, and multicontext approach

B. Strategies for Setting up Research Studies

3.7 Define and distinguish between the **correlational strategy** and the **experimental strategy**.

3.8 Explain why researchers use **random assignment** in experimental research.

3.9 Define and distinguish between **independent variables** and **dependent variables**.

3.10 Describe and evaluate the strengths and limitations of experimental and correlational strategies.

C. Time Span of Inquiry

3.11 Compare and contrast the **cross-sectional approach, longitudinal approach**, and **sequential approach** to life-span research.

3.12 Discuss the strengths and limitations of the cross-sectional and longitudinal approaches to research.

3.13 Define **cohort effects** and explain why they are important.

4.0 Research Challenges

A. Ethics in Research on Life-Span Development

4.1 Describe ethical concerns in research on life-span development.

B. Sexism in Research on Life-Span Development

4.2 Understand how research on life-span development can be sexist.

4.3 Explain Florence Denmark's three recommendations for nonsexist research.

C. Being a Wise Consumer of Information About Life-Span Development

4.4 Explain why you should be cautious about what the media reports.

4.5 Define and distinguish between **nomothetic research** and **idiographic needs**.

4.6 Explain why you should be careful about generalizing from small and clinical samples.

4.7 Explain why a single study is not the defining word about an aspect of life-span development.

4.8 Explain why causal conclusions cannot be made from correlational studies.

4.9 Explain why more credible reports appear in professional journals rather than in the popular media.

5.0 Chapter Boxes

A. Sociocultural Worlds of Development: Culture- and Gender-Based Criticisms of Freud's Theory

5.1 Summarize gender-based and sociocultural criticisms of Freud's theory.

B. *Critical Thinking About Life-Span Development: Freud and Schwarzenneger*

    5.2   Identify the sociohistorical and cultural factors highlighted by imagining how Freud would react to the sex and violence in today's films and how Schwarzenegger would have reacted to Victorian Vienna.

C. *Critical Thinking About Life-Span Development: Reading and Analyzing Reports About Life-Span Development*

    5.3   Compare and contrast a research report and a newspaper/magazine article about identical topics, and indicate what you learned by doing so.

D. *Life-Span Health and Well-Being: Cultural Expectations and Support for Health and Well-Being*

    5.4   Use the questionnaire to evaluate whether the contexts in which you live enhance your health and well-being.

Guided Review and Study

1.0 Theory and the Scientific Method

    1. A _____ is a set of concepts that help to explain observations and make predictions.   *theory*

    2. _____ are assumptions that can be tested to determine their accuracy.   *Hypotheses*

    3. The _____ method allows researchers to discover accurate information about development.   *scientific*

    4. Characterize the following four steps in the scientific method:

        identify a problem

        collect the data

        draw conclusions

        revise the theory

2.0 Theories of Development

    1. The five major theoretical perspectives on life-span development should be regarded as complementary rather than _____ .   *contradictory*

A. *Psychoanalytic Theories* earliest

    1. Indicate three basic assumptions made by psychoanalytic theorists about life-span development.

    2. Use Figure 2.1 to explain the nature and function of Freud's three personality structures:

        id

        ego

        superego

    3. According to Freud, _____ results from the wishes of the id, the demands of reality, and the constraints of the superego, and the ego reduces conflict by using _____ mechanisms.   *conflict*
        defense (unconscious methods)

4. Explain the concept of a defense mechanism in your own words.

5. According to Freud, the most powerful defense mechanism is _____ , which operates by pushing threatening impulses back into the _____ .

   repression
   unconscious

6. According to Freud, individuals go through five stages of _____ development.

   psychosexual

7. Each stage of development is influenced by parts of the body called _____ zones that yield strong pleasure.

   erogenous

8. Personality results from the resolution of the _____ between sources of pleasure and the demands of reality.

   conflict

9. When conflicts are not resolved at a particular stage, _____ occurs.

   fixation

10. Portray age ranges and the key aspects of Freud's five psychosexual stages of development, and explain how a crisis at each stage contributes to the development of the adult personality:

    oral stage *0 -18 mths*

    infants pleasure focuss around mouth

    anal stage *18 mths - 3 yrs*

    potty training

    phallic stage *3 - 6 yrs*

    latency stage *6 - puberty*

    nothing sexual in child's mind

    genital stage *puberty - adults*

11. Although the _____ remains a central part of psychoanalytic theories, contemporary versions downplay the role of sexual instincts and emphasize _____ experiences in the development of an individual.

    unconscious
    cultural

12. Explain why Erik Erikson formulated an alternative to Freudian theory.

    1902 1994

13. According to Erikson, the first psychosocial stage is one called trust versus _____ . An infant who feels that the world is predictable and that caregivers are reliable develops a feeling of _____ .

    0-1 yr.

    mistrust
    trust

14. The second stage in Erikson's theory is called _____ versus shame and doubt. In this stage, infants begin to develop a sense of independence and _____ .

    autonomy
    will

15. In the third stage of _____ versus guilt, children who discover ways of coping with feelings of helplessness develop healthy feelings of being _____ for their actions. Otherwise a sense of _____ may develop.

    Pre school

    initiative
    responsible
    guilt

16. Children develop a sense of _____ from positive comparisons of self with peers, and a sense of _____ from unfavorable comparisons. Industry versus inferiority thereby defines stage _____ in Erikson's theory.

    elementary school

    industry
    inferiority
    four

17. Life experiences produce either stable self-images called _____ or to unresolved self-images called identity _____ in Erickson's fifth stage of identity versus identity confusion.

    Jr. hi school

    identity
    confusion

18. In stage _____ , the first post-Freudian stage deemed _____ versus isolation, a young adult forms an intimate relationship.

six
intimacy

19. The central issue of stage seven is _____ which refers to helping the next generation. The absence of this is called _____ .

generativity
stagnation

20. Resolving each of the previous seven psychosocial _____ in a positive way results in satisfaction with life, and defines the eighth stage of Erikson's theory. Erikson calls this satisfaction ego _____ . If one or more of the previous crises has been resolved in a negative way, _____ may result.

crises
integrity
despair

B. Cognitive Theories

1. Cognitive theories, such as cognitive development theory and information-processing theory, focus on _____ rather than unconscious factors.

conscious

2. Explain what Jean Piaget means by saying that organization and adaptation are the two basic processes underlying a child's construction of the world.

1. organization + adaptation - grows experiences from parent to your life
2. accommodation - alter your life

3. _____ entails assimilation, a process of incorporating new information into old mental structures, and <u>accommodation</u>, a process of changing mental structures to fit new information.

Adaptation

4. Explain why pretending that a cup in the bath is a boat is an example of assimilation.

5. Explain why understanding that the thing indicated by the word "cup" may have many different shapes is an example of accommodation.

6. Piaget asserts that children's thinking in each of the four successive stages of cognitive development is _____ rather than quantitatively different.

qualitatively

7. Use Table 2.1 to specify age ranges and features of Piaget's four stages of cognitive development:

p. 44

✓ sensorimotor stage
0-2 yrs.

✓ preoperational stage *Children are learning to speak -*
2-7yrs

✓ concrete operational stage *Children can think logically what they had to do physically*
7-11 yrs. *before - a child can look + count 5 objects w/o touching to count*

✓ formal operational stage *can think in abstract and logical ways*
11-15 yrs.

8. A second cognitive theory, the _____ processing approach, focuses on the development of perception, <u>memory,</u> and reasoning.

information

9. Use Figure 2.3 to review how information processing theory models the human mind.

p. 44

C. Behavioral and Social Learning Theories

1. State basic assumptions of behavioral and social learning theories.

2. Explain B. F. Skinner's view of behaviorism in your own words.

behavior is looking at what child is doing

3. For behaviorists such as Skinner, development is _____ .   *behavior*
4. Another behavioral approach, called _____ learning theory by Albert Bandura and Walter   *social*
   Mischel, argues that behavior, environment, and _____ affect development.   *cognition*
5. Both the behavioral and the social learning approaches emphasize _____ determinants of   *environmental*
   behavior; however, the social learning approach has underscored the importance of _____   *cognitive*
   processes, and the role of _____ in controlling their own behavior.   *individuals*
6. Apply the concepts of behavior, cognition, and environment to your own achievement behavior.

7. Behavioral and social learning approaches favor an _____ approach to development.   *empirical*

NO **D. Ethological Theories**

1. Ethologists argue that sensitivities to different experiences _____ throughout the life cycle.   *vary*
2. Ethologists also stress the importance of biological and _____ determinants of behavior.   *evolutionary*
3. Provide a definition, and an example of the ethological concept of imprinting.

4. Provide a definition, and an example of the ethological concept of critical period.

5. The ethological view emphasizes the biological basis of behavior and careful _____ in   *observation*
   natural settings.

NO **E. Ecological, Contextual Theories**

1. Two examples of environmental, contextual theories of development include Urie   *ecological*
   Bronfenbrenner's _____ theory and Glen Elder's _____ theory.   *life course*
2. Bronfenbrenner's ecological theory proposes that individuals _____ their environments, and   *construct*
   that there are _____ environmental systems that define the contexts of development.   *five*
3. Characterize and illustrate the five systems in Bronfenbrenner's ecological theory:
   microsystem

   mesosystem

   exosystem

   macrosystem

   chronosystem

4. Glen Elder's _____ theory adopts a stronger orientation to life-span development than   *life course*
   Bronfenbrenner's ecological theory.

5. Elder believes that the study of development should begin with the _____ , whereas Paul Baltes believes that the point of departure should be the _____ .

environment
person

6. Explain and exemplify the four key aspects of Glen Elder's life course theory in your own terms: human lives in historical time and place

   the timing of lives

   linked lives

   human agency and social constraints

F. Analogies for Development

1. Explain each of the three analogies that have been used to describe development in your own words, and also relate them to one of the five theoretical approaches:
   staircase

   seedling in a greenhouse

   strand of ivy in a forest

G. An Eclectic Theoretical Orientation

An _____ theory tries to combine the best of several other perspectives when explaining life-span development. *selects & uses each theory + combines what is best*

eclectic

2. Explain why the author of *Life-Span Development* favors an eclectic orientation to development.

3. _____ approaches assume that development is life-long, multidirectional, multidimensional, plastic, historically embedded, contextual, and multidisciplinary.

Life-span

4. Use Table 2.2 to compare and contrast the five theories with regard to issues and methods in development.

4.0 Methods

A. Measures

1. There are various ways to make _____ observations.

systematic

2. Explain what it means to say that researchers must know what to look for, who to watch, how to record the information, and when and where to conduct their study.

3. Subjects may not behave in a natural way when brought into the _____ for observation; however, laboratories allow developmentalists to _____ various factors under scrutiny.   *laboratory*
   control
4. Identify and explain three drawbacks of laboratory research.

5. Researchers make _____ observations of people at schools, malls, hospitals, airports, and other places, but do not attempt to manipulate aspects of the situation under study.   *naturalistic*
6. One way to collect data is to use interviews or questionnaires to ask people about their attitudes or _____ .   *experiences*
7. A set of questions used in a personal meeting is called an _____ .   *interview*
8. Indicate what makes an individual a competent interviewer.

9. A _____ is similar to a structured interview; however, the subject reads the questions and marks the answers on a prepared sheet.   *questionnaire*
10. Describe advantages and disadvantages of interviews and questionnaires.

11. An in-depth look at an individual, a _____ , provides historical information about a person's emotional concerns or difficulties, childhood experiences, and family relations.   *case study*
12. Explain why researchers must be careful when making generalizations from a case study.

13. Standardized tests require individuals to answer a series of written or oral _____ .   *questions*
14. Identify and explain the two unique features of standardized tests.   SAT , ACT TEST

15. Among the most popular _____ tests are the Stanford-Binet to measure intelligence, and the Minnesota Multiphasic Personality Inventory or MMPI to measure personality traits.   *standardized*
16. Developmentalists who perform cross- _____ and ethnic minority research distinguish between emic and etic approaches.   *cultural*
17. The goal of an _____ approach is to describe the activities and behavior of a cultural or ethnic group in its own terms without reference to other groups.   *emic*
18. The goal of an _____ approach is to describe activities and behaviors in a way that allows comparisons and generalizations across cultural and ethnic groups.   *etic*
19. Cross-cultural research helps us determine to what extent aspects of development are _____ across cultures, or _____ to a particular culture.   *universal*
   specific
20. One difficulty in cross-cultural research is ethic _____ , a tendency to make group members seem more alike than they really are.   *gloss*
21. Explain why there is a need to include more ethnic minority individuals in developmental research.

22. Characterize life-history records. / archival records

23. Provide an example of physiological research. / research 4 animals

24. When developmentalists cannot do physiological research with humans, they use _____ .   *animals*

25. Indicate the advantages entailed in studying animals.

1. *What you can't use on humans you try on animals*

26. Explain why life-span researchers employ a multimeasure, multimethod, multicontext approach.

Because every method has strengths + weaknesses

B. Strategies for Setting Up Research Studies

1. Researchers employ correlational and experimental _____ in their research.   *strategies*

2. State the concept of correlational strategy in your own words.

3. _____ strategies allow investigators to predict a second variable given information about a   *Correlational*
   first variable. For example, a correlation between smoking and lung cancer leads to the prediction   *increase*
   that the likelihood of cancer will _____ the longer a person continues to smoke.   *2 items are closely related / no causal relationship*

4. Use Figure 2.8 to review the three possible explanations for an observed correlation.

✓5. The advantage of the _____ strategy over the correlational strategy is that it can   *experimental*
   demonstrate a _____ relationship between two variables.   *causal*

6. Characterize the following concepts in your own terms:

NO random assignment

independent variable

dependent variable

7. In an experiment, researchers manipulate the _____ variable, and measure its effect on the   *independent*
   _____ variable.   *dependent*

✓8. _____ assignment to conditions assures that experimental groups do not differ in any   *Random*
   systematic way.

9. Identify three situations in which a correlational strategy is preferable to an experimental strategy.
NO

C. Time Span of Inquiry

1. Life-span developmentalists employ three different time span approaches to study the relationship   *age*
   between _____ and some other dependent variable.

2. Describe the cross-sectional approach in your own terms.

✓3. Cross-sectional studies are _____ , but provide no information about how individuals   *efficient*
   change or the stability of their characteristics. *researcher does not have to wait until subject grows up.*   *negatives*

✓4. Describe the longitudinal approach in your own terms.
Same individuals are studied over a period of time (2-3yrs) - expensive
negative - Change in Culture
- death, move
- researcher becomes disinterested

19

5. Longitudinal studies are expensive and individuals commonly drop out and _____ the sample. *starts w/* — bias

6. Explain how and why sequential studies combine cross-sectional and longitudinal features.

   new groups are added later

7. _____ designs are expensive and time-consuming, but helpful in assessing cohort effects. — *Sequential*

8. When subjects belong to the same peer group, are born at the same time, or grow up in the same environment, they come from the same _____ . — *cohort*

9. Findings in a cross-sectional design easily can be due to _____ effects rather than to a relationship between age and the dependent variable under study. — *cohort*

4.0 Research Challenges

A. Ethics in Research on Life-Span Development

1. Psychologists who use human subjects in their research must take precautions to ensure the _____ of their participants. — *well-being*

2. The American Psychological Association has adopted a code of _____ to protect subjects from physical and mental harm. *Best interest of client/subject is most important* — *ethics*

3. State the concept of informed consent in your own terms.

4. If researchers want to employ children in their research, they must obtain _____ from both the parents or legal guardians and the children themselves. — *consent*

5. Researchers _____ the potential risk or harm to the child against the potential benefits. — *weigh*

6. Researchers must strive to make the subject's participation in the study a _____ experience. *+ supportive* — *positive*

B. Reducing Sexism in Research on Life-Span Development

1. Science is not _____ free. For example, much research in life-span development can be regarded as sexists because it typically has been _____ dominated and oriented. — *value* / *male*

2. Characterize Florence Denmark's guidelines for nonsexist research regarding:

   research methods

   data analysis

   conclusions

C. Being A Wise Consumer of Information About Life-span Development

1. Individuals who encounter media presentations of life-span developmental research must be _____ about simply accepting the conclusions and interpretations at face value. — *cautious*

2. Media presentations often focus on _____ findings that may go beyond the actual results. — *dramatic*

3. Explain what it means to say that media presentations may be misleading because they confuse nomothetic research with idiographic needs.

4. Media presentations may be misleading because they may _____ generalize findings from small or clinical samples. — *over*

5. Media presentations often do not describe the _____ well enough to preclude unwarranted generalizations. *sample*

6. Evaluate the contention that solid conclusions about life-span development depend more on converging evidence than the results of single studies.

✓7. Media presentations may be misleading because the _____ conclusions can not be drawn from correlational research. *causal*

8. In your own terms, explain why research reported in professional journals is more credible than research reported in the popular media.
   consider the source

5.0 Chapter Boxes

A. Sociocultural Worlds of Development: Culture- and Gender-Based Criticisms of Freud's Theory

1. Critics of Freud's theory contend that his view of the personality development of males and females _____ emphasizes biological processes such as anatomy, and _____ emphasizes cognitive and social processes entailed in culture. *over* *under*

2. Cross-cultural studies _____ support predictions of Freudian theory. For example, research by Bronislaw Malinoski demonstrated that the Oedipus complex is not _____ . *do not* *universal*

3. Karen Horney made the first _____ criticism of psychoanalysis. *feminist*

4. Explain Nancy Chodorow's feminist revision of psychoanalytic theory.

B. Critical Thinking About Life-Span Development: Freud and Schwarzenneger

1. Identify the sociohistorical and cultural factors highlighted by imagining how Freud would have reacted to the sex and violence in today's films.

2. Identify the sociohistorical and cultural factors highlighted by imagining how Arnold Schwarzenegger would have reacted to Victorian Vienna.

C. Critical Thinking About Life-Span Development: Reading and Analyzing Reports About Life-Span Development

1. Evaluate the author's claim that comparing research journal articles and newspaper/magazine accounts of a specific developmental topic will promote your learning how to make accurate observations, descriptions, and inferences about life-span development.

D. Life-Span Health and Well-Being: Cultural Expectations and Support for Health and Well-Being

1. Explain how cultural expectations influence our health and well-being.

Self Test A: Key Terms and Key Persons

Write the appropriate key term or key person in the space to the right of the definition or description.

1. The research design that tests a group of individuals at two or more separate times in their lives. _____

2. The perspective that multiple theoretical views are necessary to understand life-span development. _____

3. Erik Erikson's third stage of psychosocial development in which a child encounters a challenging social world, and may gain a sense of accomplishment or may feel guilt. _____

4. The research design that describes how strongly two or more events or characteristics of individuals are related, but does not permit causal conclusions. _____

5. The first stage in Jean Piaget's theory that lasts from birth until about two years of age. Infants construct an understanding of the world by coordinating sensation and action. _____

6. A superficial description of a cultural or ethnic group that makes the members appear to be much more similar than they really are. _____

7. The third stage in Sigmund Freud's psychosexual theory that occurs between ages of 3 and 6 years in which pleasure centers on the genital area and resolution of the Oedipal complex occurs. _____

8. An approach that favors the scientific study of observable behavior and environmental influences, and says development results primarily from conditioning and learning processes. _____

9. One of the two individuals whose behavioral theory emphasizes the roles of behavior, cognition, and environment in development. _____

10. A psychoanalytic theorist who proposed that development entails eight psychosocial stages. _____

11. One of Urie Bronfenbrenner's five systems in which experiences in another social setting, in which the individual plays no active role, influence how an individual experiences another current situation. _____

12. An approach in which researchers simply observe activities and behaviors in their normal setting, but make no attempt to control or manipulate the situation in any way. _____

13. An individual who recommended ways to conduct nonsexist research on life-span development. _____

14. A period of time early in development that is optimal for the emergence of certain behaviors. _____

15. The originator of an environmental, contextual theory of development that includes five environmental systems. _____

16. The process of obtaining information by identifying and analyzing the problem, collecting data, drawing conclusions, and revising theories. _____

17. An approach that focuses on how people attend, code, remember, and reason with information. _____

18. The individual who proposed life course theory. _____

19. Research intended to describe the activities or behavior of a particular group in a culturally and ethnically meaningful way without regard to other cultures or ethnic groups. _____

20. The research design that manipulates variables and permits causal conclusions. _____

21. The proponent of a cognitive theory of development that entails four qualitatively different stages. _____

22. A scientific approach associated with Albert Bandura and Walter Mischel that emphasizes the contributions of behavior, environment, and an individual's cognitive processes and experiences. _____

23. The research design that compares different groups of individuals from different age ranges at the same time. _____

24. Urie Bronfenbrenner's sociocultural view of development that consists of five systems. _____

25. An assumption or prediction that can be tested to determine its accuracy. _____

26. Concerns important to an individual that often are not addressed by studies of groups. _____

27. The effects of a generation or the time of an individual's birth rather than effects of age *per se*. _____

28. The variable in an experiment that is manipulated by the researcher. _____

29. Glen Elder's view of life-span development. _____

30. Erik Erikson's fifth developmental stage, typically experienced by individuals during adolescence. _____

Sample Test B: Multiple Choice

1. The science of life-span development is
   a. a systematic body of testable theories that can be verified or refuted.
   b. a set of specific, testable world views that describe life-span development.
   c. a descriptive catalogue of methods used to collect information about life-span development.
   d. a chronological identification of the stages of socioemotional, cognitive, and physical changes in children.

2. Predicting that dependent children will become alcoholics is an example of a(n)
   a. theory of personality.
   b. hypothesis.
   c. scientific fact.
   d. unscientific question.

3. Developing a study schedule is a function of the
   a. id.
   b. ego.
   c. superego.
   d. ego-ideal.

4. History reveals that Sigmund Freud's psychosexual theory may have been influenced by his childhood experiences. Apparently, Freud as a teenager was
   a. unusually shy and sexually repressed.
   b. normally expressive.
   c. oversexed and overactive.
   d. completely disinterested in sex.

5. Louella believes all boys have "cooties." She devotes herself to athletics and caring for various pets. A psychoanalyst would say Louella is
   a. behaving normally for someone in the latency stage.
   b. being overly controlled by her superego.
   c. experiencing unconscious conflicts between her ego and id.
   d. fixated at the phallic stage of development.

6. Erik Erikson's theory emphasized
   a. repeated resolutions of unconscious conflicts about sexual energy.
   b. success in confronting specific conflicts at particular ages in life.
   c. changes in children's thinking as they matured.
   d. the influence of sensitive periods in the various stages of biological maturation.

7. Bobby is interested in school; he spends a great deal of time reading and likes to do experiments. Bobby is showing signs of being in Erik Erikson's _____ stage.
   a. autonomy versus shame and doubt
   b. initiative versus guilt
   c. industry versus inferiority
   d. identity versus identity confusion

8. When a child recognizes that all four-legged creatures are animals, _____ has occurred. When the child learns that cows and horses belong in different categories, _____ has occurred.
   a. accommodation, accommodation
   b. assimilation, assimilation
   c. accommodation, assimilation
   d. assimilation; accommodation

9. If Dotty can't stand to be seen in public with her parents, she most likely is in Jean Piaget's
   a. sensorimotor stage.
   b. preoperational stage.
   c. concrete operational stage.
   d. formal operational stage.

10. The information processing approach to development emphasizes
    a. the quality of thinking among children of different ages.
    b. overcoming certain age related problems or "crises."
    c. age appropriate expressions of sexual energy.
    d. perception, memory, reasoning ability, and problem solving.

11. If you want to increase the number of times your spouse does the dishes, B. F. Skinner would tell you to
    a. yell at your spouse when he or she does not do the dishes.
    b. kiss your spouse when he or she does the dishes.
    c. leave the sink full of dishes until your spouse does them.
    d. ask your spouse nicely to do the dishes.

12. From B. F. Skinner's point of view, the best way to explain children's behavior is to
    a. pay attention to the external consequences of that behavior.
    b. pay attention to the self-produced consequences of that behavior.
    c. focus on children's cognitive interpretation of her environmental experiences.
    d. identify the biological processes that determine children's maturation.

13. The frequent finding that adults who abuse their children typically come from families in which they themselves were abused supports which theory of life-span development?
    a. Freudian psychoanalytic theory
    b. information processing theory
    c. ecological theory
    d. social learning theory

14. A social learning theorist would agree with which one of the following statements?
    a. Children are not passive responders; they judge, expect, plan and imagine behaviors.
    b. Children's behaviors change solely as a result of reward and punishment.
    c. Life-span development researchers underestimate the role of biologically based changes in behavior.
    d. An eclectic approach is always preferred in explaining a particular behavior.

15. Barbara insists that to assure bonding she must be conscious and have an opportunity to see and hold her baby immediately after its delivery. Which of the following theories would agree with Barbara?
    a. ethological theory
    b. humanistic theory
    c. psychoanalytic theory
    d. learning theory

16. A linguist who argues that to learn a language without an accent one must be exposed to it before the age of 12 has borrowed which of the following theoretical ideas from ethological theories?
    a. sensitive period
    b. critical period
    c. assimilation
    d. imprinting

17. To determine the cause of anxiety in 40-year-old men, you set out to test subjects from different cultures in different settings and under different kinds of stressful situations. Observation, interview, and a variety of structured and unstructured personality tests are used. What theoretical approach have you most likely adopted?
    a. cognitive
    b. social learning
    c. phenomenological
    d. ecological

18. The development of children in Somalia was negatively affected by the recent famine. Such events are examples of the
    a. macrosystem.
    b. exosystem.
    c. mesosystem.
    d. chronosystem.

19. A major strength of ecological theory is its framework for explaining
    a. environmental influences on development.
    b. biological influences on development.
    c. cognitive development.
    d. affective processes in development.

20. Which of the following is true about theories to explain life-span development?
    a. if theorists keep working at it they will eventually come up with one theory that explains development
    b. cognitive, psychoanalytic, and humanistic theories have nothing in common and can never be reconciled
    c. the theories proposed should be thought of as complementary rather than competitive
    d. one theory from biology, one theory from cognitive psychology, and one theory from social psychology are all that is needed to explain development

21. A theorist who holds to Erik Erikson's psychosocial stages while emphasizing the need for social learning, particularly in the study of cross-cultural settings, has adopted an _____ view.
    a. eclectic
    b. ecological
    c. environmental
    d. ethological

22. One difficulty of doing life-span research in a laboratory setting is that
    a. an unnatural behavior may occur.
    b. random assignment is impossible.
    c. extraneous factors are difficult to control.
    d. the experimenter's judgments are of unknown reliability.

23. How is a questionnaire study different from one that uses interviews?
    a. Questionnaires usually involve in-depth probing into the details of a person's life.
    b. Interviews may be carried out over the phone, while questionnaires are always completed with the researcher present.
    c. Questionnaires ask respondents to indicate their answers on paper instead of answering orally.
    d. Interviews are the preferred method for cross-cultural research.

24. An investigator interested in gender differences in helping behavior spends three hours a day in the mall watching who opens doors for shoppers burdened with packages uses which of the following methods of data collection?
    a. observational
    b. experimental
    c. correlational
    d. case studies

25. Animals are used in psychological research for all but which of the following reasons?
   a. investigators can control their genetic background
   b. experiential factors can be manipulated
   c. the entire life span of an animal can be tracked in a relatively short period of time
   d. animals always behave like humans

26. A research sample is described as "comprised of 72 blacks for an inner city area of Pittsburgh." Actually, 30 were African-Americans, 30 were West Indians, and 12 were Haitians. This study suffers from
   a. sociocultural bias.
   b. an overrepresentation of ethnic factors.
   c. ethnic gloss.
   d. a lack of standardization.

27. Which of the following questions would best be answered using a correlational study?
   a. Does depression increase with age?
   b. Are people more depressed before or after retirement?
   c. Does exercise decrease depression?
   d. How depressed are 14-year-olds?

28. An experimenter administered a placebo (inert substance) to one group of individuals, while another group received caffeine pills. In this memory experiment, the placebo group was the _____ group, and the caffeine group was the _____ group.
   a. experimental, control
   b. independent, dependent
   c. control, experimental
   d. dependent, independent

29. An experimenter compared the reading ability of two groups of children, one that regularly watched educational television, and another that never watched educational television. He concluded that watching educational television causes children's reading abilities to improve. This conclusion is faulty because
   a. a correlational strategy was used.
   b. no dependent variable was manipulated.
   c. there was no control group.
   d. the adolescents were not randomly assigned to conditions.

30. A psychologist selects three groups of children (5-, 8-, and 11-year olds) and tests each group's cognitive abilities. What can be said about this study?
   a. It does not control for cohort effects.
   b. It does identify true developmental changes.
   c. It is a longitudinal-sequence design.
   d. It is a cross-sectional design.

31. Which of the following is likely to be the most complex approach for studying changes in development with age?
   a. cross-sectional
   b. longitudinal
   c. sequential
   d. correlational

32. What is the most important principle when conducting ethical research on life-span development?
   a. Researchers must keep the best interests of their subjects in mind.
   b. Researchers must select participants in a way that allows for appropriate generalizations.
   c. Researchers must use any means to answer important development questions.
   d. Researchers must publish exclusively in professional journals.

33. Florence Denmark recommends reducing sexism in developmental research by
   a. not drawing causal conclusions from correlational strategies.
   b. selecting participants in a way that allows for appropriate generalizations.
   c. requiring participants to sign informed consent sheets.
   d. publishing exclusively in professional journals.

34. A wise consumer of information about life-span development does all of the following except
   a. draw causal conclusions from correlational strategies.
   b. regard research in professional journals as more credible than research in the popular media.
   c. be careful to distinguish between nomothetic research and idiographic needs.
   d. generalize from small or clinical samples of subjects.

35. Why was Bronislaw Malinowski's research among the Trobriand Islanders so important?
   a. He considered racial factors in personality development.
   b. He demonstrated that the concepts of the unconscious and repression were not valid.
   c. He showed that the Oedipal conflict was a culturally determined phenomenon and not biologically based.
   d. He proved that anatomical differences between the sexes were critical in explaining personality development.

Answers for Self Test A

1. longitudinal approach
2. eclectic theoretical orientation
3. initiative versus guilt
4. correlational strategy
5. sensorimotor stage
6. ethnic gloss
7. phallic stage
8. behaviorism
9. Albert Bandura or Walter Mischel
10. Erik Erikson
11. exosystem
12. naturalistic observation
13. Florence Denmark
14. critical period
15. Urie Bronfenbrenner
16. scientific method
17. information processing approach
18. Glen Elder
19. emic approach
20. experimental strategy
21. Jean Piaget
22. social learning theory
23. cross-sectional approach
24. ecological theory
25. hypotheses
26. idiographic needs
27. cohort effects
28. independent variable
29. life course theory
30. identity versus identity confusion

Answers for Self Test B

1. a LO 1.1
2. b LO 1.1
3. b LO 2.2
4. a LO 2.3
5. a LO 2.5
6. b LO 2.7
7. c LO 2.9
8. d LO 2.11
9. d LO 2.12
10. d LO 2.14
11. b LO 2.15
12. a LO 2.16
13. d LO 2.17
14. a LO 2.17
15. a LO 2.20
16. a LO 2.20
17. d LO 2.21
18. b LO 2.22
19. a LO 2.22
20. c LO 2.27
21. c LO 2.27
22. a LO 3.2
23. c LO 3.3
24. a LO 3.3
25. d LO 3.3
26. c LO 3.5
27. a LO 3.7
28. c LO 3.9
29. c LO 3.10
30. d LO 3.11
31. c LO 3.11
32. a LO 4.1
33. b LO 4.3
34. a LO 4.8
35. c LO 5.2

Chapter 3   Biological Beginnings

Learning Objectives with Key Terms in Boldface

1.0 The Evolutionary Perspective

  A. *Natural Selection*

    1.1 Define **natural selection**, and show how an evolutionary perspective explains human development.

  B. *Sociobiology*

    1.2 Define **sociobiology**, and state its purpose according to E. O Wilson.

    1.3 Give an example of a sociobiological interpretation of behavior.

    1.4 Evaluate the contributions of sociobiology to our understanding of human behavior.

    1.5 Indicate what critics say about sociobiology, and summarize sociobiologist's response to their critics.

  C. *Evolutionary Psychology*

    1.6 Define **evolutionary psychology** and distinguish it from sociobiology.

    1.7 State the central issue of evolutionary psychology.

    1.8 Identify the domain specific (modular) mechanisms revealed by evolutionary psychology.

    1.9 Apply evolutionary psychology to life-span issues such as attachment and warmth.

    1.10 Evaluate the contribution of evolutionary psychology to our understanding of human behavior.

2.0 Heredity

  A. *What Are Genes?*

    2.1 Define and distinguish **chromosomes**, **DNA**, and **genes**.

    2.2 Define **gametes** and **zygotes**, and describe the process that transforms gametes into zygotes.

    2.3 Define and distinguish between **meiosis** and **reproduction**.

  B. *Reproduction*

    2.4 Explain how technology might allow parents to select the sex of their child.

    2.5 Define *in vitro* **fertilization**, and indicate how this procedure allows an infertile couple to have a baby.

    2.6 Define infertility, and discuss its causes and cures.

    2.7 Discuss the risks of adoption to both adoptive children and their adoptive parents.

  C. *Abnormalities in Genes and Chromosomes*

    2.8 Define genetic abnormality, and contrast genetic abnormalities such as **phenylketonuria (PKU)**, **Down syndrome**, **sickle-cell anemia**, **Klinefelter syndrome**, **Turner syndrome**, and **XYY syndrome**.

    2.9 Describe the method and purpose for **amniocentesis**, **ultrasound sonography**, the **chorionic villus test**, and the **maternal blood test**.

3.0 Genetic Principles and Methods

  A. *Some Genetic Principles*

    3.1 Define and distinguish between the **dominant-recessive genes principle** and **polygenic inheritance**.

    3.2 Explain why two brown-eyed parents can have blue-eyed children, but two blue-eyed parents cannot have brown-eyed children.

    3.3 Define and distinguish between **genotype** and **phenotype**.

    3.4 Define and distinguish between **reaction range** and **canalization**.

    3.5 Indicate why Sandra Scarr says that the concept of reaction range explains why it is hard to determine the genotype given the phenotype.

  B. *Methods Used by Behavior Geneticists*

    3.6 Define **behavior genetics**.

3.7 Define and distinguish between **fraternal twins** and **identical twins**.

3.8 Compare and contrast an **adoption study** and **twin study**, and state the conclusions derived from these studies about heredity's influence on behavior.

C. *Heredity's Influence on Development*

3.9 Indicate why Arthur Jensen favors nature over nurture as an explanation of intelligence.

3.10 State the main points of Richard Hernstein and Charles Murray's book, *The Bell Curve*.

3.11 Explain why Hernstein and Murray titled their book *The Bell Curve* and why they say IQs have predictive value.

3.12 Indicate what critics say about the views expressed by Hernstein and Murray in *The Bell Curve*.

4.0 Heredity-Environment Interaction and Development

A. *Passive Genotype-Environment, Evocative Genotype-Environment, and Active Genotype-Environment Interactions*

4.1 Define and distinguish **passive genotype-environment interactions**, **evocative genotype-environment interactions**, and **active (niche-picking) genotype-environment interactions**.

4.2 Explain how the relative importance of the three types of interactions may change with age.

B. *Shared and Nonshared Environmental Influences*

4.3 Indicate Robert Plomin's view about shared and nonshared environmental influences.

4.4 Distinguish **shared environmental experiences** and **nonshared environmental experiences**.

4.5 State Eleanor Maccoby and Diana Baumrind's criticism of the concept of nonshared environmental experience.

C. *The Contemporary Heredity-Environment Controversy*

4.6 Explain Sandra Scarr's view that genotypes drive experiences.

4.7 Indicate criticisms of Scarr's view, and evaluate how well she rebuts the criticisms of her theory of genotype-environment effects.

4.8 Explain the idea that virtually all developmentalists are interactionists.

D. *Conclusions About Heredity-Environment Interaction*

4.9 Summarize the importance of genes and environment to human development.

5.0 Chapter Boxes

A. *Sociocultural Worlds of Development: The Human Species Is a Culture-Making Species*

5.1 Define and distinguish between cultural and evolutionary changes.

B. *Critical Thinking About Life-Span Development: Mate Selection: Male and Female Strategies*

5.2 Describe the role each sex plays in sexual selection according to evolutionary theory.

5.3 Pursue alternative explanations for sexual selection.

C. *Critical Thinking About Life-Span Development: Who Am I? Identity and Adoption*

5.4 Generate pro and con arguments for sealing records and withholding information in cases of adoption.

D. *Life-Span Health and Well-Being: Genetic Counseling*

5.5 Discuss what couples would learn and understand by consulting a genetic counselor.

Guided Review and Study

1.0 The Evolutionary Perspective

1. In an evolutionary calendar year, humans arrived on the scene in the month of _____ .   *December*

A. *Natural Selection*

1. Explain the concept of natural selection in your own terms.

2. Charles _____ published *On the Origin of Species* in 1859.   *Darwin*

3. Although Darwin determined that reproduction rates should result in overpopulation, he noticed   *constant*
that populations remained relatively _____ .

28

4. Darwin reasoned that the individuals who survived were best _____ to their environments, and passed their _____ on to the next generation.

adapted
genes

5. Evolutionary change generally occurs _____ according to Darwin.

slowly

6. Although _____ changes have not occurred in humans for the past 50,000 years, there have been dramatic _____ changes.

evolutionary
cultural

B. Sociobiology

1. _____ explains social behavior in terms of principles of evolutionary biology.

Sociobiology

2. State the purpose of sociobiology in your own terms.

3. One way to illustrate sociobiological inquiry is to examine the _____ behavior of various species of birds.

helping

4. Characterize some sociobiological contributions to the understanding of human behavior.

5. Indicate criticisms of sociobiology, and how sociobiologists respond to their critics.

C. Evolutionary Psychology

1. A contemporary approach, _____ psychology, emphasizes that behavior is a function of mechanisms, requires input for activation, and relates ultimately to survival and reproduction.

evolutionary

2. The central issue for evolutionary psychologists is the nature of psychological mechanisms created by selection and their _____ functions.

adaptive

3. Explain what it means to say that human psychological mechanisms are domain-specific or modular, and provide some examples.

4. One of the applications of evolutionary psychology to issues in life-span development involves _____ and warmth; other issues include the _____ from mating to parenting, and from menopause to grandparenting.

attachment
shifts

5. Evaluate the contribution of evolutionary psychology to our understanding of human behavior.

2.0 Heredity

A. What Are Genes?

1. _____ are thread-like structures that come in 23 pairs and contain deoxyribonucleic acid or DNA.

Chromosomes

2. _____ are short segments of DNA.

Genes

3. Indicate what genes do.

4. _____ are human reproductive cells created in the testes of males and the ovaries of females.

Gametes

5. The process of cell division called _____ separates pairs of chromosomes into gametes.

meiosis

6. The union of an ovum and a sperm cell produces a _____ through the process of reproduction.

zygote

7. Each parent contributes _____ of the offspring's genetic endowment.

50%

B. Reproduction
1. Normal females have two _____ chromosomes, whereas normal _____ have one X and one   *X; males*
    Y chromosome.
2. Explain how technology might allow parents to select the sex of their child.

3. Although reproduction produces more males than females, males are more likely than females to   *abort*
    spontaneously _____ .
4. Explain the process of *in vitro* fertilization.

5. Babies born through *in vitro* fertilization _____ show later developmental deficiencies.   *do not*
6. Define infertility.

7. Approximately 10 to 15 percent of human couples are _____ .   *infertile*

8. Use Table 3.1 to review the causes of and remedies for infertility in females and males.

9. A non-reproductive solution to a couple's infertility is _____ .   *adoption*
10. Adopted children typically do not know their _____ parents; however, this policy is now   *biological*
    being challenged by adoption rights activists.
11. Compared to nonadopted children, adopted children experience _____ problems.   *more*
12. The problems are most likely to be greatest during _____ when children are searching for   *adolescence*
    their identity.
13. Indicate developmentalist's advice to parents of children who have been adopted.

C. Abnormalities in Genes and Chromosomes
1. There are numerous chromosomal and _____ problems.   *genetic*
2. The _____ syndrome is a genetic disorder that results in the failure of the body to produce   *PKU*
    an enzyme.
3. An untreated PKU syndrome results in mental retardation and _____ .   *hyperactivity*
4. _____ syndrome refers to the presence of an extra chromosome that results in retardation, a   *Down*
    flattened skull, short limbs, and a protruding tongue.
5. A genetic disorder creating problems with red blood cell formation is _____-cell anemia.   *sickle*
6. Sickle-cell anemia is most likely to occur among _____ -American children.   *African*
7. Some genetic disorders are related to _____ chromosomes.   *sex*
8. _____ syndrome results from an extra X chromosome in males.   *Klinefelter*
9. _____ syndrome can cause retardation in women, and is due to the absence of an X   *Turner*
    chromosome.
10. _____ syndrome presumably is related to excessive male aggression.   *X Y Y*
11. Describe the method and purpose of the following tests for abnormalities:
    amniocentesis

ultrasound sonography

chorionic villus test

maternal blood test

3.0 Genetic Principles and Methods

A. Some Genetic Principles

1. Although determining the nature and extent of genetic influence on behavior is a complex task, researchers have identified a number of _____ : dominant-recessive _____ , polygenic inheritance, reaction _____ , and canalization.   *principles*   *genes*   *range*

2. Express the principle of dominant-recessive genes in your own terms.

3. Although two brown-eyed parents can have a blue-eyed child, two blue-eyed parents cannot have a brown-eyed child. This outcome means that the gene for brown eyes is _____ and the gene for blue eyes is _____ .   *dominant*   *recessive*

4. State the principle of polygenic inheritance in your own terms.

5. Most psychological characteristics result from _____ inheritance.   *polygenic*

6. _____ refers to an individual's actual hereditary constitution, whereas _____ refers to the observable and measurable characteristics of the individual.   *Genotype*   *phenotype*

7. Psychological _____ include intelligence, creativity, personality, and social tendencies.   *phenotypes*

8. Given a particular genotype, a wide range of _____ is possible.   *phenotypes*

9. The genotype may only set broad limits on the range of phenotypes, a phenomenon known as the _____ range.   *reaction*

10. The reaction range is largely determined by the _____ .   *environment*

11. What does Sandra Scarr mean by saying that the concept of reaction range explains why it is hard to determine the genotype given the phenotype?

12. _____ refers to characteristics minimally influenced by the environment.   *Canalization*

13. Indicate and explain Jerome Kagan's evidence for canalization.

14. Explain why developmentalists such as Gilbert Gottlieb say that genes do not directly determine human behavior.

B. Methods Used by Behavior Geneticists

1. Define behavior genetics in your own terms.

2. Behavior geneticists assume that heredity and environment _____ .   *interact*

3. Monozygotic twins are called _____ twins, and develop from _____ ova.   *identical; one*

4. Dizygotic twins are called _____ twins, and develop from _____ ova.   *fraternal; two*

5. Identical twins are genetically _____ similar than fraternal twins.   *more*

6. Behavior geneticists perform both twin and _____ studies.   *adoption*

7. _____ studies compare identical twins with fraternal twins.   *Twin*

8. If _____ twins are more similar than _____ twins, behavior geneticists infer that the behavior or trait under study is influenced by heredity.   *identical fraternal*

9. _____ studies compare adopted offspring to both their adoptive and biological parents.   *Adoption*

10. If the adopted offspring are more similar to _____ than the _____ parents, behavior geneticists infer that the behavior or trait under study is influenced by heredity.   *biological adoptive*

C. *Heredity's Influence on Development*

1. Behavior geneticists have assessed _____ influence on development by studying intelligence and temperament.   *heredity's*
   Indicate why Arthur Jensen believes that intelligence is primarily inherited.

3.. Summarize the main point of Richard Hernstein and Charles Murray's *The Bell Curve: Intelligence and Class Structure in Modern Life.*

4. The term bell curve is synonymous with the concept of the _____ distribution.   *normal*

5. Explain why Hernstein and Murray titled their book *The Bell Curve.*

6. Hernstein and Murray say IQ scores have _____ value when applied to large groups.   *predictive*

7. Indicate what critics say about the ideas expressed by Hernstein and Murray in their book.

4.0 Heredity-Environment Interaction and Children's Development

A. *Passive Genotype-Environment, Evocative Genotype-Environment, and Active Genotype-Environment Interactions*

1. State what Sandra Scarr assumes that parents contribute to their children's development.

2. According to behavior geneticists, heredity _____ with the environment in three different ways: passively, evocatively, and actively.   *interacts*

3. _____ genotype-environmental interactions refer to the environments provided by the biological parents of the children.   *Passive*

4. Provide your own example of passive genotype-environmental interactions.

5. _____ genotype-environmental interactions refer to environments resulting from the child's genotype.   *Evocative*

6. Provide your own example of evocative genotype-environmental interactions.

7. _____ genotype-environmental interactions refer to the role played by children in finding situations most comfortably and interesting to them.   *Active*

32

8. Provide your own example of active genotype-environmental interactions.

9. According to Sandra Scarr, the relative importance of passive, evocative, and active genotype-environment interactions _____ as children develop from infancy through adolescence.

change

B. *Shared and Nonshared Environmental Influences*

1. Indicate Robert Plomin's views about shared environmental experiences and nonshared environmental experiences.

2. A _____ environmental influence refers to common experiences of children in a family. Examples include the parent's _____ and the family's social class.

3. A _____ environmental influence refers to each child's unique experiences both within and outside the family. Examples include different _____ and teachers at school.

shared
personalities
nonshared
friends

C. *The Contemporary Heredity-Environment Controversy*

1. Explain why Sandra Scarr says that genotypes drive experiences.

2. Sandra Scarr argues that _____ influences within an average range can be expected to have _____ effects on their children's personality, intelligence, and interests.

3. Scarr argues that nonrisk children _____ experience prolonged, negative effects of day care.

parental
small
will not

4. Indicate the reasons that developmentalists such as Diana Baumrind, Jacquelyne Jackson, and Eleanor Maccoby criticize Sandra Scarr's viewpoint.

5. Scarr rebuts such critics by saying children's development must be understood under the umbrella of _____ theory, and that her critics largely ignore the role of _____ in understanding children's development.

evolutionary
biology

D. *Conclusions About Heredity-Environment Interaction*

1. Explain why both genes and environment are important to human development.

5.0 Chapter Boxes

A. *Sociocultural Worlds of Development: The Human Species Is a Culture-Making Species*

1. Explain why humans change primarily through cultural rather than biological evolution.

B. *Critical Thinking About Life-Span Development: Mate Selection: Male and Female Strategies*

1. Explain why males and females may have different sexual selection strategies.

C. *Critical Thinking About Life-Span Development: Who Am I? Identity and Adoption*

1. Identify what you would learn by developing pro and con arguments for closed adoptions, in which both birth and adoptive parents are unknown to one another.

D. *Life-Span Health and Well-Being: Genetic Counseling*

1. Discuss what couples would learn and understand by consulting a genetic counselor.

Self Test A: Key Terms and Key Persons

Write the appropriate key term or key person in the space to the right of the definition or description.

1. The narrow path or track that marks the development of some characteristics; these characteristics appear immune to vast changes in environmental events. _____

2. An approach that utilizes principles of evolutionary biology to explain behavior. _____

3. Aspects of a child's life inside and outside the family that are not common to other siblings. _____

4. Either of the three developmentalists who criticize Sandra Scarr's views for having loopholes. _____

5. The process of cell division which produces cells with 23 unpaired chromosomes or gametes. _____

6. A case in which the biological parents also provide the rearing environment for their children. _____

7. Twins that develop from separate eggs, and are genetically less similar than identical twins. _____

8. Twins that come from the same egg. _____

9. The most common genetically transmitted form of mental retardation that is caused by an extra chromosome. _____

10. Actions and behaviors on the part of children that put them in environments personally compatible and comfortable for them. _____

11. The individual who proposed the principle of natural selection. _____

12. The biochemical agents that are the building blocks of heredity; part of a chromosome. _____

13. Observable and measurable characteristics of an individual that are the product of heredity. _____

14. Either of the two authors of a controversial book titled *The Bell Curve*. _____

15. An evolutionary process that favors individuals of a species best able to survive and reproduce. _____

16. A prenatal test that detects genetic defects in the fetus by removing and analyzing a small sample of the placenta between the eighth and eleventh weeks of a pregnancy. _____

17. A behavior geneticist who believes that shared environments account for little of the variation in children's interests or personalities. _____

18. A research design that compares the characteristics of an adopted child to those of both the biological and the parents who reared the children. _____

19. When the ovum is surgically removed from the mother, fertilized in a laboratory medium with live sperm, stored in a solution that substitutes for the uterine environment, and then implanted back in the mother's uterus. _____

20. A behavior geneticist who believes that parental genotypes influence the environments that they provide for their offspring. _____

Self Test B: Multiple Choice

1. Which statement best depicts the process of natural selection?
   a. One species destroys another.
   b. One species produces more offspring than others.
   c. Individuals of a species adapt themselves to a changing environment and therefore survive.
   d. Environments modify heredity by causing genetic mutations.

2. A basic assumption of sociobiologists is that
   a. genes are the most important determinant of behavior.
   b. cultural evolution is the dominant type of evolution among humans.
   c. social and biological factors interact to produce human behavior.
   d. physical and psychological aspects of humans have different determinants.

3. Which one of the following is not a criticism of sociobiology?
   a. Sociobiology ignores the adaptability of human beings.
   b. Sociobiology ignores evidence from animal behavior.
   c. Sociobiological concepts can be used to justify existing social injustices.
   d. Sociobiologists cannot make theory-based predictions about behavior.

4. The approach that says behavior is a function of mechanisms, requires input for activation, and is ultimately related to survival and reproduction is called
   a. behavior genetics.
   b. evolutionary psychology.
   c. natural selection.
   d. sociobiology.

5. The fact that children imitate high-status rather than low-status models provides evidence for
   a. natural selection.
   b. domain-specific psychological mechanisms.
   c. cultural evolution.
   d. some scientific findings are politically objectionable.

6. Twenty-three pairs of threadlike structures from each parent and the fundamental unit of heredity define _____ and _____ , respectively.
   a. DNA, meiosis
   b. zygotes, gamete
   c. genotype, phenotype
   d. chromosomes, gene

7. What is the name for the process of cell division in which each pair of chromosomes separates and joins a daughter cell?
   a. reproduction
   b. mitosis
   c. meiosis
   d. gametization

8. An identical twin shares _____ of his or her genes with an identical twin and _____ with either parent.
   a. 100%, 50%
   b. 100%, 100%
   c. 50%, 100%
   d. 50%, 50%

9. *In vitro* fertilization is a possible solution to infertility that involves
   a. having sperm and egg unite outside of a woman's body.
   b. implanting a fertilized egg into a substitute mother's womb.
   c. enhancing the possibility of conception by taking fertility drugs.
   d. incubating a zygote outside of a woman's body.

10. Which of the following treatments for infertility is effective with both females and males?
    a. hormone therapy
    b. surgery
    c. antibiotics
    d. All of these answers are correct.

11. Which is a disadvantage of adoption in comparison to medical treatments for infertility?
    a. Adoptive parents tend not to try as hard as nonadoptive parents to care for their children.
    b. Adopted children are more likely than nonadopted children to have psychological problems.
    c. Adoption is more likely to involve third parties than nonadoption.
    d. Biological parents find it easier to love their child than do adopting parents.

12. Which of these syndromes is not sex-linked?
    a. Down syndrome
    b. Klinefelter syndrome
    c. Turner syndrome
    d. XXY syndrome

13. A physician orders that an amniocentesis be performed to determine whether a woman's fetus is genetically normal. This procedure will involve
    a. taking a blood sample from the mother.
    b. drawing a sample of the fluid that surrounds a baby in the womb.
    c. taking a sample of the placenta between the eighth and eleventh week of pregnancy.
    d. taking a blood sample from the fetus.

14. Traits that are produced by the interaction between two or more genes are called
    a. dominant.
    b. recessive.
    c. canalized.
    d. polygenic.

15. Assume that the gene for green hair is dominant, whereas the gene for blue hair is recessive. Which of the following statements is most accurate?
    a. Parents with green hair can have a child with blue hair.
    b. Parents with blue hair can have a child with green hair.
    c. Parents with blue hair cannot have a child with blue hair.
    d. Parents with green hair cannot have a child with blue hair.

16. A person's genetic heritage is his or her _____ , whereas the expression of the genetic heritage is his or her _____ .
    a. genotype; phenotype
    b. dominant character; recessive character
    c. phenotype; genotype
    d. recessive character; dominant character

17. Which of the following is the best example of canalization?
    a. Twins reared apart in very different environments have different temperaments.
    b. Two brown-eyed parents have a blue-eyed child.
    c. An extra X chromosome causes genetic abnormalities.
    d. Infants smile at exactly 40 weeks after conception, regardless of when they are born.

18. Behavioral geneticists believe that behaviors are determined by
    a. only biological factors.
    b. only environmental factors.
    c. biological factors at birth and environmental factors throughout the rest of life.
    d. a continuous interaction between biological and environmental factors.

19. If heredity is an important determinant of a specific behavior, what prediction can we make about expression of the behavior in identical twins reared apart compared to its expression in fraternal twins reared apart?
    a. Fraternal twins will express the behavior more similarly than identical twins.
    b. There will be little similarity in the expression of the behavior in either set of twins.
    c. Identical twins will express the behavior more similarly than fraternal twins.
    d. The behavior will be expressed as similarly by identical twins as it is by fraternal twins.

20. In an adoption study, a psychologist compares the behavior of
    a. identical fraternal twins.
    b. family members and randomly selected others.
    c. fraternal twins with each other.
    d. children living with adoptive parents and children living with biological parents.

21. Which of the following phrases best defines intelligence?
    a. a skill that favors survival and reproduction
    b. an individual's standardized test score
    c. a skill that enhances life through the use of complex objects
    d. an individual's behavior style

22. Jensen argues that heredity is a more important determinant of intelligence than environment because the
    a. educational level of biological parents correlates more strongly with children's IQs than do the IQs of adoptive parents.
    b. IQs of fraternal twins are as highly correlated as the IQs of identical twins.
    c. IQs of identical twins reared apart are as highly correlated as the IQs of identical twins reared together.
    d. correlation between fraternal twins' IQs is similar to the correlation between siblings' IQs.

23. What do Arthur Jensen's views and Richard Hernstein and Charles Murray views have in common?
    a. Their specific views illustrate the more general issue of heredity's influence on development.
    b. These individuals are on the same side with regard to the debate regarding shared and nonshared environmental influences.
    c. Their specific views illustrate the more general issue of an evolutionary perspective.
    d. These individuals are proponents of genetic counseling.

24. Children who are highly active, easily distractible, and move very fast frequently elicit adult attempts to quiet them down, punishment for lack of concentration, and angry warnings to slow down. This describes an example of a/an _____/environment interaction.
    a. passive genotype
    b. active genotype
    c. niche-picking genotype
    d. evocative genotype

25. All three of the Brodsky children grew up in the same house, went to the same school, and observed their parents' dedication to charitable work. These experiences constitute the children's
    a. shared environmental influences.
    b. nonshared environmental influences.
    c. niche-picking experiences.
    d. heritability.

26. Which of the following illustrates the idea of heredity-environment interaction most clearly?
    a. phenylketonuria
    b. Down syndrome
    c. spina bifida
    d. sickle-cell anemia

27. The key difference between evolutionary and cultural change is that evolutionary change alters _____ , whereas cultural change alters _____ .
    a. reproduction, environment
    b. heredity, environment
    c. environment, behavior
    d. development, learning

28. What would evolutionary psychologists say about mate selection?
    a. Culture plays a greater role than evolution in mate selection.
    b. Females want to spread their genes around to many males, whereas males try to attract the best female they can find.
    c. Evolution produced different mate selection strategies for males and females.
    d. Mate selection is determined by domain-specific psychological mechanisms.

29. Which of the following statements best describes the role and function of a genetic counselor?
    a. Counseling couples who have a baby that is genetically abnormal.
    b. Administering *in vitro* fertilization.
    c. Helping a couple decide how likely they are to have a genetically defective baby.
    d. Helping a couple evaluate their future as adoptive parents.

Answers for Self Test A

1. canalization
2. sociobiology
3. nonshared environmental influences
4. Diana Baumrind, Jacquelyne Jackson, or Eleanor Maccoby
5. meiosis
6. passive genotype-environment interactions
7. fraternal twins
8. identical twin
9. Down syndrome
10. active (niche-picking) genotype-environment interactions
11. Charles Darwin
12. genes
13. phenotype
14. Richard Hernstein or Charles Murray
15. natural selection
16. chorionic villus test
17. Robert Plomin
18. adoption study
19. *in vitro* fertilization
20. Sandra Scarr

Answers for Self Test B

1.	b	LO 1.1
2.	a	LO 1.2
3.	b	LO 1.5
4.	b	LO 1.6
5.	b	LO 1.8
6.	d	LO 2.1
7.	c	LO 2.3
8.	a	LO 2.3
9.	a	LO 2.5
10.	d	LO 2.6
11.	b	LO 2.7
12.	a	LO 2.8
13.	b	LO 2.9
14.	d	LO 3.1
15.	a	LO 3.2
16.	a	LO 3.3
17.	d	LO 3.4
18.	d	LO 3.6
19.	c	LO 3.7
20.	d	LO 3.8
21.	b	LO 3.9
22.	c	LO 3.9
23.	a	LO 3.11
24.	d	LO 4.1
25.	a	LO 4.4
26.	a	LO 4.8
27.	b	LO 5.1
28.	c	LO 5.2
29.	c	LO 5.5

Section II   Beginnings

Chapter 4   Prenatal Development and Birth

Learning Objectives with Key Terms in Boldface

1.0 Prenatal Development

  A. *The Course of Prenatal Development*

    1.1   Describe the **germinal period**.

    1.2   Define and distinguish between **blastocyst** and **trophoblast**.

    1.3   Define **implantation**.

    1.4   Describe the **embryonic period**, and define and distinguish among the structures of the **endoderm, mesoderm,** and **ectoderm**.

    1.5   Define **placenta** and **umbilical chord**, and explain how they prevent transmission of harmful substances from mother to infant.

    1.6   Explain the roles of the **amnion** and amniotic fluid in prenatal development.

    1.7   Define **organogenesis** and explain its importance.

    1.8   Summarize changes that occur during the **fetal period**.

  B. *Miscarriage and Abortion*

    1.9   Define and distinguish between miscarriage and abortion.

    1.10 List some causes of miscarriage.

    1.11 Discuss the medical, legal, psychological, and social aspects of the decision to have an abortion.

    1.12 Indicate what the APA review panel concluded about the psychological effects of an abortion on a woman.

  C. *Teratology and Hazards to Prenatal Development*

    1.13 Define **teratogen** and teratology, and identify the period of greatest vulnerability to teratogens.

    1.14 Discuss maternal diseases and conditions that influence prenatal development such as rubella, syphilis, herpes, and AIDS.

    1.15 Describe the incidence of AIDS among children.

    1.16 List ways a mother with AIDS may infect her offspring, and list the possible outcomes for infants born to mothers infected with AIDS.

    1.17 Discuss how age relates to both the incidence of pregnancy and to problems with the pregnancy.

    1.18 Summarize the effects of nutrition on prenatal development.

    1.19 Explain how a mother's emotional state and stress can influence prenatal development, birth, and the newborn.

    1.20 Identify and contrast the effects of thalidomide, alcohol, cigarettes, marijuana, and cocaine on prenatal development.

    1.21 Define the **fetal alcohol syndrome (FAS)**.

    1.22 Explain the relationship between alcohol consumption and risks of deformity and birth defects among younger versus older women.

    1.23 List the prenatal, birth, and postnatal consequences of smoking by pregnant women.

    1.24 Compare and contrast the effects of various drugs on fetal development and later life.

    1.25 Describe how radiation, toxic wastes, video display terminals, and hot tubs pose risks to prenatal development.

    1.26 Define **toxoplasmosis,** and explain why it is a risk to prenatal development.

    1.27 Describe how culture influences health care practices during pregnancy.

2.0 Birth

  A. *Stages of Birth*

    2.1   Describe the three stages of birth: the first stage, the second stage, and **afterbirth**.

  B. *Delivery Complications*

    2.2   List four birth complications.

    2.3   Define and distinguish between **precipitate delivery** and **anoxia**.

2.4   Explain why the **breech position** complicates delivery of a baby.

2.5   Define **cesarean section**, list factors that influence its use, and cite information regarding its overuse.

C. The Use of Drugs During Childbirth

2.6   List reasons for giving drugs such as tranquilizers, sedatives, and analgesics to a woman giving birth.

2.7   Define **oxytocin** and prostaglandins, and list pros and cons of using these drugs during the birth process.

2.8   Summarize the research findings about the effects of drugs administered to a woman during childbirth.

D. Childbirth Strategies

2.9   Describe standard childbirth, the **Leboyer method**, **prepared (natural) childbirth**, and the **Lamaze method**.

2.10   List pros and cons of each the above child birth practices.

2.11   Indicate the basic philosophies underlying the standard, Leboyer, and prepared childbirth methods.

2.12   Define **doula**, and characterize the roles of the doula.

2.13   Characterize trends in childbirth practices in the 1990s.

2.14   Explain why and how fathers have become more involved in childbirth, and list the pros and cons of a father's participation in childbirth.

E. Preterm Infants and Age-Weight Considerations

2.15   Define and distinguish between **preterm infants** and **low-birthweight infants**.

2.16   Discuss interventions for low-birthweight infants.

2.17   Discuss whether a shortened gestation period harms an infant.

2.18   Contrast the profile of preterm and full-term infants.

2.19   Indicate factors related to whether preterm infants will have developmental problems.

2.20   Explain what it means to say that whether a preterm infant will have developmental problems is a complex issue.

F. Prenatal Care

2.21   Describe the nature of prenatal care, and indicate the reasons for inadequate prenatal care.

G. Measures of Neonatal Health and Responsiveness

2.22   Define and distinguish between the **Apgar Scale** and the **Brazelton Neonatal Assessment Scale**.

2.23   Compare and contrast what you would learn about your infant from the Apgar and Brazelton scales.

3.0 The Postpartum Period

A. The Nature of the Postpartum Period

3.1   Explain why it might be helpful to call the **postpartum period** the "fourth trimester."

B. Physical Adjustments

3.2   Summarize the physical adjustments women make during the postpartum period.

3.3   Define **involution**.

C. Emotional and Psychological Adjustments

3.4   Summarize the emotional and psychological adjustments women make during the postpartum period.

3.5   Define **bonding**, and evaluate the claim that bonding between infant and parent shortly after birth is crucial to the infant's development.

4.0 Chapter Boxes

A. Sociocultural Worlds of Development: Prenatal Care in the United States and Around the World

4.1   Indicate why some countries have lower rates of low-birthweight infants than does the United States.

B. Sociocultural Worlds of Development: To Work or Not to Work

4.2   Explain how the advice of Arlene Eisenberg, Heidi Murkoff, and Sandee Hathaway may help a family decide whether a mother stays home or returns to work after the birth of her baby.

C. Critical Thinking About Life-Span Development: Cultural Beliefs About Pregnancy and Health Care

4.3   Explain why it is important for health care professionals to know their clients' cultural beliefs about pregnancy.

4.4   Identify important questions to ask concerning cultural beliefs about pregnancy.

D. Critical Thinking About Life-Span Development: Beyond the "Mommy Track"

4.5   Evaluate the "mommy track" as a way women can combine careers and families.

4.6   Suggest ways to reshape work so that it won't be a burden to women who have families.

E.   *Life-Span Health and Well-Being: The Power of Touch and Massage in Development*

    4.7   Explain why experts such as Tiffany Field believe that massage, exercise, and touch benefit preterm infants, HIV-infected infants, and children and adolescents who suffer touch aversion.

Guided Review and Study

1.0   Prenatal Development

1.   _____ occurs when one sperm from the male unites with an ovum from the female.   *Fertilization*

2.   The fertilized egg, or _____ , travels 3 to 4 days through the fallopian tube to the uterus.   *zygote*

A.   *The Course of Prenatal Development*

1.   The _____ periods of prenatal development include the germinal period, the embryonic period, and the fetal period.   *three*

2.   The first prenatal period of development, the _____ period, lasts two weeks.   *germinal*

3.   Describe the blastocyst.

4.   Describe the trophoblast.

5.   The zygote _____ itself on the uterine wall about 10 days after conception.   *implants*

6.   The second prenatal period of development, the _____ period, encompasses weeks 2 to 8 after conception.   *embryonic*

7.   During the embryonic period, cell _____ intensifies, cell support systems form, organs appear, and the zygote becomes an _____ .   *differentiation* *embryo*

8.   The embryo divides into _____ layers: the ectoderm, mesoderm, and endoderm.   *three*

9.   The _____ , or inner layer, gives rise to the digestive and respiratory systems.   *endoderm*

10. The _____ , or outermost layer, becomes the nervous system, skin, and sensory receptors.   *ectoderm*

11. The _____ , or middle layer, gives rise to muscles, bones, and circulatory system.   *mesoderm*

12. Describe the nature and function of the following components of the life-support system:

placenta

umbilical cord

amnion

13. During the first two months of prenatal development, the organs develop during the process of _____ .   *organogenesis*

14. The third prenatal period of development, the _____ period, extends from the end of the _____ month to the ninth month after conception.   *fetal* *second*

15. After _____ months, the fetus is 3 inches long and weighs 1 ounce.   *three*

16. Most physical features also have become differentiated, and _____ can be identified.   *gender*

17. By the end of the fourth month, the fetus exhibits some prenatal _____ ; the fetus is about 6 inches long and weighs about _____ ounces.   *reflexes* *4*

18. By the end of the fifth month, the infant displays a preference for a particular _____ ; the fetus is 10 to _____ inches long and weighs up to 1/2 to 1 pound.   *position* *12*

19. By the end of the sixth month there is evidence of both _____ movements and a grasping reflex; the fetus is 11 to _____ inches long and weighs up to 2 pounds.   *breathing* *12*

20. By seven month of age the fetus is 14 to _____ inches long and weighs 2.5 to _____ pounds.   *17: 3*

21. The final two months mainly produce overall growth as the fetus grows to an average of _____ inches in length and a weight of 7 to _____ pounds.

20
7.5

B. *Miscarriage and Abortion*

1. _____ abortions occur for 15 to 20 percent of all pregnancies, primarily as a result of _____ abnormalities.

Spontaneous
chromosomal

2. Indicate some causes of miscarriage.

3. Abortion became legal in the United States in _____ , and can be used to terminate unwanted pregnancies legally during the first _____ months.

1973
six

4. Summarize the APA panel's conclusions about the psychological effects of abortion on women.

C. *Teratology and Hazards to Prenatal Development*

1. An agent that can cause a birth defect is called a _____ , whereas the study of the causes of birth defects is called _____ .

teratogen
teratology

2. The possibility of structural defects by teratogens is greatest during the _____ period, the time of organogenesis.

embryonic

3. Exposure to teratogens during the _____ period is likely to stunt growth or affect organ function.

fetal

4. Various _____ diseases and conditions such as rubella, syphilis, genital herpes, and AIDS can produce birth defects.

maternal

5. An outbreak of _____ caused large numbers of birth defects in the mid-1960s.

rubella

6. Rubella, or _____ measles, causes the greatest damage during the third and fourth weeks of pregnancy.

German

7. _____ causes defects later in prenatal development and after birth.

Syphilis

8. Syphilis damages organs _____ they have been formed and can produce eye and skin lesions as well as _____ nervous system problems.

after
central

9. Genital _____ can infect the baby at birth, and result in either death or _____ damage.

herpes
brain

10. One way to prevent genital herpes from infecting newborns is to deliver the baby by _____ section.

cesarean

11. AIDS was the _____ leading cause of death among children ages 1 to 4 in 1989.

eighth

12. The usual source of the mother's infection is either use of _____ drugs or heterosexual contact with intravenous drug users.

intravenous

13. Mothers can transmit _____ to their offspring during gestation, delivery, and postpartum, through breast feeding.

AIDS

14. Describe the age-related risks of pregnancy for teenage mothers and "thirtysomething" mothers.

15. As women get older, they are _____ likely to conceive.

less

16. Maternal _____ affects the ability to reproduce, and the condition of the offspring.

nutrition

17. Maternal malnutrition can cause infants to be lighter and less vital, or _____ .

die

18. Dietary _____ to mother's diets improved the performance of their offspring through the age of 3 years.

supplements

19. Describe how a mother's emotional state and stress can influence prenatal development, birth, and the newborn.

20. Maternal consumption of _____ , such as tranquilizers, alcohol, tobacco, marijuana, heroin, and cocaine, affects _____ development.

drugs
prenatal

21. Mothers in the 1960s who took _____ , a tranquilizer to minimize morning sickness, gave birth to deformed babies.   *thalidomide*

22. Describe the fetal alcohol syndrome (FAS).

23. Even moderate drinking may _____ infant's levels of attention and alertness.   *lower*

24. In the recent decade, drinking by pregnant women has _____ , a trend that is clearest for older and more _____ women.   *decreased*
educated

25. Cigarette smoking has been associated with _____ prematurity rates and lower birth weights. _____ problems are also more common in the offspring of smokers.   *higher*
Respiratory

26. Mothers who smoke marijuana while pregnant tend to have infants who have _____ and startles as newborns, and poor verbal and _____ development at age 4.   *tremors*
memory

27. Maternal _____ use during pregnancy causes addiction, tremors, and disturbed sleep by their infants. _____ deficits may appear later in development.   *heroin*
Attention

28. Maternal use of cocaine is associated with low birthweights and _____ abnormalities.   *congenital*

29. Explain why it is difficult to determine the effects of cocaine on mothers and their offspring.

30. Maternal exposure to environmental _____ that impair prenatal development include radiation, pollutants, and toxic wastes.   *hazards*

31. _____ during pregnancy can cause gene mutations.   *Radiation*

32. Prenatal exposure to lead is associated with poor mental _____ , whereas prenatal exposure to PCBs is associated with having _____ infants who react slowly to stimuli.   *development*
premature

33. Prenatal exposure to video display terminals appears not to increase the risk of _____ ; however, working at video display terminals is associated with _____ on expectant mothers.   *miscarriage*
stress

34. _____ , an infection contracted from _____ feces, or raw meat, produces mild symptoms in adults and brain defects, eye defects, and premature birth in human infants.   *Toxoplasmosis*
cat

35. Hot tubs are an _____ hazard to fetuses because they may cause a fever in the mother.   *environmental*

36. A reasonable amount of time for a pregnant woman to spend in a hot tub is _____ minutes.   *ten*

37. Describe how culture influences health care practices during pregnancy.

2.0 Birth

A. Stages of Birth

1. The birth process occurs in _____ stages.   *three*

2. During the first and longest stage, uterine contractions _____ in frequency and intensity, and also become more regular.   *increase*

3. The first phase ends when the cervix dilates to a diameter of about _____ inches.   *4*

4. The second stage begins when the baby's _____ moves into the birth canal, and ends when the baby _____ from the mother's body.   *head*
emerges

5. During _____ , the third and shortest stage, the _____ and the umbilical cord are expelled from the mother's body.   *afterbirth*
placenta

B. Delivery Complications

1. Complications that can occur during _____ include precipitate delivery, anoxia, the breech position, and a cesarean section.   *delivery*

2. A _____ delivery is one that is too fast, and can cause hemorrhaging of the infant's head.   *precipitate*

3. A very long delivery can result in _____ , an impaired supply of oxygen to the infant.   *anoxia*

4. Explain why the breech position complicates delivery of a baby.

5. Although surgical removal of an infant from the uterus, a _____ section, is safer than a breech delivery, it does entail other complications.

cesarean

6. What do critics say about the number of cesarean sections performed in the United States?

C. The Use of Drugs During Childbirth

1. Drugs can relieve the mother's _____ and speed delivery during the birth process.

anxiety

2. One concern is that drugs can cross the _____ barrier and affect the infant.

placental

3. A drug that has been used to speed delivery is _____ ; however, it's use is controversial because it may cause _____ .

oxytocin
complications

4. Indicate four conclusions regarding the effects of drugs administered to a woman during delivery.

D. Childbirth Strategies

1. Alternative childbirth _____ include standard childbirth, the LeBoyer method, and prepared, or natural, childbirth.

strategies

2. Describe standard childbirth.

3. The _____ method eases the birth process for infants. LeBoyer characterizes standard birth practices as _____ for infants, and believes his strategy entails "birth without violence."

LeBoyer
traumatic

4. In the _____ method of childbirth, the umbilical cord is not cut right away, the baby is placed on the mother's stomach for a few minutes of _____ prior to being placed in a warm bath to relax.

LeBoyer
contact

5. In _____ childbirth, the mother knows what will happen, expects little medication, makes decisions during the birth, presumably will be helped by a _____ .

prepared
partner

6. Prepared childbirth procedures are _____ ; however, the basic element of prepared childbirth procedures is that mothers are _____ about procedures and make decisions about them. Preparing parents for childbirth now involves several _____ disciplines beyond obstetrics.

variable
informed
professional

7. The Lamaze method of childbirth, a widely used form of prepared childbirth, focuses on breathing and _____ . This method has increased the involvement of _____ in the entire process of childbirth.

relaxation
fathers

8. Explain the role of the *doula* in your own terms.

9. Review trends in childbirth for the 1990s.

10. _____ are more involved in childbirth than ever before.

Fathers

11. Fathers often participate in birth as a _____ .

coach

12. Professionals now support this involvement by stressing that birth should be an intimate, _____ event for couples; however, there is disagreement about whether _____ are the best coaches during labor.

shared
fathers

E. Preterm Infants and Age-Weight Considerations

1. Babies born before 38 weeks after conception are now referred to as _____ babies, whereas babies who weigh less than _____ pounds at birth are referred to as low-birthweight babies.

preterm
5.5

2. Both preterm and low-birthweight babies are _____ risk developmentally.

high

3. In order to enhance developmental outcomes for low-birthweight infants, mothers can learn to better understand low-birthweight infant's _____ and temperamental characteristics and cues, and how to _____ appropriately to them.

behavioral
respond

4. In one study, low-birthweight infants whose mothers had received such training scored better on _____ processing measures than low-birthweight infants whose mothers had not. *information*

5. Indicate whether a shortened gestation period necessarily harms an infant.

6. A disproportion of _____ American babies are born with low birthweights, likely to be born preterm, or likely to do die at birth. *African*

7. Indicate factors related to whether preterm infants will have developmental problems.

8. Indicate whether the effects of low-birthweight can be reversed.

F. Prenatal Care

1. Characterize the nature of prenatal care.

2. Indicate reasons for inadequate prenatal care.

G. Measures of Neonatal Health and Responsiveness

1. Indicate the purpose of the Apgar Scale and the Brazelton Neonatal Assessment Scale.

2. The _____ Scale evaluates various signs of health such as heart rate, color, respiratory effort, reflexes, and muscle tone. A score of 7 to 10 indicates a _____ baby; a score of 3 or lower indicates an _____ , and there is some question as to whether the baby will live. *Apgar* *healthy* *emergency*

3. The _____ Neonatal Behavioral Assessment Scale assesses the infant's reflexes, neurological function, and reactions to people. A very low score on the Brazelton may indicate _____ damage. *Brazelton* *brain*

3.0 The Postpartum Period

A. The Nature of the Postpartum Period

1. The _____ period lasts about 6 weeks after delivery. *postpartum*

2. Explain why it might be useful to call the postpartum period the "fourth trimester."

B. Physical Adjustments

1. A woman's body makes various _____ adjustments during the postpartum period. *physical*

2. Most women feel _____ , which may undermine their self-confidence. *tired*

3. Other physical changes include _____ , the return of the uterus to its prepregnant size, and rapid changes in _____ production. *involution* *hormone*

4. If the woman does not breast feed, _____ begins after 4 to 8 weeks. *menstruation*

5. _____ during pregnancy helps a women to recover faster, as does relaxation. *Exercise*

C. Emotional and Psychological Adjustments

1. Women make various _____ adjustments during the postpartum period. *physical*

2. Women who experience prolonged _____ fluctuations may need to obtain professional help. *emotional*

3. Pospartum _____ is a common experience for as many as 70% of birthmothers. *depression*

4. Evaluate the claim that bonding between infant and parent shortly after birth is crucial to the infant's development. *Bonding* *critical*

4.0 Chapter Boxes
  A. *Sociocultural Worlds of Development: Prenatal Care in the United States and Around the World*
    1. The number of low-birthweight infants is a measure of _____ health care.   *prenatal*
    2. The United States has _____ low-birthweight babies compared to other technologically   *more*
        advanced nations of the world.
    3. _____ American infants are twice as likely as _____ infants to be born either   *African*
        prematurely or to have low-birthweights.   *White*
    4. These conditions in the United States probably derives from the absence of a national   *health*
        _____ care social policy.

  B. *Sociocultural Worlds of Development: To Work or Not to Work*
    1. Arlene Eisenberg, Heidi Murkoff, and Sandee Hathaway provide a list of questions that new   *work*
        mothers must address about whether or not to _____ after the birth of a baby.
    2. Indicate some of the questions that mothers face when they consider whether or not to work after
        the birth of a new baby.

  C. *Critical Thinking About Life-Span Development: Cultural Beliefs About Pregnancy*
    1. Explain why health care professionals should understand their clients' cultural beliefs about
        pregnancy.

    2. Identify important questions to ask concerning cultural beliefs about pregnancy.

  D. *Critical Thinking About Life-Span Development: Beyond the "Mommy Track"*
    1. Evaluate the "mommy track" as a way women can combine careers and families.

    2. Suggest ways to reshape work so that it won't be a burden to women to have families.

  E. *Life-Span Health and Well-Being: The Power of Touch and Massage in Development*
    1. Research by Tiffany Field has produced interest in the roles of _____ and _____ in   *touch*
        improving the growth, health, and well-being of infants and children.   *massage*
    2. Massage facilitates weight _____ for preterm babies.   *gains*
    3. Touch also reduces the touch _____ of children and adolescents resulting from sexual   *aversions*
        abuse, autism, and eating disorders.

Self Test A: Key Terms and Key Persons

Write the appropriate key term or key person in the space to the right of the definition or description.
    1. A hormone administered during labor that stimulates uterine contractions.   _____
    2. The first two months of prenatal development, during which time organ systems form and are   _____
        sensitive to influence from environmental events.
    3. A newborn characterized by small heads and defective limbs, joints, face, and heart commonly   _____
        born to mothers who consumed alcoholic beverages during pregnancy.
    4. The individual who developed a way to assess the health of a newborn 1 to 5 minutes after birth.   _____
    5. A process whereby a recent mother's uterus returns to its prepregnant state about 5 to 6 weeks   _____
        after birth.
    6. The inner layer of cells that later becomes the embryo.   _____
    7. A process for giving birth in which the mother is informed about what will happen during the   _____
        procedure, accepts little medication, and makes decisions about any complications or problems.

8. A method used to assess the health of the newborn that measures heart rate, respiratory effort, muscle tone, body color, and reflex irritability. _____

9. A French obstetrician who developed a form of prepared or natural childbirth widely used today. _____

10. The outer layer of the embryo that later becomes the hair, skin, and nervous system. _____

11. The inner layer of embryonic cells that become the digestive and respiratory systems. _____

12. Infants born before they have spent at least 38 weeks in the womb. _____

13. The prenatal period lasting from about two to eight weeks after conception. _____

14. The shortest of the stages of birth, in which the placenta and umbilical cord are expelled from the mother's body. _____

15. Any of the three authors who developed a set of guidelines for helping the parents of a newborn decide whether the mother should work, or not work, outside the home. _____

16. A procedure in which a newborn baby is surgically removed from the mother's uterus. _____

17. A condition in which an infant is born buttocks first. _____

18. An infant weighing less than 5.5 pounds at birth, but having experienced a normal length gestation period. _____

19. The meeting ground for the circulatory systems of the embryo and mother; oxygen and nutrients, but not blood, pass through to the embryo. _____

20. A French obstetrician who advocated a procedure referred to as "birth without violence." _____

21. The period of time shortly after birth during which time the mother's body returns to a prepregnant state. _____

22. The researcher who has examined the role of touch and message in development. _____

Self Test B: Multiple Choice

1. The period of prenatal development that occurs in the first two weeks after conception is called the _____ period.
   a. fetal
   b. germinal
   c. embryonic
   d. blastocystic

2. A fertilized ovum is called a(n)
   a. zygote.
   b. blastocyst.
   c. egg.
   d. spermatozoon.

3. How does the placenta/umbilical cord life-support system prevent harmful bacteria from invading a fetus?
   a. Bacteria are too large to pass through the placenta's walls.
   b. The placenta generates antibodies that attack and destroy bacteria.
   c. Bacteria become trapped in the maze of blood vessels of the umbilical cord.
   d. No one understands how the placenta keeps bacteria out.

4. The fetal period is best described as a time when
   a. major organ systems emerge from the less differentiated endoderm and mesoderm.
   b. support systems that sustain the fetus become fully formed and functioning.
   c. fine details are added to systems that emerged during the embryonic period.
   d. teratogens are most likely to impair development.

5. Miscarriage is to abortion as
   a. embryo is to fetus.
   b. life is to death.
   c. environmental factors are to genetic factors.
   d. involuntary is to deliberate.

6. Theresa has been chronically depressed. Recently, she chose to have an abortion as a result of an unplanned pregnancy. How is Theresa likely to react in the months following the abortion?
   a. She will be relieved at stopping an unwanted pregnancy.
   b. She will feel guilty for a short while.
   c. She will have no feelings for a time, but then experience elation.
   d. She will be upset and possibly more depressed.

7. Which phrase best defines a teratogen?
   a. a life support system that protects the fetus
   b. an agent that stimulates the formation of organs
   c. an abnormality in infants of alcoholic mothers
   d. an environmental factor that produces birth defects

8. Which of the following statements about the relationship between age and pregnancy outcomes is most accurate?
   a. Adolescent mothers are most likely to have retarded children.
   b. More women become pregnant through artificial insemination in their thirties and forties than do women in their twenties.
   c. Mothers over age 30 are most likely to have retarded babies.
   d. Adolescent mothers suffer the lowest infant mortality rates of any age group.

9. Which statement about a mother's emotional state and prenatal development is most accurate?
   a. The emotional state of a mother influences prenatal development and birth.
   b. The emotional state of a mother influences birth but not prenatal development.
   c. The emotional state of a mother influences prenatal development but not birth.
   d. The emotional state of a mother has no influence on prenatal development or birth.

10. Which of the following statements about fetal alcohol syndrome is most accurate?
    a. The infant is often physically deformed and below average in intelligence.
    b. It commonly results in miscarriages.
    c. It causes ectopic pregnancies.
    d. Babies suffering from this syndrome are often born before term and with low birthweights.

11. A common characteristic of babies born to women who smoke during their pregnancies is
    a. a missing arm or leg.
    b. facial deformities and below-average intelligence.
    c. restlessness and irritability.
    d. lower birthweights.

12. All of the following are environmental hazards to prenatal development except
    a. cats.
    b. hot tubs.
    c. carbon monoxide.
    d. video display terminals.

13. Mrs. Peters, who is bearing down hard with each contraction, is in the _____ stage of labor.
    a. first
    b. second
    c. third
    d. final

14. A physician who has just witnessed a precipitated birth would likely say
    a. "It's OK for a child to come out feet first."
    b. "Wow, that delivery certainly went fast."
    c. "That abdominal scar will heal within a week."
    d. "One's a girl and one's a boy."

15. Why do suggest that cesarean sections are performed too often in the United States?
    a. The percentage of all deliveries that are done by cesarean section have decreased in the United States.
    b. More cesarean sections are performed in the United States than in other countries.
    c. Babies can be born without cesarean sections.
    d. Physicians are trying to reduce the use of cesarean sections.

16. What is the reason for administering analgesics to a woman during labor?
    a. to minimize the risk of cesarean sections
    b. to speed delivery
    c. to facilitate natural childbirth
    d. to lessen the pain for the mother

17. Which of the following statements about the influence on newborns of drugs used during birth is most accurate?
    a. Experiments on the effects of drugs on childbirth raise few ethical questions.
    b. Methodological problems complicate the results of studies of drug use during labor.
    c. Drugs affect all infants in the same way.
    d. Many mothers choose standard childbirth to help researchers learn about how drugs affect labor.

18. A mother delivers a baby that is placed on her stomach immediately after birth and then placed in a bath of warm water to relax. The mother is using the _____ method of childbirth.
    a. La Leche
    b. Lamaze
    c. Leboyer
    d. traditional

19. Virtually all modern birthing practices encourage relaxation by the mother. The main reason for this appears to be that it
    a. makes birth less traumatic for the infant.
    b. eliminates the mother's pain.
    c. enables the mother to participate fully in the birth.
    d. helps the attending physician to control the birth process.

20. Today more fathers are participating in childbirth because
    a. they need to do this to bond with their infants.
    b. doing so can be an important experience to share with their wives.
    c. they are the best possible support for their wives.
    d. physicians require that fathers be present.

21. A "preterm" cannot have gestated for more than _____ weeks.
    a. 38
    b. 34
    c. 30
    d. 26

22. Which of the following statements about a shortened gestation period is most accurate?
    a. It is common or low-birthweight infants.
    b. It often leads to organ malformation.
    c. It is almost always devastating.
    d. It alone does not necessarily harm an infant.

23. In contrast to the Brazelton scale, the Apgar scale primarily assesses a newborn's
    a. psychological status.
    b. reflexes.
    c. physiological health.
    d. responsivity to people.

24. All of the following are typical for a women within the first month after giving birth except
    a. the lack of a menstrual flow (especially if she is breastfeeding).
    b. a feeling of exhaustion.
    c. an increased sex drive.
    d. lower levels of estrogen.

25. Which of the following terms refers to a physical change that occurs to women after childbirth?
    a. decompression
    b. menstruation
    c. involution
    d. natural selection

26. Which of the following statements about close contact between mothers and newborns enjoys supporting evidence?
    a. Optimal development of the infants depends on close contact with mother immediately after birth.
    b. Close contact between infant and mother only can occur after standard childbirth.
    c. Close contact with mothers is helpful to preterm infants.
    d. Close contact with the mother is more important to an infant than close contact with the father.

27. Some countries have lower rates of low-birthweight infants than does the United States because these countries
    a. have banned standard childbirth practices.
    b. provide paid work leave for fathers.
    c. have outlawed natural childbirth practices.
    d. provide comprehensive prenatal care to pregnant women.

28. According to Arlene Eisenberg, Heidi Murkoff, and Sandee Hathaway, a recent mother, considering whether she should return to work, should be able to answer all of the following questions except
    a. Do I mind if someone else cares for my baby?
    b. Can I deal with the stress of work and child care?
    c. Is it moral to work and be a mother?
    d. How important is my career to me?

29. What type of research has demonstrated that massage and exercise benefit preterm infants?
    a. observational
    b. experimental
    c. correlational
    d. cross-sectional

30. On the basis of her research, Tiffany Field has argued for the inclusion of _____ into the school setting.
    a. positive touch
    b. corporal punishment
    c. prayer
    d. the feminist perspective on parenthood

Answers for Self Test A

1. oxytocin
2. organogenesis
3. fetal alcohol syndrome (FAS)
4. Virginia Apgar
5. involution
6. blastocyst
7. prepared, or natural, childbirth
8. Apgar Scale
9. Fernand Lamaze
10. ectoderm
11. endoderm
12. preterm infant
13. embryonic period
14. afterbirth
15. Arlene Eisenberg, Heidi Murkoff, or Sandee Hathaway
16. cesarean section
17. breech position
18. low-birthweight infant
19. placenta
20. Frederick LeBoyer
21. postpartum period
22. Tiffany Field

Answers for Self Test B

1. b   LO 1.1
2. a   LO 1.1
3. a   LO 1.5
4. c   LO 1.8
5. d   LO 1.9
6. d   LO 1.12
7. d   LO 1.13
8. c   LO 1.17
9. a   LO 1.19
10. a   LO 1.21
11. d   LO 1.23
12. d   LO 1.25
13. b   LO 2.1
14. b   LO 2.3
15. d   LO 2.5
16. d   LO 2.6
17. b   LO 2.8
18. c   LO 2.9
19. c   LO 2.11
20. b   LO 2.14
21. a   LO 2.15
22. d   LO 2.17
23. c   LO 2.22
24. c   LO 3.2
25. c   LO 3.3
26. c   LO 3.5
27. d   LO 4.1
28. c   LO 4.2
29. b   LO 4.7
30. a   LO 4.7

Chapter 5   Physical Development in Infancy

Learning Objectives with Key Terms in Boldface

1.0   Physical and Motor Development in Infancy

    1.1   Review the definition of infancy, and describe the physical development of infants.

A. Reflexes

    1.2   Explain the role of natural selection in the development of reflexes.

    1.3   Define and distinguish between the **sucking reflex** and **rooting reflex**, and between the **Moro reflex** and **grasping reflex**.

    1.4   Explain why some reflexes disappear during infancy whereas others persist throughout life.

    1.5   Use Figure 5.1 to compare and contrast various reflexes with regard to the nature of eliciting stimuli, infant's behavior, and the course of development.

    1.6   Discuss variation in the ability of infants to suck.

    1.7   Distinguish between nutritive sucking and **nonnutritive sucking**, and explain which of the two is more useful to developmental researchers.

B. Growth Patterns

    1.8   Define and distinguish between the **cephalocaudal pattern** and **proximodistal pattern** of growth, and explain how the development of gross motor skills and fine motor skills follows both.

    1.9   Use Figure 5.2 to describe the course of height and weight increases during infancy.

    1.10   Distinguish between **fine motor skills** and **gross motor skills**.

    1.11   Sketch the development of gross motor skills during infancy.

    1.12   Discuss the relationship between gross motor skills and the independence of infants.

    1.13   Indicate the nature of find motor skills at birth, discuss the development of reaching and grasping during infancy.

    1.14   Define and describe **developmental biodynamics**.

    1.15   Use the work of Rachel Clifton to compare and contrast the developmental biodynamics approach with more traditional accounts of motor achievement during infancy.

C. The Brain

    1.16   Define and distinguish among the **hindbrain, midbrain,** and **forebrain**.

    1.17   Define and distinguish among the **occipital lobe, temporal lobe, frontal lobe,** and **parietal lobe.**

    1.18   Define and distinguish among **neurons, dendrite,** and **axon.**

    1.19   Define **myelin sheath**, and explain its role.

    1.20   Describe how the brain changes during infancy.

D. Infant States

    1.21   Define infant state, and distinguish among Brown's seven infant states.

    1.22   Define sleep-wake cycle, and describe how sleep patterns change during the first year.

    1.23   Define **sudden infant death syndrome (SIDS)**, and list factors related to an infant's risk of SIDS.

E. Nutrition

    1.24   Relate the nutritional needs of infants to their growth during their first year of life.

    1.25   Discuss pros and cons of breast- versus bottle-feeding, and indicate sociocultural factors that encourage bottle- rather than breast-feeding.

    1.26   Define **marasmus** and describe feeding practices associated with the condition.

F. Toilet Training

    1.27   Summarize current advice regarding toilet training of 20-month-old infants.

2.0 Sensory and Perceptual Development

A. *What Are Sensation and Perception?*

2.1 Define and distinguish between **sensation** and **perception**.

B. *Theories of Perceptual Development*

2.2 Distinguish the **constructivist view** and the **ecological view** of infant perception.

C. *Visual Perception*

2.3 Discuss whether what humans see resembles or differs from a photograph.

2.4 Indicate William James's idea about the infant's perceptual world.

2.5 Compare the visual acuity of infants and adults.

2.6 Describe Robert Fantz's research method, and indicate whether his results regarding newborns viewing preferences confirm or disconfirm William James's view.

2.7 Describe the development of face perception.

2.8 Define and distinguish among **size constancy**, **shape constancy**, and **brightness constancy**.

2.9 Explain how scientists such as Eleanor Gibson and Richard Walk learn about infants' ability to perceive depth.

2.10 Indicate why Elizabeth Spelke says that infants have visual expectations.

D. *Other Senses*

2.11 Explain how we know that infants can hear before birth.

2.12 State the two conclusions derived from research on prenatal hearing.

2.13 Indicate evidence that shows infants have a sense of touch.

2.14 Discuss evidence that challenges the practice of withholding anesthesia from infants who are having operations.

2.15 Identify odors that newborns can discriminate.

2.16 Identify tastes that newborns can discriminate.

E. *Intermodal Perception*

2.17 Define **intermodal perception** and explain why it is a controversial concept.

3.0 Chapter Boxes

A. *Sociocultural Worlds of Development: Children Living Hungry in America*

3.1 Discuss the incidence of infant malnutrition and associated infant mortality in the United States.

B. *Critical Thinking About Life-Span Development: Measuring Infant Perception*

3.2 Indicate how you could think critically about development by devising ways to measure infant perception.

C. *Critical Thinking About Life-Span Development: Devising Age-Appropriate Activities to Stimulate Infants' Different Sensory Modalities*

3.3 Devise a list of age-appropriate activities for stimulating hearing and touch in newborns according to the textbook's information about these sensory modalities.

D. *Life-Span Health and Well-Being: The Right Exercise and Stimulation*

3.4 Explain why infants do not need exercise classes, and indicate appropriate activities and toys in the first year.

Guided Review and Study

1.0 Physical and Motor Development in Infancy

1. The term that refers to the first two years of life-span development is _____ .   *infancy*

A. *Reflexes*

1. Infants are born with genetically endowed survival mechani   *reflexes*
automatic and beyond the infant's control.

2. The food-getting reflex of neonates is _____ .   *sucking*

3. Stroking an infant's cheek activates the _____ reflex that orients neonates to potential   *rooting*
sources of nourishment.

4. Describe the Moro reflex, and the stimuli that activate this reflex.

5. Although some reflexes persist throughout life, other reflexes disappear during _____ .   *infancy*

6. The _____ reflex becomes part of more coordinated reaching responses.   *grasping*

7. Use Figure 5.1 to compare and contrast various reflexes with regard to the nature of eliciting stimuli, infant's behavior, and the course of development.

8. Infant's abilities to suck effectively and successfully during feeding _____ considerably.   *vary*

9. T. Barry Brazelton observed that infants often suck their _____ , or other objects, and that this behavior may continue for some time.   *fingers*

10. Indicate whether parents should worry about children who (they start school.

11. _____ sucking provides a way to measure infants' attention and learning.   *Nonnutritive*

B. Growth Patterns

ᵛ 1. The _____ principle indicates that the pattern of growth proceeds from the head downward.   *cephalocaudal*

ᵛ 2. The _____ principle indicates that the pattern of growth proceeds from the center of the body outward.   *proximodistal*

3. Provide examples of cephalocaudal and proximodistal patterns of growth.

4. The average North American newborn is ____ inches long and weighs 7.5 pounds.   *20*

5. Although infants _____ weight after birth, they soon grow rapidly.   *lose*

6. Use Figure 5.2 to describe increases in height and weight during infancy.

7. Walking and moving one's arms exemplify _____ motor skills, whereas picking up a rattle exemplifies a _____ motor skill.   *gross* *fine*

8. Review developmental milestones in gross motor skills portrayed in Figure 5.3.

9. Improved gross motor skills allow infant to be more _____ .   *independent*

10. Child experts believe that motor activity and mobility _____ development, and that the only restrictions on infants should be concerned with their _____ .   *promote* *safety*

11. Indicate the nature of fine motor skills at birth.

12. Rachel Clifton and her colleagues believe that _____ is guided by proprioception rather than vision.   *grasping*

13. Although traditional views of infant motor development have chronicled changes in posture and movement in terms of _____ , the newer perspective, developmental _____ , seeks to explain how motor skills are assembled for perceiving and acting.   *stages* *biomechanics*

14. Explain why Rachel Clifton's work is an example of biodynamic research.

E. The Brain

1. Indicate the location and function of hindbrain, midbrain, and forebrain.

2. Use Figure 5.5 to review the location and function of the occipital, temporal, frontal, and parietal lobes.

✓ 3. The receiving portion of neurons are called _____ , whereas the transmitting portion of neurons are called _____ .

dendrites
axons

✓ 4. The _____ sheath encases neurons in a layer of fat cells, and _____ the speed of impulse travel.

myelin
increases

5. Summarize knowledge about the following process in the development of neurons:

cell production

cell migration

cell elaboration

6. The brain weight of newborns is about _____ percent of their adult weight, but by 2 years of age, an infant's brain weighs _____ percent of its adult weight.

25
75

D. Infant States

1. A _____ is a synonym for consciousness—the level of awareness that characterizes an individual.

state

2. Brown identified _____ distinct infant states that included three states of sleep.

seven

3. _____ sleep exists when the infant lies motionless with eyes closed and does not respond to stimulation.

Deep

4. In _____ sleep there is little movement, and respiration may be irregular.

regular

5. During _____ sleep the eyelids may flutter, breathing is irregular, and the infant may vocalize.

disturbed

6. Brown also described _____ waking states.

four

7. _____ describes an infant with partially opened and glassy eyes, who moves little, but vocalizes more than an infant in disturbed sleep.

Drowsy

8. An alert _____ infant is awake with open and bright eyes, shows a variety of movements, frets, has reddish skin, and shows respiration changes when upset.

active

9. The alert and _____ state characterizes older infants and is much like an alert active infant except that movements are integrated around a specific activity.

focused

10. The _____ focused infant is awake but nonresponsive because attention is centered on some activity such as sucking or _____ .

inflexibly
crying

11. Describe changes in the sleep wake cycle during infancy.

✓ 12. A special concern about infant sleep is _____ , which occurs when an infant stops breathing during sleep and dies.

SIDS

13. The cause of sudden infant death syndrome is _____ .

unknown

14. List biological factors that make infants vulnerable to SIDS.

E. Nutrition

1. Although infants' nutritional needs are variable, the general rule is to feed infants about _____ calories per day for each pound of their body weight.

50

2. A long-standing controversy concerns the benefits of _____ versus _____ feeding. *bottle; breast*

3. The contemporary consensus is that breast feeding is _____ than bottle feeding; however, the proportion of mothers that nurse their babies is only about _____ percent. *healthier* *50*

4. _____ , a wasting away of an infant's body tissues, results from severe protein-calorie deficiency. *Marasmus*

5. Describe feeding practices that result in marasmus.

F. Toilet Training

1. North American parents expect their children to be toilet trained by _____ years of age, and ____ percent of three-year-old children are dry during the day. *3; 84*

2. Successful toilet training depends on muscular maturation, motivation, and also _____ maturity. *cognitive*

3. Summarize the advice developmentalists give to parents who are toilet training an infant.

2.0 Sensory and Perceptual Development

A. What Are Sensation and Perception?

1. _____ occurs when information contacts sensory receptors in the eyes, ears, mouth, nose, and on the skin. *Sensation*

2. _____ is the interpretation of what is sensed. *Perception*

B. Theories of Perceptual Development

1. Jean Piaget is the major proponent of the _____ view of perception. *constructivist*

2. Express the constructivist view of perception in your own words.

3. Eleanor and James Gibson are the major proponents of the _____ view of perception. *ecological*

4. Express the ecological view of perception in your own terms.

C. Visual Perception

1. Human vision is not like a _____ because it conveys a richer sense of depth, color, and texture. *photograph*

2. Indicate William James's idea about the infant's perceptual world.

3. Contrast the visual acuity of infants and adults.

4. Robert Fantz's pioneering device for studying infants' vision, the _____ chamber, allows researchers to determine whether infants prefer to view one of _____ stimuli. *looking* *two*

5. Fantz discovered that infants prefer to look at patterns rather than colors, and the ability to perceive visual patterns is _____ . *innate*

6. Fantz's research _____ the hypothesis of William James. *disconfirms*

7. The most important visual pattern for an infant to perceive is the _____ face. *human*

8. Infants can recognize _____ faces by 6 months of age. *familiar*

9. Explain size constancy in your own terms.

10. Explain shape constancy in your own terms.

11. Explain brightness constancy in your own terms.

12. Explain how Eleanor Gibson and Richard Walked used the visual cliff to assess the ability of infants to perceive depth.

13. Indicate what Elizabeth Spelke means by saying that infants have visual expectations.

D. *Other Senses*
    1. Immediately after birth newborns can hear; however, their sensory thresholds are _____ than those of adults.   *higher*
    2. Studies have shown that a _____ can hear sounds. For example, infants _____ hearing a story previously read to them while in the womb.   *fetus*
       preferred
    3. State the two conclusions derived from research on prenatal hearing.

    4. Touching the cheek of an infant results in head _____ .   *turning*
    5. At 6 months infants can _____ touch and vision.   *coordinate*
    6. Describe the way in which Megan Gunnar determined how healthy newborns cope with stress.

    7. Although male infants react to the pain of circumcision by crying and fussing, they cope well with this procedure by _____ deeply.   *sleeping*
    8. Indicate whether physicians should perform surgery on newborns without anesthesia.

    9. Identify odors that newborns can discriminate.

    10. When the sucking of a newborn is rewarded with a sweetened solution the amount of sucking _____ .   *increases*
    11. One study found that a sweet taste resulted in a _____ from the neonate, whereas a sour taste resulted in _____ lips.   *smile*
       pursed
E. *Intermodal Perception*
    1. _____ perception is the ability to relate and integrate information about two or more sensory modalities.   *Intermodal*
    2. Characterize the constructivist and ecological view's accounts of intermodal perception.

    3. Elizabeth Spelke demonstrated auditory-visual _____ perception in 4-month-old infants.   *intermodal*
    4. Explain what is meant by the concept of haptic-visual intermodal perception.

54

3.0 Chapter Boxes

A. *Sociocultural Worlds of Development: Children Living Hungry in America*

1. Indicate the concerns about children living hungry in America.

B. *Critical Thinking About Life-Span Development: Measuring Infant Perception*

1. Explain how devising ways to measure infant perception promotes critical thinking about life-span development.

C. *Critical Thinking About Life-Span Development: Devising Age-Appropriate Activities to Stimulate Infants' Different Sensory Modalities*

1. Propose some age-appropriate activities for stimulating hearing and touch in newborns.

D. *Life-Span Health and Well-Being: The Right Exercise and Stimulation*

1. Experts believe that babies _____ need special exercise for motor development.   *do not*

2. Some kinds of exercise may hurt infants. For example, _____ may produce water intoxication, which makes the brain swell.   *swimming*

3. Characterize developmentally appropriate activities and toys for infants in the first year of life.

Self Test A: Key Terms and Key Persons

Write the appropriate key term or key person in the space to the right of the definition or description.

1. A wasting away of body tissues caused by severe protein and calorie deficiency.   *marasmus*

2. A researcher who concludes that young infants have a biologically programmed core knowledge about the workings of the perceptual world.   *Elizabeth Spelke*

3. A pattern of growth starting at the center of the body and moving toward the extremities.   *proximodistal pattern*

4. The ability to combine and connect information from two or more sensory modalities.   *intermodal perception*

5. The startle response of the neonate triggered by the sudden loss of support, bright light, or loud noise.   *moro reflex*

6. A kind of sucking that provides a useful measure of attention and learning to researchers, but does not provide nutrition to infants.   *nonnutritive sucking*

7. Either of the two researchers who used the visual cliff to study infant depth perception.   *Gibson/Walk*

8. Motor behaviors involving small muscle groups such as scribbling with a pencil.   *fine motor skills*

9. A view that asserts infants can relate and integrate information from different sensory modalities only after extensive experience.   *constructivist view*

10. A developmental theorist who is the major proponent of the constructivist view of intermodal perception.   *Piaget*

11. An unusual and unexpected death of an apparently healthy infant who stops breathing for no apparent reason.   *SIDS sudden infant death syndrome*

12. A pediatrician who observed infants to determine the incidence of their sucking when they were nursing, and how their sucking changed as they grew older.   *Brazelton*

13. A pattern of growth occurring first at the top (or head) and gradually working downward.   *cephalocaudal pattern*

14. The interpretation of what is sensed.   *perception*

15. An experimenter who used the looking chamber to determine the visual preferences of infants.   *Fantz*

16. A researcher who studied how newborns cope with stress by observing their reactions during circumcision.   *Gunnar*

Self Test B: Multiple Choice

1. Which statement best characterizes infant reflexes?
   a. Infants once needed reflexes but no longer do.
   b. Reflexes are genetically coded survival mechanisms for all infants.
   c. Modern infants rely more on learning than on reflexes.
   d. All reflexes disappear by the end of infancy.

2. Which statement best contrasts the blinking and grasping reflexes?
   a. Sudden sounds stimulate blinking, whereas stroking the cheek stimulates grasping.
   b. Both reflexes disappear after 3 to 4 months.
   c. Stroking the side of the foot elicits grasping, whereas flashes of light elicit blinking.
   d. The blinking reflex persists throughout life, whereas the grasping reflex disappears after a year.

3. The sucking style of an infant is dependent on all but which of the following?
   a. the way the milk is coming out of the bottle or breast
   b. the infant's sucking speed and temperament
   c. the way the infant is held
   d. the nourishment being offered

4. Which principles explain why an embryo's hands develop before its fingers, and why the head develops before the body?
   a. cephalocaudal, cephalocaudal
   b. cephalocaudal, proximodistal
   c. proximodistal, cephalocaudal
   d. proximodistal, proximodistal

5. Which of the following statements most accurately describes height and weight changes during infancy?
   a. Both increase more rapidly during the second year than during the first year.
   b. Girls increase in height and weight faster than do boys during infancy.
   c. The sexes grow at the same rate during infancy.
   d. Both height and weight increase more rapidly during the first year than during the second year.

6. Finger dexterity is to walking as _____ is to _____ .
   a. gross motor skills; gross motor skills
   b. fine motor skills; fine motor skills
   c. fine motor skills; gross motor skills
   d. gross motor skills; fine motor skills

7. Which of the following is *not* one of the characteristics of the infant brain?
   a. increasing experience increases the number of neurons
   b. increasing experience increases the number of connections between neurons
   c. the dendrites branch out with increasing age
   d. neurotransmitters change with increasing age

8. Which of the following statements most accurately portrays the sleep-wake cycle of infants?
   a. Infants sleep less as they grow older.
   b. Newborn sleep is reflexive, whereas infant sleep is intentional.
   c. Infants eventually sleep more during the day than they do at night.
   d. Infants spend less time sleeping than do adults.

9. Juan was a low-birthweight infant, whereas John was a premature infant. Which of the following statements applies to them?
   a. Neither is vulnerable to SIDS.
   b. Juan is less vulnerable to SIDS than John.
   c. Juan is more vulnerable to SIDS than John.
   d. Both are vulnerable to SIDS.

10. Infants require about _____ calories a day for each pound they weigh.
    a. 25
    b. 50
    c. 75
    d. 100

11. Why is breast-feeding superior to bottle-feeding?
    a. Breast-feeding is more convenient and more adaptable to the time requirements of demand feeding.
    b. Breast milk is a superior source of the nutrients that babies need.
    c. Infants who are bottle-fed suffer psychological damage because they become only weakly attached to their mothers.
    d. Breast-feeding is not superior to bottle-feeding; this is a myth propagated by radical feminists.

12. A child who eats a low-fat, low-calorie diet endures _____ , whereas a child who eats a restricted protein diet experiences _____ .
    a. breast-feeding, bottle-feeding
    b. delirium, toxic shock
    c. malnourishment, marasmus
    d. marasmus, sudden infant death syndrome

13. Which of the following conditions is *not* necessary for a young child to be toilet trained?
    a. adequate motivation
    b. cognitive maturity
    c. passage from the anal to the phallic stage
    d. muscular control

14. Which of the following is a sensation?
    a. sound waves hitting the ear
    b. seeing your mother's face
    c. feeling the roughness of your father's beard
    d. hearing the sound of your brother crying

15. Was William James right when he proclaimed that newborns experience a blooming, buzzing confusion?
    a. No, because infants display visual preferences.
    b. Yes, because infants' visual acuity is less than that of adults.
    c. Yes, because infants sense the world but do not perceive it.
    d. No, because infants display sensitivity to pinpricks.

16. Which statement accurately compares the visual acuity of a father and son?
    a. At his son's birth, a father sees objects less clearly than does his son.
    b. When his son reaches 6 months of age, a father sees objects more clearly than does his son.
    c. When his son reaches 6 months of age, a father and son see objects equally clearly.
    d. A father sees objects more clearly than his son does throughout his son's infancy.

17. At birth an infant is capable of visually perceiving
    a. eyes versus the rest of a face.
    b. a bull's-eye versus a yellow circle.
    c. depth on a visual cliff.
    d. a dog versus a cat.

18. Which one of the following is inaccurate regarding the development of infant vision?
    a. At 3 1/2 weeks, the infant is fascinated with the eyes.
    b. At 1 to 2 months, the infant perceives contour.
    c. At 1 or 2 months, the infant differentiates facial features.
    d. At 5 months, the infant perceives the oval shape of the head.

19. When infants were placed on one side of the visual cliff, they refused to go to their mothers who were coaxing them from the other side. This result was cited as evidence for which of the following?
    a. depth perception
    b. failure of visual acuity
    c. inability to hear at a distance
    d. inability to crawl

20. What evidence indicates that a fetus can hear?
    a. A fetus moves when a loud noise occurs.
    b. Newborns prefer their mother's voice to stranger's voices.
    c. Hearing is more sensitive and better developed among newborns who have been experimentally stimulated before birth.
    d. Newborns prefer to hear stories that were read to them just before they were born.

21. What evidence challenges the practice of withholding anesthetics from newborns during surgery?
    a. Male infants increase their heart rates during circumcision.
    b. All infants cry when the umbilical cord is cut.
    c. Male infants cry and fuss during circumcision.
    d. Circumcised infants spend more time in REM sleep than do uncircumcised infants.

22. Which of the following smells did infants like the least?
    a. vanilla
    b. fish
    c. their mothers' milk
    d. strawberries

23. Research indicates that newborns respond favorably to all of the following substances except?
    a. sweetener
    b. vanilla
    c. fish
    d. strawberry

24. When an infant turns its head at the sound of footsteps in the hall and then smiles when it sees Mom come into the room, the infant is using
    a. depth perception.
    b. intermodal perception.
    c. auditory perception.
    d. visual perception.

25. According to the ecological perception view, it is true that
    a. bimodal perception is possible at birth.
    b. perceptual abilities are uncoordinated at birth.
    c. bimodal perception depends on internal representations of the perceptions from different senses.
    d. experience with all of the senses is needed before bimodal perception can occur.

26. The incidence of infant malnutrition and related death is underestimated in the United States because
    a. impoverished families often do not report the deaths of their babies.
    b. the government covers up the death rate.
    c. infant malnutrition occurs mainly in rural, isolated areas.
    d. no one has attempted to document it.

27. Which of the following statements about infant fitness classes is false?
    a. Swimming lessons can result in brain swelling because infants swallow too much water.
    b. Everyday activities are optimal for normal infant physical development.
    c. Infants are not capable of aerobic exercise.
    d. Infants exposed to swimming will be less frightened of water later in life.

Answers for Self Test A

1. marasmus
2. Elizabeth Spelke
3. proximodistal pattern
4. intermodal perception
5. Moro reflex
6. nonnutritive sucking
7. Eleanor Gibson or Richard Walk
8. fine motor skills
9. constructivist view
10. Jean Piaget
11. sudden infant death syndrome (SIDS)
12. T. Berry Brazelton
13. cephalocaudal pattern
14. perception
15. Robert Fantz
16. Megan Gunnar

Answers for Self Test B

1. b   LO 1.2
2. d   LO 1.5
3. d   LO 1.6
4. c   LO 1.8
5. d   LO 1.9
6. c   LO 1.10
7. a   LO 1.20
8. a   LO 1.22
9. d   LO 1.23
10. b   LO 1.24
11. b   LO 1.25
12. c   LO 1.26
13. c   LO 1.27
14. a   LO 2.1
15. a   LO 2.4
16. b   LO 2.5
17. b   LO 2.6
18. c   LO 2.7
19. a   LO 2.9
20. d   LO 2.11
21. c   LO 2.13
22. b   LO 2.15
23. c   LO 2.15
24. b   LO 2.17
25. a   LO 2.17
26. a   LO 3.1
27. d   LO 3.4

Chapter 6   Cognitive Development in Infancy

Learning Objectives with Key Terms in Boldface

1.0 Piaget's Theory of Infant Development

    1.1   Describe Jean Piaget's method for studying infant cognition.

    1.2   Compare and contrast qualitative and quantitative approaches to cognitive development.

    A. The Stage of Sensorimotor Development

    1.3   Explain why Piaget named the initial period of cognitive development the sensorimotor period.

    1.4   Define and give an example of the concept of **scheme** or **schema**.

    1.5   Describe observations that portray the emerging coordination of visual and motor schemes.

    1.6   Define **simple reflexes**, and explain what Piaget thought was happening when a 1-month-old sucked at the sight of a bottle.

    1.7   Define, distinguish, and give examples of **first habits and primary circular reactions**.

    1.8   Define and give examples of **secondary circular reactions**.

    1.9   Define and give examples of **coordination of secondary circular reactions**.

    1.10 Define and distinguish among the concepts of **tertiary circular reactions, novelty,** and **curiosity,** and describe observations that indicate their presence in infants.

    1.11 Define and give examples of **internalization of schemes**.

    B. Object Permanence

    1.12 Define **object permanence**, and indicate why the idea is important.

    1.13 Describe observations that indicate the presence of object permanence in infants.

2.0. The New Look in Infant Cognitive Development

    A. The Attacks on Piaget's Theory of Sensorimotor Development

    2.1   Indicate the impact of Piaget's theory of infant development on researchers' beliefs about infants' abilities to see and to think.

    2.2   Indicate the sources of attacks on Piaget's theory.

    B. Perceptual Development

    2.3   Describe new findings about infants' perceptual development that challenge Piaget's theory.

    C. Conceptual Development

    2.4   Describe new findings about infants' conceptual development that challenge Piaget's theory.

    D. The Information-Processing Perspective

    2.5   Compare and contrast the Piagetian and information-processing approaches to infant cognitive development.

    2.6   Define and distinguish between **habituation** and **dishabituation**, describe observations that indicate their presence in infants, and indicate their value to parents.

    2.7   Define **memory**, and describe observations that indicate its presence in infants.

    2.8   Define and distinguish between imitation and **deferred imitation**, and describe observations that show that newborns really can imitate facial expressions.

    2.9   Explain why Andrew Meltzhoff believes that newborn imitation is not simply a biologically based reflex.

    2.10 Indicate how information-processing discoveries support or refute Piaget's findings.

3.0 Individual Differences in Intelligence

    3.1   Compare and contrast the Piagetian, information-processing, and individual differences approaches to infant cognitive development.

    3.2   Define Arnold Gesell's **developmental quotient (DQ)** and compare it to IQ.

3.3   Compare and contrast the Gesell and Bayley approaches to testing individual differences in infant intelligence.

3.4   List the kinds of items used on Nancy Bayley's **Bayley Scales of Infant Development**.

3.5   Discuss applied and scientific uses of scales for infant mental development.

3.6   Explain why researchers believe that measures of habituation and dishabituation taken during infancy predict later intelligence during childhood.

3.7   Compare and contrast measures of cognitive development such as habituation and imitation with those on the Bayley and Gesell scales.

4.0 Language Development

4.1   List language development issues prompted by children such as the Wild Boy of Aveyron.

A. What Is Language?

4.2   Define **language** in terms of **infinite generativity** and five rule systems.

4.3   Define and give examples of **phonology**.

4.4   Sketch developmental trends in infants' ability to distinguish sounds and understand words.

4.5   Define and give examples of **morphology**.

4.6   Define and give examples of **syntax**.

4.7   Define and give examples of **semantics**.

4.8   Define and give examples of **pragmatics**.

B. Biological Influences

4.9   Describe the characteristics of human language that are evidence of a biological basis for language.

4.10   Indicate what experts believe is the evolutionary basis of language.

4.11   Describe Noam Chomsky's **language acquisition device (LAD)** and indicate its theoretical role in language development.

4.12   Describe evidence for the existence of a human LAD.

4.13   Describe attempts to teach language to chimpanzees, and evaluate whether the evidence supports any claim that a nonhuman species has been able to learn a language.

4.14   Define and give examples of the idea of a **critical period**.

4.15   Cite and evaluate evidence for the existence of a critical period for human language learning.

C. Behavioral and Environmental Influences

4.16   Indicate how behaviorists explain language acquisition.

4.17   Evaluate Roger Brown's evidence regarding the behavioral view of language acquisition.

4.18   Describe evidence that indicates that environment influences language development.

4.19   Define and distinguish among **motherese, recasting, echoing, expanding,** and **labeling**.

4.20   Explain why linguists have underplayed social interactionist views of language development.

4.21   Indicate cautions about applying knowledge about behavioral and environmental influences to encourage language development in children.

D. How Language Develops

4.22   Describe the forms of language that appear during the first year of life.

4.23   Describe evidence for the claim that the onset of babbling is determined by biological maturation, not an environmental factor.

4.24   Define and distinguish between **receptive vocabulary** and spoken vocabulary.

4.25   Define the **holophrase hypothesis**, and explain how infants and toddlers can communicate using only one- and two-word utterances and telegraphic speech.

4.26   Define and give examples of **telegraphic speech**.

4.27   Define Roger Brown's **mean length of utterance (MLU)**, and explain how it is used to measure language maturity.

5.0 Chapter Boxes
   A. *Sociocultural Worlds of Development: African American Language Traditions and Urban Poverty*
      5.1   Explain how living in poverty may impair language development.
   B. *Critical Thinking About Life-Span Development: Comparing Piaget's Methodological Strategy with a More Rigorous Experimental Strategy*
      5.2   Indicate your ability to evaluate the quality of conclusions and strategies in life-span development by comparing and contrasting the advantages and disadvantages of Piaget's methods and more rigorous experimental methods.
   C. *Critical Thinking About Life-Span Development: Comparing Piaget's Approach and the Individual Differences Approach*
      5.3   Indicate your ability to pursue alternative explanations to understand life-span development by doing your own comparison and contrast of Piaget's approach and the individual differences approach to cognitive development.
   D. *Life-Span Health and Well-Being: How Parents Can Facilitate Their Child's Language Development*
      5.4   Summarize Naomi Baron's recommendations for facilitating language development among infants, toddlers, and preschool children.

Guided Review and Study

1.0   Piaget's Theory of Infant Development
   1.   Jean Piaget based his theory of infant development on the results of interviews and _____ of his own children. *observations*
   2.   Piaget believed that children's development entails a series of _____ different stages of thought. *qualitatively*
   3.   A child's passage through a series of stages results from biological pressure to _____ to the environment and to _____ structures of thinking. *adapt* *organize*
   4.   Explain what it means to say that the stages of thought are qualitatively rather than quantitatively different from one another.

   A. *The Stage of Sensorimotor Development*
   1.   Explain why Piaget chose *sensorimotor* as the term for the initial stage of development.

   2.   The sensorimotor stage is divided into _____ qualitatively different substages. *6*
   3.   The _____ is the basic unit of sensorimotor functioning. *scheme*
   4.   Explain how and why the observations of Laurent's behavior demonstrate an emerging coordination of visual and motor schemes.

   5.   The first substage of the sensorimotor period is called _____ reflexes. *simple*
   6.   During the first month, the infant develops an ability to produce simple reflexes in the _____ of a triggering stimulus. *absence*
   7.   Provide an example of a simple reflex.

   8.   The second substage of the sensorimotor period is called _____ habits and primary _____ reactions. *first* *circular*
   9.   A _____ refers to schemes based on a reflex that is divorced from its eliciting stimulus, whereas primary _____ reactions refer to schemes derived from an infant's attempt to reproduce interesting or _____ events that happened accidentally. *habit* *circular* *pleasurable*
   10. Provide examples of a first habit and a primary circular reaction.

11. The infant about 4 to 8 months old becomes _____ -oriented in the third substage of the sensorimotor period called _____ circular reactions.

12. Piaget says simple _____ is limited to behavior already in the infant's repertoire.

13. Explain whether schemes are goal-directed during the substage of secondary circular reactions.

object
secondary
imitation

14. The fourth substage of the sensorimotor period is called the _____ of secondary circular reactions.

15. Describe the two important developments that occur for infants between the ages of 8 and 12 months during the fourth substage of sensorimotor thought.

coordination

16. The fifth substage of the sensorimotor period, _____ circular reactions, novelty, and curiosity, occurs when infants are 12 to 18 months of age.

17. Tertiary circular acts are the first to be concerned with _____ .

18. The sixth sensorimotor substage is called the _____ of schemes.

19. During months 19 to 24, the infant makes first use of primitive _____ .

20. Explain what Piaget means by the concept of symbol.

tertiary

novelty

internalization

symbols

B. Object Permanence

1. Object _____ refers an understanding that objects and events continue to exist even when they cannot be seen, heard, or touched.

2. Object permanence requires that infants distinguish _____ from the world.

3. Explain how life-span developmental psychologists study object permanence.

permanence

themselves

4. Use Figure 6.2 to review the main characteristics of sensorimotor thought.

2.0 A New Perspective on Cognitive Development in Infancy

A. The Attacks on Piaget's Theory of Sensorimotor Development

1. Jean Piaget's view of sensorimotor development was based on observations of his own children rather than on _____ studies with larger numbers of children.

2. Contemporary research regarding _____ and _____ development suggests that Piaget's ideas about sensorimotor development need revision.

laboratory

perceptual
conceptual

B. Perceptual Development

1. Explain why individuals such as Eleanor Gibson, Elizabeth Spelke, and Tom Bower believe that infants develop their perceptual abilities much earlier than Jean Piaget claimed.

C. Conceptual Development

1. The finding that six-month-olds start to use _____ language indicates that infants employ memory and other forms of _____ activity earlier than Piaget claimed.

sign
symbolic

D. The Information-Processing Perspective

1. Information processing psychologists approach infant development in terms of _____ processes rather than a series of stages.

2. Explain what it means to say that information processing psychologists believe that the young infant is more cognitively competent than Piaget realized.

cognitive

3. Researcher's examine _____ by repeatedly exposing infants to a stimulus and measuring their response. *attention*

4. If an infant's heart rate or sucking rate decreases after several presentations of the stimulus, _____ of the response has occurred. *habituation*

5. Researchers sometimes introduce a new stimulus after an infant has _____ to one stimulus. *habituated*

6. If the infant can detect a _____ between the new stimulus and the old one, the infant's heart rate or sucking rate increases, a phenomenon is known as _____ . *difference* *dishabituation*

7. Explain why parents who understand habituation and dishabituation can interact more effectively with their infant.

8. _____ pertains to retaining information over time. *Memory*

9. Describe how researchers have used televisions, mobiles, and objects making different sound to reach the conclusion that memory develops earlier than formerly believed.

10. Research by Andrew Meltzoff demonstrates that infants can _____ facial expressions. *imitate*

11. Indicate why Meltzhoff argues that imitation is biologically based, and that the ability to imitate is flexible and adaptive.

12. _____ imitation occurs over a period of hours or days. For example, Meltzhoff found that _____ month-old infants could imitate actions that they had seen performed 24 hours earlier, an outcome that occurs _____ than Piaget believed. *Deferred* *9* *earlier*

3.0 Individual Differences in Intelligence

1. Another approach to infant cognitive development involves the study of _____ differences in intelligence. *individual*

2. Investigators use infant intelligence tests or _____ scales to determine whether infants develop at a slower or faster pace than _____ . *developmental* *normal*

3. One of the early contributors to infant testing was Arnold _____ . *Gesell*

4. The current version of the Gesell test measures _____ , language, adaptive, and personal-social behavior, and permits combining these scores into an overall developmental _____ . *motor* *quotient*

5. Gesell's developmental tests _____ correlate highly with intelligence scores obtained later in childhood. *do not*

6. Nancy _____ devised today's most widely used developmental scale. *Bayley*

7. The Bayley Scales of Infant Development include a mental scale, a motor scale, and an infant behavior _____ . *profile*

8. The Bailey-II, published in _____ , provides updated norms for diagnostic assessment. *1993*

9. Indicate what 6- and 12-month-old infants should be able to do according to the Bayley Scales.

10. Describe practical uses of infant tests of intelligence.

11. Although global measures from infant developmental scales _____ predict later measures of intelligence, specific items provide information about intellectual functioning during childhood. *do not*

12. More promising measures of intelligence that use of measures of _____ called decrement of attention and measures of _____ called recovery of attention now appear to better predict standard intelligence test performance than the usual developmental scales. *habituation* *dishabituation*

13. Explain what it means to say that we should regard infant intelligence as being both continuous and discontinuous with later intelligence.

4.0 Language Development

1. Indicate issues in language raised by children such as the Wild Boy of Aveyron.

A. What Is Language?

1. A system of symbols used to communicate with others is called a _____ . — *language*
2. Language entails both _____ systems and infinite generativity. — *rule*
3. State the concept of infinite generativity in your own terms.

4. Phonology, morphology, syntax, semantics, and pragmatics exemplify the _____ systems of language. — *rule*
5. The basic speech sounds are _____ ; whereas the study of sound systems is phonology. — *phonemes*
6. Explain why it is advantageous to make a sound sequences the basis for words in language systems.

7. Sketch the developmental trends in infants' ability to distinguish sounds and understand words that have been identified by Patricia Kuhl.

8. The smallest unit of meaning in a language is the _____ , whereas _____ is the study of rules that govern the combining and sequencing of morphemes. — *morpheme* / *morphology*
9. Identify the four morphemes in the word *unwillingly*.

10. _____ refers to the rules for combining words into acceptable phrases and sentences. — *Syntax*
11. The formal description of syntactical rules is called the _____ of a language. — *grammar*
12. The term *semantics* refers to the _____ of words. — *meaning*
13. The sentence "The car looked at the mechanic" is semantically _____ even though it is syntactically _____ . — *incorrect* / *correct*
14. Pragmatics deals with rules for the _____ of language in an appropriate conversation and knowledge underlying the use of language in _____ . — *use* / *context*

B. Biological Influences

1. Indicate the strongest evidence for the biological basis of language.

2. Experts such as Noam Chomsky stress the _____ basis of language. — *biological*
3. Although the physical apparatus for human language _____ over hundreds of thousands of years, human language is an evolutionary recent acquisition, estimated to occur somewhere between _____ to 70,000 years ago. — *evolved* / *20,000*
4. Explain Noam Chomsky's concept of a language acquisition device or LAD.

5. Indicate evidence for the existence of a language acquisition device.

6. The idea that language has evolved has led researchers to study language in animals such as _____ . — *chimpanzees*

7. _____ is a chimp that has learned 160 signs and can put them together in unique ways that entails a rude form of grammar.

Washoe

8. The two-part debate concerning chimpanzee's use of language focuses on the issue of whether chimps understand the _____ they use, and the issue of whether they can use _____ .

symbols
syntax

9. There is strong evidence that chimpanzees understand the meaning of _____ , but no strong evidence that they can learn _____ .

symbols
syntax

10. Explain the concept of *critical period*.

11. Indicate what Eric Lenneberg means by saying that there is a critical period for language development.

12. The sad case of Genie illustrates the concept of a _____ period for language acquisition.

critical

13. State the most reasonable conclusion pertaining to the idea that there is a critical period for language acquisition.

C. Behavioral and Environmental Influences

1. The _____ view is that language is acquired through the process of reinforcement and imitation.

behavioral

2. Indicate what Roger Brown observed regarding how parents do and do not reinforce their children's use of language.

3. Behavioral analyses also fail to explain the _____ of language development because this approach predicts large _____ differences in language that do not appear to exist.

orderliness
individual

4. The social nature of language ensures the _____ plays an important role in language development.

environment

5. One of the many roles the environment plays in language development is through the use of _____ , a special language used by adults to communicate with children.

motherese

6. Speaking _____ entails talking in a higher-than-normal frequency, greater-than-normal pitch, and using simple words in short sentences.

motherese

7. In addition to motherese, caregivers also use _____ , echoing, expanding, and _____ to facilitate language acquisition by children.

recasting
labeling

8. _____ is phrasing the same meaning of a sentence in a different way.

Recasting

9. Repeating what the child has said to you is called _____ .

echoing

10. Restating a child's utterance in another, more sophisticated form is called _____ .

expanding

11. The process of _____ via the great word game may account for a large part of a child's early vocabulary.

labeling

12. Indicate cautions about applying knowledge about behavioral and environmental influences to encourage language development by children.

D. How Language Develops

1. Between 3 and 6 months of age infants begin to _____ .

babble

2. Infant's earlier communications aim to attract _____ .

attention

3. The shifting of eye contact between an adult and a toy involves _____ .

pragmatics

4. Between 6 to 9 months infants begin to understand _____ .

words

5. An infant's _____ vocabulary grows to about 300 words by the second year of age.   *receptive*

6. By the time that infants utter their first words between _____ to 15 months, they have already accomplished several language _____ .   *10*

   milestones

7. By 2 years of age the _____ vocabulary of infants reaches 200 to 275 words.   *spoken*

8. The possibility that the single word utterance of the one-word stage really represents a complete sentence which the baby has in her mind is called the _____ hypothesis.   *holophrase*

9. Finally, near the end of infancy, children use short and precise words combined in two- and three-word utterances in their _____ speech.   *telegraphic*

10. Telegraphic speech omits small words, and appears to be _____ .   *universal*

11. Provide some examples of telegraphic speech.

12. Roger Brown proposed that the mean length of utterance, or MLU, is a better measure of language _____ than chronological age.   *development*

13. The mean length of utterance is an _____ of language development based on the number of words per sentence than a child will produce in a sample of 50 to 100 sentences.   *index*

14. Brown also has described _____ stages of language based on the mean length of utterance or MLU.   *5*

15. The first stages involves utterances of 1+ words; the fifth stage involves utterances of _____ words.   *4*

16. Use Figure 6.8 to review the relationship between age ranges and MLUs.

5.0 Chapter Boxes

A. *Sociocultural Worlds of Development: African American Language Traditions and Urban Poverty*

1. According to Shirley Brice Heath, the tradition of Black American speech encourages children to become _____ listeners.   *active*

2. This varied and demanding language experience prepares individuals _____ for interactions in the market place, but _____ for traditional schools.   *well*

   poorly

3. This linguistically varied and strong language tradition _____ characteristic of the developmental experiences of children raised by single urban and impoverished parents.   *is not*

B. *Critical Thinking About Life-Span Development: Comparing Piaget's Methodological Strategy with a More Rigorous Experimental Strategy*

1. Indicate how comparing and contrasting the advantages and disadvantages of Piaget's methods and more rigorous experimental methods will abet your critical thinking about life-span development.

C. *Critical Thinking About Life-Span Development: Comparing Piaget's Approach and the Individual Differences Approach*

1. Indicate how comparing and contrasting Piaget's approach and the individual differences approach to cognitive development would help you think critically about life-span development.

D. *Life-Span Health and Well-Being: How Parents Can Facilitate Their Child's Language Development*

1. Indicate what Naomi Baron recommends about facilitating language development among infants, toddlers, and preschool children.

Self Test A: Key Terms and Key Persons

Write the appropriate key term or key person in the space to the right of the definition or description.

1. An index of language development that computes the average number of words per sentence from a sample of 50 to 100 sentences spoken by a child. *mean length of utterance*
2. The ability to relate and combine information about two or more sensory modalities. *intermodal*
3. The most important developmentalist who contributed to infant intelligence testing. *Gesell*
4. The sixth substage in Piaget's sensorimotor period in which infants switch their mental functioning from a purely sensorimotor plane to a symbolic plane. *internalization of schemes*
5. The first substage in Piaget's sensorimotor period in which reflexes are the basic means of coordinating sensation and action. *simple reflexes*
6. An observer's behavior that results from and is similar to the behavior of a model, but occur after a period of delay of hours or days. *deferred imitation*
7. A developmentalist who used mobiles to demonstrate detailed memory on the part of infants as young as 2 to 3 months old. *Rovee-Collier*
8. The individual who devised the infant intelligence test most commonly used nowadays. *Bayley*
9. A language rule system concerned with the meaning of words and sentences. *semantics*
10. The term that refers to a parent's repeating what a child says, especially in the case of fragmentary phrases or sentences. *echoing*
11. The stage of language development in which a single word stands for a complete sentence in the young child's mind. *holophrase hypothesis*
12. A developmentalists who studied imitation and deferred imitation by infants. *Meltzhoff*
13. The third substage in Piaget's sensorimotor period in which infants focus more on the world. *secondary circular reaction*
14. The study of the rules involved in the combining and sequencing of morphemes. *morphology*
15. A linguist who suggested ways in which parents can facilitate their child's language development. *Baron*
16. The reduced attention that results from repeated presentations of the same stimulus. *habituation*
17. The most fundamental unit for an organized pattern of sensorimotor functioning according to Jean Piaget. *scheme*
18. The individual who developed the mean length of utterance to measure the language maturity of children. *Roger Brown*
19. The researcher who studied the language traditions of African Americans in urban poverty. *Heath*
20. The hypothetical ability of the young child to detect certain language categories. *LAD language acquisition device*
21. The individual whose observations of his own children contributed to his theory of infant development.
22. The most widely used developmental scale that includes a Mental scale, a Motor scale, and an Infant Behavior Profile. *Bayley Scales of Infant development*
23. The characteristic way in which adults talk to young language learners. It involves simple, short sentences, exaggerated intonation contours, long pauses between sentences, and great stress on important words. *motherese*
24. The knowledge that objects and events continue to exist even when one is not in direct perceptual contact with the objects. *object permanence*
25. The number of words that an individual can understand; usually larger than the spoken vocabulary. *receptive vocabulary*

Self Test B: Multiple Choice

1. Jean Piaget gathered the information for his theories about cognitive development by
   a. reviewing the literature on cognitive development.
   b. surveying thousands of parents.
   c. observing his own children.
   d. testing hundreds of children in his laboratory.

2. Piaget's theory is a qualitative theory of cognitive development, which means that it
   a. uses standardized tests to measure and describe thought.
   b. explains what kinds of knowledge are typical of children at different ages.
   c. identifies different kinds of thinking children perform at different ages.
   d. provides ways to determine how well children think at different stages.

3. In terms of schemes, infants are born with
_____ and develop _____ during
infancy.
   a. reflexes; habits
   b. sensorimotor functions; circular reactions
   c. habits; secondary reactions
   d. circular reactions; symbolic functions

4. Laurent is having problems retrieving a ball that
has rolled out of his reach; he uses a Tinkertoy
stick to hit the ball. Laurent is in the
   a. primary circular reactions substage.
   b. secondary circular reactions substage.
   c. coordination of secondary reactions substage.
   d. tertiary circular reactions substage.

5. If a child is able to track an object that disappears
and reappears in several locations in rapid
succession but does not do well with invisible
displacements, she is in substage
   a. three.
   b. four.
   c. five.
   d. six.

6. Object permanence in the simple reflexes
sensorimotor substage
   a. is not apparent.
   b. is beginning to develop.
   c. is characterized by active searches for missing
objects.
   d. is fully developed.

7. Infants whose parents use sign language have been
observed to start using conventional signs at about
_____ months of age.
   a. three
   b. six
   c. ten
   d. thirteen

8. If a child is listening to a tape of a story being read
by a male voice and the voice of the storyteller
changes to a female voice, which of the following
is likely to occur?
   a. sucking rate will not change
   b. sucking will stop
   c. sucking rate will increase
   d. sucking rate will decrease

9. Evidence that infants can imitate adult facial
expressions shortly after birth indicates which of
the following?
   a. imitative abilities are learned quickly
   b. imitation has a biological base
   c. infants have a full range of emotional
expressions at birth
   d. imitation is a form of emotional expression

10. Contrary to Jean Piaget's view, it has been shown
that infants can engage in deferred imitation by the
age of
   a. 3 months.
   b. 6 months.
   c. 9 months.
   d. 18 months.

11. The developmental quotient is a global
developmental score that combines subscores in all
of the following areas except
   a. motor ability.
   b. language ability.
   c. physical ability.
   d. personal-social abilities.

12. Which one of the following has been shown to
predict academic achievement at 6 to 8 years of age?
   a. Piagetian Sensorimotor Scales
   b. Bayley Scales of Infant Development
   c. Gesell Developmental Schedules
   d. Brazelton Neonatal Behavioral Assessment
Scales

13. Infant intelligence tests are good for all but which
of the following?
   a. assessing the effects of malnutrition
   b. predicting childhood intelligence
   c. determining the developmental effects of
environmental stimulation
   d. measuring the detrimental effects of a mother's
drug-taking habits during pregnancy

14. All of the following are part of the system of rules
needed in a language except
   a. generativity.
   b. phonemes.
   c. morphemes.
   d. semantics.

15. Phonological rules ensure that
   a. word meaning will be communicated.
   b. speakers will take turns when talking.
   c. only certain sound sequences will occur in
speech.
   d. surface structure will reflect deep structure.

16. Which of the following words has more than one
morpheme?
   a. deer
   b. desk
   c. driver
   d. dance

17. Which of the following components of language is
closely related to grammar?
   a. semantics
   b. pragmatics
   c. syntax
   d. morphology

18. Which of the following sentences is semantically incorrect?
    a. The cloud covered the frog pond.
    b. The frog pond was covered by a cloud.
    c. The green frog in swam pond.
    d. The pond ate the green frog.

19. The best estimate is that human language evolved about _____ years ago.
    a. 20,000 to 70,000
    b. 70,000 to 100,000
    c. 100,000 to 500,000
    d. 500,000 to 1,000,000

20. The evidence favors the conclusion that animals other than humans
    a. cannot communicate with one another.
    b. may communicate with one another but cannot learn syntax.
    c. may communicate with one another and may learn syntax.
    d. may learn language with all of the characteristics of human language.

21. The Rumbaughs' experiments with Austin and Sherman have shown that chimpanzees are capable of
    a. simple communication via speech.
    b. learning syntax.
    c. understanding symbols.
    d. All of the answers are correct.

22. If a child were reared in isolation from people for the first ten or eleven years of life, he would likely
    a. never learn to communicate effectively with humans.
    b. learn to communicate if given speech and language therapy.
    c. learn to communicate if placed in a warm, comfortable environment.
    d. learn to communicate in his own personal language system understood by a few people.

23. The critical period for language development seems to end at about _____ years of age.
    a. 3
    b. 5
    c. 12
    d. 18

24. Dr. Jones claims that Marie can make a negative statement because that use was reinforced. Dr. Jones most likely takes the _____ view.
    a. biological
    b. behavioral
    c. cognitive
    d. interactionist

25. When Jennifer said, "The deer was running," Mother asked, "Where was the deer running?" Mother's strategy is
    a. echoing.
    b. expanding.
    c. recasting.
    d. labeling.

26.. A child's first word is uttered at around _____ months.
    a. 3
    b. 9
    c. 12
    d. 18

27. The theory that a single word may imply a whole sentence is known as the _____ hypothesis.
    a. generalization
    b. implied meaning
    c. holophrase
    d. cognitive

28. Which of the following utterances is an example of telegraphic speech?
    a. "Mama"
    b. "Big car"
    c. "Go ride McDonalds"
    d. "Billy took my ball"

29. The mean length of utterance (MLU) is a good index of
    a. holophrase speech.
    b. overextension.
    c. language maturity.
    d. language deficit.

30. A 1989 study by Shirley Brice Heath found that urban housing projects
    a. impede the ability of young children to develop cognitive and social skills.
    b. provide an opportunity for positive social interactions among children but may restrict intellectual development.
    c. enhance the cognitive development but not the social development of children.
    d. provide excellent social opportunities for parents but restrict the child's development.

31. Naomi Baron recommends all of the following ways to facilitate language development in infants *except*
    a. being an active conversational partner.
    b. avoiding sexist language.
    c. talking as if the infant understands you.
    d. using a language style comfortable to you.

Answers for Self Test A

1. mean length of utterance (MLU)
2. internalization of schemes
3. Arnold Gesell
4. infinite generativity
5. simple reflexes
6. deferred imitation
7. Carolyn Rovee-Collier
8. Nancy Bayley
9. semantics
10. echoing
11. holophrase hypothesis
12. Andrew Meltzhoff
13. secondary circular reaction
14. morphology
15. Naomi Baron
16. habituation
17. scheme
18. Roger Brown
19. Shirley Brice Heath
20. language acquisition device (LAD)
21. Jean Piaget
22. Bayley Scales of Infant Development
23. motherese
24. object permanence
25. receptive vocabulary

Answers for Self Test B

1. c   LO 1.1
2. c   LO 1.2
3. a   LO 1.4
4. c   LO 1.9
5. c   LO 1.10
6. a   LO 1.12
7. b   LO 2.4
8. c   LO 2.7
9. b   LO 2.8
10. c   LO 2.10
11. c   LO 3.2
12. b   LO 3.3
13. b   LO 3.5
14. a   LO 4.2
15. c   LO 4.3
16. c   LO 4.5
17. c   LO 4.6
18. d   LO 4.7
19. a   LO 4.10
20. c   LO 4.13
21. c   LO 4.13
22. a   LO 4.15
23. c   LO 4.15
24. b   LO 4.16
25. c   LO 4.19
26. c   LO 4.22
27. c   LO 4.25
28. c   LO 4.26
29. c   LO 4.27
30. a   LO 5.1
31. b   LO 5.4

Chapter 7   Socioemotional Development in Infancy

Learning Objectives with Key Terms in Boldface

1.0 Family Processes

  A. *Reciprocal Socialization*

    1.1 Define **reciprocal socialization** and illustrate it with examples of mother-infant interaction.

    1.2. Define **scaffolding** and illustrate it with examples of infant-parent interaction.

  B. *The Family as a System*

    1.3 Define and distinguish between dyadic and family subsystems.

    1.4 Describe direct and indirect effects in a family system, and explain how the family comprises a system of interacting individuals.

2.0 Attachment, Fathers, and Day Care

  A. *Attachment*

    2.1 Define **attachment** and describe observations that indicate its presence in an infant.

    2.2 Explain why researchers believe that contact comfort is more important than feeding to attachment.

    2.3 Compare and contrast the explanations for attachment proposed by Sigmund Freud, Harry Harlow, Konrad Lorenz, Erik Erikson, and John Bowlby.

    2.4 Define and distinguish between **secure attachment** and insecure attachment.

    2.5 Define and distinguish among **type A babies**, **type B babies**, and **type C babies**.

    2.6 Discuss possible causes of individual differences in attachment.

    2.7 Indicate how the quality of attachment relates to later social adjustment.

    2.8 Compare and contrast Jerome Kagan's view of individual differences in infants' adaptations to the social world with those of attachment theorists.

    2.9 List criticisms of attachment theory.

    2.10 Indicate why the **strange situation** is an improvement over earlier measures of attachment.

    2.11 Cite criticisms of the strange situation as a measure of attachment.

  B. *Fathers as Caregivers of Infants*

    2.12 Cite evidence that fathers can be sensitive and responsive with their infants.

    2.13 Compare and contrast fathers' and mothers' abilities to care for infants, and identify their general caregiving practices.

    2.14 Indicate evidence about which parent infants under stress prefer.

    2.15 Compare and contrast parenting practices in families that adopt traditional and nontraditional gender roles.

    2.16 Describe childcare practices in Sweden and other countries that offer both maternity and paternity leave.

  C. *Day Care*

    2.17 Compare and contrast the day-care experiences of Ellen Smith and Barbara Jones.

    2.18 Indicate the role poverty plays in the quality of daycare infants receive.

    2.19 Describe the variety of day-care services offered in the United States today.

    2.20 State Jay Belsky's point about day-care in the United States and describe evidence that supports it.

    2.21 Explain why it is hard to reach firm conclusions about the effect of day care on child development.

    2.22 Compare and contrast Jerome Kagan's criteria for high quality day-care with those provided by the National Association for the Education of Young Children.

3.0 Temperament

  A. *Temperament's Nature*

    3.1 Define **temperament**.

    3.2 Define and distinguish among Alexander Chess and Stella Thomas's **easy child**, **difficult child**, and **slow-to-warm-up child**.

3.3 Define and distinguish among Arnold Buss and Robert Plomin's dimensions of temperament called **emotionality, sociability,** and **activity level**.

3.4 Indicate additional domains of temperament that some researchers suggest are important.

3.5 Describe how the influence of heredity on temperament changes with age.

3.6 Indicate the evidence supporting the hypotheses that (a) heredity influences temperament and (b) environment influences temperament.

B. Parenting and the Child's Temperament

3.7 Explain why parents come to believe in the importance of temperament after the birth of their second child.

3.8 Indicate and explain the implications of temperamental variations for parenting.

4.0 Emotional and Personality Development

A. Emotional Development

4.1 Define and distinguish among **emotion, positive affectivity (PA),** and **negative affectivity (NA)**.

4.2 Sketch the new functionalist view of emotions.

4.3 Apply the new functionalist approach to understanding the measurement of attachment.

4.4 Indicate how emotions relate to goals.

4.5 Discuss the role of emotions or affect in infant-parent interactions.

4.6 Describe Carroll Izard's **Maximally Discriminative Facial Movement Coding System (MAX)** for coding infants' facial expressions related to emotions.

4.7 Indicate the developmental sequence for the expression of emotions in infants.

4.8 Define and distinguish among the **basic cry, anger cry,** and **pain cry**, and indicate parents' ability to discriminate them.

4.9 Indicate how behaviorists and ethologists view the pros and cons of responding to infants' cries, and explain how they can both be right.

4.10 Define and distinguish between the **reflexive smile** and **social smile**, and indicate what each reveals to parents and developmental researchers.

B. Personality Development

4.11 Compare and contrast Erik Erikson's concept of trust versus mistrust and Mary Ainsworth's concept of secure versus insecure attachment.

4.12 Discuss long term hopes and dangers for children who develop either a sense of trust or of mistrust.

4.13 Describe observations that indicate an infant has a sense of self and independence.

4.14 Compare and contrast Margaret Mahler's and Erikson's explanations for the development of independence and the self during infancy.

4.15 Describe the negativism often displayed by two-year-olds, and indicate how parents can cope with it.

C. Problems and Disorders

4.16 Evaluate the severity of child abuse, and explain why it is too simple to view child abuse as a result of the hostility of bad, sadistic parents.

4.17 Distinguish between child abuse and child maltreatment, and list the incidence of different types of maltreatment.

4.18 Explain why the severity of child abuse is perceived as greater than it is, and indicate the typical extent of abuse.

4.19 Identify cultural and social factors that relate to high and low rates of child maltreatment.

4.20 Identify family factors that relate to child abuse.

4.21 Define **infantile autism** and describe social deficiencies associated with it.

4.22 Define **echolalia** and describe other communication deficiencies associated with infantile autism.

4.23 Describe patterns of behavior associated with infantile autism.

4.24 Indicate what we know about the causes of infantile autism.

5.0 Chapter Boxes

A. Sociocultural Worlds of Development: Child-Care Policy around the World

5.1 Describe the nature and purposes of child care policies typical of European countries, Canada, Israel, and many developing nations.

B. Critical Thinking About Life-Span Development: Characteristics of Competent Caregivers

 5.2 Make up a list of five characteristics of competent caregivers and compare it to a list given in the box on Life-Span Health and Well-Being.

C. Critical Thinking About Life-Span Development: Developing a Model of Intervention for Maltreating Families

 5.3 Explain why it is difficult to intervene with maltreating families.

 5.4 Indicate your ability to apply knowledge about life-span development to improve human welfare by developing a model of intervention that would benefit maltreated children and their families.

D. Life-Span Health and Well-Being: The Personal Characteristics of Competent Caregivers

 5.5 List and describe the personal characteristics LaVisa Wilson believes define a competent caregiver.

Guided Review and Study

1.0 Family Processes

 A. Reciprocal Socialization

  1. Reciprocal socialization means that _____ socialize their children and that children socialize their _____ . *parents*
   parents

  2. Explain the concept of *mutual synchrony*.

  3. Studies of reciprocal socialization during infancy reveal that mutual _____ plays an important role in socialization. *gaze*

  4. Define *scaffolding* and illustrate the concept with examples from infant-parent interactions.

  5. Scaffolding helps children learn _____ rules such as taking one's turn. *social*

 B. The Family as a System

  1. The family can be viewed as a social _____ defined in terms of generation, gender, and role. *system*

  2. Family subsystems can be _____ or polyadic. *dyadic*

  3. Use Figure 7.1 to identify direct and indirect effects in the interactions between children and their parents.

2.0 Attachment, Fathers, and Day Care

 A. Attachment

  1. _____ generally refers to a relation between individuals in which at least one acts to maintain the relationship. *Attachment*

  2. In the context of life-span development, attachment is defined as a close emotional bond between infants and _____ . *caregivers*

  3. According to Sigmund Freud, infants become attached to a person who provides _____ satisfaction, an individual who is most likely to be the _____ . *oral*
   mother

  4. Explain how Harry Harlow and Robert Zimmerman tested the Freudian account of attachment.

  5. Harlow and Zimmerman concluded that the object of attachment is the individual who provides _____ comfort rather than oral satisfaction. *contact*

  6. Toddlers often develop a strong attachment to a soft _____ or blanket. *toy*

  7. Konrad Lorenz postulated that _____ was responsible for attachment. *familiarity*

  8. Familiarity is established in the first _____ hours after hatching for goslings and during the _____ year of life for humans. *36*
   first

  9. Indicate and explain Erik Erikson's views about the development of attachment.

  10. John Bowlby's ethological theory states that attachment has a _____ basis. *biological*

11. Bowlby believes that the _____ of the infant and the mother trigger behaviors that produce an attachment bond.   *instincts*

12. There are _____ differences in attachment.   *individual*

13. Indicate what Mary Ainsworth means by the concepts of secure attachment and insecure attachment.

14 For Ainsworth, a securely attached infant is called a type _____ infant, an anxious-avoidant infant is called a type _____ baby, and other insecurely attached infants who kick the mother when she picks them up are called type _____ babies.   *B*
    A
    C

15. Devise and explain a mnemonic device that will help your remember the distinction between type B babies, type A babies, and type C babies.

16. Ainsworth attributes the nature of an infant's attachment to the _____ and responsiveness of the primary _____ .   *sensitivity*
    caregiver

17. Characterize the behavior of the mothers of type A babies and type C babies.

18. Relate the quality of attachment to later social adjustment.

19. Jerome Kagan argues that genetic and _____ characteristics are more important in social _____ than acknowledged by attachment theorists.   *temperament*
    competence

20. Attachment theory has also been criticized for ignoring the diversity of social _____ and social _____ in the infant's environment.   *agents*
    contexts

21. Caretakers are important to infant social development; however, the debate concerns the necessity of a bond to a _____ caregiver.   *single*

22. Mary Ainsworth devised the _____ Situation to measure attachment.   *Strange*

23. Describe the Strange Situation, and explain why this procedure was superior to earlier measures of attachment.

24. Indicate and evaluate what critics say about the Strange Situation.

B. *Fathers as Caregivers for Infants*

1. Although _____ can take care of children as competently as mothers, fathers typically _____ choose to be active and nurturant caregivers.   *fathers*
    do not

2. Describe how mothers and fathers typically interact with infants.

3. In stressful situations, infants appear more attached to their _____ .   *mothers*

4. In Michael Lamb's study of nontraditional _____ couples in which the fathers took parental leave to care for their infants, fathers were _____ likely than mothers to discipline, vocalize, soothe, hold, and kiss their infants.   *Swedish*
    less

5. In Sweden and other countries fathers and mothers can have paid childcare leave for up to _____ months, whereas in the _____ there is no policy of paid leave for child care.   *9*
    USA

C. *Day Care*

1. Compare and contrast the day care experiences of Ellen Smith and Barbara Jones.

2. Relate socio-economic conditions to the quality of day care.

3. According to Jay Belsky, the quality of daycare received by most children in the United States is _____ and can have _____ developmental outcomes for the children.   *poor*
   negative
4. One study showed that children who began day care as infants were rated as _____ compliant and had poorer peer relationships; however, reviews of the research reveal _____ ill effects of daycare.   *less*
   no
5. Indicate why it is difficult to draw a conclusion about the long-term effects of day care.

6. Jerome Kagan's demonstration program at Harvard University exemplifies _____ quality day care.   *high*
7. Use Table 7.1 to review the major categories for quality daycare proposed by the National Association for the Education of Young Children and compare them with those entailed in Jerome Kagan's demonstration program.

3.0 Temperament

A. Temperament's Nature

1. _____ refers to an individual's behavioral style and characteristic pattern of responding.   *Temperament*
2. An important issue concerns the important _____ of temperament.   *dimensions*
3. Characterize the basic types of temperament according to Alexander Chess and Stella Thomas:

   the easy child

   the difficult child

   the slow-to-warm-up child

4. Use Table 7.2 to review the dimensions that underlie Chess and Thomas's types.

5. Chess and Thomas found that about _____ percent of the children they studied could be classified as easy, _____ percent could be classified as difficult, and _____ percent could be classified as slow-to-warm-up.   *40*
   10
   15
6. Investigations also reveal that temperament remains _____ throughout childhood.   *stable*
7. Arnold Buss and Robert Plomin contend that _____ can be described in terms of emotionality, sociability, and activity level.   *temperament*
8. An infant who responds with anger at unpleasant events displays _____ .   *emotionality*
9. _____ is the tendency to prefer the company of others.   *Sociability*
10. Children who are evaluated on the basis of games they prefer to play are classified by their _____ level.   *activity*
11. Recent researchers have differentiated the dimension of social _____ into subcategories of shyness, introversion, sociability, and extraversion.   *withdrawal*
12. Research using twin studies with infants and older children indicates that temperament becomes _____ changeable or malleable with experience.   *more*
13. A child whose temperament does not fluctuate much during development, probably has a temperament that _____ the parents.   *matches*
14. _____ influences temperament; however, the degree of influence depends on _____ experiences.   *Heredity*
   environmental

B. Parenting and the Child's Temperament

1. Explain when and why parents become interested in the importance of children's temperament.

2. Explain what Ann Sanson and Mary Rothbart mean by saying that parents need to attend to and respect individuality.

3. Explain what Ann Sanson and Mary Rothbart mean by saying that parents need to structure their children's environment.

4. Explain what Ann Sanson and Mary Rothbart mean by saying that parents need to consider the "difficult child" and packaged parenting programs.

4.0 Emotional and Personality Development

A. Emotional Development

1. Although it is _____ for researchers to define emotion, the accepted definitions encompass feelings, physiological _____ , and overt behavior.
2. All systems classify _____ in terms of positive and negative characteristics.
3. Define and distinguish between *positive affectivity* and *negative affectivity*.

difficult
arousal
emotions

4. The new view of emotion is that it is _____ rather than intrapsychic.
5. Indicate the premises of the new view of the nature of emotion.

relational

6.. The new approach is called _____ because the approach links emotions with behavioral goals.
7. Explain how the views and analysis of Alan Sroufe illustrate the way in which the new functionalists assess emotions.

functionalism

8. Emotions represent the first _____ used by infants and parents.
9. Describe the ways that emotions influence infant-parent and child-parent interactions.

language

10. Carroll Izard developed the _____ , or maximally discriminative facial movement coding system, to study the _____ expressions of infants.
11. Use of the MAX reveals that interest, distress, and disgust are present at _____ , and that expressions of contempt and guilt appear by the end of infancy, or about _____ years of age.
12. Use Figure 7.5 to review the timetable for the emergence of facial expressions of emotion.

MAX
facial
birth
2

13. Crying is an effective mechanism for infants to _____ with their world.
14. Infants display at least _____ types of cries that differ in frequency, intensity, and pause.
15. Characterize the following types of cries:
    the basic cry

    the anger cry

    the pain cry

16. John Watson argued that parents respond too _____ to a crying infant, and that such attention _____ and increases the incidence of crying. *much* *reinforces*

17. Mary Ainsworth and John Bowlby believe that prompt attention by the caregiver contributes to a _____ attachment between the infant and the caregiver. *secure*

18. Indicate whether research favors the behavioral or ethological view of crying.

19. Smiling comprises another important _____ behavior. *emotional*

20. Infants display reflexive smiles and _____ smiles. *social*

21. A _____ smile does not appear in response to social stimulation, but occurs _____ in development than a social smile. *reflexive* *earlier*

22. Social smiles do not usually occur until _____ months of age. *2 or 3*

B. *Personality Development*

1. The important factors in infant personality development concern _____ , the self, and independence. *trust*

2. According to Erik Erikson, the first year of life is characterized by the stage of psychosocial development called _____ versus _____ . *trust* *mistrust*

3. Indicate the conditions that promote the development of trust and mistrust according to Erikson.

4. Erikson's views are compatible with Mary Ainsworth's views on _____ attachment. That is, an infant who has a sense of _____ is likely to be securely attached. *secure* *trust*

5. Identify longer term hopes and dangers for children who develop a sense of trust or of mistrust.

6. A sense of _____ requires that individuals can distinguish themselves from others. *self*

7. To determine whether infants can recognize themselves, psychologists use _____ . *mirrors*

8. State the conclusions derived from developmental and comparative studies that employ the mirror technique.

9. Margaret Mahler believes that toddlers develop _____ by a process of separation followed by individuation. *independence*

10. In the _____ year of life, Erikson believes that independence is an important issue. *second*

11. Explain why Erik Erikson claims that the second stage of psychosocial development is one of *autonomy versus shame and doubt.*

12. Erikson also contends that the autonomy and doubt stage relates to the development of independence and identity during _____ . *adolescence*

13. Comment on the negative side of too much autonomy for children.

14. _____ -year-olds are very frustrated because they cannot control the adult world. *Two*

15. Developmentalists believe it is better to be _____ with toddlers and to set _____ on their behavior rather to make allowances for negativism. *firm* *limits*

C. *Problems and Disorders*

1. Various biological, social, and developmental characteristics of children predict problems and disturbances at age _____ . *18*

2. Some authorities say that as many as _____ children are physically abused every year in the United States. *500,000*

3. Indicate what it means to say that child abuse is a diverse condition that is only partially caused by individual personality characteristics of parents.

4   Although child abuse refers to both abuse and neglect, experts often use the term child _____ to describe both phenomena.   *maltreatment*

5. Indicate the incidence of different kinds of maltreatment.

6. _____ children are more likely to be angry than _____ children, who are more likely to be passive.   *Abused*
                                                                                                                              neglected

7. Explain why the "battered child syndrome is something of a media invention.

8. _____ children suffer no physical injuries, but they often suffer long-term psychological harm.   *Neglected*

9. Maltreatment must be considered within its _____ context.   *cultural*

10. Community support and the support of family and friends can _____ child abuse.   *reduce*

11. Maltreatment must also be considered within the _____ system.   *family*

12. Indicate some family influences on the maltreatment of children.

13. Infantile _____ is a severe developmental disturbance characterized by deficiencies in social relationships, abnormalities in communication, and stereotyped behavior.   *autism*

14. Describe the social deficiencies of autistic children.

15. Children suffering from infantile autism also usually suffer from _____ , a speech disorder in which children repeat what they hear.   *echolalia*

16. Indicate what a child suffering from echolalia would say in response to the question, "How old are you?"

17. Characterize some of the stereotyped behaviors of autistic children.

18. Autism is related to organic _____ disorders and genetic endowment, but unrelated to _____ socialization.   *brain*
                                                                                                                              family

5.0   Chapter Boxes

A.   Sociocultural Worlds of Development: Child-Care Policy Around the World

1. More than 100 countries have effective child care policies designed to get a child off to a _____ start in life and to protect _____ health.   *competent*
                                                                                                                              maternal

2. Since the 1960s maternity policies have been linked strongly with _____ .   *employment*

3. Describe the parenting policy implemented in Sweden.

4. All industrialized countries except the United States recognize the importance of parenting leave, policies that prevent the loss of _____ .   *employment*

B.   Critical Thinking About Life-Span Development: Characteristics of Competent Caregivers

1. Propose five characteristics of competent caregivers and compare your list to the one given in the box on Life-Span Health and Well-Being.

C.   Critical Thinking About Life-Span Development: Developing a Model of Intervention for Maltreating Families

1. Explain why it is difficult to intervene with maltreating families.

2. Consider what you would learn about life-span development by developing a model of intervention to benefit maltreated children and their families.

D. Life-Span Health and Well-Being: The Personal Characteristics of Competent Caregivers

1. LaVisa Wilson has suggested _____ characteristics of competent caregivers. *8*
2. Competent caregivers are mentally and physically _____ , have a positive self-image, are *healthy* flexible, are _____ , are positive models for infants, are open to learning, and enjoy *patient* _____ . *caregiving*
3. Indicate the extent to which you would be a competent caregiver.

Self Test A: Key Terms and Key Persons

Write the appropriate key term or key person in the space to the right of the definition or description.

1. Emotions such as joy and laughter that are positively toned and range from enthusiasm to calmness. *positive affectivity*
2. The creator of the Maximally Discriminative Facial Movement Coding System or MAX. *Carroll Izard*
3. Early in development this kind of smile is a common response to the appearance of a face. *social smile*
4. A relationship in which the infant uses the mother as a base from which to explore the environment; infants respond positively to being picked up and, when put down, move away freely to play. *secure attachment*
5. A child who adapts to new experiences, generally appears in a positive mood, and quickly establishes regular routines. *easy child*
6. The individual who proposed a solution to the day care needs of many families in the United States. *Edward Zigler*
7. A predisposition to prefer to be with others rather than by oneself. *sociability*
8. The view that children socialize parents just as parents socialize children. *reciprocal socialization*
9. A loud cry followed by breath holding that appears suddenly without any prior moaning. *pain cry*
10. An important role of caretakers early in the parent-child interaction. *scaffolding*
11. Infants who exhibit insecure attachment by avoiding the mother. *type A baby*
12. The researcher who devised the Strange Situation to measure attachment. *Mary Ainsworth*
13. A system for coding emotions expressed by the faces of infants. *MAX*
14. Either of the two researchers who said the three basics temperaments are the easy child, difficult child, and slow-to-warm-up-child. *Chess/Thomas*
15. A child who displays a low intensity of mood, little adaptability, and low activity levels. *slow-to-warm up*
16. The developmentalist who proposed that children go through a process of separation and individuation. *Margaret Mahler*
17. A condition in which the individual is deficient is social relationships, and often performs repetitive and stereotyped movements. *infantile autism*
18. The individual who studied nontraditional gender roles in Swedish families. *Michael Lamb*
19. A speech disorder displayed by autistic children who echo what they hear. *echolalia*
20. A procedure used to measure infant attachment by moving the infants through a series of introductions, separations, and reunions with the caregiver and a novel individual. *Strange Situation*
21. Either of the two researchers who used monkeys to test the Freudian hypothesis that oral satisfaction is the key aspect that promotes attachment to the caregiver. *Harry Harlow/Zimmerman*
22. The researcher whose work illustrates the new functionalism in emotion. *Alan Sroufe*

Self Test B: Multiple Choice

1. Reciprocal socialization is best defined in which of the following ways?
   a. children are products of their parents' socialization techniques
   b. parents are products of their children's socialization techniques
   c. socialization is bi-directional
   d. the interactions that children have with people other than their parents determines how they will be socialized

2. One of the functions of scaffolding is to
   a. introduce infants to interactive games.
   b. provide a parent support network.
   c. teach infants social rules.
   d. ensure that parents know how to care for their infants.

3. According to Jay Belsky's model of the family system, the father and one child define a _____ system, and the mother and the father define a _____ system.
   a. dyadic; polyadic
   b. dyadic; dyadic
   c. polyadic; polyadic
   d. polyadic; dyadic

4. Which of the following research techniques is used to investigate attachment?
   a. watching children as they are separated from and then reunited with their parents
   b. asking parents to describe how emotionally involved they are with their children
   c. watching children play with dolls representing adults and children to see what kinds of interactions they create
   d. asking baby-sitters about how infants behave when their parents are gone

5. Erik Erikson says that the key time for attachment is within the first _____ after birth.
   a. few minutes
   b. few hours
   c. day
   d. year

6. Life-span developmentalists agree that secure attachment
   a. is essential to adult social competence.
   b. is not essential but is a factor in adult social competence.
   c. is not an important factor in adult social competence.
   d. None of the answers is agreed upon.

7. You are asked to baby-sit your niece for the evening. When the parents put the child down so they can finish getting dressed, she heads toward her toys while she watches the parents find their coats. The child is demonstrating which of the following kinds of attachment?
   a. secure
   b. anxious-avoidant
   c. anxious-resistant
   d. insecure

8. Jeremy resists being held closely by his mother yet hangs on to her clothes when she tries to put him down. Jeremy is a type _____ baby.
   a. A
   b. B
   c. C
   d. D

9. Which of the following is a good predictor of problems and disturbances at age 18?
   a. low socioeconomic status at 2 years of age
   b. average intelligence
   c. moderate infant responsiveness at 1 year of age
   d. prenatal stress

10. Jerome Kagan has emphasized the importance of _____ as a determinant of social competence.
    a. bonding
    b. temperament
    c. peer responsiveness
    d. learning

11. All but which of the following are criticisms of the theories concerning attachment?
    a. genetics and temperament have not been accounted for and may play more of a role in development than the nature of the attachment
    b. the role of multiple social agents and changing social contexts is not included in the study of attachment
    c. cultural differences are not considered when explaining how attachment occurs
    d. the relationship between the parent and the infant is not emphasized enough

12. Given the opportunity, fathers usually will
    a. not elect caretaking roles with children.
    b. elect nurturing caretaker roles with infants.
    c. elect inactive child-caretaking roles.
    d. elect involved caretaker roles over occupational roles.

13. Which of the following is true? Infants show a preference for attention from
    a. mother when both parents are present in nonstressful circumstances.
    b. father when both parents are present in nonstressful circumstances.
    c. father when both parents are present in stressful circumstances.
    d. mother when both parents are present in stressful circumstances.

14. The results of a Swedish study indicate that if a mother works and a father stays at home with the baby, the father
    a. reverses roles and behaves like the typical mother in many respects.
    b. interacts with the baby in his usual fatherly manner.
    c. is more likely to discipline and comfort the infant than the mother is.
    d. plays with the infant in a less physical and arousing manner than does the mother.

Handwritten annotations:

Type B - secure
A - anxious avoidant - avoids mom
C - anxious resistant - cling to mom, but fights against close

Chess + Thomas
3 types of Temperment
1. Easy - positive mood, quickly establishes routine, infant
2. Difficult - reacts negatively, cries frequently, irregular daily routine, slow to accept new experiences
3. Slow to warm up - low activity level, negative, low adaptability

15. It can be concluded that day care for American children is
    a. adequate but needs to be expanded.
    b. inadequate and has negative outcomes for children.
    c. neither adequate nor inadequate; the results of studies are mixed.
    d. exemplary, a good model for the world community.

16. The research concerning the long-term effects of day care suggests which of the following?
    a. day care has long-term, detrimental effects
    b. day care has no long-term effects
    c. day care can facilitate development
    d. the effects of day care are dependent on the length and type of care given

17. Temperament is best defined as
    a. the way an individual reacts to a special person in the environment.
    b. an individual's general behavioral style.
    c. the emotions experienced by infants and children.
    d. the reaction displayed by a parent when a child engages in an unwanted activity.

18. The most typical temperament is the _____ child according to Alexander Chess and Stella Thomas.
    a. difficult
    b. easy
    c. slow-to-warm-up
    d. sociable

19. Arnold Buss and Robert Plomin use all of the following categories *except* this one to classify temperament.
    a. activity level
    b. emotionality
    c. regularity
    d. sociability

20. Emotion is a mixture of
    a. physiological arousal and cognitions.
    b. cognitions and behaviors.
    c. physiological arousal and behaviors.
    d. None of the alternatives is correct.

21. Which of the following emotions develops before the others?
    a. guilt
    b. contempt
    c. surprise
    d. shame

22. Mary Ainsworth believes that attachment security depends on
    a. how sensitive and responsive the caregiver is to infant signals.
    b. the mother's love and concern for the welfare of the child.
    c. the consistency of parental responses during the child-care routine.
    d. reinforcement of attachment behaviors by the caregiver.

23. According to Erik Erikson, children will develop an excessive sense of shame and a sense of doubt about their abilities under all but which of the following circumstances?
    a. when impatient parents do things children can do for themselves
    b. when children are consistently overprotected
    c. when accidents the children have had or caused are criticized
    d. when children are allowed to express their emotions unchecked

24. Which of the following is true about the development of trust?
    a. if infants do not develop a sense of trust they will not be able to develop one later
    b. infants given inconsistent care develop a sense of mistrust they can never overcome
    c. children who have a secure sense of trust upon leaving the infancy stage are unlikely ever to mistrust the world
    d. trust that is developed early may be shattered, and situations in which trust never developed may be overcome

25. When does the human infant learn to recognize his or her image in a mirror?
    a. 2 months
    b. 6 months
    c. 9 months
    d. 18 months

26. Reductions in incidents of child abuse have been shown to be related to all but which of the following?
    a. the presence of community support systems
    b. the availability of support from relatives and friends
    c. harsh laws punishing abusers
    d. family income

27. A child suffering form echolalia will say what in response to the question "Is that your ball?"
    a. "My ball."
    b. "Is that your ball?"
    c. "No, it is my ball."
    d. "Yes, it is your ball."

28. Which of the following has no national policy permitting paternity leave?
    a. Norway
    b. the United States
    c. Portugal
    d. Spain

29. If you were listening to LaVisa Wilson lecture on competent caregivers, you would hear her describe all of the following characteristics *except*
    a. patience.
    b. physically healthy.
    c. economically solvent.
    d. flexibility.

Buss + Plomin - 3 tempernaments:
1. Emotionality - tendency to be distressed
2. Sociability - prefers company of others to being alone
3. activity level - can't sit still

Answers for Self Test A

1. positive affectivity (PA)
2. Carroll Izard
3. social smile
4. secure attachment
5. easy child
6. Edward Zigler
7. sociability
8. reciprocal socialization
9. pain cry
10. scaffolding
11. type A babies
12. Mary Ainsworth
13. maximally discriminative facial movement coding system (MAX)
14. Alexander Chess or Stella Thomas
15. slow-to-warm-up child
16. Margaret Mahler
17. infantile autism
18. Michael Lamb
19. echolalia
20. Strange Situation
21. Harry Harlow or Robert Zimmerman
22. Alan Sroufe

Answers for Self Test B

1. c LO 1.1
2. a LO 1.2
3. b LO 1.4
4. a LO 2.1
5. d LO 2.3
6. d LO 2.4
7. a LO 2.4
8. c LO 2.5
9. a LO 2.7
10. b LO 2.8
11. d LO 2.9
12. a LO 2.12
13. d LO 2.14
14. b LO 2.16
15. c LO 2.19
16. d LO 2.21
17. b LO 3.1
18. b LO 3.2
19. c LO 3.3
20. c LO 4.1
21. c LO 4.7
22. a LO 4.11
23. d LO 4.11
24. c LO 4.12
25. d LO 4.13
26. c LO 4.19
27. b LO 4.22
28. b LO 5.2
29. c LO 5.5

Chapter 8   Physical and Cognitive Development in Early Childhood

Learning Objectives with Key Terms in Boldface

1.0 Physical Development in Early Childhood

    1.1   Compare and contrast the physical and motor development of infants and toddlers.

A. *Height and Weight*

    1.2   Describe changes in height and weight during the preschool years, differentiating between boys and girls.

    1.3   List factors associated with individual differences in height and weight among preschoolers.

    1.4   Define **deprivation dwarfism**, and explain how it reveals interaction between physical and emotional factors.

B. *The Brain*

    1.5   Explain why children lose their "top-heavy" look during the preschool years.

    1.6   Define **myelination**, and discuss its contribution to development.

    1.7   Explain how motor development is related to reading readiness and other aspects of sensorimotor coordination.

C. *Motor Development*

    1.8   List representative changes in gross motor skills between the ages of three and five years.

    1.9   Explain the importance of daily exercise during early childhood.

    1.10   List representative changes in fine motor skills between the ages of three and five years.

    1.11   List advantages and disadvantages experienced by left-handed children.

    1.12   Explain how researchers learn about the hand preferences of infants and toddlers, and describe the development of handedness for early infancy through early childhood.

D. *Nutrition*

    1.13   Indicate what we know/do not know about changing nutritional needs during the preschool years.

    1.14   Define **basal metabolism rate (BMR),** and discuss its role in establishing nutritional needs.

    1.15   Explain why early exposure to fast foods worries developmentalists.

    1.16   List recommendations to caregivers about ways to discourage eating problems for children.

E. *The State of Illness and Health in the World's Children*

    1.17   List the leading causes of death among children in the world and children in the United States.

    1.18   Define **oral rehydration therapy**, and list ways to prevent illness or improve the health of children.

    1.19   Indicate the mortality rates of children under age 5 in the United States and other countries.

    1.20   Indicate diseases that are and are not likely to be fatal to children in the United States.

2.0 Cognitive Development in Early Childhood

A. *Piaget's Stage of Preoperational Thought*

    2.1   Define **operations**, and describe the nature of preoperational thought.

    2.2   Portray the **symbolic function substage** and **intuitive thought substage** of preoperational thought.

    2.3   Distinguish between **egocentrism** and **animism**, and identify observations that indicate their presence in children's thought.

    2.4   Distinguish between **centration** and **conservation**, and describe observations that indicate their presence in children's thought.

    2.5   Explain how centration causes both failure to classify objects and inability to conserve.

    2.6   Use the concepts of intuitive thought and operations to explain why young children fail conservation tests, whereas concrete operational children pass them.

    2.7   Indicate Jean Piaget's and Rochel Gelman's views about why young children fail conservation tasks.

    2.8   Discuss what children's questions reveal about their cognition.

B. *Information Processing*

    2.9   Explain how an information-processing approach distinguishes between limitations on cognitive development and limitations on the method of study.

    2.10   Indicate how habituation and dishabituation influence attention during the preschool years, and how visual attention to television changes during the same period.

    2.11   Distinguish between salient and task-relevant dimensions, and discuss their influence on youngster's attention.

    2.12   Define **short-term memory**, list its properties, and indicate how it changes in young children.

    2.13   Explain and cite evidence about why there are differences in memory span because of age.

    2.14   Explain how task analysis has led to an understanding of children's ability to reason syllogistically.

    2.15   Describe the development of theories about the mind: the existence of a mind, its connection to the external world, inferences about mental states, separateness from the world, mental representation, and interpretation.

C. *Language Development*

    2.16   Use the mean length of utterance to describe language development from one to four years of age according to Roger Brown's five stages.

    2.17   Describe observations that indicate children understand rules of morphology, syntax, semantics, and pragmatics.

D. *Vygotsky's Theory of Development*

    2.18   Define the **zone of proximal development (ZPD)**.

    2.19   Compare and contrast uses of the zone of proximal development (ZPD) and the intelligence quotient (IQ).

    2.20   Explain how learning by toddlers exemplifies the workings of ZPDs.

    2.21   Characterize the respective activities of child and teacher as a child moves through a ZPD.

    2.22   Discuss Lev Vygotsky's conception of the developmental relationship between language and thought.

    2.23   Contrast Piaget's and Vygotsky's ideas about what causes development of thought and language.

    2.24   Indicate the role sociocultural factors play in Vygotsky's theory of cognitive development.

E. *Early Childhood Education*

    2.25   List criticisms of contemporary kindergartens.

    2.26   Define and discuss the philosophy and activities of a **child-centered kindergarten**.

    2.27   Explain the concept of **developmentally appropriate practice**, and explain what makes the kindergarten in Greensbrook School in New Jersey a developmentally appropriate class.

    2.28   Identify characteristics of developmentally inappropriate practice.

    2.29   Explain why contemporary parents may not care for their young children as well as preschools do.

    2.30   Describe evidence that formal instruction in reading should be delayed until age seven.

    2.31   Describe the controversy over preschool experience, and discuss the ideal intent of early education programs.

    2.32   Describe evidence that developmentally inappropriate schools harm their young pupils in comparison to developmentally appropriate schools.

    2.33   Assess the claim that high-achieving Japanese students attend rigid elementary schools.

    2.34   Summarize the effects of early childhood education on children's development.

    2.35   Describe the nature of **Project Head Start**, and the outcomes of **Project Follow Through**.

    2.36   List the documented benefits of compensatory education for disadvantaged children, and compare them to benefits associated with preschool attendance in general.

    2.37   State the goals of nonsexist early childhood education.

    2.38   List ways that young children's awareness of equitable gender roles can be expanded.

3.0 Chapter Boxes

A. *Sociocultural Worlds of Development: Early Childhood Education in Japan*

    3.1   Compare and contrast both schools in Japan and the United States, and mothers' involvement in early child education in both countries.

B. *Critical Thinking About Life-Span Development: Explaining to Parents Why Most 3-Year-Olds Should Not Participate in Sports*

    3.2   Indicate your ability to think critically by applying life-span developmental framework to an explanation of why 3-year-olds should not participate in sports.

C. *Critical Thinking About Life-Span Development: Giving Advice to Parents About Selecting a Good Preschool Program*

    3.3   Indicate your ability to think critically by applying life-span developmental concepts to advice you would give parents about how to select a good preschool program.

D. *Life-Span Health and Well-Being: Early Interventions That Work*

    3.4   Explain why it is important to provide health services to poor young children.

    3.5   List and describe four attributes of successful health intervention programs for poor young children.

    3.6   Describe two successful health intervention programs for poor young children, and explain how they implement the four attributes of success.

Guided Review and Study

1.0 Physical Development in Early Childhood

A. *Height and Weight*

    1. The _____ of growth begun in the second year continues in early childhood.   *slowing*

    2. The average child grows _____ inches and gains 5 to 7 pounds a year.   *2.5*

    3. Use Figure 8.1 to review changes in the height and weight of preschool girls and boys.

    4. Explain what it means to say that individual differences characterize patterns of growth.

    5. Important factors that produce individual differences in height are ethnic origin and _____ .   *nutrition*

    6. Three conditions, either congenital factors, physical problems, or _____ difficulties can produce unusually short children.   *emotional*

    7. The hormone that controls growth is secreted by the _____ gland at the base of the brain.   *pituitary*

    8. Explain why deprivation dwarfism illustrates an interaction of physical and emotional factors.

B. *The Brain*

    1. Although the brain grows more _____ in early childhood than in infancy, children have a brain _____ percent of adult size by 3 years of age, and 90 percent of adult size by age 5.   *slowly* *75*

    2. A portion of the increase in size is due to an increase in the number and size of nerve _____ within and between areas of the brain.   *endings*

    3. The process of _____ covers nerve cells with fat, and _____ the speed of information transmission in the brain.   *myelination* *increases*

    4. Indicate how myelination contributes to development.

    5. Motor development is related to _____ readiness.   *reading*

C. *Motor Development*

    1. Indicate representative gross motor skills at:

        age 3

age 4

age 5

2. It is importance for preschoolers to have daily _____ .   *exercise*

3. Children also develop their _____ motor skills such as grasping and block stacking.   *fine*

4. Three-year-olds can build block towers, but the blocks seldom occur in a _____ line.   *straight*

5. Although four-year-olds are much more _____ , they try to place each block _____ , and become upset when they fail.   *precise*
   perfectly

6. Although teachers once forced children to write with their _____ hand, today's teachers allow children to write with their _____ hand.   *right*
   preferred

7. Although the incidence of left-handed people in the general population is about _____ , the top _____ of the students who took the SAT were left-handed.   *10*
   20

8. Explain how researchers assess the hand preferences of infants and toddlers.

9. Characterize the development of handedness from early infancy through early childhood.

D. *Nutrition*

1. An individual's basal metabolism rate (BMR) is the _____ amount of energy required for resting, growth, and activity.   *minimum*

2. Explain individual differences in energy needs of children who are the same age, sex, and size.

3. One concern regarding children's eating is the consumption of excess _____ contained in fast foods.   *fat*

4. Indicate how caregivers can discourage eating problems among children.

E. *The State of Illness and Health in the World's Children*

1. _____ is the leading cause of children's death in the world.   *Diarrhea*

2. The effects of diarrhea can be prevented by use of _____ rehydration therapy.   *oral*

3. Indicate ways that parents can improve their children's health.

4. Countries with the highest mortality rates for children under age 5 include _____ and Ethiopia.   *Afghanistan*

5. The _____ mortality rates under age 5 are found in the Scandinavian countries.   *lowest*

6. Identify diseases that are and are not likely to be fatal to children in the United States.

2.0 Cognitive Development in Early Childhood

A. *Piaget's Stage of Preoperational Thought*

1. The preoperational period lasts from _____ to _____ years of age.   *2; 7*

2. The preoperational stage of cognitive development is a time when _____ are formed, reasoning begins, _____ comes and goes, and magical beliefs are apparent.

    concepts
    egocentrism

3. _____ are internalized actions that allow children to do mentally what before they could only do physically.

    Operations

4. Characterize developmental changes in operations.

5. Preoperational thought can be divided into two substages of _____ functioning and _____ thought.

    symbolic
    intuitive

6. The _____ function substage occurs roughly between the ages of 2 to 4 years.

    symbolic

7. Indicate what young children can do in the symbolic functioning substage.

8. Egocentrism and animism are two _____ that occur during the symbolic function substage.

    limitations

9. The inability to distinguish between one's own and another's perspective is called _____ .

    egocentrism

10. Explain the methods and interpretation of the three mountain task devised by Piaget and Inhelder to study egocentrism in children.

11. The view that inanimate objects are alive or that plants and similar forms have human qualities is called _____ .

    animism

12. What appears to be animism might be due to lack of _____ and understanding rather than to a view of the world.

    knowledge

13. During the _____ thought substage, children from 4 to 7 years of age are sure of their knowledge, but _____ of how they know.

    intuitive
    unaware

14. When asked to sort objects into groups of similar items the she has not yet developed the skill of _____ .

    classification

15. Although the 6-year-old child cannot cross-_____ the 9-year-old child probably can cross-classify on the basis of _____ or more properties.

    classify
    two

16. Egocentrism, animism, and difficulty with classification may represent _____ , a focus on a single dimension of a multi-dimensional object.

    centration

17. Centration is evident in the children's lack of _____ .

    conservation

18. Explain the concept of conservation by describing the method and interpretation of Piaget's water beakers task.

19. Failure to pass a conservation task test indicates that a child is in the _____ stage of cognitive development according to Jean Piaget.

    preoperational

20. According to Rochel Gelman, _____ abilities underlie conservation skills.

    attentional

21. Attentional training allows children to demonstrate conservation _____ than Piaget believed possible.

    earlier

22. About the age of _____ children begin to ask questions.

    3

23. Explain what it means to say that children's questions reveal much about mental development.

B. Information Processing

1. The thoughts of preschoolers demonstrate _____ in their information processing skills of attention and memory.

    limitations

2. Habituation refers to a _____ of attention, whereas dishabituation refers to a _____ of attention. *decrement*

   recovery

3. Both decrements and recovery of attention during infancy _____ with intelligence during preschool years. *correlate*

4. Describe changes in the ability of preschoolers to attend to objects and events.

5. Preschool children are more likely to attend to _____ rather than _____ stimuli when solving a problem. *salient*

   relevant

6. By the age of 6 or 7, children attend more efficiently to the _____ features of a task rather than the _____ features. *relevant*

   salient

7. Short-term memory retains information for up to _____ seconds, although retention duration can be increased by _____ . *30*

   rehearsal

8. Explain how to use the memory-span task to assess short-term memory.

9. Draw a graph showing the memory spans of 2-, 7-, and 13-year-olds.

10. The increase in the memory span of children as they grow older results from the use of _____ and increases in the speed and efficiency and of information processing. *rehearsal*

11. Explain what it means to say that the speed whereby a child processes information is an important aspect of the child's cognitive abilities.

12. Developmentalists perform a _____ analysis to determine how children perform on various components of a problem. *task*

13. Explain how researchers have used task analysis to determine how children reason syllogistically.

14. Investigators have become interested in children's thoughts about the human _____ . *mind*

15. The first developmental step for children is to realize minds _____ . *exist*

16. The second developmental step is for children to realize that people make cognitive _____ with events and objects. *connections*

17. Indicate evidence that shows children understand that people can be "cognitively connected" to objects and events in the external world.

18. The third developmental step entails an understanding that the mind is _____ from the physical world. *separate*

19. The fourth developmental step is for children to understand that the mind can _____ objects and events both correctly and incorrectly. *represent*

20. Indicate examples of children's understanding that the mind can represent objects and events both correctly and incorrectly.

21. The final step entails an understanding that the mind actively _____ the interpretation of reality and emotions. *mediates*

C. Language Development

1. Roger Brown identified five stages of language development, and indicates that the mean length of _____ , or MLU, is a good measure of language maturity.   *utterance*

2. Characterize Roger Brown's five stages of language development in terms of MLUs, age ranges, characteristics, and typical sentences:

Stage 1

Stage 2

Stage 3

Stage 4

Stage 5

3. Language _____ systems include morphology, syntax, semantics, and pragmatics.   *rule*

4. The correct use of plurals, possessives, and "-ed" for the past tense provides evidence that children beyond the two-word stage know some _____ rules.   *morphological*

5. Provide some examples of overgeneralizations that demonstrate preschool children understand morphological rules.

6. Explain how Jean Berko demonstrated that preschool and first-grade children understand morphological rules.

7. Similar procedures reveal that preschoolers can apply _____ rules.   *syntactical*

8. Understanding and using a wh- question requires not only the placing of a _____ word at the beginning of the sentence but also _____ the auxiliary verb.   *wh-* / *inverting*

9. Children learn to apply the inversion rule _____ than they learn to use the wh- words.   *later*

10. A growing vocabulary constitutes evidence for rules of _____ .   *semantics*

11. Regarding semantics, the _____ vocabulary of a six-year-old child has been estimated to be between 8,000 to 14,000 words.   *speaking*

12. Children acquire _____ new words per day between the ages of 1 to 6.   *5 to 8*

13. One of the most important differences between the language of infants and the language of preschoolers is the use of _____ or rules of conversation.   *pragmatics*

14. Preschoolers show evidence of _____ when they talk about things not physically present.   *displacement*

15. Describe two pragmatic abilities of later preschoolers.

D. Vygotsky's Theory of Development

1. Lev Vygotsky says tasks that are too difficult for children to handle alone, but can be done with assistance of someone more skilled fall into the zone of proximal development or _____ .   *ZPD*

2. Identify the lower and upper limits of the zone of proximal development.

3. The ZPD is a measure of learning _____ .   *potential*

4. The concept of IQ indicates that _____ is a property of the child, whereas the concept of   *intelligence*
   ZPD emphasizes that _____ is an interpersonal and social event.   *learning*

5. Describe the activities of child and teacher as a child move through a ZPD.

6. For Vygotsky, language and thought initially are _____ ; however, the two eventually   *independent*
   _____ .   *merge*

7. Two principles govern the _____ of thought and language.   *merger*

8. Explain what Vygotsky means by saying that all mental functions have external or social origins.

9. Explain what Vygotsky means by saying that the merger of thought and language requires a
   transition from external to internal speech.

10. The zone of proximal development is just one aspect of Vygotsky's theory that social and cultural   *cognitive*
    factors influence _____ development.

11. Compare and contrast Vygotsky's view of the roles of institutions and individuals in a child's
    mental development.

E. Early Childhood Education

1. Some experts on early childhood education believe that kindergartens and preschools place too   *achievement*
   much emphasis on _____ , and thereby place unnecessary pressure on children too soon.

2. _____ -centered kindergartens stress children's physical, cognitive, and social development.   *Child*

3. Child-centered kindergartens emphasize the _____ of learning rather than what is learned.   *process*

4. Express the concept of developmentally appropriate practice in your own words.

5. Developmentally _____ practices ignore the hands-on approach to learning, teach using   *inappropriate*
   paper-and-pencil activities, and teach to large groups instead of individuals.

6. Explain whether the kindergarten in Greensbrook School in New Jersey represents
   developmentally appropriate or inappropriate schooling.

7. Use Figure 8.10 to review developmentally appropriate practices and developmentally
   inappropriate practices for the six basic components of early childhood education.

8. According to David Elkind, preschool is not necessary if _____ schooling approximates the   *home*
   experiences that can be obtained at a competent preschool.

9. Explain why early childhood education should not be considered as a head start in a race.

10. Evidence that early formal education may do more _____ than _____ is that children   *harm; good*
    in countries that begin formal reading instruction early have _____ reading problems than   *more*
    children in countries that begin formal reading instruction later.

11. One of the dangers of instituting public preschools is that they will become extensions of   *traditional*
    _____ elementary education.

12. David Elkind argues that _____ childhood education should become part of public education on its own terms.   *early*

13. Diane Burts demonstrated that academic pressures on young children can produce _____ .   *stress*

14. Children in high academically oriented early education programs had _____ test anxiety, _____ creativity, and a _____ positive attitude toward school than children in low academically oriented programs.   *more* *less; less*

15. The high achievement of Japanese students _____ the result of a rigid system of schooling.   *is not*

16. Summarize the effects of early childhood education on children.

17. The first attempt at compensatory education in the United States was Project _____ .   *Head Start*

18. The purpose of Project Head Start was to provide an opportunity for children from low-income families to acquire skills important for success in _____ .   *school*

19. Explain the purpose of Project Follow Through.

20. The instructional programs of Project Follow Through produced better academic _____ and task persistence, but students in affective models were _____ less and more independent.   *performance* *absent*

21. Early childhood compensatory education programs provide benefits to both _____ and individual children.   *society*

22. Estimates indicate that every dollar spent on such programs eventually returns _____ over a lifetime.   *$5.73*

23. Irving Lazar, Richard Darlington, and their collaborators have found _____ long-term effects of _____ preschool education with low-income children.   *positive* *competent*

24. Explain why the Perry Preschool represents a model Head Start program.

25. List three important goals of nonsexist early childhood education.

26. Describe ways to expand young children's awareness of equitable gender roles.

3.0 Chapter Boxes

A. *Sociocultural Worlds of Development: Early Childhood Education in Japan*

1. Japanese and American parents have _____ reasons for sending their children to preschool.   *different*

2. Japanese parents send their children to preschool to learn persistence, concentration, and _____ experience: American parents want their children to get a good start _____ .   *group* *academically*

3. An emphasis on living and working together illustrates a _____ influence on development.   *sociocultural*

4. Both Japanese and American preschools are _____ .   *diverse*

B. *Critical Thinking About Life-Span Development: Explaining to Parents Why Most 3-Year-Olds Should Not Participate in Sports*

1. Explain why life-span developmentalists say that 3-year-olds should not participate in sports.

C. *Critical Thinking About Life-Span Development: Giving Advice to Parents about Selecting a Good Preschool Program*

1. Indicate your ability to think critically by applying life-span developmental concepts to advice you would give parents about how to select a good preschool program.

D. Life-Span Health and Well-Being: Early Interventions That Work

1. Lisbeth Schorr identified _____ reasons why early intervention programs work.   *four*

2. Effective intervention programs are _____ and intensive, build trust and respect with   *comprehensive*
children and families, regard children as part of a family, and a family as part of a _____ ,   *community*
and bridge professional and bureaucratic _____ .   *boundaries*

Self Test A: Key Terms and Key Persons

Write the appropriate key term or key person in the space to the right of the definition or description.

1. An understanding that amount remains the same without regard to changes in the shape.   _____

2. Education that includes concern for children's physical, cognitive, and social development.   _____

3. A process that produces a layer of fat cells which cover and insulate nerve cells. The results of   _____
this process is the more rapid movement of information through the nervous system.

4. A children's health expert who identified four reasons why early intervention programs work.   _____

5. An inability to distinguish one's own from another's perspective.   _____

6. Vygotsky's term for tasks too difficult to master alone, but that can be mastered with the   _____
guidance of adults or more skilled children.

7. The second part of Piaget's preoperational stage that is characterized by a child who begins to   _____
reason about various matters, and frequently asks questions.

8. A developmentalist who used fictional words such as *wur* to test children's understanding of   _____
morphological rules of language.

9. A range of techniques used to prevent dehydration during episodes of diarrhea.   _____

10. Either of the two investigators who did long-term investigations of early childhood education.   _____

11. An evaluation process to determine which educational programs were most effective in terms of   _____
the initial years of elementary school.

12. A program of compensatory education designed for children from low-income homes.   _____

13. A developmentalist who applies the information processing perspective to analyses of why   _____
children fail Piagetian conservation tasks.

14. Internalized actions that allow a child to do mentally what before the child could only do   _____
physically.

15. A developmentalist who devised the concept of MLU to measure language maturity.   _____

Self Test B: Multiple Choice

1. The rate of change in height and weight that occurs
between ages 1 and 10 appears to
   a. remain the same—the changes are roughly
   equal.
   b. decelerate—the amount of change is smaller in
   the later years.
   c. accelerate—the amount of change increases in
   the later years.
   d. accelerate, then decelerate.

2. The Nortons love their son, but are quite concerned
about his lack of height, and his slow rate of
growth. A medical examination would likely
reveal a malfunction of the
   a. pituitary gland.
   b. adrenal gland.
   c. myelinated nerves.
   d. pineal gland.

3. Myelination improves the efficiency of the central
nervous system the way that
   a. talking to an infant speeds his ability to produce
   a first word.
   b. reducing the distance between two children
   playing catch reduces the time it takes for a
   baseball to travel from one child to the other.
   c. the ingestion of certain chemicals (e.g., steroids)
   can improve overall muscle development.
   d. the insulation around an electrical extension cord
   improves its efficiency.

4. The biggest difference in gross motor skills
between 3-year-olds and 5-year-olds involves which
of the following?
   a. their adventuresome nature
   b. the addition of new skills
   c. the fear of falling while running
   d. the breakability of bones

5. Which of the following would be considered a fine motor skill?
   a. bouncing a ball
   b. walking a straight line
   c. stacking blocks
   d. throwing a ball overhand

6. Left-handedness is associated with
   a. early maturation of motor skills.
   b. delinquent tendencies.
   c. cognitive and perceptual deficits.
   d. superior scholastic aptitude.

7. What a child eats during the early childhood period affects all but which of the following?
   a. skeletal growth
   b. body shape
   c. susceptibility to disease
   d. basal metabolism rate.

8. Your child is overweight. What is the best recommendation to help him slim down?
   a. Give him snacks only when he has been good.
   b. Put him on a diet that will help him lose weight.
   c. Encourage him to get more exercise.
   d. Punish him when you find him eating snacks.

9. The most likely cause of death in the world among children younger than 5 years old is
   a. a birth defect.
   b. polio.
   c. diarrhea.
   d. German measles.

10. Which of the following countries has the lowest child mortality rate?
    a. the United States
    b. Sweden
    c. Afghanistan
    d. Japan

11. All but which of the following is characteristic of behavior from a child in the symbolic function substage of cognitive development?
    a. scribbled designs represent people
    b. pretend play becomes popular
    c. language is hampered by a lack of physical development
    d. mental representation is possible

12. The typical "human tadpole" that preschoolers draw to represent a person probably best reflects
    a. limited knowledge of the human body.
    b. a confusion between fantasy and reality.
    c. a symbolic representation of a human.
    d. limited perceptual motor skills.

13. Asked to sort a collection of plastic toy animals that is a mixture of black and white birds and mammals, a young child is likely to
    a. make smaller piles of randomly chosen animals.
    b. sort them according to just one of the features.
    c. separate the mammals from the birds because they are animistic.
    d. separate the toys into the four categories of black animals, black birds, white animals, and white birds.

14. Rochel Gelman suggests that children fail conservation tasks because they
    a. cannot think about more than one aspect of a task.
    b. do not notice important features of the tasks.
    c. cannot mentally reverse the sequence of actions in the tasks.
    d. do not understand why researchers are teasing them.

15. Which of the following questions is typical of the preoperational child?
    a. "How many different piles of toys can I make from my toys?"
    b. "How much is two plus two?"
    c. "Where does the moon go when it's light out?"
    d. "Do you see the same thing I do, Daddy?"

16. Compared to that of a toddler, a preschooler's ability to pay attention enables him to
    a. ignore unimportant but distracting details of a task.
    b. habituate more quickly to repeated stimulation.
    c. concentrate on an activity for longer periods of time.
    d. pay attention to several things simultaneously.

17. When shown red and green triangles and squares and asked to put the objects that are the same color together, preschool children will
    a. put the objects they like the best together.
    b. put the same-colored objects together because color is relevant.
    c. put the same-shaped objects together because shape is relevant.
    d. put the same-colored objects together because color is salient.

18. Information in the short-term memory is retained for approximately how long?
    a. 250 to 500 milliseconds
    b. 15 to 30 seconds
    c. 1 to 2 minutes
    d. indefinitely

19. Three-year-old Shaniqua is inspecting a bowl containing several pieces of wax fruit. After touching and smelling a wax lemon she would MOST likely tell her older brother,
    a. "That's a real lemon."
    b. "Wax tastes really bad."
    c. "Just because something looks like a lemon doesn't mean that it is a real lemon."
    d. "Lemons are alive, and they see you when you eat them."

20. Evidence that children understand the rules of their language includes all but which of the following?
    a. observations of overgeneralizations
    b. application of rules to nonsense words
    c. correct word order placement
    d. identification of the meaning of words they have never seen pictures of

21. If you show a child one of these—@—and call it an oog, then ask her to tell what two of them are and she says, "two oogs," then she has demonstrated knowledge of the rules of
    a. phonology.
    b. syntax.
    c. morphology.
    d. semantics.

22. Overgeneralizations of language rules indicate
    a. a failure to apply language rules.
    b. children's guesses about language rules.
    c. the use of language rules.
    d. the imitation of language rules.

23. After racing down the street with his uncle, Peter says, "I runned very, very fast!" The use of the term "runned" exemplifies
    a. phonological development.
    b. morphological development.
    c. syntactic development.
    d. semantic development.

24. How does a ZPD differ from an IQ?
    a. One can be determined; the other cannot.
    b. One is a property of the child; the other is not.
    c. One is a measure of language; the other is not.
    d. One is a measure of potential; the other is not.

25. Which of the following reflects Lev Vygotsky's beliefs about language and thought?
    a. Children who engage in high levels of private speech are usually socially incompetent.
    b. Children use internal speech earlier than they use external speech.
    c. All mental functions have external or social origins.
    d. Language and thought initially develop together and then become independent.

26. Vygotsky believed that cognitive development was most influenced by which of the following?
    a. biological factors
    b. social factors
    c. personality factors
    d. emotional factors

27. According to Vygotsky, an institutional context that influences cognitive development is
    a. a child's interaction with a teacher.
    b. the everyday experiences that children have with peers.
    c. the traditions of a child's ethnic group.
    d. the use of computers to teach math concepts.

28. An instructor who uses developmentally inappropriate methods for teaching the alphabet would
    a. have children recite the alphabet three times a day every day.
    b. use music to teach the alphabet.
    c. use animal names and shapes to teach the alphabet.
    d. use the sandbox to let children draw the letters.

29. Project Head Start was designed to
    a. provide low-income children a chance to acquire skills that would help them succeed at school.
    b. assess the advantages and disadvantages of preschool educational programs.
    c. give parents an educational day care center.
    d. determine the feasibility of starting formal education at an earlier age.

30. Which type of approach was related to good school attendance in Project Follow Through?
    a. an academic, direct-instruction approach
    b. a Montessori-type approach
    c. a Head Start approach
    d. an affective education approach

31. Schooling for young children in Japan is most like
    a. a developmentally appropriate kindergarten.
    b. a program of concentrated academic instruction.
    c. the kind of program most Americans want.
    d. the typical American kindergarten.

32. Which was *not* a criteria for success of early-childhood intervention presented by Lisbeth Schorr?
    a. programs that cut through bureaucracy
    b. programs that focus on the family and community
    c. programs that employ "tough love" discipline
    d. programs that are intensive and comprehensive

Answers for Self Test A

1. conservation
2. child-centered kindergarten
3. myelination
4. Lisbett Schorr
5. egocentrism
6. zone of proximal development (ZPD)
7. intuitive thought substage
8. Jean Berko
9. oral rehydration therapy (ORT)
10. Irving Lazer or Richard Darlington
11. Project Follow Through
12. Project Head Start
13. Rochel Gelman
14. operations
15. Roger Brown

Answers for Self Test B

1. a LO 1.2
2. a LO 1.4
3. d LO 1.6
4. a LO 1.8
5. d LO 1.10
6. d LO 1.11
7. b LO 1.14
8. c LO 1.16
9. c LO 1.17
10. b LO 1.19
11. c LO 2.2
12. d LO 2.3
13. b LO 2.4
14. b LO 2.7
15. c LO 2.8
16. c LO 2.10
17. d LO 2.11
18. b LO 2.12
19. a LO 2.15
20. d LO 2.17
21. d LO 2.17
22. c LO 2.17
23. b LO 2.17
24. b LO 2.19
25. c LO 2.22
26. b LO 2.24
27. d LO 2.24
28. a LO 2.28
29. a LO 2.35
30. d LO 2.35
31. a LO 3.1
32 c LO 3.5

Section IV   Early Childhood

Chapter 9   Socioemotional Development in Early Childhood

Learning Objectives with Key Terms in Boldface

1.0   Families

A. *Parenting Styles*

1.1   Sketch changes of emphasis in parenting recommendations over the past 60 years.

1.2   Define and distinguish among **authoritarian parenting, authoritative parenting, neglectful parenting, indulgent parenting**.

1.3   Describe the behavior and personalities of children who experience each type of parenting.

B. *Adapting Parenting to Developmental Changes in the Child*

1.4   Describe how competent parents adapt to their developing child.

C. *Cultural, Ethnic, and Social Class Variations in Families*

1.5   Indicate the most common parenting style in the world.

1.6   List ways in which the families of White Americans and ethnic minorities differ.

1.7   Explain how ethnic minority families can protect their children from social problems and injustice.

1.8   Characterize the child-rearing practices and values of different social classes.

D. *Sibling Relationships and Birth Order*

1.9   Explain why it is difficult to generalize about sibling influences.

1.10 Compare and contrast parent-child and sibling interactions.

1.11 Explain why siblings may be more important than parents for some aspects of socialization.

1.12 Indicate variations in sibling interactions around the world.

1.13 Explain why the firstborn child's relationship with parents is unique compared to any subsequent child.

1.14 Discuss firstborn children's relationships with later-born siblings.

1.15 List the personality and behavioral characteristics of first versus later-born children.

1.16 Compare firstborn to only children.

1.17 Explain why increasing numbers of researchers think that birth-order effects have been overemphasized.

1.18 List and discuss factors other than birth order that may influence sibling relationships.

E. *The Changing Family in a Changing Society*

1.19 Describe the variety of family structures prevalent in today's changing society.

1.20 Explain why children of two working parents may not suffer compared to children of a nonworking parent.

1.21 Discuss the various effects of a mother's working outside the home on a child's social development.

1.22 Discuss causes and cures for parents' feelings of guilt.

1.23 Characterize the **family structure model** and **multiple factor model of divorce** effects.

1.24 Discuss how age, developmental changes, and sex influence children's adjustment to divorce.

1.25 Discuss the role that conflict plays in the adjustment of children in both intact and divorced families.

1.26 Indicate how the sex of a child and the sex of the custodial parent relate to the child's adjustment to divorce.

1.27 Sketch how income is a factor in the adjustment of parents and children to divorce.

1.28 Evaluate the idea that divorce is never a good solution to marital problems when there are children in the family.

F. *Depressed Parents*

1.29 Indicate how contemporary researchers have changed our view of depression.

1.30 Explain how parental depression affects children.

2.0 Peer Relations, Play, and Television

A. *Peer Relations*

2.1 Define **peers** and indicate the roles peers play in children's development.

2.2 Evaluate the evidence that peers are necessary for adequate social development.

2.3 Compare and contrast peer and child-parent relationships.

2.4 Explain how children's relationships with their parents can influence relationships with their peers.

B. *Play*

2.5 Define **play**.

2.6 Define **play therapy**, and distinguish the functions of play according to Sigmund Freud and Erik Erikson.

2.7 State the cognitive functions of play according to Jean Piaget, Lev Vygotsky, and Daniel Berlyne.

2.8 Define and distinguish among Mildred Parten's classifications of **unoccupied, solitary, onlooker, parallel, associative,** and **cooperative play.**

2.9 Define and distinguish among play types identified by contemporary researchers: **sensorimotor/practice play, pretense/symbolic play, social play, constructive play,** and also **games**.

2.10 Explain how play fulfills both developmental and educational goals and functions.

C. *Television*

2.11 List the possible positive and negative influences of television watching on cognitive and social development.

2.12 Describe the evidence that ethnic minorities are under- and misrepresented on television.

2.13 Explain how Sesame Street is "good television" for children.

2.14 Indicate how much time three- to five-year-olds spent watching television in the 1950s, 1970s, and 1980s.

2.15 Evaluate claims that television violence causes aggression in children and that viewing prosocial behavior on television causes children to engage in prosocial behavior.

2.16 Discuss how cognitive development relates to children's television viewing experience.

2.17 State how television viewing relates to children's creativity and verbal skills.

3.0 The Self, Gender, and Moral Development

A. *The Self*

3.1 Explain Erik Erikson's concept of initiative versus guilt.

3.2 Explain how conscience relates to initiative.

3.3 Describe parenting practices that contribute to a sense of initiative.

3.4 Define and give examples of **self-understanding**.

3.5 Describe young children's self-understanding.

B. *Gender*

3.6 Define and distinguish among sex, **gender, gender identity,** and **gender role**.

3.7 Define and distinguish between androgen and estrogen.

3.8 Indicate the roles of **androgen** and **estrogen** in normal and abnormal sex organ development.

3.9 Explore the possible influence of androgen and estrogen on behavior.

3.10 Identify what is controversial about the possible influence of hormones on behavior.

3.11 Summarize Freud and Erikson's views on the influence of the genitals on gender and sexual behavior.

3.12 Interpret the phrase *biological and environmental factors interact to produce gender-related behavior.*

3.13 Identify possible social influences on gender roles.

3.14 Compare and contrast the **identification theory** and **social learning theory of gender** development.

3.15 Identify differences in parents' treatment of daughters and sons, and explain how differences in treatment may result in gender-role differences.

3.16 Summarize peer, school, teacher, and media influences on gender-role development.

3.17 Outline the **cognitive developmental theory of gender**.

3.18 Distinguish **schema** and **gender schema**, and outline **gender schema theory**.

3.19 Define sexist language, and explain how language may influence gender-role development.

C. *Moral Development*

3.20 Define **moral development**.

3.21 Distinguish the study of moral behavior from the study of moral reasoning, behavior, and emotion.

3.22 Define and distinguish among **heteronomous morality, autonomous morality,** and **immanent justice**; and describe observations that indicate their presence in children's moral reasoning.

3.23 Sketch Jean Piaget's ideas about the importance of peer versus parent relationships to moral development.

3.24 List factors that social learning theory suggests control the expression of moral behavior.

3.25 Describe the sources and effects of guilt.

3.26 Define **empathy**, and describe the part that perspective-taking plays in each.

3.27 Summarize how emotions, cognitions, and social contexts influence moral behavior and development.

4.0 Chapter Boxes

A. *Sociocultural Worlds of Development: African American and Mexican American Family Orientations*

4.1 Compare and contrast African American, Mexican American, and White American family orientations.

B. *Critical Thinking About Life-Span Development: Developing Parental TV Guidelines for Children's Viewing*

4.2 Apply life-span developmental concepts by devising a set of parental guidelines for television watching that would make television a positive influence on their children's lives.

C. *Critical Thinking About Life-Span Development: Evaluating Expectations for Girls and Boys*

4.3 Cite evidence concerning how beliefs about a baby's sex influence a person's description of a baby.

4.4 Demonstrate your appreciation of individual differences by speculating about how different expectations for boys and girls influence children's development.

D. *Life-Span Health and Well-Being: Some Working-Parent Solutions When Work/Family Interference Occurs*

4.5 Summarize Ellen Galinsky and Judy David's recommendations for overcoming work/family interference.

Guided Review and Study

1.0 Families

A. *Parenting Styles*

1. Characterize the changing kinds of advice given to parents in the past 60 years.

2. Contemporary developmentalist contend that there are _____ basic parenting styles.   *four*

3. Define each type of parenting, and describe their effects on children's behavior and personality:
   authoritarian parenting

   authoritative parenting

   neglectful parenting

   indulgent parenting

B. *Adapting Parenting to Developmental Changes in the Child*

1. Competent parents should _____ to children's developmental changes.   *adapt*

2. In the first year of a child's life interactions move away from _____ to include more play and visual-vocal exchanges.   *caretaking*
3. During the second and third years, discipline centers on physical _____ .   *manipulation*
4. Subsequently, parental discipline entails more _____ as children grow older.   *reasoning*

C. *Cultural, Ethnic, and Social Class Variations in Families*
  1. Characterize the most common parenting style in the world.

  2. The families of White American and ethnic minorities differ with regard to their size, structure and composition, reliance on _____ networks, and level of income and _____ .   *kinship* *education*
  3. Single-parent families are _____ common for White American than either Black or Latino American families.   *more*
  4. Indicate two ways in which minority families can protect their children from social injustices.

  5. Working class and low-income parents place a high value on _____ characteristics, whereas middle-class families place a high value on _____ characteristics in their children.   *external* *internal*
  6. Parents in low-income and working-class households are more likely than middle-class households to use _____ discipline with their children.   *physical*

D. *Sibling Relationships and Birth Order*
  1. The many sibling combinations make it difficult to _____ about sibling influences.   *generalize*
  2. Indicate how sibling interactions differ from parent-child interactions.

  3. Siblings can be a _____ socializing influence than parents.   *stronger*
  4. When children have questions about sex or problems with a teacher, they will probably talk to one of their _____ rather than their _____ .   *siblings* *parents*
  5. Contrast the role of siblings in industrialized versus nonindustrialized nations.

  6. Explain why the first-born child's relationship with parents is unique when compared to that of any later-born child.

  7. Birth order influences _____ relationships.   *sibling*
  8. Indicate how first-born children relate to later-born siblings.

  9. Firstborns have high standards placed on them and are more likely to excel in academic and _____ endeavors.   *professional*
  10. First-born children experience more guilt, _____ anxiety, difficulty in handling _____ , and higher admission rates to child guidance clinics.   *more* *stress*
  11. Only children are _____ oriented, and often display a desirable personality, especially in comparison to _____ children.   *achievement* *later-born*
  12. Explain why birth order effects may be overdramatized and overemphasized.

  13. How well siblings get along is affected both by the siblings' _____ traits and by the _____ treatment of siblings by parents.   *temperamental* *differential*
  14. Characterize factors that influence children's behavior and their relationships with siblings.

99

E. The Changing Family in a Changing Society

1. Characterize the various family structures prevalent in today's changing society.

2. Discuss positive and negative effects of a mother's working outside the home on her child.

3. Lois Hoffman argues that working mothers are more _____ models for the socialization of today's child than are full-time mothers, especially in the case of _____ . *realistic* *daughters*

4. Discuss the causes and cures for working parents' feelings of guilt.

5. The family _____ model and the multiple-factor model endeavor to explain the effects of _____ on children's and adolescent's development. *structure* *divorce*

6. Characterize the effects of divorce according to the family structure model.

7. Characterize the effects of divorce according to the multiple-effects model.

8. One important factor is the _____ of the child at the time of the divorce. *age*

9. Young children's cognitive immaturity may cause _____ immediate anxiety, but _____ later suffering. *more* *less*

10. Younger children remember _____ of the circumstances leading up to the divorce than older children when asked about the divorce ten years after the event. *fewer*

11. Characterize E. Mavis Hetherington's findings about children and adolescents six years after the divorce of their parents.

12. Family _____ is more important than family structure on the child's development. Adjustment problems for children are particularly evident in the _____ year after a divorce. *conflict* *first*

13. Research indicates that children living with the _____ -sexed parent were more socially competent than those with the other custody arrangements. *same*

14. Family _____ is an important influence on children's adjustment to divorce. *income*

15. State the main conclusions about the effects of divorce on children and adolescents.

F. Depressed Parents.

1. State the contemporary view of depression.

2. Parental depression is associated with children's problems of adjustment and disorders, especially with children's _____ . *depression*

2.0 Peer Relations, Play, and Television

A. Peer Relations

1. Others of about the same age or maturity level are _____ . *peers*

2. Peer groups serve as a source of _____ and comparison about the world outside the family. *information*

3. Work with animals suggests that monkeys reared with peers become _____ when separated from one another. *depressed*

4. _____ Freud's case history of six World War II orphans indicated that peer associations alone prevented delinquency and _____ . *Anna* *psychosis*

5. Explain how peer interactions relate to normal social development.

6. Children are _____ likely to engage in rough-and-tumble play with other children; however, children are more likely to approach adults in times of _____ . *more* *stress*

7. Highly aggressive boys, or _____ , are likely to have parents who rejected them, were _____ , and tolerated their sons' aggression. *bullies* *authoritarian*

8. Recipients of aggression, or _____ boy, are likely to have parents who were anxious and over protective. *whipping*

9. Indicate what research shows about how parents can help children relate to their peers.

10. Parent-child and peer worlds are _____ and connected. *coordinated*

B. Play

1. Define *play* in your own terms.

2. Developmental theorists agree that play increases the probability that children will _____ with one another. *interact*

3. According to Sigmund Freud and Erik Erikson, the function of play is to relieve _____ . *tension*

4. During play _____ , children may feel less threatened and be more likely to express their true feelings than when talking to their parents. *therapy*

5. For Jean Piaget and Lev Vygotsky, play allows children to _____ their cognitive skills. *practice*

6. According to Daniel Berlyne, play satisfies an _____ drive in all people. *exploratory*

7. Explain how Mildred Parten contributed to an understanding of play.

8. When in _____ play, a child may stand in one spot, look, or perform random movements with no goal. *unoccupied*

9. A kind of play, described by Parten, in which a child plays alone and independently of those around him is called _____ play. *solitary*

10. _____ plays describes a child who is essentially watching others play. *Onlooker*

11. In _____ play, a child plays by himself with toys similar to those being used by others. *parallel*

12. _____ play is characterized by social interaction and little or no organization. *Associative*

13. Adding group identity and organization transforms associative play into _____ play. *cooperative*

14. Contemporary perspectives on play emphasize both the _____ and social aspects of play. *cognitive*

15. Widely studied forms of contemporary play include sensorimotor/practice play, pretense/symbolic play, _____ play, constructive play, and _____ . *social* *games*

16. Infants engaged in sensorimotor/practice play select _____ objects for exploration and are particularly interested in toys that make noise and bounce. *novel*

17. Play that involves the repetition of behavior in the effort to learn new skills or the coordination of skills necessary for games or sports is called _____ play. *practice*

18. Preschool children use practice play to improve their _____ . *skills*

19. In pretense/symbolic play children transform their physical environment into _____ . *symbols*

20. A preschool child who _____ a couch is a cruise ship engages in pretense/symbolic play. *pretend/s*

21. The incidence of pretend play peaks between _____ years of age. *4 to 5*

22. Catherine Garvey indicates that pretend play involves the use of _____ , usually has a plot, *props*
   and allows children to try out different _____ . *roles*
23. Indicate Carolee Howes views about the function of pretend play.

24. Mildred Parten's play categories resembles the contemporary category of _____ play. *social*
25. When sensorimotor play is combined with symbolic representation, it is called _____ play. *constructive*
26. Constructive play can be used in elementary school to promote academic skill learning, thinking *problem*
   skills, and _____ solving.
27. _____ are activities engaged in for pleasure that include rules and competition. *Games*
28. Games are _____ salient in the preschool than the elementary school years. *less*

C. Television

1. Contemporary high school graduates have spent more hours watching television than in *parents*
   schooling or interacting with _____ .
2. Television plays many _____ in children's development. *roles*
3. Television can have a _____ influence on children's development by presenting motivating *positive*
   educational programs, increasing children's information about the world, and providing models of
   prosocial behavior.
4. Television can also have negative effects by encouraging _____ . *passivity*
5. Television can _____ because portrayed problems are often easily resolved. *deceive*
6. Explain why there is a concern about how minorities are portrayed on television.

7. *Sesame Street* demonstrates that _____ and entertainment can work well together. *education*
8. Explain what it means to say that *Sesame Street* teaches in both direct and indirect ways.

9. Children watch television a _____ . *lot*
10. Indicate how much 3- to 5-year-old children watched television in the 1950s, 1970s, and 1980s.

11. Television shows on Saturday morning average more than _____ violent acts per hour. *25*
12. Television affects both _____ and prosocial behavior by children. *aggressive*
13. Correlational studies of violence on television _____ allow investigators to conclude that *do not*
   watching violence on television causes aggressive behavior.
14. Describe the methods and results of an experiment that does allow researchers to conclude
   watching violence on television causes increased aggressive behavior.

15. Television is not the only causes of aggression because social behavior is multiply _____ . *determined*
16. Explain why some say that television can teach children to behave in prosocial ways.

17. Preschoolers and young children attend to television more, comprehend _____ central *less*
   content and _____ incidental content, and have difficulty making inferences about content. *more*
18. Indicate the relationship between viewing television and children's creativity and verbal skills.

3.0   The Self, Gender, and Moral Development

A. *The Self*

1. Explain why Erik Erikson says that the psychosocial conflict of early childhood is one of initiative versus guilt.

2. Initiative is governed by _____ .   *conscience*
3. Describe parental actions that promote initiative and minimize guilt.

4. Self-_____ is the child's cognitive representation of self.   *understanding*
5. Human infants demonstrate rudimentary self-understanding at about _____ months of age.   *18*
6. Developmentalists _____ children to learn about their self-understanding.   *interview*
7. Characterize young children's conceptions of themselves.

8. Explain why it is said that an *active dimension* is a central aspect of the self in early childhood.

B. *Gender*

1. In your own words, distinguish between sex and gender.

2. Gender _____ is the sense of being male or female, whereas gender _____ is the set   *identity; role*
    of expectations that prescribe how females and males should think, act, and feel.
3. Biological, social, and cognitive influences affect _____ identity.   *gender*
4. _____ influences on gender include genes, hormones, and anatomy.   *Biological*
5. The _____ pair of human chromosomes determine an individual's sex.   *23rd*
6. Distinguish between androgen and estrogen.

7. Evaluate the contention that sex hormones influence human behavior.

8. Both Sigmund Freud and Erik Erikson argued that *anatomy is destiny*, which implies that   *anatomical*
    psychological differences stem from _____ differences.
9. Only _____ has modified his claim and now says that cultural and psychological factors   *Erikson*
    interact to produce behavior.
10. Explain why the important issue is whether biological factors have direct or indirect effects on
    human social behavior.

11. There are various meanings to the idea that biological and environmental factors _____ to   *interact*
    produce characteristic behavior patterns.
12. _____ influences on gender include parents, peers, school and teachers, and the media.   *Social*
13. Characterize evidence that people react differently to female and male babies.

14. Two prominent theories consider how _____ influence the gender development of children. *parents*

15. According to Freud's _____ theory of gender, preschoolers identify with the _____- sex parents and unconsciously adopt their characteristics. *identification* *same*

16. Indicate what critics say about Freud's identification theory of gender.

17. According to the social learning theory of gender, boys and girls learn gender roles through _____ and _____ of gender behavior, and through the rewards and punishments they experience for gender-appropriate and gender-inappropriate behaviors. *observation* *imitation*

18. Indicate what critics say about the social learning theory of gender.

19. _____ are more involved in the socialization of their sons than their daughters. *Fathers*

20. Parents encourage boys and girls to pursue different kinds of _____ and activities. *play*

21. Parents influence gender development by allowing more independence for _____ than _____ . *boys* *girls*

22. Children show a clear preference for being with and liking _____-sexed peers. *same*

23. Playgrounds may appropriately be called gender _____ . *schools*

24. Peer demands for conformity to gender roles are intense during _____ . *adolescence*

25. Indicate ways that schools may be biased against females.

26. The media portray powerful messages about gender _____ behavior. *appropriate*

27. Describe television portrayals of males and females in the 1970s and 1980s.

28. Gender stereoptyping also appears in the _____ media. *print*

29. There are two prominent _____ accounts of how children construct their gender worlds. *cognitive*

30. According to the _____ developmental theory of gender proposed by Lawrence Kohlberg, children consistently see themselves as male or female once they organize their world on the basis of _____ . *cognitive* *gender*

31. Preschool children rely on _____ characteristics to put males and females into categories, whereas concrete operational children understand gender _____ . *physical* *constancy*

32. A _____ is a cognitive structure that guides individual perceptions. *schema*

33. Explain the concept *gender schema* in your own words.

34. State the gender schema theory of gender.

35. Use Figure 9.5 to compare and contrast the two cognitive theories of gender.

36. Gender is also a characteristic of _____ . *language*

37. Explain why your author says that children mostly hear language that is sexist.

C. Moral Development

1. The rules and conventions about how people should behave in their interaction with other people defines _____ development.   *moral*

2. Distinguish the domains of moral reasoning, moral behavior, and moral feelings.

3. Indicate how Jean Piaget studied the moral development of children.

4. Jean Piaget proposed that there are _____ stages of moral development.   *two*

5. Piaget's first stage of _____ morality encompasses the age range of 4 to 7 years.   *heteronomous*

6. Piaget's second stage of _____ morality encompasses the age range of 10 years and older.   *autonomous*

7. _____ justice is a characteristic of heteronomous rather than autonomous morality.   *Immanent*

8. Indicate the key features and developmental changes entailed in:

   heteronomous morality

   autonomous morality

9. According to Piaget, children advance their moral reasoning skills through _____ rather than parent-child relations.   *peer*

10. The study of moral reasoning identifies what children _____ is right and wrong, whereas the study of moral _____ investigates what children actually do in various situations.   *think* *behavior*

11. Explain how reinforcement, punishment, and imitation influence behavior according to social learning theorists.

12. According to Hugh Hartshorne and Mark May, moral behavior depends on the _____ .   *situation*

13. Indicate what social learning theorists say about the development of self-control.

14. Moral _____ comprise a third aspect of moral development.   *feelings*

15. Describe the sources of guilt according to Freud's psychoanalytic theory.

16. Feelings of guilt function to keep children from transgressing against _____ standards.   *social*

17. _____ refers to the understanding of another's feelings.   *Empathy*

18. Empathy depends on the skill of _____ taking.   *perspective*

19. Summarize the contemporary conception of how positive and negative feelings influence the moral development and behavior of children.

4.0 Chapter Boxes

A. Sociocultural Worlds of Development: African American and Mexican American Family Orientations

1. Compare the social and economic status of African American and White American children.

2. Extended family households often include individual such as _____ , aunts and uncles, or *grandparents* cousins who assist with basic family functions.

3. Active and involved extended-family support systems help reduce the stress of _____ and *poverty* single parenting.

4. Describe African American and Latino American family orientations.

B. Critical Thinking About Life-Span Development: Developing Parental TV Guidelines for Children's Viewing

1. Apply life-span developmental concepts by devising a set of parental guidelines for television watching that would make television a positive influence on their children's lives.

C. Critical Thinking About Life-Span Development: Evaluating Expectations for Girls and Boys

1. Cite evidence that beliefs about a baby's sex influence a person's description of a baby.

2. Demonstrate your appreciation of individual differences by speculating about how different expectations for boys and girls influence children's development.

D. Life-Span Health and Well-Being: Some Working-Parent Solutions When Work/Family Interference Occurs

1. Ellen Galinsky and Judy David provide _____ guidelines for parents who experience *six* work/family interference.

2. The guidelines range from making a list of the problems to finding _____ support. *social*

Self Test A: Key Terms and Key Persons

Write the appropriate key term or key person in the space to the right of the definition or description.

1. A psychiatrist whose case study revealed that peers play important roles in social development. _____

2. The use of play that allows children to work off frustrations and therapists to analyze children's conflicts and methods of coping with them. _____

3. Either of the two researchers who determined that moral behavior depends upon the situation. _____

4. The theory that once children consistently conceive of themselves as either male or female, they organize their world on the basis of gender. _____

5. According to Jean Piaget, the stage of moral development in which justice and rules are seen as fixed properties of the world. _____

6. The belief that, if a rule is broken, punishment will occur immediately. This view entails the belief that somehow punishment is mechanically linked to the violation. _____

7. The child repeats behavior when learning new skills, or when they require physical or mental mastery and coordination of skills for games or sports. This activity occurs throughout one's life. _____

8. The active dimension of self-understanding during early childhood in which children define themselves in terms of physical actions, body image, and material possessions. _____

9. A style of parenting in which parents place few demands on children even though they are highly involved with their children. _____

10. The theorist who contends that play satisfies an exploratory drive in each of us. _____

11. The ability to feel the distress of another. _____

12. Either of two individuals who provide solutions to parents who encounter conflicts between their work and families. _____

13. The individual who performed the classic analysis of children's play that revealed six categories. _____

14. Individuals of about the same age or maturity level. _____

15. A type of play in which the child plays alone, with toys like those other children are using or in a manner that mimics the behavior of other playing children. _____

106

16 The primary class of male sex hormones. _____

17. The use of sex as an organizing category to build a network of associations. _____

18. Activities engaged in for pleasure that often include rules and competition with other individuals. _____

19. A complex analysis of the factors entailed in divorce that includes such things as the family structure, the individual child, the nature of the divorce and custody, and the way in which family members interact after a divorce. _____

20. A parenting style in which parents encourage independence but still place limits, demands, and controls on the child. This parenting style includes extensive verbal give-and-take, and the parents demonstrate much warmth toward the child. _____

21. The theory that children's gender development results from the observation and imitation of other's behavior, and from the rewards and punishments the children receive for gender appropriate and inappropriate actions. _____

Self Test B: Multiple Choice

1. All but which of the following characterizes children of authoritarian parents?
    a. they fail to initiate activity
    b. they have poor communication skills
    c. they are anxious about social comparison
    d. they lack self-control

2. Parenting style and disciplinary action change in which of the following ways as children approach their elementary school years?
    a. physical punishment increases
    b. reasoning with the child increases
    c. physical affection increases
    d. withholding special privileges decreases

3. Which pairs of parenting styles best reflect lower-class and middle-class styles, respectively?
    a. neglectful, indulgent
    b. authoritarian, indulgent
    c. neglectful, authoritarian
    d. authoritarian, authoritative

4. It is more common for working-class families than middle-class families to use
    a. verbal praise.
    b. criticism.
    c. reasoning.
    d. asking questions.

5. Sibling interactions differ from parent-child interactions in all of the following ways except
    a. they are less positive
    b. they are more varied
    c. children pay more attention to their parents' requests than to their siblings' requests
    d. siblings behave less positively and more punitively with siblings than with parents

6. Parents are likely to treat their firstborns differently than their late-borns in that they
    a. have higher expectations.
    b. put more pressure on the firstborn to succeed.
    c. interfere less with the firstborn's activities.
    d. put more responsibility on the firstborn.

7. Compared to later-born children, firstborn children's relationships with their siblings tend to be
    a. more positive.
    b. more positive and more negative.
    c. more negative.
    d. About the same.

8. Compared to historical times, children today are growing up in _____ family structures.
    a. entirely different
    b. about the same kinds of
    c. a smaller variety of
    d. a greater variety of

9. Which of the following is *not* a good defense of the assertion that having a working mother is good for the child?
    a. The extra income will improve the standard of living for the child.
    b. Rigid sex-stereotyping is perpetrated by the division of labor in the traditional family.
    c. The mother will present a broader range of emotions and skills.
    d. The additional source of identity and self-esteem will make it easier for her to loosen her hold on the growing child.

10. Which of the following is true about the effects of the age of children on the ability to adjust to the divorce of their parents?
    a. younger children remember the conflicts surrounding the divorce longer than older children
    b. older children blame themselves more than younger children
    c. younger and older children express a desire to have grown up in an intact family
    d. older children fear abandonment more than younger children

11. Children living with the same-sex parent in single-parent families differ from children living with opposite-sex parents in all of these way except that
    a. they are more socially competent.
    b. they are less dependent.
    c. they are more mature.
    d. they have lower self-esteem.

12. You are going through a divorce and must talk to your children about it. Which of the following is a good recommendation?
    a. Encourage your children to talk about it to get their worries out of their system, then don't talk about it again.
    b. Explain that divorce is everyone's fault-both the parents and the children.
    c. Allow children a lot of time to think about the separation and how it will affect them.
    d. Realize that time heals wounds and both you and your children will feel better in the future.

13. The main function of the peer group is to
    a. foster love and understanding.
    b. act as a surrogate for the parents.
    c. teach the importance of friendship.
    d. teach about the world outside the family.

14. Experimental studies of monkeys and case studies of humans support the conclusion that
    a. peer relationships are not necessary for normal social development in children.
    b. peer relationships contribute to the normal social development of children.
    c. attachment to peers produces different effects than does attachment to adults.
    d. either loss of all peers or excessive involvement with peers produces social maladjustment.

15. The parents of bullies, whipping boys, and well-adjusted boys appear to be, respectively,
    a. neglectful, indulgent, and authoritative.
    b. permissive, neglectful, and indulgent.
    c. authoritarian, permissive, and overprotective.
    d. authoritarian, overprotective, and authoritative.

16. Play therapy is based on the notion that
    a. play relaxes children and acts as a tranquilizer.
    b. if the child feels less threatened, true feelings will be displayed.
    c. the child will model adaptive behavior during play.
    d. the increase in cognitive functioning during play allows the child to understand whatever problem is being experienced.

17. Mildred Parten's play categories are examples of increasingly complex and interactive
    a. pretense/symbolic play.
    b. social play.
    c. instructional play.
    d. games.

18. Which of the following activities requires cooperative play?
    a. jump rope
    b. puzzle building
    c. reading
    d. hopscotch

19. Practice play differs from sensorimotor play in which of the following ways?
    a. it is common in the infancy stage of development
    b. it involves coordination of skills
    c. it revolves around the use of symbols
    d. it is done for its own sake rather than as a means to an end

20. The positive aspects of television viewing by children include all but which of the following?
    a. increasing children's information about the world
    b. motivating them to learn new things
    c. encouraging them to engage in physical activity
    d. giving them models of prosocial behavior

21. Over the past forty years, the amount of television watched by preschool and elementary school children has
    a. decreased.
    b. increased.
    c. increased for younger children, but decreased for older.
    d. decreased for younger children, but increased for older.

22. Which of the following is true?
    a. Viewing television violence causes aggression.
    b. There is no relationship between watching violence on television and aggressive behavior.
    c. Children who watch violence get it out of their systems and are actually less likely to fight.
    d. Children who view violence on television are likely to engage in more aggression.

23. In dysfunctional families, television viewing by children centers on which of the following?
    a. fantasy fare that allows escape from reality
    b. violence that allows a safe expression of aggression
    c. programs that feature functional families to serve as role models
    d. educational programs to improve cognitive functioning

24. Sarah's parents openly enjoy Sarah's participation in family conversations. Although she frequently misunderstands the topic, they answer her questions, help her to join in, or simply enjoy Sarah's sometimes fantastic ideas. According to Erik Erikson, these parents are encouraging
    a. initiative.
    b. conscience.
    c. identification.
    d. self-concept.

25. Preschoolers most often describe themselves in terms of their
    a. thoughts.
    b. physical characteristics.
    c. emotions.
    d. relationships with other people.

26. Gender identity refers to the
    a. biological dimension of being male or female.
    b. social dimension of being male or female.
    c. sense of being male or female.
    d. set of expectations that prescribe how males or females should think, act, and feel.

27. Female sex hormones are called _____ ; male sex hormones are called _____ .
    a. estrogen; androgen
    b. testosterone; estrogen
    c. androgen; testosterone
    d. androgen; estrogen

28. Erikson's early belief that anatomy is destiny has been criticized because it
    a. overlooks social and cognitive factors that influence gender role.
    b. gives instinct a place in the development of gender role.
    c. it ignores connection between hormones and behavior.
    d. transcends biological heritage.

29. Which of the following statements about the identification theory and the social learning theory of gender-role development is most accurate?
    a. Both assume that children adopt the characteristics of their parents.
    b. Both assume that rewards directly shape gender-role development.
    c. Both assume that children actively acquire gender roles.
    d. Identification theory rejects the idea that anatomy is destiny, while social learning theory accepts it.

30. In which way do the media continue to discriminate between men and women?
    a. Women do not occupy high-status roles in television shows.
    b. Women appear only as housewives or lovers.
    c. Women are less competent than men in the roles they play.
    d. Women are cast primarily as sex objects.

31. During a final examination, Suzanne is observed copying information from the person sitting next to her. To which domain of the study of moral development is this observation relevant?
    a. reasoning
    b. behaviors
    c. emotions
    d. None of the other alternatives is correct.

32. Which of the following distinguishes autonomous morality from heteronomous morality? Autonomous moral thinkers focus on the
    a. consequences of behavior.
    b. intentions of someone who breaks a rule.
    c. way a specific behavior makes them feel.
    d. rewards moral behavior will bring.

33. Which cognitive ability is essential to the capacity for empathy?
    a. conservation
    b. logical reasoning
    c. decentration
    d. perspective-taking

34. Which of the following is likely to be true about a Mexican-American family?
    a. Children play more with their siblings than with schoolmates or neighborhood children.
    b. Fathers are undisputed family authorities.
    c. Children are encouraged to achieve for their families rather than for themselves.
    d. All of the other alternatives are correct.

35. "Hey, Sam, boys don't play with dolls." This statement was most likely made by Sam's
    a. teacher.
    b. sibling.
    c. father.
    d. mother.

36. Which of the following is *not* a recommendation by Ellen Galinsky and Judy David for working parents who encounter work/family interference?
    a. Select one problem at a time rather than tackling everything at once.
    b. Understand expectations and determine if they are realistic.
    c. Avoid the temptation to escape from the routines of everyday life.
    d. Form a variety of interpersonal support networks.

Answers for Self Test A

1. Anna Freud
2. play therapy
3. Hugh Hartstone or Mark May
4. cognitive developmental theory of gender
5. heteronomous morality
6. immanent justice
7. practice play
8. indulgent parenting
9. gender role
10. Daniel Berlyne
11. empathy
12. Ellen Galinsky or Judy David
13. Mildred Parten
14. peers
15. parallel play
16. androgen
17. gender schema
18. games
19. multiple-factor model of divorce
20. authoritative parenting
21. social learning theory of gender

Answers for Self Test B

1. d   LO 1.2
2. b   LO 1.4
3. d   LO 1.7
4. b   LO 1.8
5. b   LO 1.10
6. c   LO 1.13
7. b   LO 1.14
8. b   LO 1.19
9. a   LO 1.21
10. c   LO 1.24
11. d   LO 1.26
12. d   LO 1.28
13. d   LO 2.1
14. d   LO 2.2
15. d   LO 2.3
16. b   LO 2.6
17. b   LO 2.8
18. a   LO 2.8
19. b   LO 2.9
20. c   LO 2.11
21. b   LO 2.14
22. d   LO 2.15
23. a   LO 2.16
24. a   LO 3.1
25. b   LO 3.5
26. c   LO 3.6
27. a   LO 3.7
28. a   LO 3.11
29. a   LO 3.14
30. c   LO 3.16
31. b   LO 3.21
32. b   LO 3.22
33. d   LO 3.26
34. d   LO 4.1
35. c   LO 4.4
36. c   LO 4.5

Chapter 10   Physical and Cognitive Development in Middle and Late Childhood

Learning Objectives with Key Terms in Boldface

1.0 Physical Development in Middle and Late Childhood

A. *Body Changes*

   1.1   Identify average heights and weights for females and males between the ages of six and ten.

   1.2   Describe advances in gross and fine motor skills during middle and late childhood.

   1.3   Explain why elementary school children should be involved in active rather than passive activities.

B. *Exercise*

   1.4   Explain why the fitness of children from 6 to 11 years of age did not improve from 1975 to 1985.

   1.5   Describe current school fitness programs.

C. *Sports*

   1.6   List pros and cons of children's participation in sports.

D. *Stress*

   1.7   Define **stress**.

   1.8   Define **cognitive appraisal** and indicate its role in the experience of stress.

   1.9   Define and distinguish between **primary appraisal** and **secondary appraisal**, and explain how the two interact to intensify or alleviate a child's experience of stress.

  1.10   Define, distinguish between, and give examples of life events and daily hassles in children's lives.

  1.11   Define, distinguish between, and give examples of acculturative and socioeconomic stress.

  1.12   Define, distinguish between, and give examples of **acculturation** and acculturative stress.

  1.13   Discuss daily hassles and life events that constitute stressors for minorities, and discuss cultural coping mechanisms for acculturative stress.

  1.14   Indicate how poverty relates to children's experience of stress.

  1.15   Describe and give examples of factors that help children to resist threats to their health and well-being.

E. *Children with Disabilities*

  1.16   Explain why middle and late childhood is an especially difficult time for a handicapped child.

  1.17   List examples and incidences of handicapped children in America.

  1.18   Summarize **Public Law 94-142**, and explain the nature of an individualized education program.

  1.19   Define mainstreaming and indicate the role of the new term of **inclusion**.

  1.20   Define and give examples of **learning disabilities**.

  1.21   Indicate how we can improve the lives of learning disabled children.

  1.22   Define and give examples of **attention-deficit hyperactivity disorder**.

  1.23   Indicate evidence for nurture and nature explanations of attention-deficit hyperactivity disorder.

  1.24   Discuss treatments for hyperactivity.

2.0 Cognitive Development in Middle and Late Childhood

A. *Piaget's Theory and Concrete Operational Thought*

   2.1   List the characteristics of preoperational thought in contrast to the strengths of concrete operational thought.

   2.2   Indicate and critique Piaget's beliefs about the age of onset for concrete operational thought.

   2.3   Define operations and illustrate their function in conservation of matter.

   2.4   Explain why a concrete operational child understands a family tree, but a preoperational child does not.

2.5 List the three Piagetian principles of cognitive development applicable to education.

B. *Piagetian Contributions and Criticisms*

2.6 List Piaget's contributions to our understanding of cognitive development.

2.7 Describe evidence that Piaget both under- and overestimated children's cognitive development.

2.8 Define **Neo-Piagetians** and indicate how they would modify Piaget's concept of stage.

2.9 Explain why training studies challenge Piaget's theory.

2.10 Explain why the influence of culture and education challenges Piaget's theory.

C. *Information Processing*

2.11 Define **long-term memory** and characterize its development in childhood.

2.12 Define **control processes**.

2.13 Define and distinguish among rehearsal, organization, and imagery, and explain how each may be used.

2.14 Define the keyword method, indicate how it is an example of imagery.

2.15 List characteristics of the individuals that influence the memory of children.

2.16 Explain how content knowledge plays a role in memory and memory improvement.

2.17 Define and give examples of schemas.

2.18 Define story schema, and explain its role in children's comprehending, remembering, and creating stories.

2.19 Define **script** and give examples of scripts from younger and older children.

2.20 Define **metacognitive knowledge**.

2.21 Distinguish metacognitive knowledge about persons, tasks, and strategies.

2.22 Define and give examples of **cognitive monitoring**.

2.23 Define **reciprocal teaching** and explain how it promotes cognitive monitoring.

2.24 Compare and contrast children's problem solving and scientific reasoning.

2.25 Define **critical thinking**.

2.26 List important critical thinking processes.

2.27 Explain how good thinkers use more than just the right thinking processes (e.g., combining skills, using multiple perspectives).

2.28 Discuss the dynamic relationship between critical thinking and knowledge.

D. *Intelligence*

2.29 Define **intelligence** and the concept of individual differences.

2.30 Contrast the study of intelligence with the study of information processing skills and language.

2.31 Explain why intelligence is probably both a general ability and a number of specific skills.

2.32 Indicate why Alfred Binet developed an intelligence test.

2.33 Define and distinguish chronological age (CA), **mental age (MA)**, and **intelligence quotient (IQ)**.

2.34 Define **normal distribution** and explain how it could be used to measure intelligence.

2.35 Compare and contrast the Stanford-Binet and Wechsler scales of intelligence.

2.36 Define, distinguish, and illustrate the three components of Sternberg's **triarchic theory** of intelligence.

2.37 List and describe Howard Gardner's seven types of intelligence.

2.38 Explain why early intelligence tests were culturally biased.

2.39 Explain why minority groups may have difficulty with the language used on intelligence tests.

2.40 Define and give examples of **culture-fair tests**.

2.41 Explain why it may be impossible to create culture-fair tests.

2.42 Discuss how intelligence tests should be used.

2.43 Indicate the dangers of relying on a single number as an assessment of intelligence.

E. *Comparison of Approaches to Learning, Cognitive Development, and Intelligence*

    2.44 Compare and contrast the roles of stages, maturation/environmental influences, individual differences, processes/mechanisms, and the conception of the basic nature of children in the six different approaches to learning, cognitive development, and intelligence presented in *Life-Span Development*.

F. *The Extremes of Intelligence*

    2.45 Define **mental retardation**.

    2.46 Indicate the incidence of several classifications of mental retardation.

    2.47 Define and distinguish **organic retardation** and **cultural-familial retardation**.

    2.48 Define what it means to be **gifted** and indicate problems with this definition.

    2.49 Identify and challenge stereotypes about gifted people.

    2.50 Summarize and discuss findings from Lewis Terman's longitudinal study of gifted people.

G. *Creativity*

    2.51 Define and distinguish between **convergent thinking** and **divergent thinking**.

    2.52 Define **creativity** and distinguish it from intelligence.

    2.53 Explain why the concept of creativity as spontaneously bubbling from a magical well is a myth.

H. *Language Development in Middle and Late Childhood*

    2.54 Describe advances in vocabulary and grammar in middle and late childhood.

    2.55 Define and distinguish between the **whole language approach** and the **basic-skills-and-phonetics approach** to reading instruction.

    2.56 Indicate which approach to reading experts think is better.

    2.57 Define, distinguish between, and gives examples of literacy and emergent literacy.

    2.58 Discuss how advances in information processing contribute to improvements in reading ability.

    2.59 Indicate the present and future incidence of bilingual children in the United States.

    2.60 Define and explain the rationale for **bilingual education** in the United States.

    2.61 Summarize what is known about bilingualism.

    2.62 Evaluate the success of bilingual education programs.

I. *Achievement*

    2.63 Explain why it is important to study achievement.

    2.64 Define and give examples of **achievement motivation (need for achievement)**.

    2.65 Summarize the characteristics of individuals who have high achievement motivation and the parental practices that promote it.

    2.66 Define and distinguish between **extrinsic motivation** and **intrinsic motivation**.

    2.67 Discuss problems associated with extrinsic motivation.

    2.68 Explain why achievement is usually both extrinsically and intrinsically motivated.

    2.69 Characterize children who are intrinsically motivated.

    2.70 Indicate the importance of home environment in promoting intrinsic motivation.

    2.71 Explain why effort is so important to intrinsic motivation.

    2.72 Define and distinguish between **helpless orientation** and **mastery orientation** toward achievement.

    2.73 Define **performance orientation** and contrast it with mastery orientation.

    2.74 Compare and contrast mastery- and performance-oriented individuals.

    2.75 Describe evidence that differences in ethnic minority children's achievement motivation compared to White American children's motivation are probably a result of socioeconomic differences, not cultural deficits.

    2.76 Compare and contrast the achievement experiences and motivations of Black, White, and diverse Asian populations in the United States today.

3.0 Chapter Boxes

A. *Sociocultural Worlds of Development: Achievement and Learning in Asian and American Children*

    3.1 Compare and contrast the mathematics and science achievement of American and Asian students.

3.2 Sketch the nature of Asian students' educational experience.

3.3 Draw conclusions about the need for educational reform in the United States.

B. *Critical Thinking About Life-Span Development: Parents and Children's Sports*

3.4 Use knowledge about life-span development to develop a set of guidelines for parents and children's sports.

C. *Critical Thinking About Life-Span Development: Evaluating Transitions in Piaget's Stages*

3.5 Use the life-span developmental perspective to identify examples of children's shifts from preoperational to concrete operational thought.

D. *Life-Span Health and Well-Being: Madeline Cartwright: Making a Difference in North Philadelphia*

3.6 List the stressors that Madeline Cartwright removed from the lives of children at the James G. Blaine School.

Guided Review and Study

1.0 Physical Development in Middle and Late Childhood

A. *Body Changes*

1. During middle and late childhood, body changes occur in the skeletal and muscular systems and in _____ skills. *motor*

2. On average, growth is 2 to 3 inches and _____ pounds per year. *5 to 7*

3. At 11 years of age the average girl is _____ inches tall and the average boy is slightly shorter. *56*

4. By age 11, boys are _____ than girls. *stronger*

5. Motor skills _____ with age. *improve*

6. With regard to _____ motor skills, boys outperform girls *gross*

7. Explain why elementary school children should engage in active activities.

8. Fine motor skills improve as a result of increased _____ in the central nervous system. *myelinization*

9. With regard to _____ motor skills, girls generally outperform boys. *fine*

B. *Exercise*

1. Between 1975 and 1985 the physical fitness of children aged 6 to 17 _____ improve. *did not*

2. _____ is associated with the poor physical condition of American children: the more children watch television, the _____ likely they are to be overweight. *Television* *more*

3. Schools do not provide daily _____ education classes. *physical*

4. Most physical education classes do not include _____ activity. For example, children spend about _____ percent of the time in motion during physical educational classes. *vigorous* *50*

5. Parents are often _____ role models for vigorous exercise. *poor*

C. *Sports*

1. Sports are an important part of American culture, and have both positive and negative _____ for children. *consequences*

2. Indicate some positive and negative consequences of participating in sports for children.

4. Community and parental _____ should not be the focus of children's participation in sports that urge children to _____ at all costs. *prestige* *win*

D. *Stress*

1. Define *stress* in your own words.

2. Richard Lazarus hypothesized that our experience of stress is related to our _____ appraisal and interpretation of events. *cognitive*

3. Lazarus distinguished between _____ appraisal, in which individual's determine whether events involve harm, threat, or challenge, and _____ appraisal, in which individuals determine how to cope with the event in question. *primary* *secondary*

4. Provide an example of primary and secondary appraisal in your life.

5. Lazarus also hypothesized that the degree of stress relates to the _____ of primary and secondary appraisal. *balance*

6. Distinguish between major life events and daily hassles.

7. The current view is that daily hassles and life events may be culprits in _____ . *stress*

8. Sociocultural factors include _____ stress and socioeconomic status. *acculturative*

9. Define acculturation in your own terms.

10. The negative consequence of acculturation is called _____ stress, a problem for many ethnic minority group members. *acculturative*

11. Explain what it means to say that ethnic minority groups have shown remarkable resilience and adaptation in the face of severe stress and oppression.

12. Poverty is a chronic and uncontrollable _____ factor that produces stress for many ethnic minority children and their families. *socioeconomic*

13. A characteristic of individuals that helps to buffer them from adverse developmental outcomes is called _____ . *resilience*

14. Indicate and explain the three factors identified by Norman Garmezy that help children and adolescents become resilient to stress.

E. Children with Disabilities

1. Children with handicaps become _____ sensitive to their differences during the elementary school years. *more*

2. About _____ percent of the children between the ages of 5 and 18 in the United States are handicapped. *10 to 15*

3. Use Table 10.1 to review the percentage of the population with different handicaps.

4. Public Law _____ ensures a free and appropriate education to all children. *94-142*

5. An important component of the acts was the development of _____ education programs for each handicapped child. *individualized*

6. Another provision is to provide the least _____ environment for the education of handicapped children. *restrictive*

7. When handicapped children are placed in regular school classes with nonhandicapped children, they have been _____ , although the more current term is _____ .. *mainstreamed* *inclusion*

8. Children of normal intelligence, who have severe difficulty with some but not all academic areas, and who have no health or emotional condition that explains their problems are labeled _____ disabled. *learning*

9. These children often have problems _____ and in the areas of reading, spelling, and math. *listening*

10. The number of learning disabled children in the United States is about _____ million. *2*

11. Indicate ways to improve the lives of learning disabled children.

12. One kind of learning disability that specifically affects concentration and activity is attention deficit disorder, or _____ .

ADD

13. Although estimates of this disorder range from 1 to 5 percent, the disorder is much _____ common in males than in females.

more

14. ADD may be related to genes on the _____ chromosome, or to prenatal substances such as _____ , or to vitamin deficiencies.

Y

alcohol

15. ADD is frequently treated with amphetamines such as _____ , a widely prescribed and effective treatment for _____ percent of the cases.

Ritalin

80

2.0 Cognitive Development in Middle and Late Childhood

A. Piaget's Theory and Concrete Operational Thought

1. Jean Piaget says that elementary school children are entering the _____ operational thought stage of cognitive development.

concrete

2. Concrete operational thinking appears at about age 7 or 8, and entails operations, mental actions that are _____ .

reversible

3. _____ is one characteristic of the concrete operational thought stage.

Conservation

4. Review the method and interpretation of Piaget's two balls of clay task.

5. The ability to _____ is an operation that allows one to divide things into different sets and subsets on the basis of _____ characteristics.

classify

several

6. This allows the child to understand the _____ in a family tree.

relationships

7. Three Piagetian principles can be applied to _____ problems.

educational

8. First, it is important to remember that a child's _____ is not a blank slate, that children _____ see the world in the same way as adults, and that in order to meet children's educational needs there must be a great deal of communication.

mind

do not

9. Second, children acquire information, but also must _____ things as well.

unlearn

10. Third, children are naturally _____ , and the best way to take advantage of this curiosity is to allow children to spontaneously _____ with their environment.

knowing

interact

B. Piagetian Contributions and Criticisms

1. Piaget has received both commendation and _____ .

criticism

2. Piaget originated the field of _____ development, proposed a number of enduring concepts, demonstrated that children actively _____ their worlds, and astutely observed children.

cognitive

construct

3. One criticism of Piaget's approach is that children are _____ cognitively competent and adults _____ cognitively competent than Piaget supposed.

more

less

4. Explain the criticisms of Piaget's views about stages of cognitive development.

5. Neo-Piagetians are developmentalists who have _____ Piaget's theory.

elaborated

6. Neo-Piagetians also downplay the importance of _____ stages of development.

grand

7. Indicate the emphases of the neo-Piagetians.

8. A third criticism is that children can be trained to reason at a stage _____ than the one appropriate for their age.

higher

9. A fourth criticism is that studies reveal that culture and education exert _____ influences on children's development than Piaget believed.

stronger

C. Information Processing

1. Important issues regarding the information processing abilities of elementary school children concern memory, schemas and _____ , metacognitive knowledge, cognitive monitoring, _____ thinking, and scientific reasoning.

scripts

critical

2. _____-term memory is a relatively permanent and unlimited type of memory.

Long

3. Long-term memory _____ with age during middle and late childhood. *increases*

4. Long-term memory depends on _____ processes and learner characteristics. *control*

5. Rehearsal, organization, and imagery, are instances of _____ processes, ones that require work and effort on the part of the learner. *control*

6. Control processes are also called _____ . *strategies*

7. Define and illustrate the control processes of rehearsal and organization.

8. _____ is a third control process that makes use of mental, usually visual, associations. *Imagery*

9. Explain why the keyword method is an example of imagery.

10. Characteristics of the child that affect learning include age _____ , motivation, and health. *attitude*

11. What a child already _____ has a tremendous influence on what he or she remembers. *knows*

12. Explain what it means to say that children are *universal novices.*

13. Indicate the conclusion derived from the study that compared the memory for chess board arrangements by chess-playing children and novice adults.

14. Active organizations of past experiences are called _____ . *schemas*

15. When children hear stories they learn to expect a beginning, a middle, an end, a main character, and a plot because they have a _____ schema. *story*

16. Schema for events are often called _____ and may appear by the age of one year. *script*

17. Provide an original example of your own use of scripts.

18. _____ knowledge concerns the mind and how it works, and is accumulated through experience and stored in long-term memory. *Metacognitive*

19. Explain what it means to say that children have metacognitions about persons, tasks, and strategies.

20. When children assess what they are doing, determine what they need to do next, and evaluate the effectiveness of their problem-solving strategies, they engage in _____ monitoring. *cognitive*

21. Instructional programs endeavor to _____ cognitive monitoring. *promote*

22. Explain the process of reciprocal teaching, and indicate why it exemplifies cognitive monitoring.

23. Show how children's problem solving efforts resemble scientific reasoning.

24. Show how children's problem solving efforts differ from scientific reasoning.

25. Express the concept of critical thinking in your own terms.

26. Summarize Robert Sternberg's view about children's education.

27. Active thinking processes range from _____ carefully to distinguishing between _____ valid and invalid inferences.

listening
logically

28. Explain what it means to say that critical thinking programs are more effective when they are domain-specific rather than domain-general.

29. More attention needs to be paid to teaching information-processing skills in schools and also using these skills in _____ .

life

D. Intelligence

1. Verbal ability, problem solving skills, and learning from and adapting to everyday situations defines the concept of _____ .

intelligence

2. Indicate how the study of intelligence differs from the study of information processing skills and language.

3. _____ differences reflect consistent and stable ways in which we differ from one another.

Individual

4. One issue is whether intelligence entails a _____ ability or a number of _____ skills.

general
specific

5. Alfred Binet and Theophile Simon constructed the first intelligence test to determine which students would not profit from typical _____ .

schooling

6. Binet described the level of a child's intellectual functioning in terms of _____ age.

mental

7. Explain mental age (MA) and chronological age (CA) in your own terms.

8. William _____ devised the concept of intelligence quotient or IQ score.

Stern

9. Show how to compute the IQ score of a 15-year-old with a mental age of 20 years.

10. An assumption is that the distribution of intelligence in the population is _____ .

normal

11. A normal distribution is _____ , that is, the majority of scores fall in the middle and fewer scores falling in the extremes.

symmetrical

12. Give examples of the types of items on the current Stanford-Binet test.

13. The _____ revision of the Stanford-Binet, published in 1985, analyzes individual's responses into _____ area scores, and a composite score that reflects overall intelligence.

fourth
four

14. The other most widely used individual test, developed by David _____ , includes both verbal and _____ components.

Wechsler
nonverbal

15. Indicate why the Wechsler Intelligence Test includes verbal and performance subtests.

16. Use Figure 10.6 to review items on the Wechsler Intelligence Scale for Children, Revised.

17. Robert Sternberg developed the _____ theory of intelligence.

triarchic

18. According to Sternberg, the fundamental unit of intelligence is a _____ .

component

19. Define and provide your own example of componential, experiential, and contextual intelligence.

20. Howard Gardner theorized that there are _____ different kinds of intelligence. *seven*

21. Gardner cites evidence from _____ damaged individuals and *idiot savants* as support for his view that each of the seven kinds of intelligence involves unique _____ skills. *brain* *cognitive*

22. For Gardner, _____ intelligence is especially interesting. *musical*

23. Indicate what critics say about Gardner's approach.

24. Another issue is whether intelligence tests are _____ -biased. *culturally*

25. Explain the claim that early intelligence tests were culturally-biased.

26. Cultural bias can result from item content or _____ . *language*

27. A test that gives no advantage to people with a particular social background is called a culture-_____ test. *fair*

28. Another issue concerns the _____ of intelligence tests. *use*

29. Intelligence tests should not be used as the sole _____ of intelligence. *indicator*

30. The scores achieved by an individual on an IQ test should also not be regarded as a _____ indicator of his or her intelligence. *fixed*

31. Discuss the advantages of using IQ tests to evaluate an individual's intelligence.

32. Discuss the disadvantages of using IQ tests to evaluate an individual's intelligence.

E. Comparison of Approaches to Learning, Cognitive Development, and Intelligence

1. Use Table 10.2 to compare and contrast how each of the six different approaches to children's learning, cognitive development, and intelligence (Piaget's cognitive developmental theory, Vygotsky's theory, learning theory, cognitive social learning theory, information processing theory, and psychometric theory) view the role of maturation/environmental influences, stages, individual differences, cognitive processes/mechanisms, and the model of the child.

F. The Extremes of Intelligence

1. The extremes of intelligence encompass mental retardation and _____ . *giftedness*

2. A low IQ and difficulty adapting to everyday life is the currently accepted definition of mental _____ . *retardation*

3. An IQ score below _____ is usually the criterion. *70*

4. Mild retardation encompasses IQ scores of _____ , moderate retardation includes IQ scores of 40 to 54, and severe mental retardation encompasses IQ scores of _____ . *55 to 70* *25 to 39*

5. Mental retardation can result from _____ or social and cultural factors. *organic*

6. _____ causes of retardation include brain damage, or an extra chromosome in the case of the _____ syndrome. *Organic* *Down*

7. Cases of mental retardation that do not have a known organic cause are called cultural-_____ . *familial*

8. Children with cultural-familial retardation frequently come from below average _____ environments. *intellectual*

9. Individuals with well-above-average IQ scores or superior talent for something are deemed _____ . *gifted*

10. Recent studies show that giftedness _____ with mental disturbance. *is not*

11. Lewis Terman performed the classic study of _____ children by comparing them with randomly selected individuals of the same age. *gifted*

12. Summarize Lewis Terman's findings regarding men.

13. Summarize Lewis Terman's findings regarding longevity.

14. Summarize Lewis Terman's findings regarding women.

G. Creativity

1. Creativity _____ the same as intelligence. *is not*

2. Define and distinguish between convergent thinking and divergent thinking.

3. Creativity is most closely related to _____ thinking, the ability to produce many answers to one problem. *divergent*

4. _____ is the ability to think about things in novel and unusual ways and produce novel solutions to problems. *Creativity*

5. Evaluate the idea that creativity largely entails a flash of insight.

H. Language Development in Middle and Late Childhood

1. Three aspects of language development during middle and late childhood include vocabulary and grammar, reading, and _____ . *bilingualism*

2. During the elementary school years, children become more _____ in their approach to words. *analytical*

3. Provide some examples of children's improving analytical skills with language.

4. During middle and late childhood, children make gains understanding _____ , as evidenced by their use of comparative and subjective phrases. *grammar*

5. The debate about how to teach reading focuses on the _____ -language approach versus the basic-skills-and-_____ -approach. *whole* *phonetic*

6. Characterize the whole-language approach to teaching reading.

7. Characterize the basic-skills-and-phonetics-approach to teaching reading.

8. The current approach is to _____ the whole-language and basic-skills-and-phonetics methods. *combine*

9. Information-processing skills contribute to successful _____ . *reading*

10. Over _____ million children in the United States live in homes in which English is not the primary language. *6*

11. _____ education is designed for students with limited English language skills. *Bilingual*

12. In bilingual education programs, children learn concepts in their _____ language part of the time while they begin to learn things in _____ . *native* *English*

13. Investigations have shown that bilingualism _____ interfere with performance in either language.

does not

14. In general, there are positive outcomes of bilingualism on cognitive and language competency unless bilingualism is socially _____ .

stigmatized

15. Evaluate the success of bilingual education programs.

16. The United States is one of the _____ countries in the world in which most high school graduates know only their own language.

few

I. Achievement

1. The need for _____ refers to the desire to accomplish something, reach a standard of excellence, and expend _____ to excel.

achievement
effort

2. Explain how David McClelland measured achievement motivation.

3. Early research indicated that independence training by parents promoted children's achievement, but more recent research reveal that parents need to set high _____ for achievement, _____ achievement-oriented behavior, and _____ children for their achievement.

standards
model
reward

4. Describe intrinsic motivation and extrinsic motivation in your own words.

5. One study showed that the application of _____ incentives and rewards can decrease performance if the task was already _____ motivated.

external
intrinsically

6. Explain what it means to say that children's achievement is motivated by both internal and external factors.

7. Various aspects of a child's home environment can promote _____ motivation.

internal

8. A key factor in understanding internal causes for achievement is _____ .

effort

9. Children typically respond two ways to _____ circumstances.

challenging

10. Children with helpless orientations react to challenges by questioning their _____ ; children with mastery orientations react to challenges by focusing on their learning _____ .

abilities
strategies

11. Compare and contrast mastery- and performance-oriented individuals.

12. Explain why the concepts of deficit and culturally different play key roles in understanding the achievement of ethnic minority children.

13. Social _____ is a better predictor of achievement orientation than _____ because middle-class individuals do better in a variety of achievement-oriented situations than lower-class individuals.

class
ethnicity

14. Indicate why Sandra Graham contends that we should study minority-group motivation in the context of general motivational theory.

15. The Asian children characterized as _____ kids come from families that came to the United States in the 1960s and early 1970s.

whiz

16. In contrast, the Asian children whose families came to the United States in the late 1970s may struggle in the _____ system.

educational

17. Generally, American children are very _____-oriented.

achievement

3.0 Chapter Boxes

A. *Sociocultural Worlds of Development: Achievement and Learning in Asian and American Children*

1. Compare and contrast the mathematics and science achievement of American and Asian students.

2. Sketch the nature of Asian students' educational experience.

3. Draw conclusions about the need for educational reform in the United States.

B. *Critical Thinking About Life-Span Development: Parents and Children's Sports*

1. Use knowledge about life-span development to develop a set of guidelines for parents and children's sports.

C. *Critical Thinking About Life-Span Development: Evaluating Transitions in Piaget's Stages*

1. Use the life-span developmental perspective to identify examples of children's shifts from preoperational to concrete operational thought.

D. *Life-Span Health and Well-Being: Madeline Cartwright: Making a Difference in North Philadelphia*

1. Madeline _____ , an inner-city school principal, built a model school.   *Cartwright*
2. She provided a way for children to have clean _____ , and, also involved _____ in   *clothes*
   their children's schooling.   *parents*
3. She has also argued for establishing _____ houses.   *mentor*

Self Test A: Key Terms and Key Persons

Write the appropriate key term or key person in the space to the right of the definition or description.

1. Individuals with above-average intelligence and/or superior talent for something.   _____

2. The individual who created the first test to determine which children would do well In school.   _____

3. Despite varying definitions, the common element is that individuals grasp the deeper meaning of problems, keep an open mind about different approaches and perspectives, and decide by themselves what to believe.   _____

4. Intelligence tests that attempt to reduce or eliminate cultural bias.   _____

5. Programs for students with limited proficiency in English that instruct students in their own language part of the time while learning to speak English.   _____

6. This describes children who are task oriented, and who focus on their learning strategies rather than on their abilities.   _____

7. The individual who proposed a theory of seven kinds of intelligence.   _____

8. The theory that there are three types of intelligence: componential intelligence, experiential intelligence, and contextual intelligence.   _____

9. Information-processing strategies for improving learning and memory that are under the learner's conscious control.   _____

10. A subjective response to a situation in which an individual feels overwhelmed and unable to cope effectively.   _____

11. The researcher who proposed the view that stress depends upon one's cognitive appraisals.   _____

12. A subjective interpretation about whether an event already entails a past harm or loss, a threat of future harm or loss, or a challenge to be met.   _____

13. The current term for the situation in which children who need special education attend regular classes with other students rather than a special class. _____

14. The process of determining what you are doing now, what you will do next, and whether the mental activity is producing an effective result. _____

15. A type of thinking that produce many different answers to a single problem. It is commonly considered to be an example of creativity. _____

16. A desire to appear competent and be satisfied for engaging in an activity for its own sake. _____

17. The researcher who performed a longitudinal study of gifted individuals. _____

18. Binet's measure of the level of a child's intellectual functioning relative to others. _____

19. A schema for an event. _____

20. The view that reading instruction should parallel children's natural language learning. _____

21. A symmetrical distribution of scores. _____

22. The individual who created the major alternative to the Stanford-Binet intelligence test. _____

23. Richard Lazarus's term for an individual's interpretation of environmental events or situations as possible stressors and the available resources for coping. _____

24. An examination of one's personal resources available to cope with a stressful event or situation. _____

25. A type of disorder characterized by high levels of physical activity, impulsivity, distractibility, and excitability. _____

26. A form of mild retardation with no detectable brain abnormality. _____

27. The researcher who assessed achievement motivation by presenting individuals with ambiguous pictures. _____

28. Federal legislation that requires communities to provide a free, appropriate education for all children. This law contains a provision for individualized programs for each handicapped child. _____

29. Relatively permanent and unlimited type of memory. _____

30. An educational psychologist who favors interpreting achievement of ethnic minority children in terms of general motivational theory. _____

Self Test B: Multiple Choice

1. The middle and late childhood period of development is characterized by which of the following kinds of changes in the body?
   a. slow, consistent growth
   b. rapid, consistent growth
   c. rapid spurts of growth
   d. moderate growth with occasional spurts

2. Which patterns best portrays changes in gross and fine motor skills in middle and late childhood ?
   a. girls out-perform boys in gross motor skills
   b. boys out-perform girls in gross motor skills
   c. there are no sex differences in the development of gross and fine motor skills
   d. boys out-perform girls in fine motor skills

3. When results from a 1975 survey of fitness among elementary school children were compared to results of a 1985 survey, investigators found which of the following?
   a. no improvement for either boys or girls
   b. improvement for boys but not for girls
   c. improvement for girls but not for boys
   d. tremendous improvements for both boys and girls

4. Circumstances and events that threaten individuals and tax their coping abilities are called
   a. hassle factors.
   b. stresses.
   c. stressors.
   d. secondary factors.

5. All of the following are evaluated in primary appraisal except potential
   a. harm.
   b. threat.
   c. challenge.
   d. coping.

6. Whenever Roseanne plays or talks with her parents, her brother Tom interrupts. Tom's attention-seeking behavior is a(n) _____ for Roseanne.
   a. daily hassle
   b. acculturative stress
   c. conflict
   d. life event

7. African Americans living in Dubuque, Iowa who found burning crosses in their yards at night in the fall of 1991 were experiencing
   a. daily hassles.
   b. stress.
   c. frustration.
   d. socioeconomic stress.

8. The most frequent handicap among school children in the United States is
   a. visual impairment.
   b. emotional disturbance.
   c. mental retardation.
   d. speech handicap.

9. The Education for All Handicapped Children Act mandated that all states do which of the following for all handicapped children?
   a. provide free health care and free health education
   b. provide educational programs for their parents
   c. provide free testing programs
   d. provide individualized educational programs

10. Mainstreaming or inclusion refers to
    a. teaching handicapped children in public schools.
    b. assigning handicapped children to regular classrooms.
    c. giving handicapped children as high an educational priority as nonhandicapped children receive.
    d. assuring that handicapped children interact with nonhandicapped children whenever possible in school.

11. Jack, a second grader, has no trouble with math, science, or art, but he cannot spell, read, or write. Jack is likely to be found to have a(n)
    a. vision impairment.
    b. speech handicap.
    c. learning disability.
    d. attention deficit.

12. Timothy is suffering from attention-deficit hyperactivity disorder. He is most likely to be experiencing all but which of the following symptoms?
    a. he has a short attention span
    b. he is easily distracted
    c. his intelligence is below normal for his age
    d. he engages in high levels of physical activity

13. What type of drug is used to control attention-deficit hyperactivity disorder?
    a. stimulants
    b. depressants
    c. tranquilizers
    d. relaxants

14. A child who can separate playing cards by suit and number is in which of the following Piagetian stages?
    a. sensorimotor
    b. concrete operational thought
    c. preoperational thought
    d. symbolic thought

15. Reversible mental actions are called
    a. focal points.
    b. symbolic thought.
    c. abstractions.
    d. operations.

16. Which of the following is an application of Jean Piaget's ideas to education?
    a. We need to know how children understand the world to teach them effectively.
    b. Children's illogical or distorted ideas about the world make it hard for them to learn.
    c. The pattern of mental development is universal, so we can develop one curriculum for all students.
    d. By the third or fourth grade, children are ready for abstract learning.

17. All but which of the following criticisms have been applied to Piaget's work?
    a. not all aspects of a cognitive stage develop at the same time
    b. changing the tasks used to measure cognitive development changes which skills children can exhibit
    c. children can be trained to do tasks that they should not be able to do given the cognitive stage they are in
    d. some of the skills Piaget identified appear much later than he suggested

18. All but which of the following control processes are involved in memory abilities in children?
    a. rehearsal
    b. perception
    c. organization
    d. imagery

19. In order to remember the Spanish word for letter, *carta*, a child thinks of a letter in a shopping cart. This is an example of
    a. rehearsal.
    b. organization.
    c. the keyword method.
    d. metacognition.

20. Katie and her grandfather are reading a book about dinosaurs. Katie has been learning about dinosaurs in her second-grade class, but her grandfather is learning about them for the first time. When they are finished, we expect that
   a. Katie will remember more about dinosaurs, because she has had more to relate the information to.
   b. her grandfather will remember more, because he is older and processes information better.
   c. their memory for what they learned will be about equal.
   d. each will remember different things about dinosaurs.

21. Schema are used in all but which of the following circumstances?
   a. making inferences about information
   b. retrieving information in long-term memory
   c. encoding information in long-term memory
   d. receiving sensations from the environment

22. Teachers can use reciprocal teaching to improve
   a. learning.
   b. memory.
   c. cognitive monitoring.
   d. problem solving.

23. The adolescent who reflectively reads a book of essays on politics in various societies and who is open to different approaches and perspectives is exhibiting
   a. global thought.
   b. critical thinking.
   c. reflective thinking.
   d. conscious thought.

24. Compared to Jean Piaget's approach to intelligence Alfred Binet's approach was especially concerned with
   a. finding a way to describe how thought itself changes with age.
   b. developing ways to measure differences in ability.
   c. revealing how the mind works.
   d. identifying universals in cognitive growth.

25. The purpose of the first intelligence test designed by Alfred Binet and Theophile Simon was to
   a. identify students who should be placed in special classes.
   b. identify gifted students who should be placed in accelerated training programs.
   c. measure intelligence so that future success could be predicted.
   d. form a basic definition of intelligence and find definitive answers to what intelligence is.

26. A person who has a mental age of 13 and a chronological age of 10 has an intelligence quotient of
   a. 130.
   b. 10.
   c. 13.
   d. 100.

27. Many of the early intelligence tests favored urban, middle-income, White individuals. This is known as a
   a. culture-fair test.
   b. culture-biased test.
   c. cooking knowledge.
   d. cultural differentiation.

28. Why does it seem to be impossible to devise a universal, culture-fair intelligence test?
   a. We cannot establish norms for the different populations of people who take the test.
   b. Languages are so different that some languages cannot express what other languages can.
   c. Different cultures appear to encourage the development of different intellectual skills or knowledge.
   d. We are beginning to doubt that IQ tests actually measure intelligence.

29. In terms of Robert Sternberg's Triarchic theory, retarded individuals are those who are low in
   a. componential and contextual intelligence.
   b. componential and experiential intelligence.
   c. experiential and contextual intelligence.
   d. all three factors of intelligence.

30. Information about the causes of mental retardation suggests that
   a. the causes are primarily organic.
   b. environment is more important than biology.
   c. most retardation is due to genetic factors.
   d. both biological and environmental factors are involved.

31. Gary is asked to come up with as many possible uses of a paper clip as possible. This task requires Gary's
   a. verbal comprehension.
   b. convergent thinking.
   c. divergent thinking.
   d. critical thinking.

32. Bilingual education programs allow students whose native language is not English and who are not proficient in English to
   a. speak both their native language and English in classes.
   b. use their native language at school when they are not in classes.
   c. have remedial classes taught in their native language.
   d. learn most coursework in their native language.

33. Children who make an effort to reach a standard of excellence demonstrate
    a. intrinsic motivation.
    b. achievement motivation.
    c. cognitive monitoring.
    d. convergent thinking

34. Two children face a difficult series of tasks. Fred says, "I am very good at these," and Wilma says, "I can try harder and do better next time." Fred demonstrates _____ and Wilma demonstrates _____ .
    a. extrinsic motivation; intrinsic motivation
    b. a helpless orientation; a mastery orientation
    c. cognitive monitoring; metacognition
    d. contextual intelligence; experiential intelligence

35. In order to predict accurately the achievement motivation of ethnic minority children, psychologists focus on children's
    a. mastery orientation.
    b. socioeconomic status.
    c. race.
    d. intelligence.

36. When Madeline Cartwright was principal of north Philadelphia's James G. Blaine public school, located in a low-income neighborhood, she changed children's lives by reducing their
    a. crises.
    b. acculturative stressors.
    c. frustrations.
    d. daily hassles.

Answers for Self Test A

1. gifted
2. Alfred Binet
3. critical thinking
4. culture-fair test
5. bilingual education
6. mastery orientation
7. Howard Gardner
8. triarchic theory
9. control processes or strategies
10. stress
11. Richard Lazarus
12. primary appraisal
13. inclusion
14. cognitive monitoring
15. divergent thinking
16. intrinsic motivation
17. Lewis Terman
18. mental age (MA)
19. script
20. whole language approach
21. normal distribution
22. David Wechsler
23. cognitive appraisal
24. secondary appraisal
25. attention-deficit hyperactivity disorder
26. cultural-familial retardation
27. David McClelland
28. Public Law 94-142
29. long-term memory
30. Sandra Graham

Answers for Self Test B

1. a   LO 1.1
2. b   LO 1.2
3. a   LO 14
4. a   LO 1.7
5. a   LO 1.9
6. a   LO 1.10
7. d   LO 1.12
8. d   LO 1.17
9. d   LO 1.18
10. b   LO 1.19
11. c   LO 1.20
12. c   LO 1.22
13. a   LO 1.24
14. b   LO 2.1
15. d   LO 2.3
16. a   LO 2.5
17. d   LO 2.7
18. b   LO 2.12
19. c   LO 2.14
20. a   LO 2.15
21. d   LO 2.17
22. c   LO 2.23
23. b   LO 2.25
24. b   LO 2.29
25. a   LO 2.32
26. a   LO 2.33
27. b   LO 2.38
28. c   LO 2.41
29. a   LO 2.45
30. d   LO 2.47
31. a   LO 2.51
32. d   LO 2.60
33. b   LO 2.64
34. b   LO 2.72
35. b   LO 2.75
36. d   LO 3.6

Chapter 11   Socioemotional Development in Middle and Late Childhood

Learning Objectives with Key Terms in Boldface

1.0 Families

   1.1   Describe changes in the amount of time that parents spend with their children during middle childhood.

   A. *Parent-Child Issues*

   1.2   Compare and contrast issues between parents and young children, and parents and elementary school children.

   1.3   Explain how children's cognitive development during middle childhood may make parenting easier than it was or will be during other times in children's lives.

   1.4   List issues related to school and to discipline, and indicate how discipline changes as children develop.

   1.5   Define coregulation, and list guidelines for coregulation by parents.

   1.6   Describe the consequences of labeling one another for children and parents.

   B. *Societal Changes in Families*

   1.7   Explain why more older than younger children live in stepfamilies.

   1.8   Describe types of stepfamilies prevalent in today's society.

   1.9   Describe contemporary trends in remarriage.

   1.10   Define **boundary ambiguity**, and describe patterns of adjustment in stepfamilies.

   1.11   Summarize E. Mavis Hetherington's findings about the association between parenting techniques and school environment on children's coping.

   1.12   Define latchkey children.

   1.13   Describe the problems latchkey children face when their parents are away.

   1.14   Identify parenting strategies and styles that may diminish or heighten latchkey children's problems.

2.0 Peer Relations

   2.1   Indicate how much time children spend and what they do with their peers during middle childhood.

   A. *Peer Statuses*

   2.2   Indicate what makes a child popular with peers.

   2.3   Define and distinguish among **neglected children**, **rejected children**, and **controversial children**.

   2.4   Indicate the risks that neglected and rejected children face.

   2.5   Explain how to train neglected children to interact with their peers.

   B. *Social Cognition*

   2.6   Explain why children's social cognitions are important for understanding peer relations.

   2.7   List Kenneth Dodge's five steps in social cognition and explain their role in aggressive boys' behavior.

   2.8   Explain how social knowledge is involved in children's ability to get along with peers.

   2.9   Explain how social cognitive skills influence peer relations among maladjusted children.

   C. *Friends*

   2.10   Give examples of children's ideas about friends.

   2.11   Explain why children's friendships are important.

   2.12   Define **intimacy in friendships**, and explain the roles of intimacy and similarity in children's friendships.

   2.13   Discuss Harry Stack Sullivan's view of friendship's role in children's well-being and development.

3.0 Schools

  A. *The Transition to Elementary School*

    3.1 List the ways in which schools socialize children and change their lives.

    3.2 Explain why there is a concern that early schooling is based mainly on negative feedback.

    3.3 Explain what integrated learning is and why it is important.

    3.4 Compare and contrast an integrated learning classroom with one in which learning is not integrated.

  B. *Teachers*

    3.5 Illustrate how teachers influence almost everyone's lives.

    3.6 Indicate teacher characteristics associated with favorable student outcomes.

    3.7 Define and illustrate **aptitude-treatment interaction** (ATI).

  C. *Social Class and Ethnicity in Schools*

    3.8 Cite evidence that schools are middle class institutions that favor middle class students.

    3.9 Discuss how teachers' expectations influence the experience of lower class students.

    3.10 Sketch John Ogbu's view that schools provide inferior educational opportunities for ethnic minority students.

    3.11 Indicate how segregation is a factor in the education of African American and Latino students.

    3.12 Describe variations in the school experiences of children from different ethnic groups.

    3.13 Compare and contrast the opportunities of ethnic minority and White youth who graduate from school.

    3.14 Explain Margaret Beale Spencer and Sanford Dornbusch's idea that well-meaning teachers create a form of institutional racism.

    3.15 Summarize how James Comer would improve the quality of education for inner-city children.

4.0 The Self, Gender, and Moral Development

  A. *The Self*

    4.1 Indicate how elementary school children describe themselves.

    4.2 Indicate the roles that social aspects of the self and social comparison play in children's self-understanding.

    4.3 Define **perspective taking** and explain how it contributes to self-understanding.

    4.4 Indicate how Robert Selman studies perspective taking.

    4.5 Define and distinguish among Selman's five stages in the development of perspective-taking.

    4.6 Indicate how perspective taking relates to peer group status and friendships.

    4.7 Define and distinguish between **self-esteem** and **self-concept**.

    4.8 Define and assess Susan Harter's **Self-Perception Profile for Children** and its variations.

    4.9 List parenting attributes associated with boys who have high self-esteem.

    4.10 Describe Henry Tajfel's **social identity theory** and indicate how it relates group identity to self-esteem.

    4.11 Indicate how promoting social identity may lead to social conflict.

    4.12 Cite evidence that it takes very little to get people to adopt an in-group/out-group mentality.

    4.13 Define and distinguish between **ethnocentrism** and **prejudice**.

    4.14 Describe the nature of self concepts among various ethnic groups.

    4.15 Describe how to improve children's self-esteem by identifying the causes of low self-esteem.

    4.16 Describe how to improve children's self-esteem with emotional support and social approval.

    4.17 Describe how to improve children's self-esteem through achievement.

    4.18 Describe how to improve children's self-esteem through coping.

    4.19 Define and distinguish between Erik Erikson's concepts of industry and inferiority.

    4.20 Discuss experiences that promote senses of industry and inferiority.

  B. *Gender*

    4.21 Define **gender-role stereotypes**.

    4.22 Explain how stereotypes can be so general that they are ambiguous.

    4.23 Identify the consequences of labeling an individual masculine or feminine.

4.24 Indicate the extent and societal correlates of gender role stereotyping.

4.25 Indicate developmental trends in gender role stereotyping.

4.26 Identify three appropriate cautions when considering sex differences.

4.27 Identify physical and biological differences that exist between boys and girls.

4.28 Discuss the extent to which there are cognitive differences between boys and girls.

4.29 Identify socioemotional differences between boys and girls in terms of aggression, social connectedness, and emotional expression.

4.30 Identify where sex differences do and do not exist in achievement.

4.31 Explain why sex differences may be larger and more varied than they have been describe so far.

4.32 Cite evidence that supports claims about sex differences made by evolutionary psychologists (e.g., David Buss).

4.33 Explain how contexts influence whether or not males or females express helping behavior and emotions.

4.34 Describe past concepts of masculinity and femininity.

4.35 Define androgyny as an alternative to past concepts of masculinity and femininity.

4.36 Describe Sandra Bem's Sex Role Inventory and define the four gender role orientations it identifies.

4.37 Discuss how well individuals of varying gender role orientations adjust to different situations.

4.38 Indicate Joe Pleck's criticisms of **androgyny**, and explain why he favors the term **gender-role transcendence**.

4.39 Explain why we may expect different patterns of gender-related attitudes and behavior in different ethnic groups.

4.40 Indicate changes of purpose and focus in the study of African American females' gender orientation.

4.41 Discuss how racism and sexism have influenced African American females.

4.42 Identify culturally based gender expectations for Asian American women and indicate how these have changed.

4.43 Indicate how gender based expectations of women vary among Native American women.

4.44 Sketch the advantages and disadvantages of being an African American male.

4.45 Identify culturally based gender expectations for Asian American men and indicate how these have changed.

4.46 Indicate the traditional gender role orientation of Latino men.

4.47 Indicate how gender based expectations of women vary among Native American men.

C. Moral Development

4.48 Describe how Lawrence Kohlberg studies moral development.

4.49 Define **internalization** and explain why it is a key concept in Kohlberg's theory.

4.50 Define and distinguish among the stages and substages of moral development according to Kohlberg (**preconventional reasoning**: punishment and obedience orientation, individualism and purpose; **conventional reasoning**: interpersonal norms, social system morality; **postconventional reasoning: community rights versus individual rights, universal ethical principles**).

4.51 Cite evidence for Lawrence Kohlberg's claims about the sequence of moral development.

4.52 Describe the criticism that Kohlberg's theory takes too little account of moral behavior.

4.53 Explain how Kohlberg's theory may be culturally biased.

4.54 Cite evidence that Kohlberg neglected the importance of family processes in moral development.

4.55 Define and distinguish between a **justice perspective** and a **care perspective**, and explain the claim that Kohlberg neglected the care perspective in his theory.

4.56 Cite evidence supporting Carol Gilligan's claim that girls adopt a care perspective in their moral reasoning.

4.57 Indicate and explain criticisms of Gilligan's analysis of moral development.

4.58 Define and give examples of **altruism**.

4.59 Indicate the roles of reciprocity and exchange in altruism.

4.60 Describe altruism's developmental path from preschool through the middle childhood years according to William Damon.

4.61 Define and distinguish among equality, merit, and benevolence as bases for altruistic sharing.

4.62 Describe evidence that obedience to adult authority is not a primary factor in children's sharing.

5.0 Chapter Boxes

    A. *Sociocultural Worlds of Development: Gender Roles in Egypt and China*

        5.1   Compare and contrast gender roles in America, China, Egypt, and Russia.

        5.2   Assess the prospects for equal status between men and women in these countries.

    B. *Critical Thinking About Life-Span Development: Rethinking the Words We Use in Gender Worlds*

        5.3   Explain why the term relational ability has replaced the word dependent to describe females.

        5.4   Evaluate the connotations of words that you use to describe femininity and masculinity.

    C. *Critical Thinking About Life-Span Development: Moral Decision Making*

        5.5   Evaluate two moral dilemmas and place your moral decisions at one of Kohlberg's stages.

    D. *Life-Span Health and Well-Being: A Model School Health Program: Heart Smart*

        5.6   Indicate the role and activities of teachers in the Heart Smart health program.

        5.7   Describe the physical education component of the Heart Smart program.

        5.8   Indicate how the school lunch program is a component of the Heart Smart program.

        5.9   Indicate what happens to high risk children in the Heart Smart program.

Guided Review and Study

1.0   Families

1. As children move into the middle and late childhood years, parents spend _____ time with them.   *less*

    A. *Parent-Child Issues*

1. During early childhood parent-child interaction centers around issues such as _____ , bedtime regularities, control of temper, fighting, eating, autonomy in dressing, and attention _____ .   *modesty seeking*

2. In middle and late childhood, new issues emerge such as doing _____ and the possible payment for them, entertainment, and _____ outside the home.   *chores monitoring*

3. During middle and late childhood _____-related matters become prominent.   *school*

4. Problems in school are the main reason for seeking _____ help.   *clinical*

5. Explain why discipline during middle and late childhood may be easier for parents than when children are either younger or older.

6. The transition between the _____ parental control of the preschool years and the reduced supervision of the _____ years is a period of what has been called _____ .   *strong adolescent*

7. Explain the concept of *coregulation* in your own terms.

8. The way in which parents interact with children and in which children interact with their parents is influenced by _____ each attaches to the other.   *labels*

9. Portray parental life changes when children enter middle and late childhood.

    B. *Societal Changes in Families*

1. Indicate two consequences of the increasingly common situation of divorced or working-mother families.

2. Step-father families are _____ common than step-mother or blended families.   *more*

3. Summarize findings about remarriage in the United States.

5. A crucial adjustment for remarried individuals is the development of _____ expectations.   *realistic*

6. Express the meaning of *boundary ambiguity* in your own terms.

7. In comparison to studies of the effects of divorce, studies of stepfamilies are _____ .   *rare*
   Characterize the patterns of adjustment by children in stepfamilies.

8. Relationships with the custodial parents are _____ strained than those with the biological parents.   *more*

9. Relationships with the stepfather tend to be _____ .   *distant*

10. E. Mavis Hetherington demonstrated that whether children cope effectively with living in a divorced or stepfamily is associated with _____ techniques and school environment.   *parenting*

11. _____ parenting is the most effective style for stepfamilies.   *Authoritative*

12. Indicate what defines a latchkey child.

13. Interviews of latchkey children by Thomas and Lynette Long indicate that a majority had _____ experiences related to a lack of limits and _____ during the latchkey hours.   *negative*
                structure

14. Latchkey children are more likely to get into _____ ; however, the degree of developmental risk to latchkey children is largely _____ .   *trouble*
                undetermined

2.0 Peer Relations

1. The proportion of peer interaction at age 2 is _____ %, by 4 it was 20%, and between 4 and 11 it increases to more than _____ %.   *10*
                40

2. Describe what children do with their peers.

A. Peer Statuses

1. Popular children give out reinforcements to other children, listening to them, show _____ , and appear self-_____ , but not conceited.   *enthusiasm*
                confident

2. _____ children have few friends, but _____ children are more likely to be disruptive, aggressive, and overtly disliked by peers.   *Neglected*
                rejected

3. Describe *controversial children* in your own terms.

4. The key factor that predicts whether rejected children become delinquents or drop out of school later in adolescence is their _____ toward peers in elementary school.   *aggression*

5. Neglected and rejected children _____ trained to interact with their peers more effectively.   *can be*

6. Training neglected children centers around increasing their ability to attract _____ in positive ways.   *attention*

7. Training rejected children centers around decreasing their attempt to _____ peer interactions.   *dominate*

B. Social Cognition

1. Children's _____ cognitions about their peers become increasingly important for understanding peer relations.   *social*

2. Kenneth Dodge analyzes how children process information about _____ relations.   *peer*

3. Indicate the five steps in Kenneth Dodge's analysis of how children process information about their social world.

4. According to Dodge, inappropriate aggression is frequently the result of misinterpreting another child's _____ .   *intentions*

5. An inability to interact appropriately with peers may mean that a child does not have a _____ for forming a friendship.   *script*

6. Boys without peer adjustment problems demonstrate superior and more diverse _____ cognitive skills than maladjusted boys.   *social*

C. Friends

1. Friendship serves _____ different functions: companionship, stimulation, physical support, ego support, _____ comparison, and intimacy/affection.   *six*   *social*

2. One of the most important components of friendship is _____ .   *intimacy*

3. _____ in friendship is defined as self-disclosure and the sharing of private thoughts.   *Intimacy*

4. A second important aspect of a friendship is _____ .   *similarity*

5. Friends are _____ similar than dissimilar.   *more*

6. Harry Stack _____ was a psychoanalytic theorist who emphasized the importance of _____ for children's and adolescent's well-being and development.   *Sullivan*   *friendships*

7. Summarize Sullivan's ideas about friendship in children's well-being and development.

3.0 Schools

1. Explain the concern about the impact of schools on children.

A. The Transition to Elementary School

1. For most children, entering the first grade marks a change from being a "homechild" to being a _____ .   *schoolchild*

2. Early experiences in school expose children primarily to _____ feedback.   *negative*

3. Consequently, children's self-_____ is lower in the later part of elementary school than earlier in elementary school experience.   *esteem*

4. Explain what it means to say that children's learning *integrated*.

5. Indicate how curricula and classrooms can promote integrated learning.

6. Lillian Katz and Sylvia Chard described two elementary school _____ .   *classrooms*

7. In the non-integrated classroom, all of the children made _____ pictures of traffic lights, whereas in the integrated classroom, the children learned about a school bus through concrete, _____ experience.   *identical*   *hands-on*

B. Teachers

1. _____ symbolize authority, establish the classroom climate, and influence the interaction between children.   *Teachers*

2. Teacher traits associated with _____ student outcomes include enthusiasm, ability to plan, poise, adaptability, warmth, and a willingness to accept individual differences.   *positive*

3. Erik Erikson believes that good teachers should be able to produce a sense of _____ instead of _____ in their students.   *industry*   *inferiority*

4. According to Erikson, good teachers recognize _____ and help children feel good about themselves, thus building self-esteem.   *effort*

5. In an aptitude-treatment interaction, _____ refers to academic potential and personality traits, and treatment refers to the educational _____ .   *aptitude*   *technique*

6. Students with high achievement orientation do well in a _____ classroom whereas those with low achievement orientation do better in a _____ classroom.   *flexible*   *structured*

C. Social Class and Ethnicity in Schools

1. Explain why it may be appropriate to say that schools have a middle-class bias.

2. Teachers have _____ expectations for children from low-income families than for middle-class families. *lower*

3. It appears that teachers with _____-class backgrounds might make better teachers in low-income schools. *lower*

4. Explain why ethnicity is an important variable in the educational experience of children.

5. School _____ affects the educational experiences of African American and Latino children and adolescents. *segregation*

6. Illustrate what it means to say that the school experiences of children of different ethnic groups vary considerably.

7. John _____ argues that ethnic minority children experience subordination and _____ in the American educational system. *Ogbu* *exploitation*

8. Describe the range of opportunities for ethnic minority and white youth who graduate from high school or college.

9. According to Margaret Beale Spencer and Sanford Dornbusch, schools manifest _____ racism. *institutional*

10. According to Spencer and Dornbusch, all students learn most effectively when teachers provide warmth and _____ standards. *challenging*

11. James Comer's solution to the poor education of ethnic minority students involves formation of a school-_____ team. *governance*

12. Comer's goal is to create a _____ environment. *familylike*

4.0 The Self, Gender, and Moral Development

A. The Self

1. In middle and late childhood, self-understanding shifts from defining oneself in terms of _____ characteristics to defining oneself in terms of _____ characteristics. *external* *internal* *social*

2. Definitions of self in the middle and late childhood period include psychological as well as _____ characteristics. *social*

3. When children define themselves as Girl Scouts or Boy Scouts, they refer to _____ groups in the self-description. *social*

4. Explain what it meant by self-understanding in terms of social comparison.

5. _____ taking is the ability to assume another person's perspective and understand his or her thoughts or feelings. *Perspective*

6. Robert _____ has proposed a developmental theory of perspective taking. *Selman*

7. Describe and give an example of how Robert Selman studies perspective taking.

8. Use Table 11.1 to review the names, age ranges, and descriptions of Selman's five stages of perspective taking.

9. Children's perspective taking skills can increase their self-_____ , improve their peer group status, and increase the quality of their _____ .

understanding

friendships

10. Self-esteem refers to a _____ evaluation of the self, whereas self-concept refers to a domain-_____ evaluation of the self.

global

specific

11. Susan Harter replaced her Perceived Competence Scale for Children with the Self-Perception _____ for Children.

Profile

12. The Self-Perception Profile for Children measures _____ specific aspects of self-esteem of third through _____ graders.

five

sixth

13. The Self-Perception Profile for Adolescents assesses eight specific domains in addition to _____ self-worth.

global

14. Indicate parenting attributes associated with boys who have high self-esteem.

15. Indicate why it is appropriate to conclude that parental attributes relate to, but do not cause children's self-esteem.

16. Henry Tajfel proposed social _____ theory.

identity

17. According to Tajfel, members of a group conceive of themselves as part of an _____ , and thereby garner a _____ self-image.

in-group

positive

18. Social identity theory predicts that group members will _____ distinctions about opposing groups.

maximize

19. _____ is a tendency to favor one's own group over other groups, whereas _____ is an unjustified negative attitude toward an individual member of a particular group.

Ethnocentrism

prejudice

20. Describe findings about the nature of self concept among various ethnic groups.

21. Describe how to improve children's self-esteem by identifying the causes of low self-esteem.

22. Describe how to improve children's self-esteem with emotional support and social approval.

23. Describe how to improve children's self-esteem through achievement.

24. Describe how to improve children's self-esteem through coping.

25. The fourth psychosocial stage in Erik Erikson's theory is one of industry versus _____ .

inferiority

26. Describe experiences that promote senses of industry and inferiority.

B. Gender

1. Broad categories that convey impressions about males and females are termed gender-role _____ .

stereotypes

2. Labeling someone produces significant _____ reactions to the individual.

social

3. Gives some examples of how gender stereotypes are ambiguous.

4. Gender-role stereotypes are _____ throughout the world.   *pervasive*

5. As sexual equality increases, gender stereotypes and differences may _____ .   *diminish*

6. Describe developmental changes in gender-role stereotypes graphically or verbally.

7. Gender differences are based on _____ , and there is often much overlap between females   *averages*
   and males even though there is an average _____ between them.   *difference*

8. Gender _____ may be due to primarily biological factors, sociocultural factors, or both.   *differences*

9. Indicate three physical sex differences.

10. A classic study of cognitive gender differences by Eleanor Maccoby and Carol Jacklin indicated   *verbal*
    that females are more _____ than males, and males are more _____ and better at   *mathematical*
    _____ skills than females.   *visuospatial*

11. Indicate why Janet Hyde believes that the cognitive differences between females and males have
    been exaggerated.

12. One consistent finding is that males are more active and _____ than females.   *aggressive*

13. A social gender difference is that _____ are more active and aggressive than _____ .   *males*
    females

14. Explain what it means to say that females and males differ in social connectedness.

15. One prevalent gender stereotype is that females are emotional, and males are not even though   *similarities*
    research reveals more _____ than _____ between males and females in their global   *differences*
    experience of emotion.

16. Summarize Alice Eagley's position on the controversy over whether sex differences are rare and
    small or frequent and large.

17. Summarize David Buss's position on the controversy over whether sex differences are rare and
    small or frequent and large.

18. _____ affect gender.   *Contexts*

19. Indicate the helping behaviors typical of males and females.

20. Males are more likely than females to display _____ toward strangers.   *anger*

21. Females are more likely than males to include emotional descriptions of their _____   *interpersonal*
    relationships.

22. Indicate the most appropriate conclusion regarding gender d:

23. Gender-role classifications have _____ over time.   *changed*

24. Although boys long have been encouraged as a group to be _____ , and girls have been   *masculine*
    encouraged to be _____ ; contemporary gender-roles are more diverse.   *feminine*

25. The traditional masculine orientation was labeled _____ , and focused on the attainment of   *instrumental*
    goals and emphasized a person's accomplishments.

26. The traditional feminine orientation was labeled _____ , and emphasized the facilitation of   *expressive*
    social interaction, interdependence, and relationships.
27. Stereotypes are more harmful to females than to males because they promote _____ .   *sexism*
28. _____ refers to the negative treatment of individuals on the basis of sex.   *Sexism*
29. In the 1970s, the either/or dichotomy for gender classification yielded to the view that an   *expressive*
    individual can show both _____ and _____ traits.   *instrumental*
30. Define the concept of *androgyny* in your own words.

31. Sandra Bem developed the Bem Sex-Role Inventory that classifies gender-orientation into four   *feminine*
    categories: masculine, _____ , androgynous, and _____ .   *undifferentiated*
32. An _____ individual is a female or male who has a high degree of both feminine and   *androgynous*
    masculine traits, whereas an individual who has neither masculine more feminine characteristics is   *undifferentiated*
    said to be _____ .
33. Individuals who are _____ are the least competent, whereas _____ individuals are   *undifferentiated*
    more flexible and more mentally healthy than either masculine or feminine oriented individuals.   *androgynous*
34. Explain what it means to say that the context influences which gender role is most adaptive.

35. Joe Pleck favors replacing the concept of androgyny with the concept of gender-role _____ .   *transcendence*
36. State the concept of gender-role transcendence in your own terms.

37. Explain the need to study the relationship between ethnicity and gender.

38. Characterize the behavioral and gender orientations of:
    African American females

    Asian American females

    Latino American females

    Native American females

39. Characterize the behavioral and gender orientations of:
    African American males

    Asian American males

    Latino American males

Native American males

C. Moral Development

1. Lawrence Kohlberg stressed that moral development is based on moral _____ and unfolds in three _____ , each of which entails two stages.

   reasoning
   levels

2. Kohlberg used _____ for much of his research into the moral reasoning of children, and based much of his theory on the key concept of _____ .

   interviews
   internalization

3. Kohlberg's first level of preconventional reasoning demonstrates _____ internalization.

   no

4. Characterize preconventional reasoning entailed in:

   Stage 1: Punishment and obedience orientation

   Stage 2: Individualism and purpose

5. Kohlberg's second level of conventional reasoning demonstrates _____ internalization.

   intermediate

6. Characterize conventional reasoning entailed in:

   Stage 3: Interpersonal norms

   Stage 4: Social systems morality

7. Kohlberg's third level of postconventional reasoning demonstrates _____ internalization.

   complete

8. Characterize postconventional reasoning entailed in:

   Stage 5: Community rights versus individual rights

   Stage 6: Universal ethical principles

10. Kohlberg's research indicates that advancement through the stages is related to _____ and occurs in a particular _____ .

    age
    sequence

11. One criticism of Kohlberg's work is that he did not pay enough attention to moral _____ , that is, moral _____ does not always ensure moral behavior.

    behavior
    reasoning

12. A second criticism is that Kohlberg's view is culturally _____ .

    biased

13. Describe the cross-cultural evidence that indicates that Kohlberg's method of scoring does not recognize higher-level moral reasoning by certain cultural groups.

14. A third criticism is that Kohlberg _____ the importance of family processes in moral development.

    underestimated

15. A fourth criticism, expressed by Carol Gilligan, is that Kohlberg's data and theory is biased against _____ .

    females

16. Carol Gilligan proposed that there are two _____ in moral reasoning.

    perspectives

17. Characterize Gilligan's distinction between a justice perspective and a care perspective.

18. Kohlberg's approach exemplifies the _____ perspective, whereas Gilligan's approach adopts a _____ perspective.

justice

care

19. Research supports Gilligan's claim that there are _____ differences in moral reasoning, but does not support her claim of bias against _____ .

gender

females

20. _____ is an unselfish interest to help someone.

Altruism

21. Altruism involves both _____ and exchange.

reciprocity

22. Explain what is meant by *reciprocity*.

23. William _____ described a developmental model of children's altruism.

Damon

22. At about 4 years of age _____ awareness along with parental encouragement results in more frequent sharing behavior.

empathetic

24. _____ is the first principle of sharing used regularly by elementary school-aged children.

Equality

25. Mid- to late elementary school children also use the principles of merit and _____ .

benevolence

26. Express the meaning of *merit* and *benevolence* in your own terms.

27. William Damon's analysis of the development of altruism does not incorporate the motivation to _____ adult authority figures.

obey

28. Although parents may encourage sharing, children _____ their own fairness standards through daily interactions.

construct

5.0   Chapter Boxes

A.   *Sociocultural Worlds of Development: Gender Roles in Egypt and China*

1. Although gender roles in the United States have become more _____ , gender roles elsewhere in the world remained more gender-specific.

androgynous

2. In _____ , gender roles are clearly defined rather than androgynous.

Egypt

3. In _____ , females have made progress toward equality; however, complete equality does not exist.

China

B.   *Critical Thinking About Life-Span Development: Rethinking the Words We Use in Gender Worlds*

1. Explain why the term relational ability has replace the word dependent to describe females.

2. Evaluate the connotations of words that you use to describe femininity and masculinity.

C.   *Critical Thinking About Life-Span Development: Moral Decision Making*

1. Evaluate two moral dilemmas and place your moral decisions at one of Kohlberg's stages.

D.   *Life-Span Health and Well-Being: A Model School Health Program: Heart Smart*

1. Indicate the role and activities of teachers in the Heart Smart health program.

2. Describe the physical education and school lunch components of the Heart Smart program.

3. Indicate what happens to high risk children in the Heart Smart program.

Self Test A: Key Terms and Key Persons

Write the appropriate key term or key person in the space to the right of the definition or description.

1. In Kohlberg's theory, a kind of morality that is internalized and based on the development of a moral code derived from an active exploration of alternative moral courses and options.   _____

2. The global evaluative dimension of the self that is also called self-image.   _____

3. The individual who possesses desirable feminine and masculine traits.   _____

4. The individual who proposed a developmental theory of perspective taking.   _____

5. A critic of Lawrence Kohlberg who distinguished between justice and care perspectives.   _____

6. In Kohlberg's theory, a kind of morality in which the individual abides by internalized standards that have been dictated by others.   _____

7. Behaviors intended to help another individual without concern for potential external reward.   _____

8. An unjustified negative attitude toward an individual on the basis of that individual's group membership.   _____

9. Susan Harter's new measure that assesses a child's sense of self-confidence across five specific domains.   _____

10. The individual who favors the concept of gender-role transcendence over that of androgyny.   _____

11. In Kohlberg's theory, a kind of morality in which the child does not internalize moral values.   _____

12. In Gilligan's view of moral reasoning, people are distinguished from other people and stand alone. The focus emphasizes the rights of an individual.   _____

13. The developmentalist who devised an inventory to measure one's gender orientation.   _____

14. The belief that a person's competence should be judged on an individual basis rather than on the basis of gender orientation.   _____

15. A social psychological theory that members of a group regard themselves as members of an in-group and thereby accrue positive self-image.   _____

16. An anthropologist who claims American educational institutions exploit and subordinate ethnic minority children.   _____

17. Children who are ignored by their peers.   _____

18. The idea that the outcome of a particular educational intervention depends on the level of the students and the nature of the treatment.   _____

19. The ability to assume another person's point of view and understand his or her thoughts and feelings.   _____

20. An individual's knowledge about the social world and interpersonal relationships.   _____

21. Either of the two researchers who interviewed over 1,500 latchkey children.   _____

Self Test B: Multiple Choice

1. Which of the following parent-child topics of discussion is most likely to occur in the middle and late childhood period?
   a. getting dressed
   b. getting the chores done
   c. attention-seeking behavior
   d. bedtime

2. During the elementary school years, coregulation results in which of the following?
   a. more control taken by parents
   b. moment-to-moment control taken by children, with parents taking care of general supervision
   c. transfer of control to children
   d. no change from early childhood in the amount of control exercised by parents

3. Compared to preschool children, elementary schoolchildren are more likely to live in
   a. stepfamilies.
   b. families split by divorce.
   c. mother-only families.
   d. families filled with conflict.

4. Which is a good example of boundary ambiguity?
   a. parents in a blended family deciding on who should discipline the children
   b. children of divorce who are deciding which parent they will stay with
   c. fighting parents who are unsure if they should divorce or separate
   d. children from a blended stepfamily attending a birthday party

5. Marlene is a single parent who works full time. As a result, her eleven-year-old daughter Lee Anna is an after-school latchkey child. In order to minimize the negative impact of this situation, Marlene should
   a. closely monitor her daughter's behavior.
   b. encourage her daughter to make friends that she can hang out with after school.
   c. explain to Lee Anna that independence is an important trait and provide her with a lot of at-home responsibility so she gets some practice in independent living.
   d. All of the answers are correct.

6. Which statements about peer interactions is false?
   a. they usually occur at one of the children's homes
   b. they occur more often in private places than public places
   c. they are most often with members of the same sex
   d. they usually involve play, socializing, or going places

7. All of the following children will be popular with their peers except
   a. those who give out lots of reinforcement.
   b. those who listen carefully to what others have to say.
   c. those who try to please others even if it means compromising themselves.
   d. those who are self-confident.

8. Samantha has few friends at school. Other children pay little attention to her and no one invites her home. Samantha is probably a(n)
   a. rejected child.
   b. neglected child.
   c. latchkey child.
   d. controversial child.

9. When teaching a neglected child how to gain popularity with peers, a counselor should encourage the child to
   a. avoid asking his peers questions.
   b. gain some status by talking about items of personal interest, even if they are of no interest to others.
   c. get peers to pay attention to her through some positive activity (e.g., giving everyone in class a cookie).
   d. All of the answers are correct.

10. Which is the correct order of Kenneth Dodge's (1983) stages of processing of social information?
    a. enacting, searching for a response, decoding social cues, interpreting, selecting an optimal response
    b. decoding social cues, interpreting, searching for a response, selecting an optimal response, enacting
    c. searching for a response, decoding social cues, selecting an optimal response, enacting, interpreting
    d. interpreting, selecting an optimal response, decoding social cues, enacting, searching for a response

11. Friendships from ages 6 to 12 are most frequently based on which of the following?
    a. one-way assistance
    b. proximity
    c. two-way cooperation
    d. intimacy

12. Tamara's friend Shelly is someone she can confide in and get good advice from, whereas her friend Tanya is interesting and introduces her to many new things to do. The functions each of these friendships serve, respectively, are
    a. companionship and social comparison.
    b. intimacy/affection and stimulation.
    c. ego support and physical support.
    d. intimacy and similarity.

13. Who provides the best example of the text definition of intimacy in friendships?
    a. Sven, who wants to hug his best friend
    b. Zelda, who tells her friend, "I'm afraid of growing up"
    c. Iggy, who is planning a romantic dinner with his girlfriend
    d. Charolette, who gives her best friend part of a stick of gum that she has been chewing

14. The school environment forces children to do all but which of the following?
    a. develop new relationships with new significant others
    b. adopt new reference groups
    c. develop new standards by which to judge themselves
    d. adjust to increasing self-esteem

15. Children who have high achievement motivation do well in what kind of classroom?
    a. structured classrooms with structured curricula
    b. flexible classrooms with flexible curricula
    c. structured classrooms with flexible curricula
    d. flexible classrooms with structured curricula

16. Teachers who implement an aptitude-treatment interaction approach in their teaching rely on their
    a. ability to plan.
    b. awareness of individual differences.
    c. adaptability.
    d. flexibility.

17. John Ogbu's controversial argument is that racial minorities are _____ in American schools.
    a. exploited
    b. treated with complete equity
    c. given preferential treatment
    d. perseverance of their personality

18. James Comer's (1993) program for improving the quality of education for poor inner-city youths is based on the premise
    a. "all for one and one for all."
    b. "Black power."
    c. "money makes the world go around."
    d. "what's good for business, is good for America."

19. When asked how he did in a spelling bee, 10-year-old Billy is most likely to say which of the following?
    a. "I did better than last week."
    b. "I hope to do better next week."
    c. "I did real well."
    d. "I did better than Sally."

20. In Chapter 10, your author indicates that handicapped children are increasingly aware of the deficits they suffer compared to nonhandicapped children. Which new process involved in self-understanding probably generates this sensitivity?
    a. perspective taking
    b. use of abstractions to describe the self
    c. awareness of social aspects of the self
    d. social comparison

21. In response to the "save the kitten or obey the father dilemma" described in your text, a child says, "Holly knows her dad will understand how much she wants to save the kitten. So she knows she won't get into trouble for breaking her promise." Which stage of perspective taking best applies to her statement?
    a. egocentric
    b. social informational
    c. self-reflective
    d. mutual

22. The parenting attributes that are associated with high self-esteem are characteristic of a parenting style called
    a. protective.
    b. indulgent.
    c. authoritarian.
    d. authoritative.

23. The basic premise of Henry Taifel's (1978) social identification theory is that when individuals are assigned to a group, they automatically
    a. strive to get into a better group.
    b. view the group as an in-group for purposes of improving self-image.
    c. assume that they will eventually lead the group.
    d. question the nature of the group.

24. _____ is best thought of as an unjustified negative attitude a person holds toward any out-group.
    a. Discrimination
    b. Stereotyping
    c. Racism
    d. Prejudice

25. Clella is a single mother with one child, fifteen-year-old Hossein. In order to improve Hossein's self-esteem, Clella decides to enroll Hossein in a local Boy's Club program. In doing so, Clella is putting faith in the ability of _____ to increase self-esteem.
    a. achievement
    b. coping
    c. emotional support
    d. ethnocentrism

26. Children in the middle and late childhood period of development are also in which Eriksonian psychosocial stage?
    a. trust versus mistrust
    b. autonomy versus doubt and shame
    c. industry versus inferiority
    d. identity versus identity confusion

27. J. O. Halliwell's (1844) poem in which he describes girls as being made of "Sugar and spice and all that's nice" provides a good example of
    a. gender-role transcendence.
    b. androgyny.
    c. gender-role stereotyping.
    d. gender-based prejudice.

28. When reviewing research comparing males versus females, it is important to keep in mind that
    a. even when differences are found, most of the individuals in the groups are virtually identical.
    b. it is unfair to compare the groups since almost all gender differences are a result of uncontrollable biological factors.
    c. it is only when statistically significant scores are found that you can conclude that their is little overlap between male and female scores.
    d. All of the answers are correct.

29. For which of the following do investigators almost always find gender differences?
    a. verbal skills
    b. math skills
    c. social skills
    d. suggestibility

30. A child who is concerned about how well children get along in the classroom is most likely to have which of the following orientations?
    a. undifferentiated
    b. instrumental
    c. expressive
    d. androgynous

31. The term androgyny refers to a gender role that is
    a. highly masculine.
    b. highly feminine.
    c. both highly masculine and highly feminine.
    d. neither masculine nor feminine.

32. Which statistic concerning Black males in America if *false*?
    a. over half of the men executed during the past 50 years were Black males
    b. death by murder is the leading cause of death for Black males between ages 15 and 19
    c. Black males are victims of "double jeopardy"
    d. Black heads of households earn about 70 percent of what White heads of households earn

33. Lawrence Kohlberg's theory of moral development stresses that a child's moral level is determined by
    a. how well the child defends the correct answer to a moral dilemma.
    b. the nature of the child's ideas about morality.
    c. how a child processes information about moral problems.
    d. the child's reasoning about moral decisions.

34. "Heinz should steal the drug. It isn't like it really cost two thousand dollars, and he'll be really unhappy if his wife dies." This statement is characteristic of a stage of morality called
    a. punishment and obedience orientation to morality.
    b. individualism and purpose morality.
    c. interpersonal norms morality.
    d. social system morality.

35. A pacifist who is thrown in jail for refusing to obey the draft laws is at what stage of moral development?
    a. community rights versus individual rights
    b. punishment and obedience
    c. interpersonal norms
    d. universal ethical principles

36. Carol Gilligan argues that Lawrence Kohlberg's theory is limited because it does not
    a. indicate how moral reasoning relates to moral behavior.
    b. include a role for reasoning about relationships between people in evaluating moral decisions.
    c. capture the moral thinking of all cultures; some moral systems do not "fit" Kohlberg's theory.
    d. indicate how moral reasoning relates to moral feeling.

37. The basic premise of reciprocal altruism is best expressed by the statement
    a. "A bird in the hand is worth two in the bush."
    b. "Why ask why?"
    c. "Share and share alike."
    d. "The meek shall inherit the earth."

38. All but which of the following contribute to a child's willingness to share?
    a. the belief that everyone should be treated equally
    b. an understanding that people who do not have as much as he or she does need extra help
    c. the belief that helping someone else will please his or her parents
    d. an understanding that people who work harder deserve more

39. A surprise in research on sharing is that children do not share simply because they
    a. are concerned for others.
    b. felt obligated to share.
    c. are obeying adult demands.
    d. want to get their own way.

Answers for Self Test A

1. postconventional reasoning
2. self-esteem
3. androgyny
4. Robert Selman
5. Carol Gilligen
6. conventional reasoning
7. altruism
8. prejudice
9. Self-Perception Profile for Children
10. Joe Pleck
11. preconventional reasoning
12. justice perspective
13. Sandra Bem
14. gender role transcendence
15. social identity theory
16. John Ogbu
17. neglected children
18. aptitude-treatment interaction (ATI)
19. perspective taking
20. controversial children
21. Thomas or Lynette Long

Answers for Self Test B

1. b LO 1.2
2. b LO 1.5
3. a LO 1.7
4. a LO 1.10
5. a LO 1.14
6. a LO 2.1
7. c LO 2.2
8. b LO 2.3
9. c LO 2.5
10. b LO 2.7
11. c LO 2.10
12. b LO 2.11
13. b LO 2.12
14. d LO 3.1
15. b LO 3.7
16. b LO 3.7
17. a LO 3.10
18. a LO 3.15
19. d LO 4.2
20. d LO 4.2
21. c LO 4.5
22. d LO 4.9
23. b LO 4.10
24. d LO 4.13
25. c LO 4.16
26. c LO 4.19
27. c LO 4.21
28. a LO 4.26
29. b LO 4.28
30. c LO 4.36
31. c LO 4.38
32. c LO 4.44
33. d LO 4.49
34. d LO 4.50
35. d LO 4.50
36. b LO 4.55
37. c LO 4.58
38. c LO 4.61
39. c LO 4.62

Chapter 12   Physical and Cognitive Development in Adolescence

Learning Objectives with Key Terms in Boldface

1.0 The Transition to Adolescence

    1.1 Indicate evidence that adolescence is both continuous and discontinuous with childhood.

2.0 Physical Development

    2.1 Define **menarche** and summarize its trends during the past 150 years in Norway and the United States.

   A. Pubertal Change

    2.2 Define **puberty** and explain why it is difficult to know when puberty begins and ends.

    2.3 Define and distinguish between **estradiol** and **testosterone**.

    2.4 Indicate how estradiol and testosterone affect the physical development of adolescent boys and girls.

    2.5 Indicate the nature and timing of physical changes during puberty.

   B. Psychological Accompaniments of Physical Changes

    2.6 Discuss relationships among puberty, body image, and self-esteem during adolescence.

    2.7 Define and distinguish among early, late, and on-time maturation.

    2.8 Summarize the negative and positive consequences for on- and off-time maturation.

   C. Are Puberty's Effects Exaggerated?

    2.9 Explain why some researchers now question whether puberty has strong psychological effects.

3.0 Cognitive Developmental Changes

   A. Formal Operational Thought

    3.1 Characterize formal operational thought.

    3.2 Define and give an example of **hypothetical-deductive reasoning**.

    3.3 Explain some of the challenges to Jean Piaget's ideas about formal operational thought.

   B. Social Cognition

    3.4 Define and distinguish among **adolescent egocentrism**, **imaginary audience**, and **personal fable**.

    3.5 Explain how adolescent egocentrism could be caused by formal operations and perspective taking.

    3.6 Explain how egocentrism may account for adolescents' reckless behavior.

    3.7 Explain how adolescents' interpretations of personality are similar to personality theorists' interpretations.

4.0 The Nature of Adolescents' Schooling

   A. The Controversy Surrounding Secondary Schools

    4.1 Sketch the evolution of American secondary schools from 1900 to the present.

    4.2 Explain why some question whether schools actually benefit adolescents, and indicate their proposed remedies.

    4.3 Describe the controversy surrounding the back-to-basics movement and its view of American secondary education.

   B. The Transition to Middle or Junior High School

    4.4 Explain why junior high schools emerged.

    4.5 Explain why middle and junior high schools should not be "watered down versions of high schools."

    4.6 Explain why the transition to middle or junior high school can be stressful.

    4.7 Define the **top-dog phenomenon**.

   C. Effective Schools for Young Adolescents

    4.8 List the characteristics of effective middle schools according to Joan Lipsitz.

4.9   Summarize the Carnegie Report's recommendations for middle schools.

4.10   Cite institutions that are leading the way to better middle schools.

D. High School Dropouts

4.11   Describe changes in the incidence of high school dropouts over the past 40 years.

4.12   Evaluate the claim that dropout rates are comparable for ethnic majority and minority students.

4.13   List reasons that dropouts give for leaving school.

4.14   Indicate ways to reduce the high school dropout rate according to the William T. Grant Foundation.

5.0 Adolescent Problems and Disorders

A. Drugs

5.1   Describe trends in teenage drug use during the last 30 years.

5.2   Describe trends and risks in alcohol consumption by adolescents in the last decade.

5.3   Describe effects, trends and risks in cocaine consumption by adolescents in the last decade.

5.4   Explain why drug use early in adolescence is more worrisome than drug use later in adolescence.

5.5   Indicate age trends for adolescent drug use according to Lloyd Johnston, Patrick O'Malley, and Gerald Bachman.

5.6   Discuss parental and social factors that encourage or discourage drug use by adolescents.

B. Juvenile Delinquency

5.7   Define and distinguish among **juvenile delinquency**, **index offenses**, and **status offenses**.

5.8   Indicate age differences for limits of delinquency among the Untied States.

5.9   Discuss antecedents of delinquency such as family processes, social class, and neighborhood quality.

5.10   Characterize rates of youth violence.

5.11   Describe and evaluate Positive Adolescents Choices Training (PACT) as an antidote to youth violence.

5.12   Indicate how the Safe Schools Act can foster programs such as PACT.

5.13   Describe what we do/do not know about how to reduce delinquency.

5.14   List points that deserve attention as delinquency intervention and prevention possibilities.

5.15   List what has not worked in preventing delinquency.

C. Adolescent Pregnancy

5.16   Compare and contrast the incidence of adolescent sexual activity and pregnancy in the United States and in countries such as England, France, Canada, Sweden, and the Netherlands.

5.17   List issues that make adolescent pregnancy a delicate topic.

5.18   Compare and contrast adolescent pregnancy and its consequences in the 1950s and today in the United States.

5.19   Discuss the consequences of pregnancy for a young woman's health, social development, and future.

5.20   Discuss ways to reduce teenage pregnancy.

5.21   Describe adolescents' experience of sex and sex education in Holland and Sweden.

D. Suicide

5.22   Describe the incidence, correlates, and methods of suicide among today's adolescents.

5.23   Define and distinguish between distal and proximal factors in explanations of adolescent suicide.

5.24   Use Table 12.1 to review what you should and should not do when you deal with a potentially suicidal individual.

E. Eating Disorders

5.25   Define and give examples of **anorexia nervosa** and **bulimia**.

5.26   Indicate the incidence and correlates of anorexia nervosa and bulimia.

5.27   Speculate about causes of anorexia nervosa and bulimia.

6.0 The Current Status of Adolescents and At-Risk Youth

A. The Current Status of Adolescents

6.1   Evaluate stereotypes of adolescence using contemporary findings about adolescent self-images.

6.2   Indicate how too many adolescents lack adequate support and opportunities to become competent adults.

B. *Idealized Images of Adolescence and Society's Ambivalent Messages to Adolescents*

    6.3   Give examples of society's idealized image of adolescence and ambivalent messages to adolescents.

C. *At-Risk Youth*

    6.4   Define and distinguish between very high-risk and high-risk youth.

    6.5   Provide five examples of individual attention and community-wide interventions for at-risk youth.

7.0 Chapter Boxes

A. *Sociocultural Worlds of Development: Cross-Cultural Comparisons of Secondary Schools*

    7.1   Compare and contrast secondary schools in Australia, Brazil, Germany, Japan, Russia, and the United States.

B. *Critical Thinking About Life-Span Development: Seeking to Explain the Advantageous Identity Development of Late-Maturing Boys*

    7.2   Formulate an alternative to Harvey Peskin's explanation of the benefit of late maturation to adolescent boys' identity development in early adulthood.

C. *Critical Thinking About Life-Span Development: Why Is a Course of Risk Taking in Adolescence Likely to Have More Serious Consequences Than in the Past?*

    7.3   Identify the sociocultural and historical contexts that make risk taking riskier today than ever before.

D. *Life-Span Health and Well-Being: Some Guidelines for Seeking Therapy When an Adolescent Shows Problem Behaviors*

    7.4   Describe five circumstances under which parents should seek help for their adolescents' problems.

Guided Review and Study

1.0 The Transition to Adolescence

    1. _____ is a period between the ages of 13 and 18 marked by the interaction among genetic, biological, and experiential factors.   *Adolescence*

    2. Explain what it means to say that adolescence is both continuous and discontinuous with childhood.

2.0 Physical Development

    1. During adolescence, girls experience _____ , their first menstrual period.   *menarche*

    2. The average age of menarche has _____ steadily since the 1900s, an apparent result of improved health and _____ .   *declined*
        nutrition

A. *Pubertal Change*

    1. _____ is a period of rapid change in physical and sexual maturation.   *Puberty*

    2. Explain why it is difficult to know when puberty begins and ends.

    3. The endocrine glands release their secretions, called _____ , directly into the bloodstream.   *hormones*

    4. _____ is responsible for the development of genitals, an increase in height, and a change in boys' voices, whereas _____ is a hormone associated with breast, uterine, and skeletal development in girls.   *Testosterone*
        estradiol

    5. Use Figure 12.1 to review the nature and timing of physical changes during puberty for boys and girls.

B. *Psychological Accompaniments of Physical Changes*

    1. An adolescent's physical changes are accompanied by a variety of _____ changes.   *psychological*

    2. For example, adolescents are preoccupied with their _____ .   *bodies*

    3. The _____ of puberty can have differing psychological effects.   *timing*

4. According to the California Longitudinal Study, early-maturing boys view themselves more _____ and have better _____ relations than late-maturing boys. In their 30s, however, late-maturing boys have a stronger sense of _____ .

positively
peer
identity

5. Most research confirms that, at least during adolescence, it is better to be an _____ - maturing boy than a _____-maturing boy.

early
late

6. _____ maturation for girls is a mixed blessing because they experience more popularity with _____ and more problems in school.

Early
boys

7. Explain how early versus later development influences the body image of girls in the sixth and tenth grades.

8. Early maturation for girls is associated with vulnerabilities to _____ , and with _____ levels of educational and occupational attainment.

problems
lower

C. Are Puberty's Effects Exaggerated?

1. Indicate and explain what contemporary researchers now say about the overall effects of pubertal change and variation.

3.0 Cognitive Developmental Changes

A. Formal Operational Thought

1. The fourth stage of Piaget's theory of cognitive development, _____ thought appears between the ages of 11 and 15.

formal

2. Formal operational thought is more _____ than children's thought.

abstract

3. Adolescents increasingly think about _____ and its abstractness.

thought

4. _____ is another characteristic of adolescent thinking.

Idealism

5. In addition to thinking more abstractly and ideally, adolescents think more _____ . Explain Jean Piaget's concept of hypothetical-deductive reasoning in your own words.

logically

7. Indicate what critics say about Jean Piaget's view of formal operational thought.

8. Early formal operational thought entails an excess of _____ , and late formal operational thought involves accommodation.

assimilation

B. Social Cognition

1. Changes in _____ cognition include a special type of egocentrism, new views of personality, and an ability to monitor the social world in a sophisticated way.

social

2. According to David Elkind, adolescent _____ is composed of both imaginary audiences and the personal fable.

egocentrism

3. Explain the concepts of *imaginary audience* and *personal fable* in your own words.

4. Describe your own examples of imaginary audience and personal fable.

5. David Elkind argues that adolescent egocentrism is a _____ phenomenon, whereas other researchers indicate that adolescent egocentrism results from the combination of formal operational thought and _____ taking.

cognitive
perspective

6. Explain how egocentrism in adolescence may result in recklessness.

7. Indicate and explain the three domains in which adolescents begin to interpret their personality and the personality of others like personality theorists.

4.0 The Nature of Adolescents' Schooling

A. The Controversy Surrounding Secondary Schools

1. From 1890 through 1920, states adopted laws that required _____ to attend school. *adolescents*
2. In the 1920s, secondary schools became charged with training adolescents intellectually as well as _____ and socially. *vocationally*
3. Explain why some question whether secondary schools benefit adolescents.

4. One proposal is to offer adolescents educational _____ to the comprehensive high school. *alternatives*
5. Explain the back-to-basics movement in your own words.

6. Indicate the controversial views regarding the goals of schooling for adolescents.

B. The Transition to Middle or Junior High School

1. The junior high school and sometimes the middle school were created because the students are going through _____ and experiencing physical, cognitive, and social changes. *puberty*
2. One concern about junior high schools and middle schools is that they not become _____ down versions of high schools. *watered*
3. The transition to middle school or junior high school from elementary schools is a _____ experience for virtually all children. *normative*
4. Summarize the changes that make the transition from elementary school to middle school or junior high school stressful.

5. _____ makes the transition to junior high school more difficult as does the appearance of formal operational thought, the increase of responsibility and _____ , the move to a larger school, and an increased focus on _____ . *Puberty* *independence* *achievement*
6. Express the *top-dog phenomenon* in your own terms.

C. Effective Schools for Young Adolescents

1. Joan Lipsitz and her colleagues found that effective middle schools were _____ and able to adapt all school practices to the individual _____ in physical, cognitive, and social development of their students. *willing* *differences*
2. Another aspect of effective middle schools was that they created environments supportive of adolescent's social and _____ development. *emotional*
3. Summarize the 1989 Carnegie Report's recommendations for middle schools.

4. The major conclusion about middle schools is that they need a major _____ if they are to help adolescents become effective adults in the twenty-first century. *redesign*

1. In the 1940s, approximately _____ percent of all individuals dropped out of high school, whereas in the mid-1980s approximately _____ percent of all individuals dropped out of high school. *60* *14*

2. The dropout rates for minority group and low-income students is _____ than those for White adolescents.   *higher*

3. Indicate the reasons students give for dropping out of school.

4. Reducing the drop out rate requires lowering the barriers between _____ and _____ .   *work; school*

5. Indicate ways to reduce the high school dropout rate according to the William T. Grant Foundation.

5.0 Adolescent Problems and Disorders

1. Prominent adolescent problems include _____ abuse, juvenile delinquency, pregnancy, suicide, and _____ disorders such as anorexia nervosa and bulimia.   *drug* *eating*

A. Drugs

1. Characterize Lloyd Johnston, Patrick O'Malley, and Gerald Bachman's findings about teenage drug use from the 1960s through the mid-1990s.

2. _____ is the most commonly abused drug by adolescents.   *Alcohol*

3. Although the consumption of alcohol by high school seniors _____ from 1980 to 1994, a substantial sex difference, in which males drink _____ heavily than females, remains.   *decreased* *more*

4. _____ drinking by college students has remained relatively constant.   *Heavy*

5. _____ is a derivative of the coca plant, the extreme effects of which involve heart attacks, strokes, brain seizures, or death.   *Cocaine*

6. Cocaine use by high school and college students has _____ steadily since 1987 and continues to do so.   *declined*

7. Indicate the concerns about adolescents who use drugs to reduce stress.

8. Summarize the age trends in adolescent drug use.

9. Indicate parental and social factors that encourage or discourage drug use by adolescents.

B. Juvenile Delinquency

1. A child or adolescent who engages in socially unacceptable behavior, commits status offenses, or commits criminal acts is called a juvenile _____ .   *delinquent*

2. Express the concepts of *index offenses* and *status offenses* in your own words.

3. Either juveniles or adults can commit _____ offenses; however, only juveniles can commit _____ offenses.   *index* *status*

4. Indicate antecedents of delinquency other than the two detailed in your textbook (i.e., family processes, and also social class and neighborhood quality).

5. Recent research on family processes associated with juvenile delinquency has focused on family _____ and family _____ practices.   *support* *management*

149

6. List four family support and management practices associated with delinquency.

7. The most important family factor that predicts delinquency is parental _____ .   *monitoring*

8. Explain what it means to say that some characteristics of the lower-class culture are likely to promote delinquency.

9. The nature of the _____ may contribute to delinquency.   *community*

10. Describe the problem of violent adolescents.

11. Positive Adolescents Choices Training (PACT) is an _____ program designed to help 12- to 15-year-old _____ Americans learn to manage anger and resolve conflicts peacefully.   *intervention*
   African

12. Describe how the Safe Schools Act foster programs such as PACT.

13. Attempts to reduce juvenile delinquency have taken _____ forms.   *various*

14. Joy Dryfoos has identified _____ points that delinquency experts regard as likely candidates for successful prevention and intervention.   *seven*

15. List examples of various attempts that have failed to reduce delinquency.

C. Adolescent Pregnancy

1. Adolescent _____ constitutes a national dilemma in the United States.   *pregnancy*

2. Pregnancy occurs for about one in _____ American adolescents a year, and some _____ percent of these pregnancies are unintended.   *ten*
   80

3. The rate of adolescent pregnancy in the United States is the _____ in the western world.   *highest*

4. Explain why adolescent pregnancy is a delicate topic in this country.

5. Compare and contrast the incidence of adolescent pregnancy and its consequences in the 1950s and today in the United States.

6. Only about _____ percent of pregnant adolescents give their babies up for adoption.   *5*

7 Adolescent pregnancy is a _____ risk for both the baby and mother.   *health*

8. Adolescent mothers also have less _____ and lower-status jobs.   *education*

9. Experts recommend reducing the high rate of adolescent pregnancy through improved sex _____ , family planning, available _____ , and community involvement and support.   *education*
   contraception

10. Sexual _____ is also a theme in contemporary sex education classes.   *abstinence*

11. Holland and _____ have social policies regarding sex education that produce very low rates of adolescent pregnancy.   *Sweden*

12. Describe sex education in Holland and Sweden.

D. Suicide

1. One of the leading causes of death among adolescents is _____ .   *suicide*

2. The suicide rate begins to rise rapidly at about _____ years of age.   *15*

3. More males than females _____ suicide, a difference   *commit*
   efficient means by _____ .   *males*

4. Explain why it is helpful to think of suicide in terms of proximal and distal factors.

5. Genetic factors are associated with both depression and _____ .   *suicide*

6. Use Table 12.1 to review what you should and should not do when you deal with a potentially suicidal individual.

E. Eating Disorders

1. Adolescent eating disorders include anorexia nervosa and _____ .   *bulimia*

2. Anorexia nervosa is the condition of extreme, apparently voluntary _____ , a disorder more   *starvation*
   characteristics of females and than males.

3. Identify and explain societal, psychological, and physiological factors that may cause anorexia nervosa.

4. _____ is a syndrome that repeats a cycle of heavy eating followed by induced vomiting.   *Bulimia*

5. Bulimia is _____ characteristic of females than males.   *more*

6. Unlike anorexics, bulimics cannot _____ their eating.   *control*

7. _____ is a common characteristic of bulimics.   *Depression*

6.0 The Current Status of Adolescents and At-Risk Youth

A. The Current Status of Adolescents

1. A _____ represents beliefs and impressions about the typical member of a particular group.   *stereotype*

2. Contrary to stereotypes that adolescents are _____ and highly stressed, the majority of   *incompetent*
   contemporary adolescents negotiate their way to adulthood _____ .   *successfully*

3. Indicate evidence that today's adolescents confront a more unstable world than ever before.

4. Adolescents are not a _____ group.   *homogenous*

5. Important variables include _____ , culture, _____ , socioeconomic status, age, and   *ethnicity*
   life-style.   *gender*

B. Idealized Images of Adolescence and Society's Ambivalent Messages to Adolescents

1. Explain what it means to say that society's idealized image of adolescence and ambivalent messages contribute to the problems of today's adolescents.

C. At-Risk Youth

1. The concerns for _____ youth pertain to delinquency, substance abuse, pregnancy, and   *at-risk*
   dropping out of school.

2. Serious multiple behavior problems affect _____ percent of the youth population.   *5 to 10*

3. Programs for the treatment of troubled adolescents require _____ attention, and   *individual*
   _____-wide interventions according to Joy Dryfoos.   *community*

4. Identify and explain community-wide interventions to improve the lives of at-risk youth.

7.0 Chapter Boxes

A. *Sociocultural Worlds of Development: Cross-Cultural Comparisons of Secondary Schools*

   1. Compare and contrast the following aspects of secondary schools in Australia, Brazil, Germany, Japan, Russia, and the United States:

     mandatory age

     number of levels

     entrance and exit exams

     sports

     content and philosophy

     foreign languages

B. *Critical Thinking About Life-Span Development: Seeking to Explain the Advantageous Identity Development of Late Maturing Boys*

   1. Formulate an alternative to Henry Peskin's explanation of the benefit of late maturation to adolescent boys' identity development in early adulthood.

C. *Critical Thinking About Life-Span Development: Why Is a Course of Risk Taking in Adolescence Likely to Have More Serious Consequences Than in the Past?*

   1. Identify sociocultural and historical contexts that make risk taking riskier today than ever before.

D. *Life-Span Health and Well-Being: Some Guidelines for Seeking Therapy When an Adolescent Shows Problem Behaviors*

   1. Laurence Steinberg and Ann Levine developed _____ guidelines for when to get _____ help   *5*
      for an adolescent who displays problem behaviors.   *professional*
   2. Describe five circumstances under which parents should seek help for their adolescents' problems.

Self Test A: Key Terms and Key Persons

Write the appropriate key term or key person in the space to the right of the definition or description.

   1. A way of thinking by 11- to 14-year olds that includes the imaginary audience and personal fable.   _____

   2. Criminal acts committed by juveniles or adults.   _____

   3. The developmentalist who contends that the imaginary audience and personal fable are two parts of adolescent egocentrism.   _____

   4. The first menstruation of pubertal females.   _____

5. David Elkind's concept that each adolescent believes he or she will be the center of everyone's attention. _____

6. The individual who identified the best middle schools in the United States. _____

7. A form of voluntary starvation that leads to severe malnutrition and emaciation. _____

8. An adolescent who engages in socially unacceptable behavior, commits status offenses, or commits a crime. _____

9. The individual who identified possibilities for the prevention or intervention of juvenile delinquency.

10. The experience of moving from the highest status position to the lowest status position. _____

11. Either of the three researchers who survey adolescents and adults about their drug use. _____

12. A hormone associated with breast, uterine, and skeletal development in girls. _____

Self Test B: Multiple Choice

1. The age at which puberty arrives is _____ with each passing decade.
   a. increasing
   b. decreasing
   c. staying the same
   d. approaching a plateau

2. Wet dreams, first menstruation, skeletal growth, and changing body shape are events that occur in
   a. late childhood.
   b. puberty.
   c. menarche.
   d. adolescence.

3. _____ triggers breast and skeletal development in females.
   a. Progesterone
   b. Estradiol
   c. Serotonin
   d. Dopamine

4. The most noticeable changes in body growth for females include all but which of the following?
   a. height spurt
   b. tendencies towards obesity
   c. breast growth
   d. menarche

5. The information about body satisfaction in early- and late-maturing females best supports the generalization that
   a. body satisfaction is highest among adolescents who look most like attractive adults.
   b. early maturation produces lasting body satisfaction.
   c. body satisfaction is not consistently related to other positive psychological outcomes.
   d. puberty influences body satisfaction more strongly than any other set of bodily changes during the life span.

6. Recent research about puberty suggests all but which of the following?
   a. early puberty is better than late puberty during the adolescent period
   b. pubertal variations are less dramatic than commonly thought
   c. adolescents are affected by puberty as well as by cognitive and social changes
   d. the onset of puberty is related to self-esteem throughout adolescence and into early adulthood

7. At age 13, Sheila still has not entered puberty. What is she likely to experience by the time she reaches tenth grade?
   a. an increase in popularity and self-esteem
   b. a sharp drop in self-confidence, because boys will be attracted primarily to the more mature girls
   c. a strong sense of identity
   d. an increase in problems at school

8. In recent years developmental researchers have begun to view the effects of puberty as
   a. overrated.
   b. identical for early-and late-maturing individuals.
   c. positive for males and negative for females.
   d. more dramatic than they had expected.

9. A child in the formal operational thought stage of cognitive development is most likely to engage in which of the following activities?
   a. using building blocks to determine how houses are constructed
   b. writing a story about a clown that wants to leave the circus
   c. drawing pictures of a family using stick figures
   d. writing an essay about patriotism

10. Jean Piaget's ideas on formal operational thought are being challenged in all but which of the following ways?
    a. not all adolescents are capable of formal thought
    b. not all adults in every culture are formal operational thinkers
    c. there is more individual variation in the development of formal operations than Piaget thought
    d. only those with scientific training use hypothetical-deductive reasoning

11. The personal fable represents an adolescent's attempt to
    a. accommodate his beliefs about his life's course to new information about life.
    b. assimilate new information about life to personal beliefs about his own life's course.
    c. imagine possible, ideal futures for his life.
    d. develop a theory about what has created his personality.

12. Which has been conceptually linked to adolescent egocentrism?
    a. reckless sexual behavior
    b. suicidal thoughts
    c. drug use
    d. All of the answers are correct.

13. Unlike children, adolescents who interpret personality information concerning another person
    a. rely heavily on the current situation and ignore past experiences with the individual.
    b. realize that personality traits are highly consistent.
    c. tend to incorporate traditional sex-role stereotypes into their analysis.
    d. often attempt to identify the "hidden cause" of the person's behavior.

14. In the 1970s, three separate evaluations of American high schools concluded that high schools
    a. need to focus more on basic intellectual skills.
    b. do not help adolescents enter adulthood.
    c. allow adolescents to spend too many hours in part-time work.
    d. are too concerned with the social and emotional lives of students.

15. A trend in adolescent development that has stimulated the creation of middle schools is
    a. an increase in formal operational thinking among early adolescents.
    b. the appearance of greater autonomy from adults.
    c. the earlier and highly variable beginning of puberty.
    d. the fact that today's teens spend more time with peers than with parents or adults.

16. Students experiencing the top-dog phenomenon are most likely to exhibit which of the following?
    a. high achievement orientation
    b. little satisfaction with school
    c. good relations with peers
    d. power over other students

17. Joan Lipsitz said that the common thread among schools that have been successful in diminishing the trauma often associated with the middle-school experience was that they all emphasized
    a. gender equity.
    b. curricular flexibility.
    c. discipline.
    d. the importance of high academic standards.

18. Which *is not* one of the Carnegie Corporation's (1989) recommendations for improving middle schools in the United States?
    a. lower the student counselor ratio to 10 to 1
    b. get parents involved
    c. integrate physical health into the curriculum
    d. promote continuity by keeping all class sessions the same length

19. During the last 40 years, the dropout rate of American school children has
    a. increased significantly.
    b. increased slightly.
    c. decreased slightly.
    d. decreased significantly.

20. The William T. Grant Foundation on Work, Family, and Citizenship (1988) suggested that the critical factor in reducing the dropout rate involves
    a. improving the connection between schooling and work.
    b. a significant increase in the amount of money the government is willing to spend on education.
    c. ending racial inequity in the classroom.
    d. increasing the school year.

21. The most widely used drug by adolescents is which of the following?
    a. alcohol
    b. marijuana
    c. cocaine
    d. speed

22. Which person is engaged in an index offense?
    a. fourteen-year-old Dutch, who is swearing in church
    b. seven-year-old Bonnie, who was just sent to the principal's office
    c. four-year-old Al, who is committing his first lie by telling his mom that the cat knocked over his glass of milk when he actually did it
    d. ten-year-old Clyde, who is robbing a bank

154

23. Among the causes of delinquency mentioned in your text, the one that apparently has received the least attention is
    a. genetics.
    b. personality development.
    c. social class.
    d. parenting practices.

24. The causes of juvenile delinquency include all but which of the following?
    a. heredity
    b. identity problems
    c. family experiences
    d. boredom

25. A parenting practice that is associated with an adolescent becoming delinquent is
    a. use of punishment to control behavior.
    b. indulgence of a child's wants.
    c. lazy supervision of a teen's whereabouts.
    d. restrictively controlling an adolescent's behavior.

26. The issue of teenage pregnancy is complex because it involves all but which of the following?
    a. the undeveloped reproductive system of the adolescent
    b. the issue of abortion
    c. the issue of sex education in the schools
    d. the issue of contraceptive use

27. When comparing the overall pregnancy rates of American teenagers with the rates in Sweden and Holland, and then focusing on cultural differences as possible contributors, it appears that the high pregnancy rate in American teens may result from the
    a. fact that teens in the United States have sex at a much earlier age than teens in other countries.
    b. massive exposure to graphic sex found on American television.
    c. fact that American children receive information on the biological nature of reproduction (through sex-education classes) early in life.
    d. fact that American culture is very closed-minded when it comes to sex.

28. Which method of suicide is more likely to be used by a male?
    a. sleeping pills
    b. automobile "accident"
    c. carbon monoxide poisoning
    d. poison

29. Which is not a recommendation for dealing with a suicidal adolescent?
    a. Ask if the person has a plan for killing himself.
    b. Heed warning signs and take them seriously.
    c. Assure the person everything is under control.
    d. Help the person find appropriate counseling.

30. Anorexics are likely to have all but which of the following characteristics?
    a. they are male
    b. they are White
    c. they are well educated
    d. they come from the middle or upper class

31. Which statement is true of teenagers who suffer anorexia nervosa?
    a. They know they are too thin but think they look good anyway.
    b. They frequently are depressed.
    c. They want to be sexually desirable.
    d. They have an intense interest in food.

32. Which statement most accurately summarizes what we know about the causes of anorexia nervosa?
    a. Anorexics strive to be fashionably thin.
    b. Abnormal function of the hypothalamus causes anorexia.
    c. Anorexics strive to gain control of their lives.
    d. We do not know the cause of anorexia nervosa.

33. Which is *not* a good example of the type of ambivalent messages sent to today's youth?
    a. professional basketball players who never graduated from college telling children that education is important
    b. having former alcoholics teach kids about the importance of sobriety
    c. when a person who got AIDS from unprotected sex outside of marriage tells kids about the importance of abstinence
    d. having super-thin models telling you to drink diet pop

34. In order to be classified as a "very high-risk youth," 15-year-old Wayne would have to
    a. commit a serious crime.
    b. be a heavy drug user.
    c. be sexually active, but not using contraceptives.
    d. All of the answers are correct.

35. Laurence Steinberg and Ann Levine say parents should send their child to a professional
    a. only after they have identified the basic problem.
    b. whenever a child experiences any traumatic event (e.g., the death of a grandparent).
    c. only after they have attempted to "treat" the problem on their own.
    d. whenever a child is displaying a severe problem (e.g., depression, drug addiction).

Answers for Self Test A

1. adolescent egocentrism
2. index offenses
3. David Elkind
4. menarche
5. imaginary audience
6. Joan Lipsitt
7. anorexia nervosa
8. juvenile delinquency
9. Joy Dryfoos
10. top-dog phenomenon
11. Lloyd Johnston, Patrick O'Malley, or Gerald Bachman
12. estradiol

Answers for Self Test B

1. b LO 2.1
2. b LO 2.2
3. b LO 2.3
4. b LO 2.5
5. a LO 2.6
6. d LO 2.6
7. a LO 2.7
8. a LO 2.9
9. d LO 3.1
10. d LO 3.3
11. b LO 3.4
12. d LO 3.6
13. d LO 3.7
14. b LO 4.2
15. c LO 4.4
16. b LO 4.7
17. b LO 4.8
18. d LO 4.9
19. d LO 4.11
20. a LO 4.14
21. a LO 5.2
22. d LO 5.7
23. a LO 5.9
24. d LO 5.9
25. c LO 5.13
26. a LO 5.17
27. d LO 5.21
28. b LO 5.22
29. c LO 5.24
30. a LO 5.25
31. d LO 5.26
32. d LO 5.27
33. d LO 6.3
34. d LO 6.4
35. d LO 7.4

Chapter 13   Socioemotional Development in Adolescence

Learning Objectives with Key Terms in Boldface

1.0 Families

A. *Autonomy and Attachment*

1.1 Explain why adolescents' push for autonomy puzzles and angers parents.

1.2 Describe appropriate adult reactions to an adolescent's desire for control.

1.3 Explain how attachment promotes the personal development of adolescents.

1.4 Cite evidence for the claims that secure attachment promotes competent peer relations and positive relationships with other people.

B. *Parent-Adolescent Conflict*

1.5 Explain how biological change, cognitive change, social change, and personality change each could cause increased conflict between children and their parents during adolescence.

1.6 Sketch developmentally appropriate responses by parents to conflict.

1.7 Outline developmental trends for parent-adolescent conflict over the teen years.

1.8 Explain how everyday conflicts may serve positive developmental functions.

1.9 Use Figure 13.1 to compare and contrast old and new models of parent-adolescent relationships.

1.10 Indicate the incidence and correlates of unhealthy conflicts between parents and their adolescents.

C. *The Maturation of Adolescents and Parents*

1.11 Indicate concurrent changes in adolescents and their parents that influence their interactions.

2.0 Peers

A. *Peer Pressure and Conformity*

2.1 Explain how conformity to peer pressure in adolescence can be both positive and negative.

2.2 Compare and contrast conformity in childhood and adolescence.

B. *Cliques and Crowds*

2.3 Define and distinguish between **crowds** and **cliques**.

2.4 Explain how clique or crowd membership could increase parent-adolescent conflict.

2.5 Describe leading crowds in American high schools.

2.6 List the typical types of crowds found in high schools.

2.7 Describe how crowd membership relates to self-esteem.

C. *Adolescent Groups versus Children Groups*

2.8 Compare and contrast children's and adolescents' groups.

2.9 Speculate on the impact of ethnic status on peer group formation in ethnically mixed schools.

2.10 Explain why ethnic youth may have two or more social networks.

2.11 Describe trends during adolescence for opposite-sex participation in groups during adolescence.

D. *Youth Organizations*

2.12 Characterize the nature and extent of youth organizations in the United States.

2.13 Indicate characteristics of adolescents who participate in youth organizations.

2.14 Describe what Girls Clubs and Boys Clubs are doing to involve low-income and ethnic minority students in youth organizations, and the effects of their efforts.

E. *Dating*

2.15 List the functions of dating.

2.16 Describe the onset and incidence of dating in the United States during adolescence.

2.17 Define **dating scripts** and give examples of male and female dating scripts.

2.18 Compare the dating standards of White, Asian, and Hispanic adolescents to show how sociocultural context exerts an influence on dating patterns.

3.0 Culture and Adolescent Development

A. Cross-Cultural Comparisons and Rites of Passage

3.1 Explain how cross-cultural studies expand our knowledge about adolescence and guard against overgeneralizations.

3.2 Define **cross-cultural studies**.

3.3 Define **rites of passage** and explain its function.

3.4 Indicate where rites of passage still exist today.

3.5 Discuss whether there are any universal rites of passage in the United States.

3.6 Explain how the absence of clear cut passages can make the transition to adulthood ambiguous.

B. Ethnicity

3.7 Explain the idea that social class confounds ethnic explanations for adolescent development.

3.8 Explain the concept of "model minority" and discuss why middle class minorities cannot escape their ethnic minority status.

3.9 Identify the double disadvantage ethnic minority adolescents experience.

3.10 Discuss why it is important to recognize differences between ethnic groups.

3.11 Explain why it is important to recognize diversity within an ethnic group.

3.12 Give an example of how value conflicts are involved when individuals respond to ethnic issues.

3.13 Define and distinguish between **assimilation** and **pluralism**.

3.14 Discuss how the assimilation approach to ethnic issues is resurfacing with a more complex face.

3.15 Discuss Stanley Sue's view of how to resolve the conflict between the assimilation and pluralism views.

4.0 Identity

4.1 Sketch Erik Erikson's view of the experience of adolescence.

A. Some Contemporary Thoughts About Identity

4.2 Identify important considerations about the process of identity formation suggested by contemporary views of adolescence.

4.3 Identify the core elements of identity.

B. The Four Statuses of Identity

4.4 Define and distinguish between **crisis** and **commitment**.

4.5 Define and distinguish among **identity diffusion**, **identity foreclosure**, and **identity moratorium**, and **identity achievement**.

C. Developmental Changes

4.6 Explain why researchers such as Alan Waterman think that the most important changes in identity happen during youth, not adolescence.

4.7 Explain the concept of "MAMA."

D. Family Influences on Identity

4.8 Relate parenting styles to identity status outcomes.

4.9 Define and distinguish between **individuality** and **connectedness**, and discuss their role in identity development.

E. Cultural and Ethnic Aspects of Identity

4.10 Note Erik Erikson's views on how struggle for identity relates to cultural development.

4.11 Explain why adolescence is special to the development of ethnic minority individuals.

4.12 Explain how discrimination may influence ethnic minority youths' identities.

4.13 Explain how lack of successful ethnic minority role models is a concern for ethnic minority youth.

4.14 Compare and contrast the identity concerns of Asian, Black, Hispanic, and White American adolescents.

4.15 Indicate how context is important to the development of identity in ethnic minority youth.

4.16 Indicate how youth organizations may play a role in the identity of ethnic minority youth.

F. *Gender and Identity Development*

4.17 Indicate Erik Erikson's views on sex differences in identity development.

4.18 Cite evidence that the order of Erikson's developmental stages is different for males and females.

4.19 Discuss whether finding an identity is equally difficult for females and males.

5.0 Religious Development

5.1 Discuss evidence that religious indoctrination works.

5.2 Cite evidence that religious issues are important to adolescents.

A. *Developmental Changes*

5.3 Explain why adolescence is an important juncture in religious development.

5.4 Describe Piagetian cognitive stages in the development of religious thought.

B. *Religiousness and Sexuality in Adolescence*

5.5 Discuss religion's influence on diverse aspects of adolescent sexual activity.

C. *Fowler's Developmental Theory*

5.6 Describe the six stages of James Fowler's theory of religious development.

5.7 Indicate concerns about Fowler's theory.

6.0 Chapter Boxes

A. *Sociocultural Worlds of Development: Education and the Development of Ethnic Minority Adolescents*

6.1 Indicate how parenting style relates to academic achievement.

6.2 Indicate how variations in parenting style and family structure relate to achievement in various ethnic minority adolescents.

6.3 Describe Dr. Henry Gaskins's after school tutoring program in Washington, D.C.

B. *Critical Thinking About Life-Span Development: Age Trends in Parents of Adolescents and Parent-Adolescent Relationships*

6.4 Use life-span developmental concepts to speculate about how the relatively older age of future adolescents' parents will affect the nature of parent-adolescent relationships.

C. *Critical Thinking About Life-Span Development: Exploring Your Identity Development*

6.5 Use life-span development concepts to explore your own identity formation.

D. *Life-Span Health and Well-Being: El Puente*

6.6 Describe the needs that led to the establishment of El Puente, its nature, and its successes to date.

Guided Review and Study

1.0 Families

A. *Autonomy and Attachment*

1. Explain why adolescents' push for autonomy and responsibility angers many parents.

2. Parents can foster autonomy in adolescents by relinquishing _____ in areas in which _____ decisions can be made and guiding decisions in areas in which the adolescent's knowledge is more _____ .

3. A secure _____ and conntectedness to parents during adolescence provides a base from which adolescents can explore their widening _____ world.

4. Secure attachment promotes both _____ relations and positive close relationships _____ the family.

5. Characterize the relationship between secure and insecure attachment and peer relations and positive close relationships outside the family.

control
reasonable
limited
attachment
social
peer
outside

B. Parent-Adolescent Conflict

1. The _____ between parents and adolescents may be due to the biological changes of puberty, cognitive changes, social changes, maturation in parents, and violated expectations.   *conflict*

2. Characterize alternative parental approaches to dealing with conflicts with their adolescents.

3. The everyday conflicts between parents and adolescents _____ involve dilemmas like drugs and delinquency.   *rarely*

4. Conflict between parents and adolescents reaches its peak in _____ adolescence.   *early*

5. Explain how everyday conflicts between adolescents and their parents contribute to adolescents' identity development.

6. The _____ model of parent-adolescent relations suggested that conflict is intense and stressful throughout adolescence.   *old*

7. The _____ model of parent-adolescent relations emphasizes that conflict is moderate and may facilitate the development of autonomy.   *new*

8. Approximately _____ percent of American families experience intense and prolonged conflict between adolescents and parents.   *20*

9. Prolong, intense conflict is associated with adolescent _____ .   *problems*

C. The Maturation of Adolescents and Parents

1. Summarize the concurrent changes in adolescents and their parents that influence their interactions.

2.0 Peers

A. Peer Pressure and Conformity

1. Define *peer pressure* in your own terms.

2. Conformity to peer pressure can be positive or _____ .   *negative*

3. Conformity to peer pressure is _____ in the eighth and ninth grades.   *greatest*

B. Cliques and Crowds

1. The _____ exists as a result of a mutual interest in activities, whereas the members of a _____ are attracted to each other.   *crowd*
   clique

2. Cliques are _____ , involve greater intimacy, and have more group _____ than crowds.   *smaller*
   cohesion

3. Explain why group identity often overrides personal identity among adolescents.

4. The classic study by James Coleman found that the leading crowds in high school were likely to be composed of _____ and _____ girls.   *athletes*
   popular

5. _____ membership has been shown to be related to self-esteem.   *Clique*

6. The self-_____ of jocks and populars was higher than any other group except _____ who claimed that clique membership was not important to them.   *esteem*
   independents

7. The relationship between clique membership and self-esteem is _____ so no causal statements can be made.   *correlational*

C. Adolescent Groups versus Children Groups

1. Contrast childrens' and adolescents' groups.

2. Ethnic minority children become more aware of their ethnic minority _____ during adolescence. *status*

3 Explain why ethnic minority children may belong to one peer group at school and another peer group in their community.

4. Dexter Dunphy observed that during _____ adolescence, same-sex cliques begin to interact with each other; however, in _____ adolescence, the crowd begins to dissolve and couples begin to emerge. *early* *late*

D. Youth Organizations

1. Youth organization encompass career groups, _____ groups, and ethnic groups. *political*

2. Characterize the benefits to adolescents of belonging to youth organizations.

3. Boys and Girls Clubs are examples of _____ organizations established in a number of cities to enhance low-income and ethnic minority adolescents' educational and _____ development. *youth* *personal*

4. Boys and Girls Clubs _____ vandalism, drug abuse, and delinquency. *reduce*

1. Indicate four functions of dating.

2. Most _____ begin to date at age 14, whereas _____ begin between 14 and 15. *girls; boys*

3. Most adolescents have their first date between the ages of _____ . *12 and 16*

4. Three out of _____ high school students have gone steady at least once by the end of high school. *4*

5. Female adolescents bring a _____ desire for intimacy and personality exploration to dating than do male adolescents. *stronger*

6. Explain what it means to say that adolescent dating is a context that intensifies gender-role expectations.

7. Dating _____ are cognitive models that individuals use to guide their dating interactions. *scripts*

8. Explain what it means to say that males follow a proactive dating script whereas females follow a reactive dating script.

9. _____ contexts influence adolescent dating patterns. *Sociocultural*

3.0 Culture and Adolescent Development

A. Cross-Cultural Comparisons and Rites of Passage

1. Studies of adolescents in a single culture are likely to produce _____ -generalizations about adolescents. *over*

2. _____-cultural studies identify which aspects of development are universal and which aspects are culture-_____ . *Cross* *specific*

3. A _____ of passage is a ceremony or a ritual that marks an individual's transition from one status to another, and is usually characterized by some form of ritual death and _____ . *rite* *rebirth*

4. Indicate possible rites of passage for American adolescents.

5. The absence of clear-cut rites of passage make the attainment of adult status _____ . *ambiguous*

B. Ethnicity

1. _____ refers to membership in a particular group with distinctive cultural heritage, nationality characteristics, race, religion, and language.

    Ethnicity

2. Distinguish between ethnicity and social class.

3. Much research on ethnic minority adolescents does not distinguish the influences of ethnicity from those due to _____ class.

    social

4. Explain the concept of *model minority*.

5. In addition to _____ , many ethnic minority individuals in the United States continue to experience prejudice, _____ , and bias.

    poverty
    discrimination

6. Historical, economic, and social influences produce legitimate _____ between various ethnic minority groups, and between ethnic minority groups and the majority White group.

    differences

7. Indicate what it means to say that the behavior of individuals living in a particular ethnic or cultural group is often functional for them.

8. The concept of ethnic diversity implies that ethnic minority groups have _____ social, historical, and economic backgrounds.

    different

9. Indicate why Asians are an ethnically diverse group.

10. Explain why it is important to recognize diversity within an ethnic group.

11. Stanley Sue proposes that _____ conflicts enter into many ethnic issues.

    values

12. _____ refers to an ethnic minority group's absorption by the dominant group, whereas _____ refers to a coexistence between distinct ethnic and cultural groups.

    Assimilation
    pluralism

13. Explain how proponents of assimilation and pluralism appear to be on opposite sides of a values conflict when discussing the best approach to ethnic diversity.

14. Stanley Sue proposes that the resolution of value conflicts about sociocultural issues requires _____ issues, or considerable open mindedness.

    redefining

4.0 Identity

1. Erik Erikson produced the most comprehensive and provocative theory of _____ development.

    identity

2. According to Erikson, _____ versus identity _____ is the fifth psychosocial stage that occurs during adolescence.

    identity
    confusion

3. According to Erikson, the adolescent enters a psychological _____ during which he or she tries several _____ .

    moratorium
    roles

4. Adolescents who cope with the conflicting identities develop a new sense of _____ ; however, adolescents who do not successfully resolve their identity _____ remain confused and may withdraw from society or lose themselves in the _____ .

    self
    crisis
    crowd

A. Some Contemporary Thoughts About Identity

1. Contemporary views indicate that identity development is a _____ process, and one that is also extraordinarily _____ .

    lengthy
    complex

2. Identity development begins _____ adolescence, and also continues _____ adolescence.

    before; after

3. Identity development minimally entails a _____ direction, an ideological stance, and a _____ orientation.   *vocational*
   sexual

B. *The Four Statuses of Identity*

1. James Marcia believes that Erikson's theory allows _____ statuses of identity or ways of resolving identity crisis.   *four*

2. Marcia's four identity statuses are defined in terms of an adolescent's _____ and _____ .   *crisis*
   commitment

3. Indicate how identity theorists define the concepts of *crisis* and *commitment*.

4. When adolescents have neither experienced a crisis nor made any commitments, they experience identity _____ . For example, adolescents who show little or no interest in choosing an occupation or adopting a belief system are experiencing identity _____ .   *diffusion*
   diffusion

5. Adolescents who make a commitment without having gone through a crisis are experiencing identity _____ . For example, an adolescent who decides to go into the family business without exploring other options is most likely experiencing identity _____ .   *foreclosure*
   foreclosure

6. Adolescents who are in the midst of the crisis but have not yet made a commitment are in the identity _____ status. For example, an adolescent who wants to be a lawyer one day, a stay-at-home parent the next, and an interior designer the next is experiencing identity _____ .   *moratorium*
   moratorium

7. Adolescents who have undergone a crisis and made a commitment to a career path or a life-style have experienced identity _____ . For example, the adolescent who considers all the options and then chooses to attend college after high school has undergone identity _____ .   *achievement*
   achievement

C. *Developmental Changes*

1. Three aspects of a young adolescent's identity development include confidence in _____ support, a sense of industry, and a self-reflective perspective on the _____ .   *parental*
   future

2. Summarize the research by Alan Waterman that shows the most important changes in identity occur in youth rather than adolescence.

3. Many researchers contend that the common pattern for individuals who develop a positive identity is one called _____ , and that MAMA cycles _____ throughout one's life.   *MAMA*
   repeat

D. *Family Influences on Identity*

1. Family _____ affect identity development.   *influences*

2. Democratic parenting encourages identity _____ , autocratic parenting fosters identity foreclosure, and permissive parenting encourages identity _____ .   *achievement*
   diffusion

3. Individuality is composed of self-assertion and _____ ; whereas connectedness includes _____ and permeability in parent-child relationships.   *separateness*
   mutuality

4. Express the meaning of *individuality* and *connectedness* in your own terms.

5. Identity formation is _____ by family relationships that are both individuated and connected.   *enhanced*

E. *Cultural and Ethnic Aspects of Identity*

1. Erik Erikson is _____ to the role of culture in identity development. For example, he claims that the struggle for inclusive _____ has been the driving force in the founding of churches, empires, and revolutions.   *sensitive*
   identity

2. Adolescence is an important time for ethnic minority individuals who must confront their _____ and associated negative appraisals, _____ values, and career considerations.   *ethnicity*
   conflicting

3. One concern is that ethnic minority youth lack _____ models with whom to identify.   *role*

4. Research has shown that identity exploration is _____ among ethnic minority than White American college students.   *greater*

5. Compare and contrast concerns for adolescents who are African American, Asian American, and Latino American.

6. Social _____ also influence identity development.   *contexts*
7. Indicate what Shirley Heath and Milbrey McLaughlin learned about the relationship between youth organizations and the identity development of ethnic minority youths.

F. Gender and Identity Development

1. Although Erikson initially proposed that identity development is largely determined by one's _____ , recent studies have revealed that sex differences have turned into _____ .   *gender*
   similarities
2. The contemporary view is that identity formation precedes the stage of intimacy for _____ , whereas intimacy precedes identity for _____ .   *males*
   females
3. Identity formation may be _____ complex for females than males.   *more*

5.0 Religious Development

1. Summarize evidence that religious indoctrination works.

2. Evidence indicates that religious issues are _____ to adolescents.   *important*

A. Developmental Changes

1. Adolescence is an important juncture in _____ development.   *religious*
2. Jean Piaget identified _____ cognitive stages in the development of religious thought.   *three*
3. Characterize preoperational intuitive religious thought according to Jean Piaget.

4. Characterize concrete operational intuitive thought according to Jean Piaget.

5. Characterize formal operational religious thought according to Jean Piaget.

6. Research reveals _____ religious developmental changes in children and adolescents.   *similar*

B. Religiousness and Sexuality in Adolescence

1. The extent to which adolescents participate in religious organizations relates to their _____ sexual attitudes and behavior.   *premarital*
2. Indicate the relationship between religious participation and sexual activities among adolescents.

C. Fowler's Developmental Theory

1. Label and then characterize James Fowler's six stages in religious development:
   Stage 1

   Stage 2

Stage 3

Stage 4

Stage 5

Stage 6

2. Critics say Fowler's theory does not adequately address _____ differences in religious   *individual*
development.

6.0   Chapter Boxes

 A. *Sociocultural Worlds of Development: Education and the Development of Ethnic Minority Adolescents*

  1. Relate parenting styles to the academic achievement.

  2. Single-parent families and _____ contribute to poor school performance by ethnic minority   *poverty*
adolescents.

  3. Describe Dr. Henry Gaskins's after school tutoring program in Washington, D.C.

 B. *Critical Thinking About Life-Span Development: Age Trends in the Parents of Adolescents and Parent-Adolescent Relationships*

  1. Use life-span developmental concepts to speculate about how the relatively older age of future
adolescents' parents will affect the nature of parent-adolescent relationships.

   Critical Thinking About Life-Span Development: Exploring Your Identity Development

  1. Indicate what you learned by exploring your own identity formation.

 D. *Life-Span Health and Well-Being: El Puente*

  1. El Puente was the result of community _____ with health, education, and social services   *dissatisfaction*
for youth in New York City.

  2. Describe the El Puente approach.

Self Test A: Key Terms and Key Persons

Write the appropriate key term or key person in the space to the right of the definition or description.

1. A group whose members share a mutual interest in activities rather than a mutual attraction.   _____

2. The individual who contends that value conflicts often occur whenever individuals respond to   _____
ethnic issues.

3. In James Marcia's theory, this term describes adolescents who have undergone a crisis and have   _____
made a commitment.

4. A social condition in which various distinct cultural, ethnic, or religious groups coexist within a single nation. _____

5. The psychologist who says that Erik Erikson's theory contains four different developmental statuses. _____

6. Cognitive models that individuals use to guide and evaluate their dating interactions. _____

7. In James Marcia's theory, an adolescent who has neither experienced a crisis nor made a commitment. _____

8 The author of a widely cited study of adolescent cliques and crowds. _____

9. The process by which members of one culture become completely absorbed into a more dominant culture. _____

10. A group whose members are attracted to one another on the basis of similar interests and social ideals. _____

11. A concept that consists of the two dimensions of mutuality and permeability. _____

12. Either of the two individuals who studied over 24,000 adolescents in 60 different youth groups over a period of five years. _____

Self Test B: Multiple Choice

1. Parents who want their adolescents to make the smoothest transition into adulthood should
   a. relinquish control in all areas and let the adolescent take over.
   b. maintain control in as many areas as possible for as long as possible.
   c. relinquish control in areas that the adolescent has shown some competence and maintain control in those areas where the adolescent's knowledge is limited.
   d. maintain control for issues having to do with family and relinquish control for those issues having to do with peer relations.

2. If 16-year-old Talia has a secure attachment with her parents, one might predict that she will also
   a. have trouble breaking away from her parents to form relationships with age-peers.
   b. tend to be more dependent in her relationship with her best friend.
   c. have a lower sense of her self-worth.
   d. have a secure relationship with her spouse.

3. Conflicts between parents and adolescents are most likely to revolve around all of the following except
   a. keeping bedrooms clean.
   b. getting home on time.
   c. taking drugs.
   d. talking on the phone.

4. A parent who storms at her daughter, "You're 14 now I shouldn't have to tell you to pick up your room!" probably
   a. recognizes that reasoning is essential to disciplining a child.
   b. provides an appropriate change in demands that will foster greater autonomy.
   c. is unusual and probably harming her daughter's sense of responsibility.
   d. needs to realize that mastering the tasks of adolescence takes time.

5. Which of the following *has not* been associated with long-term, negative parent-adolescent interactions?
   a. joining religious cults
   b. drug abuse
   c. refusing to move away from home
   d. teenage pregnancy

6. The effects of parent-adolescent conflict on the parents' marriage
   a. bring the parents closer together.
   b. cause minor marital dissatisfaction.
   c. are the major cause of divorce.
   d. lead to greater levels of marital dissatisfaction than any other period of development.

7. A ninth grader hanging around with other ninth graders is likely to be found
   a. arguing over the latest political issues.
   b. deciding who is going to be first to steal their teacher's hubcap.
   c. helping the others do their chores.
   d. playing at the local playground.

8. Compared to children's cliques, adolescents' cliques are more likely to
   a. be made up of many types of individuals.
   b. have both male and female members.
   c. contain individuals who are not friends.
   d. be smaller.

9. In 1961 James Coleman found that high-school leaders were most often
   a. athletes.
   b. females.
   c. intelligent.
   d. rich.

10. A study of clique membership revealed that the individuals with the lowest self-esteem were the
    a. jocks.
    b. populars.
    c. druggies.
    d. nobodies.

11. Which of the following school groups appears to enjoy the highest self-esteem?
    a. normals
    b. druggies
    c. brains
    d. independents

12. Children's groups differ from those formed by adolescents in that they
    a. have fewer rules.
    b. rely more on the leaders of the groups.
    c. have more interests in common.
    d. include more minorities.

13. Ethnic-minority adolescents are more likely than White students to
    a. have a separate set of community peers of the same ethnic background.
    b. be classified as a "popular".
    c. hang around in same-sexed groups.
    d. be unconcerned about their ethnic status.

14. About three out of every four high school students
    a. have gone steady by the end of high school.
    b. date more than once a week.
    c. have dated before the age of 12.
    d. date less than once a month.

15. Dating entails all of the following except
    a. stronger desire for intimacy by females
    b. stronger desire for personality exploration by males
    c. pressure to perform in a gender-appropriate manner for males
    d. pressure to perform in a gender-appropriate manner for females

16. Culture can influence
    a. when a person can date.
    b. whom a person can date.
    c. what conditions must be in effect when dating takes place.
    d. All of the answers are correct.

17. Rites of passage into adulthood are usually
    a. continuous and peaceful.
    b. discontinuous and forceful.
    c. tied to intellectual readiness.
    d. initiated by the adolescent.

18. What feature of adolescence in American culture is highlighted by the existence of rites of passage in other cultures?
    a. There are many points of transition to adulthood in American culture.
    b. Abrupt entry into adulthood in American culture.
    c. The end of adolescence in American culture is more clearly marked by biological change than by social milestones.
    d. No specific event marks the end of adolescence in American culture.

19. One of the major limitations of studies on the effects of ethnicity is that the factor of _____ may play a larger causal role than ethnic heritage, but it is very difficult to tease the two variables apart.
    a. race
    b. innate physical variation
    c. language
    d. socioeconomic level

20. The term *model minority* best fits
    a. Carlos, who is Mexican.
    b. Akayo, who is Japanese.
    c. Marinella, who is Italian.
    d. Sandrine, who is French.

21. If a government decided to incorporate a new ethnic-minority group through assimilation, one of the first laws passed might be to
    a. require that several museums dedicated to that culture be set up in major cities.
    b. make racially motivated crimes punishable by death.
    c. ban use of that minority's language in schools.
    d. select at least one of the minority group's celebrations and make it a national holiday.

22. Which would you likely find in a country driven by ethnic pluralism?
    a. high schools being required to teach courses in the history of minority cultures
    b. tremendous internal racism
    c. great consensus on what the "average" person within that country is like
    d. virtually no foreign characters on prime-time television shows

23. Stanley Sue (1990) suggests that the assimilation/pluralism aspect of ethnic integration can best be dealt with by
    a. restricting immigration for a period of time.
    b. a national referendum designed to determine what the majority of individuals within a culture believe is appropriate.
    c. eliminating all culturally specific institutions.
    d. a fluctuating set of characteristics for defining what functional skills are necessary for success within a culture.

24. The adolescent identity crisis is a period
    a. of confusion during which youth are choosing between attachment and autonomy.
    b. when adolescents are actively making decisions about whom they want to be.
    c. when adolescents actively avoid commitment to ideas or occupations.
    d. of intense turmoil and stress that lasts a short time and determines an adolescent's identity status.

25. Erikson says it ". . . is never established in the form of a personality armor, or anything static and unchangeable." He is describing the
    a. psychological moratorium.
    b. nature of identity.
    c. nature of crisis.
    d. influence of culture on identity.

26. According to Erikson, the individual who is caught between the security of childhood and the autonomy of adulthood is in
    a. adolescence.
    b. a diffused state.
    c. a psychological moratorium.
    d. early adulthood.

27. James Marcia (1966, 1991) uses the term _____ to refer to the amount of personal investment a person has about an idea or issue.
    a. value
    b. desire
    c. commitment
    d. involvement

28. Asked about whether they ever had doubts about their religion, four students gave the following answers. Who has arrived at identity achievement?
    a. Kristin: "Oh, I don't know. It really doesn't bother me. I figure one's about as good as another."
    b. Joe: "No, not really. Our family is pretty much in agreement about these things."
    c. Alicia: "Yes, I guess I'm going through that right now. How can there be a God and so much evil in the world?"
    d. Phil: "Yeah, I even started wondering whether there was a God. I've pretty much resolved that, though."

29. A high school student who has explored all of the employment and educational options and has chosen to attend the state college near home is experiencing identity
    a. diffusion.
    b. foreclosure.
    c. moratorium.
    d. achievement.

30. It is believed that the most common identity-status pattern involves a _____ cycle.
    a. moratorium-achiever-moratorium-achiever
    b. diffusion-foreclosure-diffusion-foreclosure
    c. moratorium-foreclosure-moratorium-foreclosure
    d. diffusion-achiever-diffusion-achiever

31. Authoritarian parents are most likely to have adolescents experiencing identity
    a. diffusion.
    b. foreclosure.
    c. moratorium.
    d. achievement.

32. Parent-adolescent relations that involve mutuality and permeability enhance
    a. attachment.
    b. individuation.
    c. connectedness.
    d. self-assertion.

33. Another way of stating Cooper and Grotevants's point about the need for connectedness and individuation in adolescent identity development is that identity development requires
    a. separation and conflict.
    b. obedience and self-regulation.
    c. family and peer relations.
    d. attachment and autonomy.

34. Which statement best reflects Erik Erikson's (1968) hypothesis concerning the relationship between culture and identity development?
    a. Culture plays a critical role in identity development
    b. In some individuals, cultural factors may play a role in identity development
    c. For all individuals, cultural factors play a minor role in identity development
    d. Cultural factors have no influence on identity development

35. Most ethnic minorities first consciously confront their ethnicity in
    a. early childhood.
    b. middle childhood.
    c. adolescence.
    d. young adulthood.

36. When compared to Black, White, and Hispanic American adolescents, Asian adolescents raised in America are concerned most with
    a. prejudice.
    b. academic achievement.
    c. job discrimination.
    d. standards of comparison for beauty.

37. Several research studies carried out in the late 1980s and early 1990s suggest that positive female identity may be related to
    a. a strong bond with a female mentor.
    b. the ability to deal effectively with interpersonal relationships.
    c. a strong need for career achievement.
    d. a masculine gender-orientation.

38. Henry Gaskins (1983) has designed an effective minority program based on
    a. one-on-one tutoring with adult volunteers.
    b. emphasizing the importance of being proud of one's ethnic heritage.
    c. the principles of Head Start.
    d. pairing troubled minority youths with high-functioning White youths during an intensive summer-camp experience.

Answers for Self Test A

1. crowd
2. Stanley Sue
3. identity achievement
4. pluralism
5. James Marcia
6. dating scripts
7. identity diffusion
8. James Coleman
9. assimilation
10. clique
11. connectedness
12. Shirley Heath or Milbrey McLaughin

Answers for Self Test B

1. c   LO 1.2
2. d   LO 1.4
3. c   LO 1.7
4. d   LO 1.9
5. c   LO 1.10
6. d   LO 1.11
7. b   LO 2.1
8. b   LO 2.5
9. a   LO 2.5
10. d   LO 2.5
11. d   LO 2.7
12. a   LO 2.8
13. a   LO 2.9
14. a   LO 2.16
15. b   LO 2.17
16. d   LO 2.18
17. b   LO 3.3
18. d   LO 3.5
19. d   LO 3.7
20. b   LO 3.8
21. c   LO 3.13
22. a   LO 3.13
23. d   LO 3.15
24. b   LO 4.1
25. b   LO 4.1
26. c   LO 4.1
27. c   LO 4.4
28. d   LO 4.5
29. d   LO 4.5
30. a   LO 4.7
31. b   LO 4.8
32. c   LO 4.9
33. d   LO 4.9
34. a   LO 4.10
35. c   LO 4.11
36. b   LO 4.14
37. d   LO 4.18
38. a   LO 6.3

Chapter 14   Physical and Cognitive Development in Early Adulthood

Learning Objectives with Key Terms in Boldface

1.0 The Transition from Adolescence to Adulthood

  A. *Youth and the Criteria for Becoming an Adult*

   1.1 Explain why it is hard to determine the beginning of adulthood.

   1.2 Define **youth** according to Kenneth Kenniston and distinguish it from adolescence and adulthood.

   1.3 Identify markers for entering adulthood.

   1.4 Explain how the transition from adolescence to adulthood is continuous and produces stability, but may be discontinuous and produce change.

  B. *The Transition from High School to College*

   1.5 Compare and contrast the transition from high school to college with the transition from elementary school to middle school or junior high school.

   1.6 Indicate recent trends in college students' experience of stress and depression.

   1.7 Define **burnout**, describe its incidence, and discuss how college students can deal with it.

2.0 Physical Development

  A. *The Peak and Slowdown in Physical Performance*

   2.1 Compare and contrast peak ages for strength and speed events versus events requiring diverse motor and cognitive skills for athletic performances of men and women.

   2.2 Describe college students' health, their knowledge about healthy behavior, and their ability to assess their own health risks.

   2.3 Describe developmental trends in drug use during youth.

   2.4 Sketch aspects of unhealthy life-styles among college students.

   2.5 Describe declines in physical performance during adulthood.

  B. *Obesity and Dieting*

   2.6 Describe and evaluate evidence for heredity as a factor in human obesity.

   2.7 Define and distinguish between **set point** and **basal metabolism rate (BMR).**

   2.8 Discuss the roles of set point and BMR in weight gain during early adulthood.

   2.9 Indicate sociocultural factors likely to be involved in weight gain and obesity.

   2.10 State the economic cost of obesity.

   2.11 Identify controversies concerning the value of dieting.

   2.12 Indicate the incidence of concern for weight and dieting among men and women.

   2.13 Evaluate presently available data on whether dieting is a health risk.

   2.14 Indicate what we know about whether diets work.

   2.15 Indicate possible harmful outcomes of dieting.

   2.16 Evaluate the contribution of exercise to weight loss efforts.

   2.17 Indicate whether we know who should diet.

  C. *Exercise*

   2.18 Define **aerobic exercise**, show how to calculate optimal levels of it, and indicate evidence that it prevents heart disease.

   2.19 Describe relatively painless forms of healthy exercise.

   2.20 List mental health benefits of exercise, and indicate evidence that moderate exercise produces the best results.

   2.21 State optimal levels of exercise for American adults.

  D. *Addiction and Recovery*

   2.22 Define **psychoactive drug.**

2.23 Define and distinguish among **tolerance, physical dependence**, and **psychological dependence** on drugs.

2.24 Indicate the incidence and consequences of alcohol abuse.

2.25 Describe the effects of alcohol use, and explain how alcohol, a depressant, loosens inhibitions.

2.26 Discuss explanations of alcoholism.

2.27 Evaluate the success of Alcoholics Anonymous (AA).

2.28 Compare and contrast AA with alternative programs.

3.0 Sexuality

A. *Heterosexual Attitudes and Behavior*

3.1 Describe and evaluate the evidence for two important trends in heterosexual behavior between 1900 and 1980.

3.2 Cite key findings in the 1994 sex in America survey.

3.3 Contrast the findings of the 1994 sex survey with those reported in magazine polls and Alfred Kinsey's data.

B. *Homosexual Attitudes and Behavior*

3.4 Explain why it is difficult to distinguish heterosexual and homosexual orientations, and define **bisexual**.

3.5 Indicate the prevalence of homosexual adults and recent trends in acceptance of them.

3.6 Discuss what we do and do not know about the causes of sexual orientation.

3.7 Explain how adopting a bicultural identity can help gays and lesbians adapt to being a minority.

3.8 Explain how heterosexuals can better understand lesbian and gay realities.

C. *AIDS*

3.9 Define **AIDS** and describe its prevalence in the United States.

3.10 List ways AIDS can be transmitted and explain why there is no such thing as "safe sex."

3.11 Cite evidence that young adults are not truthful to each other about their sexual histories.

3.12 Characterize the course of AIDS.

D. *Sexual Knowledge*

3.13 Describe the sexual knowledge of adolescents and adults in the United States.

3.14 Define and distinguish between sexual messages and sexual facts, and discuss which are more influential in the United States.

3.15 Explain why it is so difficult to develop a sexual identity.

E. *The Menstrual Cycle and Hormones*

3.16 Discuss what we do and do not know about mood changes women experience during the menstrual cycle.

F. *Forcible Sexual Behavior*

3.17 Define and distinguish between **rape** and **date or acquaintance rape**, and indicate their incidence.

3.18 List reasons why rape is pervasive in American culture.

3.19 Describe the consequences of rape suffered by its victims, and characterize varieties of rape experienced by men and women.

G. *Sexual Harassment*

3.20 Describe the nature and incidence of sexual harassment.

3.21 Suggest ways to eliminate sexual harassment.

4.0 Cognitive Development

A. *Cognitive Stages*

4.1 Compare and contrast adolescent and adult thoughts according to the theories of Jean Piaget and Gisela Labouvie-Vief.

4.2 Evaluate the claims of Piaget's and Labouvie-Vief's theories.

4.3 Define and distinguish among William Perry's dualistic thinking, multiple thinking, relative subordinate thinking, and relativism.

4.4 Sketch Jan Sinott's views of cognitive change in early adulthood.

4.5 Define and distinguish among K. Warner Schaie's **achieving stage, responsibility stage, executive stage**, and **reintegrative stage** of adult cognitive development.

4.6 Use Table 14.2 to compare and contrast the ideas of Piaget, Labouvie-Vief, Perry, and Schaie.

B. *Creativity*

4.7 Describe various courses of creativity in different fields during adult life.

5.0 Careers and Work
  A. Theories of Career Development
    5.1 Define and distinguish among the fantasy stage, tentative stage, and realistic stage of Eli Ginzberg's **developmental theory of career choice**.
    5.2 Discuss criticisms of Ginzberg's theory.
    5.3 Define and distinguish among the concepts of crystallization, specification, implementation, stabilization, and consolidation in Donald Super's **career self concept theory**.
    5.4 Define and distinguish among the realistic, investigative, artistic, social, enterprising, and conventional career personalities in John Holland's **personality type theory**.
    5.5 Evaluate personality type theory.
  B. Exploration, Planning, and Decision Making
    5.6 Explain why career counselors recommend exploring career options, and describe the usual career planning of adolescents and young adults.
  C. The Life Contour of Work and Adulthood
    5.7 Define and distinguish between selection/entry and adjustment to an occupation in adulthood.
    5.8 Describe variability in levels of attainment reached by individuals in their early thirties.
  D. Women and Work
    5.9 Explain why women have new work roles in modern America.
    5.10 Describe women's involvement in the work force over the past 30 years.
    5.11 Define the "glass ceiling" that professional women encounter.
    5.12 Sketch the major career choices of modern women.
    5.13 Discuss the advantages and disadvantages of dual-career marriages for wives and husbands.
6.0 Chapter Boxes
  A. Sociocultural Worlds of Development: Juggling Roles
    6.1 Characterize the pleasures and pains of being a "juggler," a woman who is involved both in raising a family and pursuing a career.
    6.2 Discuss how the lives of jugglers could be improved through improved daycare and social policy.
  B. Critical Thinking About Life-Span Development: Evaluating the Accuracy of Claims About Sexuality
    6.3 Identify questions you should ask about cause-effect claims relating to sexuality (and any other claim about cause and effect).
  C. Critical Thinking About Life-Span Development: Career Goal Setting
    6.4 Use life-span concepts to identify your specific work, job, and career goals for the next 20, 10, and 5 years.
  D. Life-Span Health and Well-Being: Women's Health Issues
    6.5 Identify special concerns about women's health.
    6.6 Discuss what the women's health movement has done to improve women's health.
    6.7 Sketch how women experience gender bias when they seek medical help.
    6.8 Discuss concerns about the fact that women are underrepresented in health research.

Guided Review and Study

1.0 The Transition from Adolescence to Adulthood
  A. Youth and the Criteria for Becoming an Adult
    1. Explain why it is difficult to determine when adolescence ends and adulthood begins.

    2. Kenneth Kenniston calls the transitional time between adolescence and adulthood _____ .   *youth*
    3. _____ struggle with developing an autonomous self and becoming socially involved, whereas _____ struggle with self-definition.   *Youths*
          adolescents
    4. List some of the criteria that mark the end of youth and the beginning of adulthood.

5. Change characterizes the transition from adolescence to adulthood; however, considerable _____ makes the transition a little smoother. *continuity*

6. A longitudinal study of males demonstrated more _____ than _____ over an 8-year period. *stability* *change*

7. For example, the relative levels of _____ and achievement orientation do not change from the tenth grade after eight years. *self-esteem*

B. *The Transition from High School to College*

1. Going from being a senior in high school to a freshman in college exemplifies the _____ phenomenon. *top-dog*

2. Characterize the transition from high school to college.

3. Today's college freshman seem to be experiencing more _____ and depression than before. Some college students also report that they feel _____ . *stress* *burned-out*

4. Explain *burnout* in your own terms.

5. Burnout is one of the _____ frequent reasons for leaving college before earning a degree. *most*

2.0 Physical Development

A. *The Peak and Slowdown in Physical Performance*

1. Physical performance reaches its _____ during early adulthood, and also starts its decline. *peak*

2. Richard Schultz and Christine Curnow have shown that the age of Olympic winners has remained _____ for a given sport. *constant*

3. Summarize the evidence that physical activities requiring speed and strength peak earlier than physical activities requiring more diverse motor and cognitive skills.

4. In addition to achieving peak physical performance during early adulthood, individuals are also at their _____ . *healthiest*

5. Most college students know what is required to prevent illness and promote _____ , but do not practice what they know. *health*

6. Describe college students ability to assess their future health risks.

7. When compared with adolescents, individuals in early adulthood _____ their use of drugs. *increase*

8. Peak drug use typically occurs during the period that defines _____ . *youth*

9. Of particular concern is the increase in party _____ by college students and more frequent use of _____ by young adults than the general population. *drinking* *cocaine*

10. Explain why college students often have unhealthy life-styles.

11. Studies of the relationship between life-styles and health indicate that physical health at age _____ predicts life satisfaction at age _____ , a finding that is stronger for males than females. *30* *70*

12. Summarize the declines in physical performance that occur during adulthood.

B. *Obesity and Dieting*

1. The causes of _____ are complex and involve genetics, physiological mechanisms, cognitive factors, and environmental influences. *obesity*

2. Indicate the evidence for a genetic contribution to obesity.

3. A body's _____ is the weight maintained when no effort is made to gain or lose weight. *set point*

173

4. Obese individuals have _____ fat cells than normal-weight counterparts.   *more*

5. The _____ metabolism rate or BMR is the minimum amount of energy an individual uses in a resting stage.   *basal*

6. Use Figure 14.1 to relate BMR with both age and sex.

7. Environmental factors involved in weight and shape include _____ preferences, the greater availability of food, energy-saving devices, and _____ physical activity.   *taste* *declining*

8. Indicate what it means to say that there are economic costs associated with obesity.

9. Indicate the concerns of the proponents and opponents of dieting.

10. National surveys reveal that _____ is a pervasive concern for both men and women.   *dieting*

11. The available data present a _____ picture of whether weight loss is related to mortality.   *mixed*

12. Indicate what we know about whether diets work.

13. Indicate what we know about whether diets are harmful.

14. Exercise helps individuals lose weight by burning calories and lowering their _____ .   *set points*

15. When _____ is a component of a weight loss program, the weight is more likely to stay off.   *exercise*

16. Researchers _____ answered the question of who should lose weight.   *have not*

C. *Exercise*

1. _____ exercise refers to sustained exercise that stimulates heart and lung activity.   *Aerobic*

2. Swimming, running, and cycling are examples of _____ exercise.   *aerobic*

3. Calculate your own exercise heart rate.

4. Experts believe that if you exercise enough to burn more than _____ calories per week, the risk of having a heart attack is cut by two-thirds.   *2000*

5. Describe some relatively painless forms of healthy exercise.

6. The current conclusion is that Americans should exercise _____ minutes on most, preferably all, days of the week.   *30*

7. Exercise produce both physical and _____ health.   *mental*

8. For example, regular exercise increases self-concept, and _____ anxiety and depression.   *decreases*

D. *Addiction and Recovery*

1. _____ drugs alter states of consciousness, modify perceptions, and change moods.   *Psychoactive*

2. _____ results in a need to take a greater amount of a drug to produce the same effect.   *Tolerance*

3. Express the concepts of *physical dependence* and *psychological dependence* in your own words.

4. The most widely used psychoactive drug is _____ .   *alcohol*

5. Indicate the incidence and consequences of alcohol abuse.

6. Alcohol _____ brain activity and impairs judgment. *depresses*

7. Although some regard alcoholism as a _____ , others believe that sociocultural factors are as important as hereditary and biological factors in determining whether someone will become an alcoholic. *disease*

8. Recovery from addiction is _____ . *difficult*

9. Alcoholics _____ is a widespread self-help support group for alcoholics and people with other problems. *Anonymous*

10. The average length of sobriety for members of Alcoholics Anonymous is _____ months. *52*

11. Indicate what critics say about Alcoholics Anonymous.

12. Characterize the approach of the three non-spiritually oriented self-help support groups for alcoholics that have appeared in recent years.

3.0 Sexuality

A. Heterosexual Attitudes and Behavior

1. One trend is that college students in 1980 reported an _____ in the frequency of sexual intercourse when compared with those of 1900. *increase*

2. A second trend is that the proportion of _____ reporting sexual intercourse has increased more rapidly than for _____ . *females* *males*

3. Describe and evaluate the results of Morton Hunt's survey in the 1970s.

4. Describe and evaluate the results of Robert Michael's survey in 1994.

5. The main conclusion of the 1994 survey was that American's sex lives are _____ conservative than previously believed. *more*

B. Homosexual Attitudes and Behavior

1. Alfred Kinsey defines sexual orientation in terms of a _____ , with the anchor points of exclusive heterosexuality at _____ and exclusive homosexuality at _____ . *continuum* *0; 6*

2. _____ are attracted to both females and males, and constitute approximately _____ percent of the population. *Bisexuals; 1*

3. According to Kinsey's research, about _____ percent of males and _____ percent of females are exclusively homosexual. *5; 2*

4. There _____ firm answers to the question of why some individuals are homosexual and others are heterosexual. *are not*

5. Homosexual and heterosexual males display _____ physiological responses during sexual arousal, and _____ differ with regard to a wide range of attitudes, behaviors, and adjustments. *similar* *do not*

6. Homosexuality _____ considered as a form of mental illness. *is not*

7. Summarize the findings regarding a possible biological basis for homosexuality.

8. An individual's _____ orientation probably is determined by a combination of genetic, hormonal, cognitive, and environmental factors. *sexual*

9. Although researchers do not know what causes homosexuality, they do know that the possible causes do not include the sexual _____ of the parents, the dominance levels of the parents, or the choice of _____ models. *orientation* *role*

10. Lesbians and gays experience life as a _____ . *minority*

11. Explain what Laura Brown means by saying that homosexuals can cope most effectively by developing a bicultural identity.

12. One special concern regards _____ and discrimination against lesbians and gays.   *bias*

C. *AIDS*

1. The sexually transmitted disease caused by the human immunodeficiency virus (HIV) is _____ .   *AIDS*

2. AIDS impairs the body's _____ system.   *immune*

3. Current estimates indicate about _____ million Americans are infected with AIDS, even though they do not show clinical symptoms.   *1 to 1.5*

4. The incidence of AIDS is high in _____ minority populations.   *ethnic*

5. Estimates indicate that approximately one in every _____ college students is infected with AIDS.   *560*

6. List ways that AIDS can be transmitted.

7. Explain the difference between *safe* sexual behavior and *safer* sexual behavior in your own terms.

8. Asking a date about his or her sexual behavior _____ guarantee protection from AIDS and other sexually transmitted diseases.   *does not*

7. Males are three times _____ likely than females to say they had lied to sexual partners.   *more*

8. Males and females were equally likely to understate the number of previous sexual partners; however, males were _____ likely than females to say they would lie about blood test results.   *more*

9. Characterize the two stages in the course of AIDS.

10. One treatment for the symptom of AIDS is _____ or AZT.   *zidovudine*

D. *Sexual Knowledge*

1. According to June Reinisch, both adult and adolescent Americans are inundated with sexual _____ , but not sexual _____ .   *messages*
    facts

2. Explain what it means to say that much of the sexual information is actually misinformation.

3. Seth Kalichman believes that the most difficult aspect of developing a sexual _____ is the lack of opportunity to define values for ourselves.   *identity*

4. Explain the value of sex education classes.

E. *The Menstrual Cycle and Hormones*

1. In comparison with other times in the menstrual cycle, women show _____ levels of self-esteem and confidence during ovulation.   *higher*

2. Mood changes during the menstrual cycle affect about _____ percent of all women.   *75*

3. Summarize the relationship between hormone levels and mood changes throughout the menstrual cycle.

F. *Forcible Sexual Behavior*

1. _____ is forcible sexual intercourse with a person who does not give consent.   *Rape*

2. The incidence of rape is _____ in every 10,000 for females over 12 years old.   *8*

3. Distinguish between rape and date (or acquaintance) rape.

4. Males who rape are generally _____ at women and want to _____ their victims.   *angry; hurt*

5. Describe the consequences of rape for the victim and those close to her or him.

6. Of all rape victims, _____ percent are female and _____ percent are male.   *95; 5*

G. *Sexual Harassment*
   1. Indicate what constitutes sexual harassment.

   2. Sexual _____ is an expression of individual power and domination that can result in   *harassment*
      serious _____ consequences for the victim.   *psychological*

4.0 Cognitive Development

A. *Cognitive Stages*
   1. Although Jean Piaget believed that an adolescent and an _____ think the same way, other   *adult*
      developmentalists believe that individuals consolidate their _____ operational thinking   *formal*
      only in adulthood.
   2. According to Gisela Labouvie-Vief, a new _____ of thought takes place in early adulthood.   *integration*
   3. Explain what Labouvie-Vief means by saying that adult thinking relies less on logical analysis in
      problem solving.

   4. William Perry believes that adolescents and adults think _____ .   *differently*
   5. According to Perry, adolescents view the world in terms of _____ ; however, this dualistic   *polarities*
      thinking yields to _____ thinking as individuals enter early adulthood.   *multiple*
   6. Dualistic and multiple thinking are followed by relative _____ thinking, in which an   *subordinate*
      analytical, evaluative approach to knowledge is pursued.
   7. Finally, when an adult understands that truth is relative, that the context of an event and the   *relativism*
      knowledge of the perceiver influence thoughts about the event, they have reached full

      _____ .

   8. Portray Jan Sinnott's views of cognitive change in early adulthood.

   9. K. Warner Schaie, who also believes that adolescents and adults think _____ , says that   *differently*
      adults in early adulthood switch from acquiring knowledge to _____ knowledge.   *applying*
   10 Characterize the following four stages in Schaie's theory of adult cognitive development:

      the achieving stage

      the responsibility stage

      the executive stage

      the reintegrative stage

   11. Schaie's reintegrative stage of thinking is akin to Erik Erikson's _____ versus _____   *integrity*
      stage, the eighth and final stage of psychosocial development.   *despair*
   12. Use Table 14.2 to compare and contrast the views of Jean Piaget, Gisela Laouvie-Vief, and K.
      Warner Schaie regarding the cognitive stages of adulthood.

B. Creativity
  1. The quality of productivity in adults is usually highest when the adults are in their _____ .   *thirties*
  2. Describe the courses of creativity in different endeavors throughout adulthood.

  3. It is _____ to conclude that there is a linear decrease in creativity during the adult years.   *inappropriate*

5.0   Careers and Work

A. *Theories of Career Development*
  1. Eli Ginzberg proposed the _____ theory of career choice.   *developmental*
  2. Ginzberg's developmental theory of career choice claims that individuals go through _____   *three*
     career stages: fantasy, tentative, and realistic.
  3. Characterize the following stages in developmental career choice theory:
     fantasy stage

     tentative stage

     realistic stage

  4. Critics of Ginzburg's developmental career theory indicate that the original sample as limited to   *middle*
     _____ -class youth, the _____ frames were too rigid, and _____ differences   *time*
     were ignored.   *individual*
  5. Despite the criticisms, Ginzberg's main point remains that realistic career choices occur only   *adulthood*
     during late adolescence or early _____ .
  6. Donald Super proposed career _____ theory.   *self-concept*
  7. Super's career _____ theory entails _____ phases, and assumes that a number of   *self-concept*
     developmental changes occur during adolescence and early adulthood.   *5*
  8. Characterize the following phases in career self-concept choice theory:
     crystallization phase

     specification phase

     implementation phase

     stabilization phase

     consolidation phase

  9. Super devised the Career _____ Inventory to help counselors promote adolescent   *Development*
     development.
 10. John Holland proposed _____ type theory.   *personality*
 11. Holland's personality type theory involves _____ basic personality types.   *six*
 12. Holland's personality type theory assumes it is important to match individuals' _____ type   *personality*
     with their career choices.

13. Characterize the following personality types in Holland's theory:
realistic

intellectual

social

conventional

enterprising

artistic

14. One criticism is that individuals are more varied and _____ than Holland suggests.   *complex*
15. Holland's personality types are incorporated into the Strong-Campbell _____ Interest   *Vocational*
    Inventory.
B. *Exploration, Planning, and Decision Making*
    Career counselors recommend exploring a number of career _____ .   *options*
    2. Explain why career advising is a complex task.

C. *The Life Contour of Work and Adulthood*
    1. The _____ cycle has four main stages: selection and entry, adjustment, maintenance, and   *occupational*
       retirement.
    2. Characterize the initial two stages of the occupational cycle experienced most frequently by
       individuals in early adulthood:
       selection and entry

       adjustment

    3. Individuals in their thirties achieve _____ levels of attainment.   *variable*
D. *Women and Work*
    1. The situation for _____ has changed dramatically as a result of effective contraception,   *women*
       easier births, and childrearing options.
    2. Explain why these various changes have created a society that makes vastly different task
       demands on men and women in comparison to the past.

    3. Nowadays approximately _____ percent of the women with preschool children worked outside   *61*
       the home.
    4. The _____ ceiling in management poses a barrier to many women and members of ethnic   *glass*
       minority groups.

5. Explain the concept of *glass ceiling* in your own words.

6. A _____ -career marriage refers to one in which both the husband and wife work outside the home.   *dual*

7. Summarize the questions that confront women who pursue careers.

8. Although one of the main advantages of dual-career marriages is _____ , other advantages include more equal relationships between husbands and wives and _____ feelings of self-esteem for women.   *financial* *enhanced*

9. Some _____ of dual-career marriages include conflict between work and family roles, competition between husbands and wives, and adequate attention to children.   *disadvantages*

10. Describe how men react to their wive's employment.

6.0 Chapter Boxes

A. Sociocultural Worlds of Development: Juggling Roles

1. Characterize the pleasures and pains of being a "juggler."

2. The lives of jugglers could be enhanced as a result of a better national child-care policy and improved _____ .   *day care*

B. Critical Thinking About Life-Span Development: Evaluating the Accuracy of Claims About Sexuality

1. Indicate what you could learn by identifying questions that you should ask about cause-effect claims relating to sexuality.

C. Critical Thinking About Life-Span Development: Career Goal Setting

1. Explain what you could learn by identifying the specific work, job, and career goals that you have for the next 20, 10, and 5 years.

D. Life-Span Health and Well-Being: Women's Health Issues

1. Women and men _____ in their experience of health and the health care system.   *differ*

2. Explain what the women's health movement has done to improve women's health.

3. Explain the concern over the fact that medicine remains a male-dominated field.

4. There is a growing awareness about sex and gender _____ in medical research.   *bias*

Self Test A: Key Terms and Key Persons
Write the appropriate key term or key person in the space to the right of the definition or description.

1. A drug that alters states of consciousness, modifies perceptions, and changes moods.   _____

2. K. Warner Schaie's stage of cognitive development in which an adult is responsible for societal systems and organizations.   _____

3. The director of the Kinsey Institute who claims that Americans have woefully inadequate sexual knowledge.   _____

4. A subjective craving and perceived need for a drug.   _____

5. The transition period between adolescence and adulthood according to Kenneth Kenniston.   _____

6. A physical craving for a drug that is accompanied by unpleasant withdrawal symptoms when the drug is unavailable. _____

7. A feeling produced by relentless, work-related stress. _____

8. The primary investigator who surveyed American sexual patterns in 1994. _____

9. A cognitive developmental theorists who believes adolescents view of the world in terms of polarities eventually yields to a fully relativistic position in adulthood. _____

10. The minimum amount of energy expended by an individual in a resting state. _____

11. The individual who proposed the personality type theory of career development. _____

12. Donald Super's theory of career development, an alternative to either developmental or personality-type theory. _____

13. Coerced sexual activity by an individual familiar to the victim. _____

14. A sexually transmitted disease that is caused by a virus that destroys the human immune system. _____

Self Test B: Multiple Choice

1. According to Kenneth Kenniston, which of the following questions would not be included in those asked by young adults?
   a. How do I relate to society?
   b. What should my vocation be?
   c. How do I define myself?
   d. What life-style should I choose?

2. In what way does the move from high school to college differ from the move from elementary school to junior high school?
   a. Junior high school students experience the top-dog phenomenon, but college freshmen do not.
   b. College freshmen experience increased achievement pressure, but junior high school students do not.
   c. College freshmen have opportunities to explore life-styles, but junior high school students do not.
   d. Junior high school students are challenged by academic work, but college freshmen are not.

3. At many colleges students are dropping because of
   a. stress.
   b. burnout.
   c. depression.
   d. lack of preparation.

4. Evidence from records for track and field events suggests that the age for peak performance in strength and speed events is
   a. biologically determined.
   b. determined by an interaction of biological factors and experience.
   c. variable and unpredictable.
   d. getting lower as training methods improve.

5. Now in her middle twenties, Harriet exercises rarely, skips breakfast to get to work early, and parties hard on weekends to compensate for the long hours of hard work she must put in to support her ambitious career plans. Late in life, when she has achieved success and retired, Harriet will be
   a. relatively healthy, because in her youth peak resources protected her against the stress she experienced.
   b. in satisfactory health, because her stressful living makes up for early success.
   c. vigorous, because she has trained herself for the demands of a successful career.
   d. relatively less healthy and dissatisfied with her life.

6. Between the ages of 16 and 21, all but which of the following behaviors increase?
   a. use of alcohol
   b. smoking
   c. calories consumed
   d. exercise

7. With increasing age the basal metabolism rate
   a. increases steadily.
   b. reaches a peak and levels off.
   c. declines steadily.
   d. does not change.

8. All of the following are sociocultural influences on body weight except
   a. basal metabolism rate.
   b. declining physical activity.
   c. energy saving devices.
   d. greater availability of food

9. Which of the following statements is most accurate?
   a. Longitudinal studies with random assignment to weight-loss and no-weight-loss groups show that weight loss reduces health risks.
   b. Some research shows that low-calorie diets combined with intensive education and behavior produce good long-term results.
   c. Moderate exercise reduces calorie consumption.
   d. Researchers recommend that everyone should go on a diet.

10. At age 30 you find that you are a successful, hardworking executive, but also that you are slightly overweight and having more and more difficulty coping with the tension in your life. What can you do that will help you with both problems and possibly improve your job performance?
    a. Lose weight.
    b. Start a program of weight lifting and stretching exercises.
    c. Begin walking or jogging at a moderate pace three to five times a week.
    d. Push yourself to jog fast three to five times a week.

11. Experts recommend that American adults engage in at least _____ minutes of exercise or more on a _____ basis.
    a. 15; daily
    b. 30; daily
    c. 30; every other day
    d. 60; weekly

12. Which is not a criteria for a psychoactive drug?
    a. acts on the nervous systems to create an altered state of consciousness
    b. modifies perceptions
    c. is physically addicting
    d. changes mood

13. Which individual provides the best examples of a drug-related psychological dependence?
    a. Charles, who uses drugs because he can't cope with everyday stressors without them
    b. Benjamin, who uses drugs because when he stops he becomes very ill
    c. Margaret, who has decided that she needs to start taking drugs to make her feel better
    d. Francis, who is concerned because his wife is addicted to painkillers and her behavior is threatening to destroy their family

14. Alcohol is a
    a. stimulant.
    b. depressant.
    c. hallucinogen.
    d. antipsychotic agent.

15. Who would most likely have a philosophical disagreement with the "twelve-step" approach emphasized by Alcoholics Anonymous?
    a. Artie, who is poor
    b. Dan, who doesn't believe in God
    c. Goldie, who is a strong feminist
    d. Dick, who believes in the power of abstinence

16. Since the 1940s sexual intercourse among college students has
    a. decreased steadily.
    b. increased more for men than for women.
    c. increased more for women than for men.
    d. increased substantially for both men and women.

17. Which statement concerning homosexuality is *false*?
    a. The incidence of homosexual behavior increases in individuals denied access to the opposite sex.
    b. An early, positive homosexual relationship virtually guarantees that a homosexual preference will remain for life.
    c. The percent of the population practicing exclusively homosexual behavior has remained constant during most of this century.
    d. Male homosexuals tend to be more sexually active than lesbians.

18. AIDS cannot be transmitted by
    a. intimate sexual contact.
    b. blood transfusions.
    c. contact with urine.
    d. sharing needles.

19. You cannot contract AIDS from
    a. a kiss.
    b. heterosexual intercourse.
    c. contact with AIDS-infected blood.
    d. oral sex.

20. Studies of the human menstrual cycle indicate that hormonal changes during the cycle
    a. cause mood changes.
    b. produce depression and irritability.
    c. result in higher confidence and self-esteem.
    d. are associated with mood changes.

21. What percentage of college men admit to forcing sexual activity on their dates?
    a. 10 percent
    b. 25 percent
    c. 50 percent
    d. 75 percent

22. Rapists share all but which of the following characteristics?
    a. anger toward women
    b. a desire to hurt their victim
    c. feelings of aggression that enhance the rapist's sense of power
    d. a history of being abused as children

23. Gisela Labouvie-Vief believes that, when compared to those in adolescence, thought processes of individuals in early adulthood are
    a. more pragmatic.
    b. more logical.
    c. more idealistic.
    d. more optimistic.

24. Dr. Lopez, a new university professor, has established a research program and is comfortable with her teaching responsibilities. Now she is concentrating on helping her advisees and training graduate students. Dr. Lopez is in which of Schaie's stages?
    a. achieving
    b. responsibility
    c. executive
    d. reintegration

25. Introductory psychology students often complain, "Why do we have to learn all of these theories? Why don't you just teach us the right one?" According to William Perry, this complaint reflects
    a. dualistic thinking.
    b. multiple thinking.
    c. relative thinking.
    d. undifferentiated thinking.

26. Which of the following disciplines shows the earliest decline in productivity?
    a. art
    b. humanities
    c. social sciences
    d. business

27. When children say they want to grow up to be a doctor, they are in Eli Ginzberg's _____ stage of career choice.
    a. tentative
    b. fantasy
    c. realistic
    d. imaginative

28. Matt is in his last year of college and is now doing a teaching internship. He also is preparing letters for fourth-grade teaching positions. Matt is in Donald Super's vocational phase called
    a. crystallization.
    b. specification.
    c. implementation.
    d. stabilization.

29. According to John Holland, the person with a conventional personality is most likely to be a
    a. bank teller.
    b. artist.
    c. social worker.
    d. carpenter.

30. The first two stages of work in adulthood, selection/entry and adjustment, appear to require Schaie's stage of cognitive development called
    a. achieving.
    b. responsibility.
    c. executive.
    d. reintegration.

31. Women who experience comparatively less stress in male-dominated fields tend to be
    a. masculine.
    b. feminine.
    c. androgynous.
    d. undifferentiated.

32. Advantages of dual-career marriages include all but
    a. financial benefits.
    b. increased self-esteem for men.
    c. a more equal relationship between men and women.
    d. more commitment to work by women.

Answers for Self Test A

1. psychoactive drug
2. executive stage
3. June Reinisch
4. psychological dependence
5. youth
6. physical dependence
7. burnout
8. Robert Michael
9. William Perry
10. basal metabolism rate (BMR)
11. John Holland
12. career self-concept theory
13. date or acquaintance rape
14. AIDS

Answers for Self Test B

1.	c	LO 1.2
2.	c	LO 1.5
3.	b	LO 1.7
4.	b	LO 2.1
5.	a	LO 2.2
6.	d	LO 2.4
7.	c	LO 2.7
8.	a	LO 2.9
9.	b	LO 2.14
10.	c	LO 2.18
11.	b	LO 2.21
12.	c	LO 2.22
13.	b	LO 2.23
14.	b	LO 2.25
15.	b	LO 2.27
16.	c	LO 3.1
17.	b	LO 3.6
18.	c	LO 3.10
19.	a	LO 3.10
20.	d	LO 3.16
21.	c	LO 3.17
22.	d	LO 3.18
23.	a	LO 4.1
24.	b	LO 4.1
25.	a	LO 4.3
26.	c	LO 4.7
27.	b	LO 5.1
28.	c	LO 5.3
29.	a	LO 5.4
30.	a	LO 5.7
31.	a	LO 5.10
32.	b	LO 5.13

Chapter 15   Socioemotional Development in Early Adulthood

Learning Objectives with Key Terms in Boldface

1.0 Attraction, Love, and Close Relationships

  A. *What Attracts Us to Others in the First Place?*

  1.1   Explain why physical proximity does not guarantee a positive relationship with someone.

  1.2   Cite evidence that we like to associate with people who are similar to us.

  1.3   Define **consensual validation**, and discuss how it explains the role similarity in friendship and love.

  B. *The Faces of Love*

  1.4   Define **friendship** and explain how it is both different from and similar to love.

  1.5   Define **romantic love** and discuss its importance in adults' lives.

  1.6   List the emotions associated with romantic love, giving special attention to sexual desire.

  1.7   Define **affectionate love** and indicate its developmental relationship to romantic love.

  1.8   Discuss how previous relationships may influence new relationships.

  1.9   Define Robert Sternberg's **triangular theory of love**.

  1.10   Show how passion, commitment, and intimacy combine in different types of love.

  C. *Relationship Cognition*

  1.11   Discuss the role attributions play in marital satisfaction.

  1.12   Discuss the role of memories in close relationships, giving special attention to sex differences.

  1.13   Indicate the role of relationship schemas in understanding individual differences in relationships, using attachment security and relationship trust as examples.

  D. *Loneliness*

  1.14   List the social and personal correlates of loneliness.

  1.15   Describe and discuss the causes of loneliness in college freshmen.

  1.16   Indicate how to measure loneliness, and discuss two general ways to reduce it.

2.0 Marriage and the Family

  A. *The Family Life Cycle*

  2.1   Define **leaving home and becoming a single adult**, with special attention to the idea of **launching**.

  2.2   Define the **new couple**, indicating how this stage involves creating a third family system by joining two separate systems.

  2.3   Define **becoming parents and a family with children**, citing the special demands of this stage.

  2.4   Define the **family with adolescents**, indicating how parents cope with noncompliance.

  2.5   Define the **family at midlife**, indicating new trends in this stage of the family life cycle.

  2.6   Define the **family in later life**.

  B. *Trends in Marriage*

  2.7   Describe historical trends and sociocultural influences on marriage.

  C. *Marital Expectations and Myths*

  2.8   Discuss how marital expectations and myths may influence the course of a marriage.

  2.9   Take and score the marriage quiz in Figure 15.4 and evaluate your realism about marriage.

  D. *Gender, Intimacy, and Family Work in Marriage*

  2.10   Compare and contrast men's and women's experience of intimacy in marriage.

  2.11   Compare and contrast men's and women's experience of family work.

E. *Parental Roles*

    2.12 Indicate variations in expectations about the parental role.

    2.13 List myths about parenting.

    2.14 Discuss how changes in women's career expectations have influenced patterns of child-bearing and child-rearing.

    2.15 Compare and contrast the effects of early versus late child-bearing.

    2.16 Indicate how motherhood has relatively low prestige in our society.

    2.17 Indicate changes in the father's role over the course of American history.

    2.18 Cite the benefits to children of active fathering and mother-father cooperation.

3.0 The Diversity of Adult Lifestyles

A. *Single Adults*

    3.1 Describe the experience of becoming single.

    3.2 Indicate recent trends in the numbers of single adults.

    3.3 Discuss the advantages and disadvantages of being single.

B. *Divorced Adults*

    3.4 Describe modern trends in divorce.

    3.5 Describe the lives of people who get divorced.

    3.6 Indicate special problems that divorced homemakers face.

4.0 Intimacy, Independence, and Gender

A. *Intimacy*

    4.1 Review Erik Erikson's idea about the place of intimacy in development.

    4.2 Discuss how achieving intimacy versus isolation may influence a person's life.

    4.3 Define and distinguish among Jacob Orlofsky's **intimate style, preintimate style, stereotyped style, pseudointimate style,** and **isolated style** of intimate relationships.

    4.4 Define and distinguish among Kathleen White's **self-focused level, role-focused level,** and **individuated-connected level** of relationship maturity.

B. *Intimacy and Independence*

    4.5 Discuss the dynamic interplay of needs for intimacy and commitment versus needs for independence and freedom that occurs in early adulthood.

C. *Women's Development, Men's Development, and Gender Issues*

    4.6 Review the problems women face in contemporary society.

    4.7 Sketch Jean Baker Miller's ideas on the importance of psychological issues from a female view.

    4.8 Explain why it is important for women to be self-motivated.

    4.9 Compare and contrast the men's and women's movements.

    4.10 Discuss Herbert Goldberg's views on the critical difference between men and women.

    4.11 List Goldberg's ideas on how men can live more physically and psychologically healthy lives.

    4.12 Describe and evaluate Robert Bly's approach to men's issues.

5.0 Continuity and Discontinuity from Childhood to Adulthood

    5.1 Summarize what we currently believe about the influence of early versus late experiences on adult personality.

6.0 Chapter Boxes

A. *Sociocultural Worlds of Development: Marriage Around the World*

    6.1 List the traits of a desirable marriage partner that vary widely from culture to culture.

    6.2 Compare and contrast trends in marriage in Scandinavian countries versus Hungary.

B. *Critical Thinking About Life-Span Development: Evaluating Domestic Violence*

    6.3 Use your knowledge about life-span development to speculate about the causes and cures of domestic violence.

C. *Critical Thinking About Life-Span Development: Evaluating Intimacy and Close Relationships in Our Lives*

    6.4 Evaluate the nature of intimacy and close relationships in your life.

D. Life-Span Health and Well-Being: Reducing Loneliness

    6.5   Discuss how to recognize and to reduce loneliness.

Guided Review and Study

1.0 Attraction, Love, and Close Relationships

A. *What Attracts Us to Others in the First Place?*

1. Attraction to others results from physical _____ and perceived similarity.   *proximity*

2. Physical _____ does not guarantee that we will develop a positive relationship with an   *proximity* individual; however, _____ is a necessary condition for a close relationship to develop.   *familiarity*

3. We share _____ attitudes, behaviors, and characteristics with those to whom we are close.   *similar*

4. Explain the concept of *consensual validation* in your own words.

B. *The Faces of Love*

1. The four forms of _____ include: altruism, friendship, romantic or passionate love, and   *love* affectionate or companionate love.

2. _____ is a form of close relationship that involves enjoyment, acceptance, trust, respect,   *Friendship* confiding, understanding, and spontaneity.

3. Indicate how friendship differs from love.

4. _____ and lovers are alike in that they share the characteristics of acceptance, trust,   *Friends* confiding, understanding, spontaneity, mutual assistance, and happiness.

5. _____ love has strong sexual and infatuation components and often predominates in the   *Romantic* early part of a love relationship.

6. Romantic love is also called _____ .   *eros*

7. When we say we are "in love" with someone we are experiencing _____ love.   *romantic*

8. Romantic love is the main reason given for getting _____ .   *married*

9. When asked to identify their closest relationship, most college students name their _____   *romantic* partners rather than parents, siblings, or friends.

10. Ellen Berscheid claims that romantic love is 90 percent _____ desire.   *sexual*

11. Romantic love may be contrasted with _____ love or _____ love, a type of love that   *affectionate* occurs when individuals desire to have the other person near and have a deep, caring affection for   *companionate* the person.

12. Summarize Phillip Shaver's view of the developmental course of love.

13. When affectionate love fails, wives are _____ as likely as husbands to initiate divorce.   *twice*

14. Indicate how previous relationships influence new relationships.

15. Robert Sternberg proposed the _____ theory of love.   *triarchic*

16. Sternberg's triarchic theory of love has _____ main components: passion, _____ , and   *3; intimacy* commitment.

17. Explain what Robert Sternberg means by *passion, intimacy,* and *commitment.*

18. Different combinations of passion, intimacy, and commitment produce different kinds of   *love* _____ according to Sternberg.

19. For example, a relationship is marked by _____ if only passion is present.　　*infatuation*

20. If a relationship has intimacy and commitment but little passion, _____ love is present.　　*companionate*

21. When both passion and commitment are present in a relationship but intimacy is absent, the relationship is called _____ .　　*fatuous*

22. When all three components of love are present, the relationship entails _____ love.　　*consummate*

C. Relationship Cognition

1. Define *attributions*, and discuss the role they play in marital satisfaction.

2. Another aspect of relationship cognition is relationship _____ .　　*memories*

3. Explain what it means to say that women have more highly developed relationship schemas.

4. Two aspects of relationship schemas include attachment security and relationship _____ .　　*trust*

D. Loneliness

1. Society's emphasis on self-fulfillment, the importance of commitment in relationships, and the decline in stable close relationships all contribute to _____ .　　*loneliness*

2. Indicate some social and personal correlates of loneliness.

3. College freshmen are often _____ , and ore than _____ percent of the college freshmen said their loneliness was moderate to severe.　　*lonely; 40*

4. To reduce _____ , individuals can change their social relations or change their social needs and desires.　　*loneliness*

5. To change social _____ , individuals can form new relationships, use existing social networks more competently, or create surrogate relationships with pets.　　*relations*

6. To change social _____ , one can select activities that can be pursued alone.　　*needs*

7. Although not always healthy, individuals can _____ or become workaholics to reduce their loneliness.　　*drink*

2.0 Marriage and the Family

A. The Family Life Cycle

1. The family life cycle includes _____ stages.　　*6*

2. The first stage of the family life cycle entails leaving home and becoming a _____ adult.　　*single*

3. Describe the phenomena of *launching* in your own terms.

4. The second stage involves marriage and a new _____ system.　　*family*

5. Families and friends realign themselves to accommodate the _____ .　　*spouse*

6. Indicate how men and women experience marriage differently.

7. In the third stage of the family life cycle, adults become _____ to the new generation.　　*caregivers*

8. Families with _____ define the fourth stage of the family life cycle.　　*adolescents*

9. Indicate the relative effectiveness of the alternative ways that parents can cope with noncompliant adolescents.

10. _____ children, linking of generations, and adapting to mid-life changes, occur in the fifth stage of the family life cycle. *Launching*

11. Activities such as _____ and _____ typify the family in later life, the sixth stage in the family life cycle. *retirement grandparenting*

B. *Trends in Marriage*

  1. Describe the nature and consequences of a changing norm in male-female equality in marriage.

  2. Only about _____ percent of women never marry. *7*

  3. _____ contexts strongly influence the nature of marriage. *Sociocultural*

C. *Marital Expectations and Myths*

  1. The high divorce rate and the high degree of dissatisfaction in many marriages may result from strong _____ about marriage. *expectations*

  2. A _____ is a widely held belief supported by facts. *myth*

  3. Take the marriage quiz and compare and contrast your score with those for the college students in the Jeffrey Larson study.

D. *Gender, Intimacy, and Family Work in Marriage*

  1. Female and male marriage partners _____ with regard to the expression of intimacy and performance of family work. *differ*

  2. More men than women view their spouses as best friends; however, _____ disclose more to their partners than do _____ . *wives husbands*

  3. Women are _____ expressive and affectionate than men. *more*

  4. Men typically do _____ family work than women. *less*

  5. Indicate some examples of family work typically performed by women and men.

  6. Family work is intertwined with _____ and embedded in family relations, and thereby has complex and contradictory meanings for _____ . *love women*

E. *Parental Roles*

  1. Some marriage partners plan and _____ parental roles; however, few ever receive any _____ education in parenting. *coordinate formal*

  2. Note some myths about parenting.

  3. The smaller number of _____ per family and reduced demands of child care have led to increases in women working, more time spent in fathering, and parental care supplemented by institutional care. *children*

  4. Some advantages of having children _____ include more physical energy, fewer pregnancy-related medical problems, and lack of built-in expectations for the children. *early*

  5. Some advantages of having children _____ include more time for parents to consider their goals, more competent parenting, and better finances. *later*

  6. Attributing the problems of children to their mothers ignores the important psychological lesson that behavior is _____ determined. *multiply*

  7. Motherhood entails both benefits as well as _____ . *limitations*

  8. Father's role in parenting has changed from being the _____ teacher in colonial American times to being _____ , and actively involved with children in contemporary times. *moral nurturant*

  9. Specify how interactions with fathers influence the social development of children.

10. Indicate the benefits to children of mother-father cooperation.

3.0 The Diversity of Adult Lifestyles

  A. *Single Adults*

   1. Explain what it means to say that adult lifestyles are diverse.

   2. The number of people living _____ increased substantially in the 1970s. *alone*
   3. The number of individuals living alone is a symptom of _____ birth rates, high divorce *low*
      rates, long lives, and _____ marriages. *late*
   4.. Indicate some myths and stereotypes associated with being single.

   5. _____ adults have problems in developing intimate relationships with other adults, finding *Single*
      a place in a marriage-oriented society, and confronting loneliness.
   6. By the time single adults reach the age of _____ , there is increasing pressure to make a *30*
      conscious decision to get married or remain single.

  B. *Divorced Adults*

   1. Divorce rates are now _____ more slowly than previously. *increasing*
   2. Identify factors associated with higher divorce rates.

   3. Explain why separation and divorce are emotionally charged and complex.

   4. Evidence that separated and divorced individuals are _____ psychologically appears in the *at risk*
      form of higher rates of admission to psychiatric hospitals, clinical depression, alcoholism, and
      sleep disturbances.
   5. Evidence that separated and divorced individuals are at risk _____ is apparent in their *physically*
      impaired immune systems.
   6. Divorce poses special _____ for both women and men. *problems*
   7. Divorced _____ have to overcome loneliness, lack of autonomy, and financial hardships; *women*
      whereas divorced _____ have fewer rights to their children, lower incomes, and receive little *men*
      emotional support.

4.0 Intimacy, Independence, and Gender

  A. *Intimacy*

   1. Erik Erikson says _____ should come after individuals have established their identity. *intimacy*
   2. If an individual does not develop _____ in early adulthood, the individual may be left in a *intimacy*
      stage of _____ . *isolation*
   3. Indicate what Erikson says is the result of an inability to develop intimacy for an individual.

   4. Jacob Orlofsky's classification system for intimacy includes _____ styles. *5*
   5. According to Orlofsky, the _____ style is a form of social interaction in which an *intimate*
      individual maintains at least one deep and long-lasting love relationship.
   6. Individuals who have mixed emotions about a relationship that results in offering love without *preintimate*
      obligation of a long-lasting bond represents the _____ style.
   7. The _____ style refers to an individual engaged in superficial relationships that tend to be *stereotyped*
      dominated by same-sex friendships.

8. When individuals maintain long-lasting attachments with little depth or closeness, they display the _____ style.   *pseudointimate*

9. The _____ style describes individuals who withdraw from social encounters and have few or no attachments to any individuals.   *isolated*

10. A model of relationship _____ by Kathleen White suggests that individuals move through _____ levels: self-focused, role-focused, and individuated-connected.   *maturity*
    3

11. According to White, a _____ -focused individual is concerned only with how the relationship affects him- or herself.   *self*

12. A _____ -focused individual considers the other's perspective, but still maintains a stereotyped and socially acceptable perspective.   *role*

13. The _____ -connected individual enjoys a mature relationship, understands the needs of both partners, and anticipates the needs and emotional concerns of the partner.   *individuated*

14. White indicates that the individuated-connected level is typically reached in _____ .   *adulthood*

B. Intimacy and Independence

1. Explain why development in early adulthood often involves the delicate balance of intimacy and commitment on one hand, and independence and freedom on the other hand.

C. Women's Development, Men's Development, and Gender Issues

1. Identify some of the problems feminist scholars say women face in contemporary society.

2. Feminists have also argued that gender _____ , male-imposed standards, and devaluation of feminine qualities have made women _____-class citizens.   *stereotyping*
    second

3. Jean Baker Miller's studies of how women spend their lives make it clear that they spend much of their time participating in the emotional, intellectual, and social _____ of others.   *development*

4. Feminists also advocate increased self-_____ for women.   *motivation*

5. The author of *The Dance of Intimacy*, Harriet Lerner, argues that competent relationships are those that contain both _____ and emotional connectedness.   *separateness*

6. Compare and contrast the men's movement and the women's movement.

7. Herbert Goldberg argues that men differ from women because they are unable to _____ their feelings and problems.   *articulate*

8. Characterize the consequences of masculinity according to Goldberg.

9. Goldberg contends that men can live more physically and psychologically _____ lives by doing such things as avoiding the suicidal "success" syndrome and developing friendships with other males.   *healthy*

10. Robert Bly contends that contemporary men are too _____ , and that the fundamental lack of a deep _____ identity can be overcome by ritual gatherings.   *soft*
    masculine

11. Indicate what critics say about Robert Bly's views.

5.0 Continuity and Discontinuity from Childhood to Adulthood

1. Explain what it means to say that we no longer believe in the infant determinism of Sigmund Freud's psychosexual theory.

2. In determining the personality of the young adult, it is important to look at early _____ as   *experiences*
   well as the present circumstances or _____ .   *contexts*
3. Adult _____ development lies somewhere between the infant determinism of Freud and the   *personality*
   contextual approach that altogether ignores early _____ .   *experiences*

6.0 Chapter Boxes

A. *Sociocultural Worlds of Development: Marriage Around the World*

1. Explain why the most desirable characteristics of a marriage partner differ around the world.

2. Compare and contrast trends in marriage in Scandinavian countries versus Hungary.

B. *Critical Thinking About Life-Span Development: Evaluating Domestic Violence*

1. Indicate what you could learn by speculating about the causes and cures of domestic violence.

C. *Critical Thinking About Life-Span Development: Evaluating Intimacy and Close Relationships in Our Lives*

1. Use your answers to the questions as a basis for evaluating the nature of intimacy and close relationships in your life.

D. *Life-Span Health and Well-Being: Reducing Loneliness*

1. Distinguish feeling lonely from being alone.

2. Indicate some signs of loneliness.

3. For people who experience intense feelings of loneliness over long periods of time, one effective   *strategy*
   _____ entails engaging in interactions with others, or enhancing one's social _____ .   *network*

Self Test A: Key Terms and Key Persons

Write the appropriate key term or key person in the space to the right of the definition or description.

1. The second stage in the family life cycle in which two individuals unite to form a new family.   _____
2. A men's movement theorist who says that men differ from women because they are unable to   _____
   articulate their feelings and problems.
3. A type of love in which an individual has a deep, caring affection for another person.   _____
4. Jacob Orlofsky's classification of intimacy in which an individual maintains a long-lasting sexual   _____
   attachment with little or no depth or closeness.
5. The individual who developed a model of relationship maturity.   _____
6. A concept that explains why similar individuals are attracted to one another.   _____
7. A love researcher who contends that romantic love is 90 percent sexual desire.   _____
8. According to Kathleen White's analysis, a type of relationship in which an individual considers   _____
   the other's perspective, but still maintains a stereotyped and social acceptable perspective.
9. A type of love in which an individual experiences strong sexual desires and infatuations.   _____
10. An individual who proposed that there are five different styles of intimacy.   _____

Self Test B: Multiple Choice

1. Which of the following statements most closely illustrates the formula for interpersonal attraction?
   a. 2 + 2 = 4
   b. opposites attract
   c. blue + yellow = green
   d. hammers are often found with nails

2. Consensual validation refers to
   a. the adolescent's first experience of sexual intercourse.
   b. a high level of agreement among members of a social group.
   c. parental acceptance of their offspring as independent adults.
   d. attraction among similar individuals.

3. Which of the following is true about friendship between spouses?
   a. more men than women consider their wives to be their best friends
   b. men gain most of their emotional support in relationships outside of the marriage
   c. more women than men consider their husbands to be their best friends
   d. women gain most of their emotional support from their husbands

4. When we say that we are in love, we are most likely referring to _____ love.
   a. compassionate
   b. affectionate
   c. romantic
   d. consummate

5. When unattached college students identified their closest relationship, most named
   a. a friend.
   b. parents.
   c. a close but nonparent relative.
   d. a romantic partner.

6. According to Ellen Berscheid romantic love cannot be experienced without
   a. sexual desire.
   b. a strong sense of personal identity.
   c. consensual validation.
   d. trust.

7. A desire to have a partner who is adored and will be near is the basis of
   a. affectionate love.
   b. altruism.
   c. friendship.
   d. romantic love.

8. If the only real attraction that Richard and Jamie feel toward each other is sexual, Robert Sternberg would ague that they are
   a. experiencing infatuation.
   b. experiencing companionate love.
   c. experiencing fatuous love.
   d. not experiencing love.

9. Research has shown that people feel lonely for all of the following reasons except
   a. the society's emphasis on self-fulfillment.
   b. the importance attached to relationships.
   c. a decline in stable, close relationships.
   d. the rising divorce rate.

10. Which of the following statements regarding loneliness and college is more accurate?
    a. Students become more lonely as they approach graduation.
    b. Loneliness remains of little concern for college students.
    c. A lonely high school student is likely to be a lonely college student.
    d. Males are likely to be more lonely than females.

11. According to your textbook, an individual may try to reduce loneliness by
    a. changing his or her social relations.
    b. reducing his or her desire for social contact.
    c. becoming a workaholic.
    d. All of these are correct.

12. Which process in the "family life cycle" is also called launching?
    a. birth
    b. leaving home and becoming a single adult
    c. taking one's first job and entering the workforce
    d. losing one's episodic memory in later adulthood

13. Which phase would many individuals begin to hear during the sixth stage of the "family life cycle?"
    a. "How come I have to clean my room? I'm almost in the fifth grade."
    b. "I now pronounce you husband and wife."
    c. "Hi, grandpa and grandma."
    d. "Honey, I'm pregnant."

14. The developmental course of marriage is
    a. varied both within and across cultures.
    b. the same across cultures.
    c. easy to predict once a couple falls in love.
    d. determined by the individuals involved.

15. Compared to marriages earlier in the twentieth century, today's marriages are
    a. more stable.
    b. longer lasting.
    c. more fragile.
    d. less intense.

16. In a study of beliefs in marriage myths among college students, Jeffrey Larson found that
    a. college students' beliefs about marriage were surprisingly realistic.
    b. females tended to approach the subject of marriage more realistically than males.
    c. highly romantic students are likely to experience more marital stability.
    d. the low participation rate in the study indicates a low interest in the subject of marriage seems characteristic among college students.

17. The idea of an equal sharing of family work is
    a. an ideal.
    b. a reality in most contemporary marriages.
    c. held only by couples who have careers outside the home.
    d. associated more with upper-class families.

18. Men working around the house are most likely to
    a. do the dishes.
    b. take out the garbage.
    c. straighten up.
    d. go shopping.

19. Which statement is not a myth about parenting?
    a. the birth of a child will save a failing marriage
    b. children will take care of parents in their old age
    c. when children fail, the parent is not entirely to blame
    d. mothers are naturally better parents than fathers

20. American women have fewer children than in the past. One repercussion of this is that
    a. men are putting more time into child-rearing.
    b. fewer women are entering the workforce.
    c. institutionalized day care use is on the decline.
    d. women have lost a great deal of status.

21. The biggest increase in the number of people living alone occurred in the
    a. 1950s.
    b. 1960s.
    c. 1970s.
    d. 1980s.

22. Divorced men and women have higher rates of all of the following except
    a. clinical depression.
    b. alcoholism.
    c. sleep disturbances.
    d. immunity to disease.

23. Thirteen-year-old Allison is experiencing some difficulty in establishing close friendships. Erikson's theory would say she
    a. is likely to be aggressive as an adult.
    b. had poor relationships with childhood peers.
    c. is normal at this point in her life.
    d. is likely to be somewhat isolated in adulthood.

24. According to Erik Erikson, if individuals are unable to develop intimacy in early adulthood, they are left with feelings of
    a. despair.
    b. stagnation.
    c. isolation.
    d. confusion.

25. Partners who have stressful intimate interactions often have a(n)
    a. isolated style relationship.
    b. stereotyped style relationship.
    c. pseudointimate style relationship.
    d. preintimate style relationship.

26. For women, the threat of disruption of the sense of connectedness is perceived as
    a. a loss of relationship.
    b. a loss of purpose.
    c. a loss of self.
    d. a loss of intimacy.

27. The feminist perspective places emphasis upon women as
    a. authorities about their own experiences.
    b. seekers of careers outside the home.
    c. members of a family unit.
    d. All of these are correct.

28. *The Dance of Intimacy* argues that competent relationships are those in which
    a. separateness and connectedness strike a balance.
    b. that intimacy versus isolation conflict is resolved.
    c. self-determination is sacrificed for intimacy with others.
    d. individuality is sacrificed for the good of the relationship.

29. Robert Bly argues that the reason why American men are "soft" is that, unlike in centuries past, men today
    a. are often shamed into submission by politically correct feminists.
    b. do not participate in any rituals of manhood.
    c. rely too heavily on technology and not enough on physical strength.
    d. typically bond with their mothers and not with their fathers.

30. If appears that the more often personality is assessed over a person's lifetime, the more
    a. stable personality appears.
    b. Freud appears to have been right.
    c. psychological differences appear to have biological origins.
    d. it appears that adult behaviors seldom have origins in childhood.

Answers for Self Test A

1. new couple
2. Herbert Goldberg
3. affectionate love
4. pseudointimate style
5. Kathleen White
6. consensual validation
7. Ellen Berscheid
8. role-focused level
9. romantic love
10. Jacob Orlofsky

Answers for Self Test B

1.	a	LO 1.2
2.	d	LO 1.3
3.	a	LO 1.4
4.	c	LO 1.5
5.	d	LO 1.6
6.	a	LO 1.6
7.	a	LO 1.7
8.	c	LO 1.10
9.	d	LO 1.14
10.	a	LO 1.15
11.	d	LO 1.16
12.	b	LO 2.1
13.	c	LO 2.6
14.	a	LO 2.7
15.	c	LO 2.7
16.	b	LO 2.9
17.	a	LO 2.11
18.	b	LO 2.11
19.	c	LO 2.13
20.	a	LO 2.14
21.	c	LO 3.2
22.	d	LO 3.5
23.	c	LO 4.1
24.	c	LO 4.2
25.	a	LO 4.3
26.	c	LO 4.4
27.	d	LO 4.7
28.	a	LO 4.8
29.	b	LO 4.12
30.	c	LO 5.1

Chapter 16   Physical and Cognitive Development in Middle Adulthood

Learning Objectives with Key Terms in Boldface

1.0   Changing Middle Age

    1.1   Compare and contrast the boundaries of middle age 90 years ago and today.

    1.2   Define **middle adulthood**.

2.0   Physical Development

  A.   Physical Changes

    2.1   Describe changes in vision, hearing, and height during middle adulthood.

    2.2   Indicate the physiological correlates of vision, hearing, and height changes in middle age.

  B.   Health Status

    2.3   List health and physical self-esteem challenges that occur to men and women during middle age.

  C.   Stress and Illness

    2.4   Describe evidence for biological pathways that link stress and illness.

    2.5   Describe evidence for behavioral pathways that link stress and illness.

    2.6   List interventions that break down the stress-illness connection.

  D.   Life-Style, Personality, and Health

    2.7   Describe changes in cardiovascular function among middle-aged people.

    2.8   Sketch evidence that culture influences cardiovascular health.

    2.9   Define the **Type A behavior pattern** and state its link to coronary disease.

    2.10 Evaluate the link between Type A behavior and coronary disease.

    2.11 Define **Type C behavior** and indicate its significance.

    2.12 Define **hardiness**, and indicate how it relates to health in middle adulthood.

  E.   Sexuality

    2.13 Define **menopause** and characterize variations in women's experience of it.

    2.14 Compare and contrast erroneous beliefs and reality concerning menopause.

    2.15 Explain why erroneous beliefs about menopause persist.

    2.16 Describe the pros and cons of hormonal treatment for the consequences of menopause.

    2.17 Discuss whether there is a male menopause.

    2.18 Sketch trends for the sexual behavior of men and women during middle adulthood.

    2.19 Explain sex differences in sexual behavior during middle adulthood.

    2.20 Indicate the physiological correlates of declining sex drive in men during middle adulthood.

3.0   Cognitive Development

    3.1   Describe ways that memory may decline during middle age.

    3.2   Indicate what adults can do about memory decline.

4.0   Careers, Work, and Leisure

  A.   Job Satisfaction

    4.1   Describe the course of job satisfaction from early through middle adulthood.

  B.   Career Ladders

    4.2   Indicate major predictors of and limitations on progress up the career ladder.

C. MidLife Career Changes

    4.3   Indicate experiences associated with mid-life career changes in a small percentage of Americans.

D. Work Pathways of Men and Women

    4.4   Compare and contrast the continuity of work pathways among men and women.

    4.5   Define and distinguish among the regular, interrupted career, second career, and modified second career work pathways of professional women.

    4.6   Explain why women go back to work during middle adulthood.

E. Leisure

    4.7   Define **leisure** and state its importance.

    4.8   List examples of adult leisure activity.

    4.9   Explain why leisure is important during middle age.

5.0   Religion and Meaning in Life

A. Religion and Adult Lives

    4.10   Characterize the extent of religion's influence on adult Americans' lives.

    4.11   Indicate individual differences and variations of involvement in religion among American adults.

B. Religion, Happiness, and Coping

    4.12   Indicate how religious faith relates to happiness.

    4.13   Describe variations in the relationship between religion and the ability to cope with stress.

5.0   Chapter Boxes

A. Sociocultural Worlds of Development: Health Promotion in African Americans, Latinos, Asian Americans, and Native Americans

    5.1   Compare and contrast challenges to and opportunities for good health experienced by Black, Hispanic, Asian, and Native Americans.

B. Critical Thinking About Life-Span Development: Exploring Sexual Attitudes

    5.2   Relate three sexual attitudes prevalent in America to your own sexual attitude.

    5.3   Speculate about how age relates to sexual attitudes.

C. Critical Thinking About Life-Span Development: The Balance and Imbalance of Work, Family, and Leisure in Our Lives as We Develop

    5.4   Describe your current balance of work, family, and leisure commitments.

    5.5   Speculate about your future balance of work, family, and leisure commitments.

D. Life-Span Health and Well-Being: Toward Healthier Lives

    5.6   Explain why health professionals believe that the next step in improving Americans' health will be behavioral, not medical.

    5.7   List the Society for Public Health Education's objectives for the year 2000.

    5.8   Explain the advantage of prevention as a means to good health.

Guided Review and Study

1.0   Changing Middle Age

    1. In 1900 average life expectancy was _____ ; today, it is _____ years of age.   *47; 75*

    2. Summarize issues involved in the definition of middle age.

    3. Middle adulthood is a time of physical _____ and expanding responsibility.   *decline*

2.0   Physical Development

A. Physical Changes

    1. Accommodation of the eye _____ sharply between the ages of 40 and 59.   *declines*

2. Middle aged individuals find it harder to view _____ objects. *nearer*

3. Sensitivity to _____ frequency pitches usually declines first. *high*

4 _____ usually lose sensitivity to high-pitched sounds earlier than _____ . *Men; women*

5 With age the visual _____ decreases, and the _____ becomes less light sensitive. *field; retina*

6 Explain what causes individuals to shrink in middle age.

B. Health Status

1. People in middle adulthood worry more about _____ than people in early adulthood. *health*

2. The number one killer of middle aged adults in the United States is _____ . *cardiovascular*

3. Summarize how men and women react to the signs of aging.

4. Facial wrinkles and gray hair may be perceived as _____ in women. *unattractive*

5. There are large individual _____ in ability to deal with physical change in middle age. *differences*

C. Stress and Illness

1. Biological pathways that link stress and illness include the autonomic, endocrine, and _____ systems. *immune*

2. Summarize three lines of support for stress-mediated immune response.

3. Two lines of research reveal the role of _____ in health. *stress*

4. _____ is a behavior that may be a behavioral pathway that links stress and illness. *Eating*

5. Poor health behaviors can _____ the effects of stress on illness. *magnify*

6. The behavioral effects of cancer treatment can lead patients to _____ with treatment. *not comply*

7. Therapy components that can reduce stress in cancer patients include _____ support, coping strategies, and relaxation training. *emotional*

D. Life-Style, Personality, and Health

1. A 40-year-old's heart pumps about _____ as much blood per minute as a 20-year-old's. *half*

2. Describe arterial changes that make cardiovascular problems more likely in middle age.

3. _____ plays a role in coronary disease. *Culture*

4. Describe cross-cultural variations in Japanese men that illustrate how culture influences cardiovascular health.

5. Because they have changed their _____ , Japanese-American men suffer fewer strokes than their counterparts in Japan. *behavior*

6. Personality appears to contribute to _____ difficulties. *cardiovascular*

7. The Type A behavior pattern includes excessive competitiveness, _____ , and hostility. *impatience*

8. The component of Type A behavior most closely associated with hear disease is _____ . *hostility*

9. Some argue that if we can control our _____ , we can reduce our risk of heart disease. *anger*

10. The behavioral style prone to cancer is called the _____ pattern. *Type C*

11. Type C people are more likely to develop cancer than more _____ people. *expressive*

12. Explain why hardiness may buffer people against illness.

E. Sexuality

1. Menopause is the time between _____ to _____ years in a women's life when menstruation _____ and childbearing is no longer possible.   *40; 50*
   ceases
2. During menopause, _____ decline accompanies hot flashes, nausea, fatigue, and rapid heart beat.   *estrogen*
3. Research indicates that menopause does not produce _____ or physical problems for most women, but that stereotypes about it exist due to research on _____ samples of women.   *psychological*
   small
4. Estrogen _____ may help women who experience difficulties with menopause.   *replacement*
5. One concern about estrogen replacement is that is associated with breast and uterine _____ .   *cancer*
6. _____ begins to decline in middle aged men.   *Testosterone*
7. The male menopause mainly concerns _____ changes.   *psychological*
8. Summarize trends in sexual activity as found in the Sex in America survey.

9. One reason for sex differences in sexual activity during middle age is the male _____ rate.   *mortality*
10. An important point to remember is that middle-aged people are _____ active.   *sexually*

3.0 Cognitive Development

1. The most studied aspect of middle adulthood cognition is _____ .   *memory*
2. Memory decline in middle adulthood is likely to occur mainly for _____ memory.   *long-term*
3. Middle-aged people are less likely to remember _____ used information.   *infrequently*
4. Sketch the role that memory strategies play in adult memory failure or success.

5. A noncognitive factor declining memory during middle adulthood is _____ .   *poor health*

4.0 Careers, Work, and Leisure

A. Job Satisfaction

1. Job satisfaction _____ with age due to higher pay, status, and security.   *increases*
2. Older individual show higher job _____ .   *commitment*
3. Measures of job commitment include taking jobs seriously, low rates of absenteeism, and _____ .   *involvement*
4. Middle-aged adults focus on what is _____ about their jobs in contrast with younger adults.   *right*

B. Career Ladders

1. Explain the concept of a *career ladder*.

2. Having _____ education predicts earlier and greater career advancement.   *college*
3. _____ promotion predicts further career advancement than _____ promotion.   *early; late*
4. Most career achievement occurs by _____ years of age.   *40 to 45*

C. Mid-Life Career Changes

1. About _____ percent of Americans change jobs at mid-life.   *10*
2. Career change may be brought on by feelings of _____ from bosses, wives, or children.   *constraint*

D. Work Pathways of Men and Women

1. Woman are more likely than men to show a _____ pattern of work.   *discontinuous*
2. More than middle income men, low income men are likely to have an _____ work history.   *unstable*
3. Identify and describe four career patterns found among women.

4. Women return to work because of _____ , loneliness, and desire for new interests.   *boredom*

5. Employment plays an important role in a middle-aged woman's _____ well-being.   *psychological*

E. Leisure

1. _____ is a pleasant time after work when people choose and pursue their own interests.   *Leisure*

2. Compared to 90 years ago, contemporary adults enjoy _____ leisure time.   *more*

3. Describe typical modern leisure activities.

4. Leisure activity helps adults deal with _____ in middle adulthood.   *changes*

5. Leisure activity helps to prepare middle-aged adults for _____ .   *retirement*

5.0 Religion and Meaning in Life

A. Religion and Adult Lives

1. About _____ percent of Americans believe in God or a universal spirit.   *95*

2. Three out of four Americans _____ or engage in some spiritual practice.   *pray*

3. Females have a _____ interest in religion than do males.   *stronger*

4. Americans are becoming less committed specific religious _____ .   *denominations*

5. Involvement in religion may _____ during an individual's life-span.   *vary*

B. Religion, Happiness, and Coping

1. Happy people tend to have a meaningful _____ faith.   *religious*

2. An important point to remember is that research on religion and happiness is _____ .   *correlational*

3. Discuss whether or not religious faith plays a positive or negative role in coping with stress.

5.0 Chapter Boxes

A. Sociocultural Worlds of Development: Health Promotion in African Americans, Latinos, Asian Americans, and Native Americans

1. Differences _____ ethnic groups are factors in an ethnic minority group member's health.   *within*

2. Black American's health has suffered from _____ and racial segregation.   *prejudice*

3. A barrier to obtaining health care among Hispanic Americans is _____ .   *language*

4. A special characteristic influencing their access to health care is Asian American's _____ .   *diversity*

5. Different ethnic groups have different ideas about the _____ of disease.   *causes*

6. Native Americans are likely to think of medicine as a _____ fix.   *quick*

7. Physicians should _____ ethnic minority beliefs about medicine into their regular practice.   *integrate*

B. Critical Thinking About Life-Span Development: Exploring Sexual Attitudes

1. Sexual attitudes prevalent in America today are the traditional, relational, and _____ .   *recreational*

2. Relate your sexual attitudes to the three sexual attitudes prevalent in America.

3. Speculate about how age relates to sexual attitudes.

C. Critical Thinking About Life-Span Development: The Balance and Imbalance of Work, Family, and Leisure in Our Lives as We Develop

1. As individuals age, the _____ of work versus leisure may change.   *priority*

2. Describe your current balance of work, family, and leisure commitments.

3. Speculate about your future balance of work, family, and leisure commitments.

D. Life-Span Health and Well-Being: Toward Healthier Lives
1. Advances in general health will most likely result from _____ interventions.   *behavioral*
2. Behavioral interventions will be important because they deal with diseases caused by _____   *lifestyle*
.
3. Many _____ have begun health promotion programs for their employees.   *corporations*

Self Test A: Key Terms and Key Persons
Write the appropriate key term or key person in the space to the right of the definition or description.
1. These researchers invented the concept of Type A behavior.   _____
2. People who feel committed rather than alienated, experience control rather than powerlessness, and perceive problems as challenges rather than threats, are said to have this trait.   _____
3. A twisting, turning life-span developmental period that begins between ages 35 and 45.   _____
4. This theorist describes the mid-life career-change experience as a turning point in adulthood.   _____
5. A hospital administrator who worries that estrogen replacement might increase the risk of breast cancer.   _____
6. The time when women lose their ability to have children.   _____
7. According to his work, competent middle-aged men and woman are likely to be involved in religion.   _____
8. A cluster of personality characteristics that include excessive competitiveness, impatience, and hostility, and that are related to coronary disease.   _____
9. The pursuit of activities and interests of ones own choosing.   _____
10. A cancer-prone personality consisting of being inhibited, uptight, and emotionally inexpressive.   _____

Self Test B: Multiple Choice

1. Contemporary advances in health and health care have caused the boundaries of middle age to
   a. move downward.
   b. move upward.
   c. become confused and indistinct.
   d. stay the same, but apply to more people.

2. A person between the ages of 40 and 49 is going to have the most difficulty
   a. reading a wall chart at the eye-care professional's office.
   b. reading the telephone book.
   c. reading a newspaper.
   d. watching television at a distance.

3. The leading cause of death in the United States is cancer.
   b. cardiovascular disease.
   c. weight-related problems.
   d. accidents.

4. Which of the following is a behavioral link between stress and illness?
   a. religious faith
   b. immune system response
   c. eating habits
   d. respiratory infection

5. Facial wrinkles and gray hair symbolize
   a. maturity and strength in men.
   b. maturity and strength in women.
   c. the beginning of the end for men.
   d. the beginning of the end for women.

6. Which of the following occupations is least likely to attract people with Type A personalities?
   a. lawyers
   b. bank executives
   c. college professors
   d. novelists

7. Linda is characterized by control, commitment, and seeing problems as challenges. It is most likely that she will
   a. remain healthy.
   b. develop heart disease.
   c. develop breast cancer.
   d. become obese.

8. In an extensive survey of women who had experienced menopause, most reported that menopause was a _____ experience.
   a. positive
   b. negative
   c. neutral tending toward positive

d. neutral tending toward negative

9. Why do erroneous beliefs about menopause exist?
    a. Badly controlled research supports them.
    b. The beliefs conform well with gender-typed beliefs about middle age women.
    c. The essence of the menopause experience appears in them.
    d. Physicians promote them to guard against use of estrogen therapy.

10. When compared to that in early adulthood, sexual activity during middle adulthood is
    a. more frequent.
    b. less frequent.
    c. more dependent on physical ability.
    d. almost absent.

11. Which of the following memory tasks would be the most difficult for an individual in the middle adulthood period?
    a. remembering a phone number long enough to dial it
    b. remembering a grocery list being given over the phone
    c. remembering the date of a son-in-law's birthday
    d. remembering the name of someone you just met so you can introduce him or her to your spouse

12. Job satisfaction increases with age for all but which of the following reasons?
    a. job security
    b. higher pay
    c. higher positions within the company
    d. work is a good escape from the problems of raising a family

13. Boris is 45 years old. He is most likely to
    a. continue up the corporate ladder.
    b. remain at his present level in the corporation.
    c. change jobs.
    d. increase his savings for retirement.

14. Upon finishing undergraduate school, Joan enrolls in the Metropolitan School of Law. According to Golan she is in the _____ career pattern.
    a. regular
    b. interrupted
    c. second
    d. modified second

15. If the current trend in work-force entry for women continues,
    a. more women than ever before will enter the work force.
    b. there will be an increasing demand by women for part-time jobs.
    c. women will soon outnumber men in many professions.
    d. women will enter the work force at younger ages.

16. All but which of the following are leisure activities for a computer programmer?
    a. fishing
    b. playing computer games
    c. writing computer programs for home use
    d. reading

17. The percentage of Americans who believe in God is _____ the percentage who attend religious services.
    a. less than
    b. greater than
    c. equal to
    d. changing in comparison to

18. The strongest statement we can make about the relationship between involvement in religion and happiness is that
    a. involvement in religion causes people to be happy.
    b. happiness leads people to become involved in religion.
    c. there is no meaningful relationship between involvement in religion and happiness.
    d. people who are involved in religion tend to be happy.

19. One way to promote access to health care for Hispanic Americans would be to
    a. print information about health care in Spanish.
    b. desegregate clinics for ethnic minorities.
    c. teach Hispanic Americans not to use medical care as a quick fix.
    d. use Hispanic Americans' belief in the supernatural in treatment.

20. If you believe that sexual activity is one of several ways to spice up a relationship, your attitude is
    a. traditional.
    b. relational.
    c. recreational.
    d. irresponsible.

21. Which of the following is the best example of the next step toward improved health among people in middle adulthood?
    a. Cures will be found for heart disease and cancer.
    b. The federal government will develop an effective national insurance plan.
    c. Corporations will help ethnic minorities gain access to the medical system.
    d. More effective ways to help people stop smoking will be found.

Answers for Self Test A

1. Meyer Friedman and Ray Rosenman
2. hardiness
3. middle adulthood
4. Daniel Levinson
5. Veronica Ravniker
6. menopause
7. John Clausen
8. Type A behavior pattern
9. leisure
10. Type C behavior

Answers for Self Test B

1. b   LO 1.1
2. c   LO 2.1
3. b   LO 2.3
4. c   LO 2.5
5. a   LO 2.8
6. d   LO 2.9
7. a   LO 2.12
8. a   LO 2.13
9. a   LO 2.15
10. b   LO 2.18
11. c   LO 3.1
12. d   LO 4.1
13. b   LO 4.2
14. a   LO 4.5
15. a   LO 4.6
16. c   LO 4.7
17. b   LO 4.10
18. d   LO 4.12
19. a   LO 5.1
20. c   LO 5.2
21. d   LO 5.6

Chapter 17   Socioemotional Development in Middle Adulthood

Learning Objectives with Key Terms in Boldface

1.0 Close Relationships

  A. *Love and Marriage at Midlife*

    1.1 Compare and contrast the roles of romantic and companionate love among early versus middle adult couples.

    1.2 Indicate evidence for age and sex differences in satisfying love relationships.

    1.3 Define and give examples of stability (or *working through*) in the family life-cycle.

    1.4 Discuss the advantages and disadvantages of a midlife divorce.

  B. *The Empty Nest and Its Refilling*

    1.5 Define and evaluate the idea of the **empty-nest syndrome**.

    1.6 Indicate reasons that some young adults delay leaving home.

    1.7 Describe the pluses and minuses for family life that occur when adult children return to live at home.

  C. *Sibling Relationships and Friendships*

    1.8 Characterize sibling relationships in adulthood

    1.9 State the significance of friendships in adulthood.

  D. *Intergenerational Relationships*

    1.10 List ways that younger and older generations are similar and different.

    1.11 Indicate sex differences in the quality of intergenerational relationships.

    1.12 Explain why middle-aged adults may experience more intergenerational stress than younger and older adults.

2.0 Personality Theories and Development in Middle Age

  A. *The Adult Stage Theories*

    2.1 Define Erik Erikson's stage of generativity versus stagnation.

    2.2 List ways adults are concerned about and achieve generativity.

    2.3 Use Table 17.1 to review Roger Gould's seven stages of adult life.

    2.4 Sketch Daniel Levinson's method for discovering the seasons of a man's life.

    2.5 List Levinson's developmental tasks for male adulthood.

    2.6 Indicate the four conflicts that occur at mid-life and how men resolve them.

    2.7 Evaluate Levinson's data.

    2.8 Define and distinguish between George Vaillant's ideas about **career consolidation** and **keeping the meaning versus rigidity**.

    2.9 Identify common themes in the theories of Erikson, Gould, Levinson, and Vaillant.

    2.10 List concerns about the theories of Erikson, Gould, Levinson, and Vaillant.

  B. *Crisis and Cohort*

    2.11 Compare and contrast Daniel Levinson's and Roger Gould's views of the mid-life crisis.

    2.12 Explain how changing times may relate to how different age groups move through the life cycle.

    2.13 Use the concept of **social clock** to explain why the results of Levinson's, Gould's, and Vaillant's studies may not generalize to other age cohorts.

  C. *Gender, Culture, and Middle Age*

    2.14 List feminist criticisms of contemporary stage theories of adult development.

    2.15 Evaluate the "normative sequence of development" assumption characteristic stage theories.

    2.16 Indicate how the women's movement changed the lives of traditionally raised women.

    2.17 Indicate Valory Mitchell and Ravenna Helson's evidence that mid-life is a new prime of life for women.

2.18 List and explain the advantages Judith Brown says that women in nonindustrialized countries enjoy at mid-life.

2.19 Explain why it is hard to identify a mid-life crisis in cultures other than our own.

2.20 Illustrate how another culture represents life transitions with Gusii culture.

D. The Life-Events Approach

2.21 Define the contemporary life-events approach to adult development.

2.22 List criticisms of the **contemporary life-events approach** to adult development.

2.23 Illustrate the daily hassles approach to adult adaptation to stress with research examples.

2.24 List criticisms of the daily hassles approach to adult adaptation to stress.

E. Individual Variation

2.25 Explain what it means to focus on individual variation in adult personality development.

2.26 Illustrate the individual differences approach to adult development with an example from Vaillant's Grant Study.

3.0 Longitudinal Studies of Personality Development in Adulthood

A. Neugarten's Kansas City Study

3.1 Summarize Bernice Neugarten's longitudinal study of adult personality development.

B. Costa and McRae's Baltimore Study

3.2 List and describe the five personality dimensions measured in Paul Costa and R. R McRae's study.

3.3 Summarize Costa and McRae's longitudinal study of adult personality development.

C. Berkeley Longitudinal Studies

3.4 Summarize Eichorn's report of the Berkeley longitudinal studies.

3.5 Summarize John Clausen's conclusions about the life histories of men and women who participated in the Berkeley longitudinal studies.

3.6 Define planful competence and explain how it relates to adult development.

3.7 Explain Clausen's view that too much attention has been given to discontinuities in adult development.

D. Helson's Mills College Study

3.8 Summarize Ravenna Helson's longitudinal study of women's adult personality development.

3.9 Explain Helson's concept of mid-life consciousness as it relates to women's personality development.

E. Overview of Constancy and Change

3.10 Show how the lives of Richard Alpert and Jerry Rubin illustrate continuities in personality development.

3.11 Cite theory and evidence that adult personality is continuous.

3.12 Cite evidence that adult personality changes as people age.

3.13 Summarize the relationship of continuity and change in adult personality development.

4.0 Chapter Boxes

A. Sociocultural Worlds of Development: Intergenerational Relationships in Mexican American Families —The Effects of Immigration and Acculturation

4.1 Describe variations in intergenerational relationships that occur in response to within-family and across-generation differences in acculturation among members of immigrant Mexican-American families.

B. Critical Thinking About Life-Span Development: Seasons of a Woman's Life

4.2 Develop an argument about whether David Levinson's stages apply as well to women as they do to men.

C. Critical Thinking About Life-Span Development: Are There Distinguishable Subphases Within Middle Adulthood?

4.3 Develop a description of two subphases of middle adulthood.

4.4 Discuss whether there is too much individual variation to delineate clear subphases of middle adulthood.

D. Life-Span Health and Well-Being: Engaging in a Life Review

4.5 Define and distinguish between a life review and a "life line" summary of a person's life.

4.6 Discuss the benefits of reviewing one's life.

Guided Review and Study

1.0 Close Relationships

  A. *Love and Marriage at Mid-life*

    1. _____ love becomes more important than romantic love in middle adulthood.   *Affectionate*

    2. Compare and contrast romantic and companionate love.

    3. _____ occurs when partners share knowledge, are responsible for each other's satisfaction,   *Mutuality*
and share private information that governs their _____ .   *relationship*

    4. Emotional _____ is the most important characteristic of love at all ages.   *security*

    5. Marriages often become better _____ during middle adulthood.   *adjusted*

    6. For _____ individuals, divorce may hold fewer perils than it would for younger people.   *mature*

    7. An example of _____ is when couples accommodate to changing goals.   *stability*

    8. In contrast to the divorcer, a divorced person may regard a divorce as a _____ .   *betrayal*

  B. *The Empty Nest and its Refilling*

    1. The idea of the _____ syndrome is that marital satisfaction decreases when children leave.   *empty nest*

    2. The reality is that marital satisfaction usually _____ when children leave home.   *increases*

    3. A recent trend is that children _____ home after a failure or a divorce.   *return*

    4. One reason that children stay home is that they cannot meet _____ needs.   *financial*

    5. Research shows that substantial numbers of adults have _____ conflicts with their   *serious*
_____ children living at home.   *adult*

    6. A concern of both adults living at home and their parents is loss of _____ .   *privacy*

    7. When adult children live with their parents, it is best when there is enough _____ .   *space*

    8. List the pros and cons of living at home with one's parents as an adult child.

  C. *Sibling Relationships and Friendships*

    1. In adulthood _____ relationships may be close, apathetic, or rivalrous.   *sibling*

    2. Most adult sibling relationships are _____ , although they tend not to be if they were not   *close*
when the individuals were _____ .   *children*

    3. The friendships of middle adulthood are usually _____ than those of early adulthood.   *deeper*

  D. *Intergenerational Relationships*

    1. Family members usually maintain close _____ across generations.   *contact*

    2. List areas in which parents and children are most and least similar.

    3. The closest intergenerational relationships occur between _____ and daughters.   *mothers*

    4. Married men are more involved with their wives' _____ than their own.   *kin*

    5. The mid-life well-being of women is related only to their relationships with their _____ .   *mothers*

    6. Middle-aged adults are called the _____ generation because they must care for both their   *sandwich*
children and their _____ , a situation that causes much stress.   *parents*

2.0 Personality Theories and Development in Middle Age

  A. *The Adult Stage Theories*

    1. According to _____ , the issue of middle adulthood is generativity versus stagnation.   *Erik Erikson*

    2. Define and give examples of generativity versus stagnation.

3. Carol Ryff found that _____ was a major concern of middle-aged men and women. *generativity*

4. Roger Gould combines stages and _____ in his view of developmental transformations. *crises*

5. List and describe Gould's seven stages of adult development.

6. Criticisms of Gould's study include middle class bias, no tests of the _____ of clinical judgments, and no statistical analyses. *reliability*

7. Daniel Levinson conducted detailed _____ to find out about men's lives. *interviews*

8. Levinson emphasizes that _____ tasks must be mastered at stages of adult life. *developmental*

9. List and describe Levinson's developmental tasks for adult male life.

10. One of the four conflicts of middle adulthood is being _____ versus being old. *young*

11. Another conflict of middle adulthood is being separated versus being _____ . *attached*

12. Like Gould's work, Levinson's has been criticized for failure to include _____ analyses. *statistical*

13. George Vaillant added stages of career _____ and keeping the meaning versus rigidity to Erik Erikson's adult stages. *consolidation*

14. Identify the major similarities among the three theories of adult personality development.

15. Critics claim that the theories of adult personality development are not very _____ . *scientific*

16. Critics also contend that the adult theories focus too much on _____ . *crises*

17. A third criticism of the adult theories is that they neglect individual _____ . *variation*

B. Crisis and Cohort

1. In contrast to Levinson, Gould found few individuals who experienced a _____ . *mid-life-crisis*

2. Different generations may have different lives because they belong to different _____ . *cohorts*

3. Neugarten emphasizes that our development is influenced by the _____ in which we live. *times*

4. Explain the concept of *social clock*.

5. Neugarten argues that the social environment of an age group can alter its _____ . *social clock*

6. Findings about one cohort may not _____ to another cohort. *apply*

7. Currently, there is _____ agreement about major life events than ever before. *less*

C. Gender, Culture, and Middle Age

1. Critics say that adult theories of stage development have a _____ bias. *male*

2. Some critics say that stage theorists do not address women's concerns about _____ . *relationships*

3. Critics also argue that women's _____ roles have been neglected in adult stage theories. *family*

4. Summarize how women's adult lives may differ from men's adult lives.

5. Women may not experience a _____ sequence of adult development. *normative*

6. Many of today's mid-life women experienced a _____ in their earlier adult lives. *role shift*

7. Mitchell and Helson found the early 50s to be a _____ of life for many women. *prime*

8. _____ is a cultural characteristic that influences women's adult lives. *Modernity*

9. Women in nonindustrialized countries may experience _____ status in middle age. *improved*

10. Indicate three changes that improve middle-aged women's lives in nonindustrialized countries.

11. Some cultures do not appear to have a concept of _____ age.   *middle*
12. In the Gusii culture females and males follow _____ life courses.   *different*
13. Among the Gusii, _____ , not age, lead to changes in adult status.   *life events*

D. *The Life-Events Approach*
   1. An alternative to stage theories is a _____ approach to adult development.   *life events*
   2. Define and give examples of the contemporary life events approach to adult development.

   3. A criticism of the life events approach is that emphasizes _____ at the expense of stability. *change*
   4. _____ experiences may be as powerful as life events in shaping personality.   *Daily*
   5. A study of Florida police officers showed how daily _____ were very stressful.   *hassles*
   6. Knowing about daily hassles needs to be supplemented by information about how people   *cope*
      _____ with and perceive them.

E. *Individual Variation*
   1. Another important focus of research on adult personality is individual _____ .   *variation.*
   2. A focus on individual variation emphasizes that people are _____ in their own lives.   *active agents*
   3. In Valliant's study, personal preoccupations were _____ for college students after   *maladaptive*
      graduation.

3.0 Longitudinal Studies of Personality Development in Adulthood
A. *Neugarten's Kansas City Study*
   1. Bernice Neugarten found that _____ characteristics were the most stable in adulthood.   *adaptive*
   2. Personality changed from active to passive _____ in Neugarten's study.   *mastery*
   3. Draw appropriate conclusions about continuity in adult personality based on Neugarten's study.

B. *Costa and McRae's Baltimore Study*
   1. Costa and McRae identified _____ stable dimensions of personality in the adult years.   *five*
   2. Being soft-hearted is a component of a personality factor called _____ .   *agreeableness*
   3. Identify and describe the other four personality factors identified by Costa and McRae.

C. *Berkeley Longitudinal Studies*
   1. The _____ longitudinal studies are the longest running studies of adult personality.   *Berkeley*
   2. The Berkeley studies _____ support the debate about stability versus change.   *did not*
   3. The consistent dimensions of personality in the Berkeley studies concerned the _____ .   *self*
   4. John Clausen reports that planful competence in _____ is associated with adult successes.   *adolescence*
   5. Planful competence consists of self-confidence, dependability, and _____ investment.   *intellectual*
   6. Explain how planful competence contributes to success in the adult years.

   7. Clausen emphasizes _____ over similarity as a characteristic of adult personality.   *variation*

D. *Helson's Mills College Study*
   1. Ravenna Helson found _____ groups of women among the Mills students she studied.   *three*

2. Identify and characterize the three groups of women identified by Helson.

3. In all three groups there was a shift toward _____ traditionally feminine attitudes. *less*
4. In contrast to mid-life crisis, Helson found mid-life _____ in Mills college sample. *consciousness*

E. *Overview of Constancy and Change*

1. The lives of Richard Alpert and Jerry Rubin illustrate _____ in adult personality. *constancy*
2. William James believed that personality does not _____ in middle age. *change*
3. Costa and McRae's research _____ James's contentions. *supports*
4. The Berkeley studies suggest that personality change is _____ and adaptive. *possible*

4.0 Chapter Boxes

A. *Sociocultural Worlds of Development: Intergenerational Relationships in Mexican American Families —The Effects of Immigration and Acculturation*

1 _____ separates Mexican-Americans from their extended families. *Immigration*
2. When their lives become stable, Mexican families may _____ immigration of other family members. *sponsor*
3. There are _____ levels of acculturation in a Mexican-American family. *three*
4. Mother and grandparents are likely to be at the _____ level of acculturation. *beginning*
5. Different levels of acculturation may lead to _____ in a Mexican American family. *conflict*
6. Middle-age Mexican Americans are better _____ than they are couples. *parents*

B. *Critical Thinking About Life-Span Development: Seasons of a Woman's Life*

1. According to data in the textbook, Daniel Levinson's argument _____ apply to women. *does not*
2. Show how textbook material relates to the idea of *Seasons in a Woman's Life*.

C. *Critical Thinking About Life-Span Development: Are There Distinguishable Subphases Within Middle Adulthood?*

1. Indicate what you would learn by developing a description of two phases of middle adulthood.

2. Discuss whether there is too much individual variation to identify clear subphases of middle age.

D. *Life-Span Health and Well-Being: Engaging in a Life Review*

1. In contrast to a life line summary, a life review summarizes one's life in terms of _____ . *segments*
2. A life review may help someone _____ many goals. *achieve*
3. Life reviews and life lines help people to _____ their thoughts about their lives. *organize*

Self Test A: Key Terms and Key Persons

Write the appropriate key term or key person in the space to the right of the definition or description.

1. An implicit schedule for when events such as marriage or having children should occur. _____
2. Famous American psychologist who maintained that personality sets by age 30. _____
3. The idea that marital satisfaction decreases after children leave home. _____
4. Life-span psychologist who found that middle-aged adults viewed themselves as leaders and decision makers. _____
5. The view of life span development that holds that life events, mediating factors, individual adaptation, life-stage context, and sociohistorical context influence adult personality development. _____

6. Researchers who developed evidence for stability in five personality factors during middle age. _____

7. An adult career stage occurring between ages 23 and 35 when a person's career becomes stable. _____

8. Theorist who added to stages to Erikson's theory of personality development. _____

9. An adult stage of development occurring between ages 45 to 55 when adults relax if they have met their goals, or accept that they have not. _____

10. Researcher who pioneered longitudinal studies of adult personality development. _____

Self Test B: Multiple Choice

1. During the middle years _____ love increases.
   a. affectionate or companionate
   b. romantic or passionate
   c. intimate
   d. committed

2. Satisfying relationships in early adulthood and middle adulthood share all of the following characteristics except
   a. emotional security.
   b. passion.
   c. sexual intimacy.
   d. respect.

3. The empty nest syndrome usually accompanies
   a. increased marital satisfaction.
   b. decreased marital satisfaction.
   c. increased conflict between adult siblings.
   d. decreased conflict between adult siblings.

4. _____ percent of the adult population has at least one living sibling.
   a. Twenty-five
   b. Sixty-five
   c. Eighty-five
   d. Ninety-five

5. Parents and their adult children are most likely to disagree about
   a. choice of life-style.
   b. church attendance.
   c. political party.
   d. abortion.

6. Married men are more likely to be involved with
   a. their wives' relatives than their own.
   b. their own relatives than their wives'.
   c. their paternal grandparents than their maternal grandparents.
   d. their parents than their wives' parents.

7. Ann experiences great satisfaction through nurturing, guiding, and teaching skills to her children. According to Erik Erikson, Ann is dealing successfully with which psychological task?
   a. initiative versus guilt
   b. industry versus inferiority
   c. identity versus role confusion
   d. generativity versus stagnation

8. An adult who has successfully resolved the conflicts of the generativity versus stagnation psychosocial stage is most likely to
   a. donate money to a scholarship fund.
   b. buy a piece of a football franchise.
   c. spend time and money on exercise programs.
   d. hire consultants to teach junior executives the finer points of business management.

9. According to Daniel Levinson, the major issue that the middle-aged man must face is
   a. mortality versus immortality.
   b. sexual and physical decline.
   c. empty nest syndrome.
   d. industry versus inferiority.

10. According to Daniel Levinson, the success of the mid-life transition is dependent upon how effectively the individual
    a. accepts polarities of the conflicts as an integral part of their being.
    b. chooses the most troublesome conflict and resolves it.
    c. learns to pay more attention to the needs of others than to his or her own needs.
    d. realizes the sense of urgency in his or her life and comes to peace with it.

11. According to George Vaillant, the stage of development that occurs from approximately 23 to 35 years of age, in which careers become more stable and coherent, is
    a. settling down; acceptance of one's life.
    b. generativity versus stagnation.
    c. career consolidation.
    d. goal realization.

12. Stage theories of adult development have been criticized for all but which of the following reasons?
    a. the research upon which they are based is not very scientific
    b. the tendency is to see the stages of development as crises
    c. life events may be more important than stages in development
    d. the clinical skills of the investigators are questionable

13. Evidence from an accumulation of studies indicates that the mid-life crisis is
    a. a universal phenomenon.
    b. present in a majority of individuals but not all.
    c. dependent on the cohort that is currently middle aged.
    d. nonexistent.

14. A distinctly feminist critique of stage theories of adult development is that such theories
    a. place too little stress on similarities in women's and men's development.
    b. neglect the complexity of women's lives.
    c. disregard personality variation in favor of personality continuity.
    d. focus too much on crisis at the expense of adaptation.

15. The nature of middle age for women in other cultures is
    a. dependent upon the theoretical position of the researcher and cultural values.
    b. highly similar due to shared values and behavioral expectations.
    c. a function of how cultures deal with the empty nest syndrome and mid-life crisis.
    d. dependent upon how modern the culture is and its view of gender roles.

16. When women in nonindustrialized countries reach middle age, their status improves for all but which of the following reasons?
    a. they are freed from cumbersome restrictions placed on them when they were younger
    b. they have authority over younger relatives
    c. they have opportunities to gain status outside the home that younger women do not have
    d. they are no longer able to bear children

17. According to the life events approach, individuals may differ in the way they deal with divorce for all but which of the following reasons?
    a. the status of their health
    b. their previously established coping mechanisms
    c. their developmental stage
    d. societal acceptance of the divorce

18. The group most often citing body-weight and health-status concerns as frequent daily hassles (Kanner et al.) was
    a. college students.
    b. middle-aged adults.
    c. divorcees.
    d. adults experiencing the empty nest syndrome.

19. Regarding age changes in personality, Bernice Neugarten in the Kansas City Study found that
    a. personality remains fairly constant, but age changes do exist.
    b. significant gender differences in personality were present, but mostly at younger ages.
    c. neurosis increases with age, but social inhibitions in personality decline.
    d. depression increases with age, but only in the personalities of elderly who are widowed.

20. Paul Costa and R. R. McRae determined that the "big five" personality factors
    a. showed different patterns of development during middle adulthood.
    b. became the "big three" as adults matured.
    c. go through a series of developmental stages.
    d. are all stable during the middle adult years.

21. All but one of the following is an aspect of planful competence. Which one is the exception?
    a. self-concept
    b. dependability
    c. high intelligence
    d. intellectual investment

22. Ravenna Helson described an awareness of limitations and death as a mid-life
    a. consciousness.
    b. stage.
    c. crisis.
    d. transformation.

23. The lives of Ram Dass (Richard Alpert) and Jerry Rubin tend to support which theory of personality?
    a. change
    b. stability
    c. introversion/extroversion
    d. neuroticism/openness

24. Mexican American families with strong ties to Mexican values may find it very stressful when
    a. the husband's parents come to live with them.
    b. their female children choose to further their education over raising a family.
    c. their male children feel the urge to return to their Mexican homeland.
    d. the parents of the wife come to live with them.

25. Which research reported in our text best supports the idea that there are seasons in a woman's life?
    a. Neugarten's Kansas City study
    b. Costa and McRae's Baltimore study
    c. the Berkeley longitudinal studies
    d. Helson's Mills College study

26. A life review focuses on
    a. segments of a person's life.
    b. a chronological list of life events.
    c. important life transformations.
    d. formative life crises.

Answers for Self Test A

1. social clock
2. William James
3. empty nest syndrome
4. Carol Ryff
5. contemporary life-events approach
6. Paul Costa and R. R. McRae
7. career consolidation
8. George Vaillant
9. keeping the meaning versus rigidity
10. Bernice Neugarten

Answers for Self Test B

1. a LO 1.1
2. b LO 1.2
3. a LO 1.5
4. c LO 1.8
5. a LO 1.10
6. a LO 1.11
7. d LO 2.1
8. a LO 2.2
9. a LO 2.5
10. a LO 2.6
11. c LO 2.8
12. d LO 2.10
13. c LO 2.12
14. b LO 2.14
15. d LO 2.18
16. d LO 2.19
17. c LO 2.21
18. b LO 2.23
19. a LO 3.1
20. d LO 3.3
21. c LO 3.6
22. a LO 3.9
23. b LO 3.10
24. b LO 4.1
25. d LO 4.2
26. a LO 4.5

Chapter 18   Physical Development in Late Adulthood

Learning Objectives with Key Terms in Boldface

1.0 Longevity

A. *Life Expectancy and Life Span*

1.1   Explain why the concept of late adulthood is a recent one.

1.2   Define and distinguish between **life span** and **life expectancy**, and indicate Americans' current life expectancy.

1.3   Identify the correlates of long life suggested by the Social Security Administration's interviews of people who lived to be 100.

1.4   Study the Basic Life Expectancy Test in Table 18.1 to identify correlates of long life.

1.5   List the predictors of long life found in the Duke Longitudinal Study.

1.6   Compare the longevity of men and women.

1.7   Discuss why women have a longer life expectancy than men do.

B. *The Young Old, the Old Old, and the Oldest Old*

1.8   Define and distinguish among the young old, old old, and oldest old.

1.9   Explain the value of the distinctions among the subphases of old age.

1.10   Sketch characteristics of the oldest old.

1.11   Discuss how the oldest old are a heterogeneous, diversified group.

1.12   Cite evidence that a substantial portion of the oldest old function effectively.

C. *Biological Theories of Aging*

1.13   Define and distinguish **microbiological theories of aging** and **macrobiological theories of aging**.

1.14   Describe microbiological processes that are associated with aging.

1.15   Indicate the human life span suggested by microbiological studies.

1.16   Describe macrobiological processes associated with aging.

1.17   Discuss controversies concerning the number and nature of biological clocks.

2.0 The Course of Physical Development in Late Adulthood

2.1   Describe the nature of physical changes in late adulthood.

2.2   List factors associated with individual variation in physical changes in late adulthood.

A. *The Brain and Nervous System*

2.3   Describe changes in the brain and nervous system during late adulthood.

2.4   Evaluate the myth that elderly adults lose the majority of their brain cells or experience dramatic deterioration in brain functions.

2.5   List factors associated with the prevention or delay of loss of brain function.

B. *Sensory Development*

2.6   Describe changes in vision, hearing, taste, smell, and touch during old age, and indicate associated physiological changes.

2.7   Use Table 18.3 to compare and contrast perceptual decline in old age and late old age.

C. *The Circulatory System*

2.8   Compare and contrast what we used to believe with what we now know about normal blood circulation and blood pressure among the elderly.

D. *The Respiratory System*

2.9   Indicate the loss of lung capacity between 20 and 80 years of age.

E. Sexuality

 2.10 Describe changes in sexual performance associated with age.

 2.11 Explain limitations of our knowledge of sexuality among the very old.

 2.12 Indicate whether therapy improves interest in sex and sexual functioning in the very old.

3.0 Health

 A. Health Problems

  3.1 Define **chronic disorders**.

  3.2 Describe the incidence of various disorders among men and women 45-64 years of age versus those 65 years of age and older.

  3.3 Describe the association of chronic disorders with work limitations and low income.

 B. Causes of Death in Older Adults

  3.4 Indicate the leading causes of death among older adults.

  3.5 Discuss how reductions in causes of death could increase or have increased longevity.

 C. Arthritis

  3.6 Indicate the nature and experience of **arthritis**.

  3.7 Indicate what people can do about arthritis.

 D. Osteoporosis

  3.8 Indicate the nature, incidence, and causes of **osteoporosis**.

  3.9 Indicate what people can do about osteoporosis.

 E. Accidents

  3.10 Indicate the prevalence of accidents among older adults.

  3.11 Explain how accidents are followed by slow recovery or even death in older adults.

 F. The Robust Oldest Old

  3.12 Indicate myth and reality about the nature and incidence of the "robust old".

  3.13 Discuss what can be done to make more old people robust.

4.0 Health Treatment

 A. Health Costs

  4.1 Indicate the health care and nursing home costs for elderly adults.

  4.2 Discuss how health costs are and could be met by present and new government programs.

 B. Nursing Homes

  4.3 Indicate age changes in the percentages of adults who live in nursing homes.

  4.4 Define and distinguish among skilled, intermediate or ordinary, and residential nursing facilities.

  4.5 Explain how the quality of nursing homes for the elderly varies and why it is a continuing national concern.

  4.6 Explain why the decision to place an elderly person in a nursing home is often long and stressful.

  4.7 Explain why older adults may experience financial barriers to obtaining nursing home care.

  4.8 List and sketch the advantages of alternatives to residential care for the elderly.

 C. Giving Options for Control and Teaching Coping Skills

  4.9 Indicate evidence for the claim that feelings of control and self-determination are good for nursing home patients' health and survival.

  4.10 Explain how feelings of control may contribute to better health and survival.

  4.11 Cite evidence that feelings of control contribute to better health and survival.

 D. The Older Adult and Health-Care Providers

  4.12 Explain how attitudes and stereotypes impede delivery of health care to the elderly.

  4.13 Describe failures of communication that impede delivery of health care to the elderly.

  4.14 Indicate how the elderly may impede delivery of health care to themselves.

5.0 Exercise, Nutrition, and Weight

  A. *Exercise*

    5.1   Indicate evidence that regular exercise may lead to a healthier late adulthood and possibly extend life.

    5.2   Indicate whether strength training can slow or prevent muscle loss.

  B. *Nutrition and Weight*

    5.3   Indicate evidence that restricting food intake may increase longevity.

    5.4   Cite evidence that weight is related to long life.

  C. *The Growing Controversy About Vitamins and Aging*

    5.5   Indicate what we do and do not know about the capacity of vitamin supplements to slow the aging process and improve the health of older adults.

    5.6   List recommended doses of specific vitamin supplements for older adults.

6.0 Chapter Boxes

  A. *Sociocultural Worlds of Development: Aging in Russia, Ecuador, and Kashmir*

    6.1   Describe and evaluate claims of extreme old age by people in Russia, Ecuador, and India.

  B. *Critical Thinking About Life-Span Development: How Long Would You Like to Live?*

    6.2   Identify issues involved in determining how long you would like to live.

  C. *Critical Thinking About Life-Span Development: Old Age in the Past and the Future*

    6.3   Develop a description of the lives of 70-year-olds in the year 2050.

    6.4   Delineate the life-span developmental concepts you used to develop your description.

  D. *Life-Span Health and Well-Being: Explorations in the Health Care of the Elderly*

    6.5   List facts that support the claim that elderly people get shoddy health care.

    6.6   Explain why improving the health care of the elderly starts with training and research.

    6.7   Discuss how and why physicians both undertreat and overtreat their elderly patients.

Guided Review and Study

1.0 Longevity

  A. *Life Expectancy and Life Span*

    1. The concept of _____ adulthood is a twentieth century phenomenon.   *late*

    2. Life _____ is the upper boundary of life, the maximum number of years an individual can live.   *span*

    3. The maximum life span of humans is approximately _____ years.   *120*

    4. Life _____ refers to the number of years of life for the average person born in a particular year.   *expectancy*

    5. Improvements in medicine, nutrition, exercise, and life-style have increased our life expectancy about _____ years since the turn of the century.   *22*

    6. Identify the correlates of long life suggested by the Social Security Administration's interviews of centenarians, people who lived to be 100.

    7. Use the Basic Life Expectancy Test in Table 18.1 to predict your own longevity.

    8. Both insurance actuaries and life-span developmentalists are interested in predicting _____ .   *longevity*

    9. The Duke Longitudinal Study, the most comprehensive inv that _____ is the best predictor of longevity.   *longevity* *health*

   10. In addition, _____ predicted longevity for men, whereas _____ level predicted longevity for women.   *finances* *activity*

11. Beginning at the age of _____ , females begin to outnumber males, and by the time adults are 75 years of age, almost 70 percent of the population is _____ .

25

female

12. Explain why women have a longer life expectancy than men.

13. The increased number of women entering the work force has not affected the gap between male and female life _____ .

expectancy

14. Gender differences in longevity may be related to _____ factors associated with the X chromosome.

biological

B. *The Young Old, the Old Old, and the Oldest Old*

1. _____ adulthood is the longest period of life-span development.

Late

2. Some researchers have distinguished the _____ old from the old old; however, others have added a third division called the _____ old.

young

oldest

3. Characterize the oldest old.

4. One characteristic of individuals in the three subperiods of late adulthood is their _____ .

heterogeneity

5. Explain why the distinctions among the young old, old old, and oldest old are important.

6. Cite evidence that a substantial portion of the oldest old function effectively.

C. *Biological Theories of Aging*

1. _____ biological theories explain aging at the cellular level, whereas _____ biological theories explain aging in terms of more global analyses.

Micro

macro

2. The _____ accumulation theory of aging is a _____ biological theory that assumes cell waste collects in the system and slows down cellular functioning.

garbage

micro

3. The cross-_____ theory of aging is a _____ biological theory that assumes aging cells link up with one another and cause cellular dysfunction.

linkage

micro

4. Both garbage accumulation and cross-linkage may be _____ rather than _____ of aging.

consequences

causes

5. Indicate why Leonard Hayflick says that a biological clock within our cells may cause us to age.

6. An impaired _____ system theory is a _____ biological theory that assumes the immune system becomes less able to recognize and attack bacterial and other unfriendly cells.

immune

macro

7. An aging immune system may also begin to attack _____ cells.

healthy

8. The aging _____ theory is a _____ biological theory that assumes there is a biological clock in the hypothalamus which eventually shuts down hormonal production.

timer

macro

9. Describe the methods and conclusions of David Rudman's study of human growth hormone.

10. According to Rudman, one clock in the _____ may determine longevity; however, a second clock in the _____ systems also influences aging via an adrenal hormone, DHEA.

genes

neuroendocrine

11. The organ _____ theory is a _____ biological theory that assumes aging results from a decline in the body's reserve that makes homeostasis increasingly difficult.

reserve

macro

12. Use Figure 18.1 to review the theories of aging.

2.0 The Course of Physical Development in Late Adulthood

1. Describe the nature of physical changes in late adulthood.

2. Indicate factors related to individual variation in physical changes in late adulthood.

A. The Brain and Nervous System

1. The current consensus is that brain cells may _____ or go dormant in old age, but _____ die off in large quantities.   *shrink*
   do not
2. Unlike other cells in the body, a dying _____ does not replace itself.   *neuron*
3. Through the seventies, _____ growth may compensate for neuron loss.   *dendritic*
4. Characterize Stanley Rapaport's conclusions about the aging brain.

5. Contrary to myths, the aging brain can function _____ despite some neuron loss.   *effectively*
6. Describe the contributions of the Mankato, Minnesota nuns to understanding the aging brain.

7. The capacity of the brain to _____ offers new possibilities for preventing and treating brain _____ .   *change*
   diseases

B. Sensory Development

1. In late adulthood, the decline in _____ that began earlier in adulthood becomes more pronounced.   *vision*
2. List some of the visual declines that occur in late adulthood.

3. Visual decline derives from reductions in the quality or intensity of light that reaches the _____ .   *retina*
4. _____ blindness is defined as corrected distance of 20/200.   *Legal*
5. The _____ problems that began in middle adulthood become troublesome in late adulthood.   *hearing*
6. By the time adults reach the age of 75, about _____ percent have a hearing problem.   *75*
7. As we age we may become less sensitive to _____ and smell.   *taste*
8. Bitter and sour tastes are _____ to perceive than sweet and salty tastes.   *easier*
9. Older adults are _____ sensitive to pain than younger adults.   *less*
10. Explain why the distinction between young old age and late old age is important when discussing declines in the perceptual system.

C. The Circulatory System

1. In the absence of heart disease, the amount of blood pumped remains the _____ throughout the life span.   *same*
2. Nowadays high blood pressure is treated with _____ rather than just accepted as a condition of old age.   *medication*

D. The Respiratory System

1. Although lung capacity _____ , older adults can improve lung functioning with diaphragm-strengthening exercises.   *drops*

E. Sexuality

1. The changes in sexual performance with increased age are more pronounced for _____ than for _____ .

    males
    females

2. Explain why the view that sexuality can be lifelong is one contrary to many people's beliefs.

3. _____ education increases sexual interest, sexual knowledge, and sexual activity.

    Sex

3.0 Health

A. Health Problems

1. As we age, we are more likely to suffer from _____ disorders that have a slow onset and a long duration.

    chronic

2. _____ disorders rarely develop in early adulthood, increase during middle adulthood, and become _____ in late adulthood.

    Chronic
    common

3. Use Figure 18.3 to determine the least and most common chronic disorders in late adulthood.

4. The chronic illness most likely to keep an older person from working is _____ disease.

    heart

5. Older adults with low incomes have _____ health problems than older adults with higher incomes.

    more

B. Causes of Death in Older Adults

1. Use Table 18.4 to review the leading cause of death among older persons.

2. If cardiovascular and kidney diseases were eliminated, the life expectancy of older adults would increase by _____ years.

    10

3. The decline in _____ over the last several decades has been due to improved high blood pressure treatments, lower smoking rates, better diet, and an increase in exercise.

    strokes

C. Arthritis

1. _____ entails an inflammation of the joints that produces pain, limited motion, and stiffness, typically in the hips, knees, ankles, fingers, and vertebrae.

    Arthritis

2. The _____ of arthritis can be reduced by drugs, range-of-motion exercises, weight reduction, and replacement of crippled joints.

    symptoms

D. Osteoporosis

1. If the loss of bone tissue exceeds normal levels, an older adult may suffer from _____ .

    osteoporosis

2. Characterize the symptoms of osteoporosis.

3. Osteoporosis is associated with deficiencies in _____ , vitamin D, estrogen depletion, and lack of _____ .

    calcium
    exercise

4. Describe and evaluate alternative ways to prevent osteoporosis.

E. Accidents

1. _____ are the seventh leading cause of death in older adults and may occur at home, in the car, or on the sidewalk.

    Accidents

2. Exercise programs can reduce the risk of _____ by elderly adults.

    falls

F. The Robust Oldest Old

1. Indicate the myth and the reality regarding both the characteristics and incidence of the oldest old.

2. A longitudinal study of adults in their eighties and older revealed that _____ percent were robust.   *33*

3. Indicate techniques of prevention and intervention for making elderly adults more robust.

4.0 Health Treatment

A. Health Costs

1. Compared with adults under the age of 65, older adults spend _____ days in bed, have _____ stays in the hospital, and consume _____ medications.   *more*   *more; more*

2. Health care for older adults now costs an average of _____ dollars per year.   *5,000*

3. One solution to rising health care costs is government funded _____ care, and a second solution is some form of national health _____ .   *home*   *insurance*

B. Nursing Homes

1. About _____ percent of people over the age of 65 reside in nursing homes at any one time.   *5*

2. There are three kinds of nursing facilities: a _____ nursing facility, an ordinary nursing facility, and a _____ nursing facility.   *skilled*   *residential*

3. In a _____ nursing home, care is extensive and heavily monitored by federal agencies.   *skilled*

4. In an _____ nursing facility, care is moderate, federal monitoring is moderate, and costs, although high, are lower than those in a skilled nursing facility.   *intermediate*

5. Costs are less prohibitive and care is more routine and directed toward day-to-day needs in a _____ nursing facility.   *residential*

6. Characterize the quality of nursing homes.

7. The decision to place an elderly person in a nursing home is often _____ .   *stressful*

8. The average cost of staying in a nursing home for one year is in the range of _____ thousand dollars.   *25 to 34*

9. Many people incorrectly believe that _____ will cover their nursing home costs.   *Medicare*

10. List alternatives to nursing homes.

C. Giving Options for Control and Teaching Coping Skills

1. An important factor related to health and survival in a nursing home is the patient's feelings of _____ and self-determination.   *control*

2. Describe the methods and conclusions of the classic study of self-determination by elderly nursing home residents.

3. Ellen Langer says that aging adults need to understand they can _____ the way they think.   *choose*

4. Explain why Langer says many people act old.

5. Richard Schulz demonstrated that nursing home residents that had control over visits by _____ students made them more active, happier, and healthier.   *college*

6. A follow-up study revealed that the individuals who lost their control over the visits were psychologically _____ than others.   *worse*

7. Judith Rodin says that the perception of control may reduce _____ and related hormones.   *stress*

8. Her research showed that nursing home residents who had received assertiveness training had _____ levels of cortisol, were healthier, and needed fewer medications than _____ residents without assertiveness training.   *lower*   *control*

D. The Older Adult and Health-Care Providers

1. The _____ of both the health-care provider and the older adult patient influence older adult's health care. *attitudes*

2. For example, health-care personnel are more likely to be interested in treating _____ persons who have more acute problems than _____ persons who are more likely to have chronic problems. *younger* *older*

3. Explain how physicians communicate differently with younger and older patients.

4. Older patients should take an _____ role in their health care. *active*

5.0 Exercise, Nutrition, and Weight

A. Exercise

1. To prevent or decrease the severity of _____ problems during late adulthood, experts recommend a regimen of exercise, nutrition, and weight-control. *health*

2. Describe the method and conclusion of a study of the cardiovascular fitness of 101 older men and women.

3. A large study of middle-aged and older adults showed that those who led sedentary lives were _____ times more likely to die within eight years of the start of the study than those who exercised. *2*

4. In addition to aerobic activity and stretching, gerontologists increasingly recommend _____ training such as lifting weights. *strength*

5. Exercise is an excellent way to maintain _____ . *health*

B. Nutrition and Weight

1. In laboratory animals, food restriction can _____ longevity by 40 percent; however, it is not known if food restrictions _____ human longevity. *increase* *increase*

2. The best diet for an older adult is a well-balanced, _____ diet that includes the foods needed to maintain good health. *low-fat*

3. Indicate the relationship between body weight and longevity.

C. The Growing Controversy About Vitamins and Aging

1. Previously experts have recommended a healthy, well-balanced diet rather than _____ supplements for successful aging. *vitamin*

2. New results suggest that vitamin supplements in the form of _____ , such as vitamin C, vitamin E, and beta-carotene, may slow the aging process and improve the health of older adults. *antiodxidants*

3. Antioxidants presumably counter the cell damage produced by _____ radicals. *free*

4. Although antioxidants reduce the risk of becoming _____ and sick in later years, there is no evidence that they increase the human life span. *frail*

5. Indicate what critics say about vitamin supplement research.

6. List the recommended doses of vitamin supplements for older adults.

6.0 Chapter Boxes

A. Sociocultural Worlds of Development: Aging in Russia, Ecuador, and Kashmir

1. In Russia, Ecuador, and Kashmir, large numbers of individuals live to be very _____ ; however, there is reason to believe some claims that individuals live more than 120 years are _____ . *old* *false*

B. Critical Thinking About Life-Span Development: How Long Would You Like to Live?

1. Explain what you would learn by identifying issues involved in determining how long you would like to live.

C. Critical Thinking About Life-Span Development: Old Age in the Past and the Future

1. Indicate what you would learn by speculating about the lives of 70-year-olds in the year 2050.

D. Life-Span Health and Well-Being: Explorations in the Health Care of the Elderly

1. Summarize evidence for the claim that elderly people get shoddy health care.

2. Explain what it means to say that improving the health care of the elderly starts with training and research.

3. Physicians both _____ treat and _____ treat their elderly patients.   *under; over*

4. The elderly need better and more informed _____ -care treatment.   *health*

Self Test A: Key Terms and Key Persons

Write the appropriate key term or key person in the space to the right of the definition or description.

1. A class of theories that explain aging in cellular rather than more global terms.   _____

2. A health problem in which there is a loss of bone tissue from the skeletal system.   _____

3. An individual who believes that many of our habits are mindless, and people need to become mindful of why they are engaging in a habit.   _____

4. Disorders with a slow onset and long duration.   _____

5. The researcher who believes that there are biological clocks within our cells that cause us to age.   _____

6. A psychologist who showed that teaching coping skills to nursing home residents lowered their stress-related hormones.   _____

7. The number of years of life that an average person born in a particular year will probably live.   _____

8. The researcher who observed the effects of human growth hormone on elderly men.   _____

Self Test B: Multiple Choice

1. With improvements in medicine, nutrition, exercise, and life-style,
   a. our life span has increased.
   b. our life expectancy has increased.
   c. our life expectancy has stayed the same, but our lives are healthier.
   d. our life expectancy has dropped, but the quality of life has improved.

2. If the present trend in life expectancies continues, by the year 2020
   a. males are likely to live as long as females.
   b. individuals will be more resistant to infectious and chronic diseases.
   c. older persons will be in nursing homes.
   d. the average number of years between life span and life expectancy will be fewer.

3. Women outlive men for all but which of the following reasons?
   a. financial status
   b. health attitudes
   c. occupation
   d. habits

4. Women tend to outlive men because
   a. they carry two X chromosomes.
   b. they have stronger immune systems.
   c. estrogen helps protect against arteriosclerosis.
   d. All of the answers are correct.

5.. Who would be classified as the "oldest old?"
   a. Methuselah, who is 78
   b. Eve, who is 83
   c. Noah, who is 88
   d. All of these answers are correct.

6. As more information is gathered concerning the life and abilities of individuals over age 85, a more _____ picture is beginning to emerge.
   a. optimistic
   b. homogenous
   c. depressing
   d. psychopathic

7. Macrobiological theories of aging focus on
   a. the cell.
   b. genetics.
   c. systems within the body.
   d. cellular interaction.

8. Leonard Hayflick found that embryonic cells can divide about _____ times before they stop.
   a. 50
   b. 500
   c. 1,000
   d. 100,000

9. Which of the following is associated with aging?
   a. height decreases
   b. slowing of reflexes
   c. brain cell decreases
   d. All of the answers are correct.

10. Before the age of 70 we lose about _____ percent of our neurons.
    a. 10
    b. 20
    c. 40
    d. 50

11. In the aging brain, it appears that
    a. dendritic expansion compensates for neural loss.
    b. neural cell size is compensated for by myelin loss.
    c. neural efficiency is compensated for by neural size.
    d. neural transmitter production increases as neural numbers are lost.

12. Sixty-five-year-old Julia does not hear high-frequency sounds quite as well as she did at 25. Regarding this change in hearing,
    a. she would be a good candidate for two hearing aids, which would correct each ear separately.
    b. she is typical of her age group.
    c. people should speak more loudly to her.
    d. she will find reading more enjoyable than watching TV.

13. Physiological changes that affect sexual behavior
    a. are more prevalent in men than in women.
    b. are more prevalent in women than in men.
    c. cannot be corrected in men and limit their sexual activity.
    d. cannot be corrected in women and limit their sexual activity.

14. The most common chronic disorder in late adulthood is
    a. hypertension.
    b. arthritis.
    c. diabetes.
    d. heart conditions.

15. The chronic illness that puts the greatest limitation on work is
    a. asthma.
    b. arthritis.
    c. a heart condition.
    d. diabetes.

16. The decline in strokes over the last several decades is due to all but which of the following?
    a. a decrease in smoking
    b. improved treatment of high blood pressure
    c. better diet programs
    d. fewer older adults overexercising

17. An aging disorder that is associated with calcium and vitamin D deficiencies, estrogen depletion, and lack of exercise is
    a. arthritis.
    b. osteoporosis.
    c. pernicious anemia.
    d. depression.

18. To prevent osteoporosis young and middle-aged women should do all but which of the following?
    a. avoid weight-bearing exercises
    b. eat foods rich in calcium
    c. avoid smoking
    d. subscribe to estrogen replacement therapy

19. Compared to younger persons, elderly adult accident victims are likely to spend more time in the hospital because
    a. recovery is often complicated by mental depression.
    b. Medicare focuses mainly on long-term treatments.
    c. healing rates are slower in older adults.
    d. family members feel that the older adult is safer in the hospital.

20. Engaging in an exercise program has been shown to have all but which of the following effects on older adults?
    a. reduced blood pressure
    b. lower cholesterol levels
    c. better oxygen uptake
    d. more frequent bone injuries

21. In a residential nursing facility
    a. personal care is given to meet day-to-day needs.
    b. medical care is extensive and closely monitored.
    c. nursing care is moderate.
    d. patients care for themselves and meet for meals.

22. Bill's adult children realize that he needs some nursing assistance in meeting daily needs but requires only a least restrictive nursing facility. They should look for which of the following types of nursing homes?
   a. skilled
   b. intermediate
   c. residential
   d. practical

23. Alternatives to nursing homes include all but which of the following?
   a. home health care
   b. day care centers
   c. long-term care facilities
   d. preventative medicine clinics

24.. Judith Rodin and Ellen Langer found that nursing home patients who were given some responsibility and control over their lives became
   a. more difficult to manage.
   b. more likely to want to return home.
   c. healthier.
   d. happier but lived no longer than those individuals who were given no responsibility and self-control.

25. In comparing physician responsiveness to older versus younger patients, Green et al. found that physicians were
   a. more responsive to older patients.
   b. more responsive to younger patients.
   c. equally responsive to patients of both ages.
   d. more responsive depending upon the severity of the disease.

26. Blumental et al. (1989) found that older individuals who _____ experienced significant improvement in cardiovascular fitness.
   a. were in a yoga class
   b. were taught transcendental meditation
   c. engaged in moderate aerobic exercise
   d. All of the answers are correct.

27. Older adults who subscribe to a low-calorie diet
   a. have been shown to live substantially longer than those who do not.
   b. are likely to die sooner than those who do not.
   c. may be risking their health, because not much is known about the long-term effects of low-calorie diets.
   d. should be on high-protein diets with vitamin supplements.

28. The vitamin supplements called antioxidants may affect health by counteracting the effects of
   a. white corpuscles.
   b. DNA changes.
   c. free radicals.
   d. cholesterol.

29. Which statement concerning health care and the elderly is true?
   a. Elderly individuals are least likely to be given prescription drugs.
   b. Elderly individuals are often excluded from research to cure ailments that are common to their age group.
   c. Women over age 65 are least likely to get breast cancer and the most likely to be treated for it.
   d. Elderly people tend to overreport vision and hearing ailments because they believe that such problems are normal.

Answers for Self Test A

1. macrobiological theories of aging
2. osteoporosis
3. Ellen Langer
4. chronic disorder
5. Leonard Hayflick
6. Judith Rodin
7. life expectancy
8. Daniel Rudman

Answers for Self Test B

1. b   LO 1.2
2. d   LO 1.2
3. a   LO 1.6
4. d   LO 1.7
5. c   LO 1.8
6. a   LO 1.12
7. c   LO 1.13
8. b   LO 1.15
9. d   LO 2.1
10. a   LO 2.3
11. a   LO 2.5
12. b   LO 2.6
13. a   LO 2.10
14. b   LO 3.2
15. c   LO 3.3
16. d   LO 3.5
17. b   LO 3.8
18. a   LO 3.9
19. c   LO 3.11
20. d   LO 3.13
21. a   LO 4.4
22. c   LO 4.4
23. c   LO 4.8
24. c   LO 4.11
25. b   LO 4.13
26. c   LO 5.1
27. c   LO 5.4
28. a   LO 6.1
29. b   LO 6.6

Chapter 19   Cognitive Development in Late Adulthood

Learning Objectives with Key Terms in Boldface

1.0 Cognitive Functioning in Older Adults

A. *The Debate about Intellectual Decline in Late Adulthood*

1.1 Define and distinguish between **crystallized intelligence** and **fluid intelligence**.

1.2 Describe how each type of intelligence changes with age in late adulthood.

1.3 Indicate how the method used to collect data about age changes in intelligence relates to what researchers learn.

B. *The Multidimensional, Multidirectional Nature of Intelligence*

1.4 Define and distinguish between **cognitive mechanics** and **cognitive pragmatics**.

1.5 Discuss how cognitive and pragmatic mechanics may be involved in changes in intelligence during old age.

1.6 Indicate how speed of processing and memory processes change with age.

1.7 Indicate and illustrate how laboratory findings about processing speed may give only a rough indication of a person's ability in the real world.

1.8 Define **wisdom** and discuss whether it increases across the life span.

1.9 Discuss the relevance of experience to developmental changes in problem solving.

C. *Education, Work, and Health*

1.10 Indicate how education relates to age, intelligence and mental processing performance.

1.11 List reasons older adults seek more education.

1.12 Speculate about how the changing nature of jobs/careers contributes to intellectual strength over the life span.

1.13 Critically discuss how health and exercise relate to measures of intelligence and cognitive performance among older adults.

D. *Terminal Drop*

1.14 State the **terminal drop hypothesis**, and indicate how it relates to data on intellectual declines among the aged.

E. *Training Cognitive Skills*

1.15 Cite evidence that cognitive skills can be retrained in late adulthood.

1.16 Define and distinguish among **mnemonics**, the method of loci, and chunking.

1.17 Summarize the success of efforts to train reasoning, mnemonic, and problem-solving skills in older adults.

1.18 Explain how cognitive training research contributes to understanding the cognitive mechanisms of old age.

2.0 Work and Retirement

A. *Work*

2.1 Compare and contrast older adults involvement in work today and 100 years ago.

2.2 List the correlates of working into late adulthood.

B. *Retirement in the United States and Other Countries*

2.3 State why more Americans retire today than did 100 years ago.

2.4 Describe changes in U. S. government policy concerning retirement.

2.5 Indicate how several European governments have made retirement attractive.

C. *Phases of Retirement*

2.6 Define and distinguish among the **remote phase, near phase, honeymoon phase, disenchantment phase, reorientation phase, stability phase,** and **termination phase** of retirement.

D. *Adjustment to Retirement*

2.7 Indicate the correlates of satisfactory versus unsatisfactory retirement.

3.0 The Mental Health of Older Adults

A. *The Nature of Mental Health in Older Adults*

    3.1   Explain why it is important to promote mental health among older adults.

    3.2   Define mental health.

    3.3   Indicate the overall incidence of mental disorders among older adults.

B. *Depression*

    3.4   Define **major depression** and indicate its incidence in older adults.

    3.5   Indicate the problems and correlates of major depression.

C. *Dementia and Alzheimer's Disease*

    3.6   Define **dementia** and indicate its incidence among the elderly.

    3.7   Define **Alzheimer's disease** and indicate its incidence among the elderly.

    3.8   Describe what we know about Alzheimer's physiological correlates and causes.

    3.9   Sketch problems and solutions in the care of Alzheimer patients.

D. *Fear of Victimization and Crime*

    3.10   Indicate how real and imagined fears of crime influence the lives of the elderly.

E. *Meeting the Mental Health Needs of Older Adults*

    3.11   Indicate the distribution of mental health services to older adults.

    3.12   Discuss obstacles to providing mental health services to older adults.

    3.13   List ways to improve mental health services for older adults.

4.0 Religion in Late Adulthood

    4.1   Indicate how older adults participate in religion.

    4.2   Indicate general specific ways that religion is significant in the lives of older adults.

5.0 Chapter Boxes

A. *Sociocultural Worlds of Development: Work and Retirement in Japan, the United States, England, and France*

    5.1   Compare and contrast retirement rates and values in Japan, the United States, England, and France.

B. *Critical Thinking About Life-Span Development: A Challenging Intellectual Life in Old Age*

    5.2   Develop a list of older adults who have made important intellectual contributions.

C. *Critical Thinking About Life-Span Development: Evaluating General Statements about Cognitive and Work Decline in Older Adult*

    5.3   Evaluate the accuracy of generalizations about the intelligence, wisdom, and productivity of older adults.

D. *Life-Span Health and Well-Being: Trends in the Metal Health Care of Older Adults*

    5.4   Indicate recent trends in delivery of mental health services to older adults.

    5.5   List three important points for evaluating the intersection of health and mental health systems.

    5.6   Discuss the relationship between physical and mental health as a factor in delivering services for both.

    5.7   Indicate both current and possible future ways to improve delivery of mental health services to elderly adults.

Guided Review and Study

1.0 Cognitive Functioning in Older Adults

A. *The Debate About Intellectual Decline in Late Adulthood*

    1.   David Wechsler, the author of the Wechsler Scales of Intelligence, concluded that adulthood entails an intellectual _____ as a result of the aging process.   *decline*

    2.   Alternatively, John Horn believes that some intellectual abilities _____ , whereas other abilities do not.   *decline*

    3.   _____ intelligence refers to an individual's accumulated information and verbal skills, whereas _____ intelligence refers to an individual's ability to reason abstractly.   *Crystallized fluid*

4. According to John Horn, crystallized intelligence _____ with increasing age, and fluid intelligence _____ with increasing age.

increases
decreases

5. Use Figure 19.2 to explain why K. Warner Schaie questions John Horn's findings.

6. Explain what Paul Baltes means by saying that developmentalists need to recast the issue of cognitive decline in other terms.

B. The Multidimensional, Multidirectional Nature of Intelligence

1. Paul _____ distinguishes between cognitive mechanics and cognitive pragmatics.

Baltes

2. Explain the concept of cognitive mechanics in your own terms.

3. Explain the concept of cognitive pragmatics in your own terms.

4. Although cognitive _____ may decline in old age, cognitive _____ may actually improve.

mechanics
pragmatics
decline

5. Speed of processing seems to _____ in late adulthood.

6. A study of typing revealed that the reaction time of older subjects was _____ than reaction time for younger subjects; however, the typing speed for the older and younger subjects was

_____ .

slower
equal

7. Older individuals appear to maintain their skills by substituting _____ for speed.

experience

8. Characterize changes in memory during adulthood.

9. People who have expert knowledge about the practical aspects of life possess _____ .

wisdom

10. _____ involves exceptional insight into life matters, good judgment, and coping with difficult life problems.

Wisdom

11. Nancy Denny used _____ problem-solving scenarios to assess problem-solving skills in older and younger adults.

practical

12 Denny found that the ability to solve practical problems _____ through the 40s and 50s and that 70-year-olds were _____ worse at solving practic

increases
no

C. Education, Work, and Health

1. The three factors of education, work, and health affect the _____ functioning of older adults.

cognitive

2. Educational experiences correlate _____ with scores on intelligence tests and information processing tasks.

positively

3. Indicate some of the reasons that older adults tend to seek more education.

4. Since the 1900s, work experiences have entailed more _____ oriented and less manual labor.

cognitively

5. An increased emphasis on cognitive abilities at work has likely enhanced individual's _____ abilities.

intellectual

6. Better medical treatment has produced successively _____ generations who enter late adulthood.

healthier

7. Some of the decline in intellectual ability in older adults may result from _____ factors rather than age per se.

health

8. Indicate what Timothy Salthouse and K. Warner Schaie say about the relationship between cognitive performance and health.

9. In a study in which _____ exercise was defined as engaging in strenuous exercise more than one and a quarter hours per week, older adults who exercised vigorously performed _____ on tests of reasoning, memory, and reaction time than those who exercised little or not at all.

vigorous

better

10. Additional research _____ the finding that exercise improves the _____ functioning of older adults.

confirms

cognitive

D. Terminal Drop

1. The terminal _____ hypothesis states that death is preceded by a decrease in cognitive function about _____ years prior to death.

drop

5

2. The findings that older adults perform more poorly on some cognitive tasks than younger adults may be due to chronic _____ that decrease their motivation, alertness, and energy.

diseases

3. The terminal drop hypothesis receives support from studies of vocabulary, but not studies for _____ facility and _____ speed.

numerical

perceptual

E. Training Cognitive Skills

1. Describe how Sherry Willis and K. Warner Schaie reached the conclusion that there is plasticity, and that training can improve the cognitive skills of many older adults.

2. _____ , any technique that makes an individual's memory more efficient, can be used to improve an older person's memory ability.

Mnemonics

3. Grouping items on a grocery list together by category to help remember everything on the list is an example of a _____ technique.

mnemonic

4. Individuals using the mnemonic called the method of _____ pair items to be remembered with a location.

loci

5. When information is organized into meaningful or manageable units to improve recall of that information, the mnemonic technique is called _____ .

chunking

6. Telephone numbers, car license plates, and social security numbers exemplify _____ .

chunking

7. Describe how Sherry Willis and Carolyn Nesselroade reached the conclusion that cognitive training helps maintain fluid intelligence with increasing age.

8. According to Sherry Willis, _____ training research helps researchers better understand the cognitive mechanisms of old age.

cognitive

9. One aspect concerns _____ , a second aspect concerns _____ -related changes, and a third aspect concerns potential remedial training programs.

plasticity

age

2.0 Work and Retirement

A. Work

1. The percentage of men over the age of 65 who continue to work full-time has _____ since the 1900s.

decreased

2. The percentage of men over the age of 65 who continue to work part-time has _____ since the 1960s.

increased

3. Indicate factors related to working into late adulthood.

4. _____ workers have better attendance records and fewer accidents than _____ workers.

Older; younger

B. Retirement in the United States and Other Countries

1. The Social _____ system, which provides benefits for older workers when they retire, was implemented in 1935.

Security

2. Today's workers will, on the average, spend 10 to 15 percent of their lives in _____ .

retirement

3. Indicate the policy decisions implemented in 1967, 1978, and 1986 by the government regarding retirement in the United States.

4. The United States has encouraged _____ retirement, whereas many European companies have encouraged _____ retirement.

later

earlier

C. Phases of Retirement

1. Robert Atchley proposed that people go through _____ phases of retirement; however, there _____ a particular timing or sequencing of these seven stages because individuals retire at different times and for different _____ .

7

is

reasons

2. In the _____ phase of retirement, most individuals are not concerned about retirement and do little to prepare for it.

remote

3. In the _____ phase of retirement, workers begin to participate in a preretirement program.

near

4. In the _____ phase of retirement, people are able to do things they never had time to do before.

honeymoon

5. People in the _____ phase of retirement recognize that their fantasies about retirement were unrealistic.

disenchantment

6. In the _____ phase of retirement, individuals develop more realistic life-styles and adopt those habits that bring them life satisfaction.

reorientation

7. In the _____ phase of retirement, retirees develop more realistic life alternatives.

stability

8. When individuals are no longer functioning autonomously and are not self-sufficient they are most likely in the _____ phase of retirement.

termination

D. Adjustment to Retirement

1. Indicate the factors that predict who will and who will not adjust well to retirement.

3.0 The Mental Health of Older Adults

A. The Nature of Mental Health in Older Adults

1. Indicate the concerns regarding the mental health of older adults.

2. At least _____ percent of people over the age of 65 have _____ health problems severe enough to warrant attention by professionals.

10

mental

B. Depression

1. Major _____ is a mood disorder in which an individual is deeply unhappy, demoralized, self-derogatory, and bored.

depression

2. List the symptoms of major depression.

3. Major depression is called the common _____ of mental disorders.

cold

4. The four greatest risk factors associated with _____ by older adults are: living alone, being male, losing a spouse, and failing health.

suicide

C. Dementia and Alzheimer's Disease

1. Define *dementia* in your own terms.

2. Dementia affects about _____ percent of individuals over 80 years of age.

20

3. _____ disease is a progressive, irreversible brain disorder characterized by gradual deterioration of memory, reasoning, language, and physical functioning.

Alzheimer's

4. Alzheimer's disease affects about _____ million individuals over 65 years of age.

2.5

5. Alzheimer's entail a deficiency in _____ , and can be treated with a drug called Tacrine.

acetylcholine

6. Indicate what researchers know about the physical basis of Alzheimer's disease.

7. Indicate the concerns regarding the care of Alzheimer's patients.

D. *Fear of Victimization and Crime*
1. The fear of being a victim of _____ may deter travel, attendance at social events, and the pursuit of an active life-style by older adults.   *crime*
2. In reality, older adults are _____ likely than younger adults to be victims of crime.   *less*

E. *Meeting the Mental Health Needs of Older Adults*
1. The proportion of older adults who obtain services from mental health professionals is _____ than would be expected.   *less*
2. Explain why the attitudes of mental health professionals provide a barrier to good mental health for older persons.

3. List four mechanisms of change that improve the mental health of older adults.

4. To better serve the mental health needs of the elderly, _____ must be encouraged to treat older adults, who, in turn, must be convinced that they can benefit from treatment, and mental health care must be _____ .   *psychologists*   *affordable*

4.0 Religion in Late Adulthood
1. Indicate how older adults participate in religion.

2. Indicate the significance of religion in the lives of older adults.

3. Religious practices are related to well-being and life _____ in old age.   *satisfaction*
4. Indicate what it means to say that religion can meet some important psychological needs in older adults.

5.0 Chapter Boxes

A *Sociocultural Worlds of Development: Work and Retirement in Japan, the United States, England, and France*
1. There are _____ workers over the age of 60 in France, England, and the United States as compared to Japan.   *fewer*
2. Indicate what the results of the cross-cultural study reveal about the attitudes and values of workers in England, France, Japan, and the United States.

B. *Critical Thinking About Life-Span Development: A Challenging Intellectual Life in Old Age*
1. Indicate what you would learn by developing a list of older adults who have made important intellectual contributions.

C. *Critical Thinking About Life-Span Development: Evaluating General Statements about Cognitive and Work Decline in Older Adults*

2. Evaluate the accuracy of generalizations about the intelligence, wisdom, and productivity of older adults

D. *Life-Span Health and Well-Being: Trends in the Metal Health Care of Older Adults*

1. Margaret Gatz, a mental health and aging expert concerned with trends in the mental health services for older adults, has identified a _____ of coordination or cooperation among components of the mental health system.   *lack*

2. List three ways to evaluate the intersection of health and mental health systems.

3. Effective services for older adults must consider the _____ of physical and mental conditions.   *interaction*

4. Indicate ways to improve the delivery of mental health services to elderly adults.

Self Test A: Key Terms and Key Persons

Write the appropriate key term or key person in the space to the right of the definition or description.

1. Techniques and procedures designed to aid memory.   _____

2. A gerontologist who described the seven phases of retirement.   _____

3. A mental health problem that typically affects older adults who display symptoms such as feeling ill, loss of stamina, loss of appetite, and listlessness.   _____

4. One of Robert Atchley's seven phases of retirement in which the individual experiences great joy, and the freedom to do things previously precluded by obligations and responsibilities.   _____

5. A hypothesized decline in cognitive functioning during the five-year period prior to death.   _____

6. A researcher who investigated the effects of training on the cognitive skills of the elderly.   _____

7. The culture-based "software" of the mind.   _____

8. The sum of one's knowledge and verbal skills that typically increases with age.   _____

9. The individual who distinguished between cognitive mechanics and cognitive pragmatics.   _____

10. One of Robert Atchley's seven phases of retirement in which the individual has adopted criteria for evaluating choices in retirement and how the individual will perform once having made these choices.   _____

11. A mental health problem that typically affects older adults who display symptoms such as impaired memory, reasoning, and language, and, eventually, physical functioning.   _____

12. The individual who argues that crystallized intelligence increases with age while fluid intelligence declines steadily from middle adulthood.   _____

Self Test B: Multiple Choice

1. Lisa finds that as she enters middle adulthood, her ability to reason abstractly is declining. This decline is occurring in
   a. crystallized intelligence.
   b. fluid intelligence.
   c. intelligence A.
   d. intelligence B.

2. Which task requires crystallized intelligence?
   a. doing algebra problems
   b. interpreting metaphors
   c. writing a short story
   d. proving a theorem in geometry

3. John Horn says _____ increases with age.
   a. fluid intelligence
   b. crystallized intelligence
   c. chunking of information
   d. long-term memory

4. Which type of study shows general intellectual decline associated with aging?
   a. cross-sectional
   b. longitudinal
   c. quasi-experimental
   d. naturalistic observation

5. Which factor plays the biggest role in determining the pattern of cognitive pragmatics in adulthood?
   a. evolution
   b. culture
   c. early neural development
   d. inheritance

6. In older adulthood,
   a. cognitive pragmatics can be more important to performance than cognitive mechanics.
   b. cognitive mechanics can be more important to performance than cognitive pragmatics.
   c. the relative influences of cognitive pragmatics and mechanics on performance may be virtually identical.
   d. All of the answers are correct.

7. Which of the following tasks will be most difficult for older adults?
   a. problem solving in a natural setting
   b. problem solving in a laboratory setting
   c. speeded tasks in a laboratory setting
   d. speeded tasks in a natural setting

8. Older subjects are brought into the laboratory and given a list of nonsense syllables to remember. They are then given a list of groceries to pick up at the store, and their ability to remember the items is recorded. Research on memory ability in older adults would predict that their memory of the nonsense syllables will be _____ their memory of the grocery items.
   a. about the same as
   b. better than
   c. worse than
   d. poor, but better than

9. Expert knowledge about the practical aspects of life is known as
   a. the stability phase.
   b. fluid intelligence.
   c. crystallized intelligence.
   d. wisdom.

10. Which of the following tasks would most likely require wisdom?
   a. remembering a grocery list
   b. braking when a pedestrian steps out in front of your car
   c. helping a son keep his marriage from falling apart
   d. helping a granddaughter with her algebra

11. When investigating real-world problem solving, Denny found all but which of the following?
   a. practical problem-solving ability increased through the forties and fifties
   b. 70-year-olds performed as well as 20-year-olds
   c. 20-year-olds and 70-year-olds performed the task quite well
   d. subjects at all ages did quite well on the task, but 20-year-olds did substantially better than subjects in the other age groups

12. Which of the following characteristics is positively correlated with IQ scores?
   a. introversion
   b. well-rounded personality
   c. job experience
   d. educational experience

13. Your text noted that older adults return to school because they
   a. become obsolescent due to technological advances.
   b. want to learn more about aging.
   c. have a desire to learn more effective cognitive and social-coping skills.
   d. All of the answers are correct.

14. Clarkson-Smith and Hartley, in their study of the effects of exercise on cognitive functioning, found that
   a. vigorous compared to low exercisers showed improvement.
   b. both vigorous and low exercisers showed similar improvement.
   c. there was improvement in the elderly but not in other age groups.
   d. only those in good health showed improvement.

15. The terminal drop hypothesis claims that death is preceded by a decrease in
   a. physical functioning.
   b. cognitive functioning.
   c. social interaction.
   d. emotional attachment.

16. Which statement is most accurate concerning cognitive skills in the elderly?
   a. Training has little effect upon slowing declines.
   b. They can be retrained, according to an increasing number of developmentalists.
   c. Memory is the only cognitive skill that can be improved by training.
   d. A shift from factual knowledge to wisdom occurs in most elderly adults.

17. The mnemonic being used when an item to be remembered is paired with a location is
   a. chunking.
   b. organizing.
   c. rehearsing.
   d. the method of loci.

18. All of the following are true when older workers are compared to younger workers except
    a. they have better attendance records.
    b. they have fewer accidents.
    c. they have more disabling injuries.
    d. they are more productive.

19. Increases in part-time employment among older adults have been
    a. greatest for females.
    b. greatest for males.
    c. about equal for both females and males.
    d. difficult to clearly determine due to frequent job changes among older adults.

20. The 1986 United States ban on any type of age-related, mandatory retirement would not apply to
    a. Harpo, who was the president of 3-M.
    b. Groucho, who was a college professor.
    c. Chico, who was a mail carrier.
    d. Zeppo, who was a fire fighter.

21. In which of Robert Atchley's retirement phases do workers begin attending pre-retirement seminars?
    a. honeymoon
    b. near
    c. remote
    d. stability

22. In the reorientation phase of retirement, individuals
    a. develop realistic life alternatives for how to spend their time.
    b. adjust to engaging in all of the activities they eagerly anticipated when they were working.
    c. adjust to the many illnesses that accompany increasing age.
    d. begin to look forward to retirement with eager anticipation.

23. Who *is not* exhibiting a symptom of major depression?
    a. Jasmine, who is not eating
    b. Ariel, who is making self-derogatory comments
    c. Belle, who cannot remember things she learned yesterday
    d. Jafar, who is completely unmotivated

24. _____ *is not* part of the definition of Alzheimer's disease.
    a. Irreversibility
    b. Genetically based
    c. Brain disorder
    d. Deterioration of memory and physical functioning

25. Upon autopsy, concentrations of plaque and amyloid protein were found in the patient's brain. The most likely diagnosis was that the patient had
    a. a major depression.
    b. Alzheimer's disease.
    c. arteriosclerosis.
    d. brain toxicity.

26. Older adults may feel more vulnerable to crime due to
    a. physical declines.
    b. inability to crime-proof their homes.
    c. the fact that most neighborhoods they live in have deteriorated and become high-crime areas.
    d. large amounts of cash kept at home due to their general distrust of banks.

27. When compared to younger adults, adults over the age of 65 receive _____ their share of psychological services.
    a. more than
    b. less than
    c. about the same amount
    d. substantially more than

28. Psychotherapists have been accused of failing to accept many older adult clients because
    a. they believe the prognosis for the older adult is poor.
    b. fewer techniques for treating mental problems among older adults exist.
    c. older clients, compared to younger clients, are less likely to pay the therapists for services rendered.
    d. older clients typically forget appointments.

29. When asked at what age they preferred to retire, respondents from which country gave the highest age?
    a. United States
    b. England
    c. France
    d. Japan

30. Which people believe that older people's income should come from savings while employed?
    a. United States and Japan
    b. Japan and England
    c. England and France
    d. France and the United States

31. Margaret Gatz argues that in order for the current health care system to meet the needs of older adults with mental disorders, it has to
    a. allow physicians to provide prescriptions over the phone.
    b. create eldercare centers in the workplace.
    c. consider limiting the types of psychological care covered by Medicare.
    d. All of the answers are correct.

Answers for Self Test A

1. mnemonics
2. Robert Atchley
3. major depression
4. honeymoon phase
5. terminal drop hypothesis
6. Sherry Willis
7. cognitive pragmatics
8. crystallized intelligence
9. Paul Baltes
10. stability phase
11. Alzheimer's disease
12. John Horn

Answers for Self Test B

1. b LO 1.1
2. c LO 1.1
3. b LO 1.2
4. a LO 1.3
5. b LO 1.4
6. d LO 1.5
7. c LO 1.6
8. c LO 1.7
9. d LO 1.8
10. c LO 1.8
11. a LO 1.9
12. d LO 1.10
13. d LO 1.11
14. a LO 1.13
15. b LO 1.14
16. b LO 1.15
17. d LO 1.16
18. c LO 2.2
19. a LO 2.2
20. d LO 2.4
21. b LO 2.6
22. a LO 2.6
23. c LO 3.2
24. b LO 3.5
25. b LO 3.6
26. a LO 3.8
27. b LO 3.9
28. a LO 3.10
29. c LO 5.3
30. a LO 5.3
31. b LO 5.7

Chapter 20   Socioemotional Development in Late Adulthood

Learning Objectives with Key Terms in Boldface

1.0 The Social Worlds of Older Adults

A. *Social Theories of Aging*

    1.1 Define and critique the **disengagement theory** of aging.

    1.2 Define and distinguish between the **activity theory** and **social breakdown-reconstruction theory** of aging.

    1.3 Indicate how activity and social breakdown-reconstruction theories could improve the lives of older adults.

B. *Stereotyping Older Adults*

    1.4 Define and list varieties of **ageism**.

    1.5 List seven stereotypes of the aged found among adults of all ages.

    1.6 Indicate how older adults have tried to combat ageism.

C. *Police Issues in an Aging Society*

    1.7 Evaluate the claim that old people are an economic burden on society because they do not work and suffer poor health.

    1.8 Indicate how a "care" rather than a "cure" model is more appropriate for the health needs of the elderly.

    1.9 Define **eldercare**, and discuss policies that may facilitate or hinder it.

    1.10 Define **generational inequity** and identify its several facets.

D. *Income*

    1.11 Indicate the nature and incidence of poverty among the elderly.

    1.12 Discuss the income needs of older adults and deficiencies in planning for them.

E. *Living Arrangements*

    1.13 Indicate the nature and incidence of various living arrangements among older adults.

2.0 Ethnicity, Gender, and Culture

A. *Ethnicity and Gender*

    2.1 Explain the double jeopardy faced by aging ethnic minority individuals.

    2.2 Describe the double jeopardy faced by aging women.

    2.3 Indicate the triple jeopardy faced by aging ethnic minority women.

    2.4 Explain how ethnic minorities cope with the difficulties of aging.

B. *Gender Roles*

    2.5 Critically discuss how gender roles change in old age.

C. *Culture*

    2.6 Compare and contrast respect for the elderly in Japan and the United States.

    2.7 List cultural correlates of high status for the elderly.

3.0 Families and Social Relationships

A. *The Aging Couple and Friendship*

    3.1 Indicate problems retirement poses to married couples.

    3.2 Compare and contrast various adaptations of married versus single old people.

    3.3 Indicate the nature and importance of dating and friendship to older adults.

B. *Grandparenting*

    3.4 Indicate the incidence and nature of grandparenting.

    3.5 Discuss three meanings of the grandparent role.

3.6   Describe ethnic variations in grandparenting.

3.7   Define and distinguish between formal, fun-seeking, and distant figure styles of grandparenting, and indicate the prevalence of each.

3.8   Speculate about how grandparenting will change in the future.

4.0   Personality Development, Life Satisfaction, and Successful Aging

  A.   *The Nature of Personality Development*

4.1   Sketch Sigmund Freud's and Carl Jung's visions of old age.

4.2   Define and distinguish between integrity and despair in Erik Erikson's theory of personality development.

4.3   Define and distinguish **differentiation versus role preoccupation, body transcendence versus body preoccupation**, and **ego transcendence versus ego preoccupation** in Robert Peck's reworking of Erikson's concept of integrity versus despair.

4.4   Define **life review** and indicate events that prompt it.

4.5   Discuss how a life review influences relationships with other people.

  B.   *Life Satisfaction*

4.6   Define **life satisfaction** and indicate its correlates.

4.7   Compare older adults' and younger adults' view of late-life development.

  C.   *Successful Aging*

4.8   Summarize the bases of successful aging.

4.9   Define and illustrate the **selective optimization with compensation model** of aging.

5.0   Chapter Boxes

  A.   *Sociocultural Worlds of Development: Being Female, Ethnic, and Old*

5.1   Discuss the advantages and disadvantages old African American women experience in comparison to the experience of other old ethnic females.

5.2   Indicate survival strategies of aging African American women.

  B.   *Critical Thinking About Life-Span Development: Evaluating Stereotypes of the Elderly*

5.3   Compare and contrast portrayals of the elderly in contemporary and earlier magazines of the 20th century.

5.4   Draw appropriate conclusions about how images of the elderly have changed in the 20th century.

  C.   *Critical Thinking About Life-Span Development: Middle-Aged Baby Boomers and Their Grandparents*

5.5   Compare and contrast the values and attitudes of baby boomers and their grandparents.

  D.   *Life-Span Health and Well-Being: Social Support and Health in Late Adulthood*

5.6   Explain how social support might improve the health of older adults.

Guided Review and Study

1.0   The Social Worlds of Older Adults

  A.   *Social Theories of Aging*

1. _____ social theories of aging include disengagement theory, activity theory, and social breakdown-reconstruction theory.   *Three*

2. Explain disengagement theory of aging.

3. Disengagement theory _____ supported by research showing that life satisfaction _____ for individuals who live active, energetic, and productive lives.   *is not*   *increases*

4. Activity theory predicts a _____ correlation between involvement and aging and a _____ correlation between involvement and satisfaction with life.   *negative*   *positive*

5. Activity theory also suggests that older adults who lose a role should find a _____ role.   *substitute*

6. Social _____ -reconstruction theory argues that a negative view of older adults by society and inadequate services lead to poor psychological functioning.   *breakdown*

7. Social _____ may occur when a society changes its views of older adults and provides them with adequate support services.   *reconstruction*
8. Indicate how activity and social breakdown-reconstruction theories could improve the lives of older adults.

B. Stereotyping Older Adults

1. Prejudice against older adults is called _____ .   *ageism*
2. Firing people because of their age or denying them access to services or products exemplify _____ .   *ageism*
3. List seven stereotypes of the aged found among adults of all ages.

4. The _____ number of older age adults has prompted active efforts to improve the image of the elderly.   *increasing*
5. A political group promoting the concerns of older adults is the American Association of _____ Persons.   *Retired*

C. Police Issues in an Aging Society

1. The major _____ issues relating to an aging society revolve around the economy, the viability of the Social Security system, health care, eldercare, and generational inequity.   *policy*
2. Concerns about the _____ focus on the possible inability of the younger generation to provide the money necessary to provide for the older generation.   *economy*
3. Currently, the Social Security system _____ in jeopardy.   *is not*
4. Explain why an aging society prompts concerns about the availability and cost of health care.

5. A health _____ model is more appropriate than a health _____ model for the health needs of the elderly.   *care*
   cure
5. The _____ is the only industrialized nation that provides health insurance to older adults and not to the entire population.   *USA*
6. Despite the fact than many older people suffer from _____ illnesses, the medical system is set up to deal only with acute illnesses.   *chronic*
7. In other words, the system is oriented toward _____ rather than _____ .   *cure; care*
8. A _____-based system of care requires a new type of cooperative relationship among patients, medical care practitioners, and families.   *home*
9. Express the concept of *eldercare* in your own words.

10. Government assistance to families for home support of the elderly has developed _____ .   *slowly*
11. When older adults receive advantages and a disproportionately larger amount of the resources, generational _____ becomes an issue.   *inequity*
12. Identify the conflicts that generational inequity produced in American society.

13 Bernice Neugarten suggests that the society would profit by thinking about what the _____ aspects of aging would mean to America.   *positive*
14. Neugarten also believes that positive view would _____ the range of options for individuals of all different age groups.   *increase*

D. Income

1. Indicate the incidence of poverty in the United States.

2. Compared with people under 65, people over 65 spend a _____ portion of their income for food, utilities, and health care and a _____ portion for transportation, clothing, and entertainment.   *greater*
   smaller

3. Middle-aged adults who will retire in the next twenty years will need a retirement that is _____ percent of their current income.   *75*

E. Living Arrangements

1. Although one stereotype is that older adults are all in residents institutions, nearly _____ percent of older adults live in the community.   *95*

2. About one-third of the elderly live _____ , and most of them are widowed.   *alone*

3. Older adults who live _____ are usually in good health, have few disabilities, and have regular social exchanges with friends and relatives.   *alone*

4. The vast majority of older adults favor living _____ .   *independently*

2.0 Ethnicity, Gender, and Culture

A. Ethnicity and Gender

1. African American and Latino elderly are _____ likely than White American elderly to be poor.   *more*

2. Explain what it means to say that ethnic minority individuals face a double jeopardy.

3. Although elderly women face the _____ jeopardy of ageism and sexism, elderly women who belong to a minority group face the _____ jeopardy of ageism, sexism, and racism.   *double*
   triple

4. Describe coping mechanisms of elderly ethnic minority individuals.

B. Gender Roles

1. Gender roles may _____ with increasing age.   *change*

2. Older _____ become more feminine and show more sensitivity and more nurturance, but older _____ do not become more masculine.   *men*
   women

3. Explain the role of cohort effects when interpreting age effects in gender roles.

C. Culture

1. Characterize the lives of elderly Japanese.

2. Although Americans' images of the elderly in _____ is probably idealized and overexaggerated, the elderly receive more respect in _____ than the _____ .   *Japan*
   Japan: US

3. Review the _____ factors associated with higher status for the elderly members of a culture.

3.0 Families and Social Relationships

A. The Aging Couple and Friendship

1. Indicate how retirement alters a couple's life-style and changes the marriage relationship.

2. Individuals who are married in late adulthood are usually _____ than those who are single.   *happier*

3. Marital satisfaction is _____ for women than for men.   *greater*

4. Older adults who have never married seem to have the least difficulty dealing with _____ in old age.   *loneliness*

6. There is a larger number of older adults who _____ .

date

6. Regardless of their age, people seem to put a high priority on time spent with _____ .

friends

7. Characterize the friendships of the elderly.

B. Grandparenting

1. About _____ of every four adults over the age of 65 have at least one live grandchild.

3

2. About 80 percent of _____ say that they are happy in their relationships with their grandchildren.

grandparents

3. Grandfathers are _____ satisfied with their role as grandparent than grandmothers.

less

4. Maternal grandparents spend _____ time with their grandchildren than paternal grandparents.

more

5. Grandparenting means _____ things to different people.

different

6. For some, grandparenting is a source of _____ reward.

biological

7. For others, it is a source of _____ fulfillment.

emotional

8. Finally, for some it is only a _____ role.

remote

9. Describe ethnic variations in grandparenting.

10. Grandparenting can entail either a _____ , fun-seeking, or _____ style.

formal; distant

11. Grandparents who perform the formal grandparenting role, are proper, show a strong interest in their children, but who leave the parenting to the parents have a _____ style of grandparenting.

formal

12. Grandparents who spend time with grandchildren engaged in activities the children enjoy have a _____ style of grandparenting.

funloving

13. Grandparents who do not see their grandchildren very often, but are very kind to them when they do get together have a _____ figure style of grandparenting.

distant

14. Grandparents over the age of 65 were more likely to be _____ ; grandparents under the age of 65 more likely to be _____ .

formal
funloving

15. Speculate about the future of grandparenting.

4.0 Personality Development, Life Satisfaction, and Successful Aging

A. The Nature of Personality Development

1. Although Sigmund Freud and Carl Jung say old age is similar to _____ , recent theorists have emphasized the constructive and _____ nature of personality development in late adulthood.

childhood
adaptive

2. According to Erik Erikson, individuals in late adulthood must resolve the psychosocial conflict regarding _____ versus _____ .

integrity
despair

3. Summarize Erikson's views about the eighth and final psychosocial stage of development.

4. Robert Peck reworked Erikson's eighth psychosocial stage by describing _____ developmental tasks of late adulthood.

3

5. According to _____ , the differentiation versus role preoccupation stage involves the discovery of self-worth in terms of something other than _____ roles.

Peck
work

6. When older adults' view of themselves depends on their physical appearance and their health, they have trouble resolving the conflicts that occur at the body _____ versus body _____ stages of development.

transcendence
preoccupation

7. In the ego transcendence versus ego preoccupation stage, the developmental task is to recognize that _____ is inevitable, but that you have contributed to the future in a variety of ways.

death

8. A common theme in theories of personality development in late adulthood is the _____ *life* review.
9. State the concept of *life review* in your own words.

10 According to Robert Butler, life review is activated by a vision of _____ . *death*
11. Indicate how a life review influences relationships with others.

B. *Life Satisfaction*
1. Express the concept of *life satisfaction* in your own terms.

2. Income, health, life-style, and social networks are all positively associated with life _____ . *satisfaction*
3. Older adults often have a _____ optimistic perception of later-life development than middle- *more* aged adults.

C. *Successful Aging*
1. _____ aging occurs when older adults enjoy proper diet, exercise, mental stimulation, and *Successful* good social relationships and support.
2. Successful aging also requires _____ and _____ skills. *effort*
   coping
3. Paul Baltes believes that selection, _____ , and compensation contribute to successful *optimization* aging.
4. Explain, and provide an example of what Baltes means by:
   selection

   optimization

   compensation

5. The selective optimization with compensation model for successful aging is especially applicable *loss* in the case of _____ .

5.0 Chapter Boxes

A. *Sociocultural Worlds of Development: Being Female, Ethnic, and Old*
1. One's life as an ethnic female in late adulthood may be made difficult by negative stereotypes of *unimportant* the ethnic group and a cultural view that define older women's roles as _____ .
2. In the case of the Black culture, an older woman's status _____ . *improves*
3. Describe the survival strategies of aging African American women.

B. *Critical Thinking About Life-Span Development: Evaluating Stereotypes of the Elderly*
1. Indicate what you would learn by comparing and contrasting portrayals of the elderly in contemporary and earlier magazines of the 20th century.

C. *Critical Thinking About Life-Span Development: Middle-Aged Baby Boomers and Their Grandparents*

  1. Indicate what you would learn by comparing and contrasting the values and attitudes of baby boomers and their grandparents.

D. *Life-Span Health and Well-Being: Social Support and Health in Late Adulthood*

  1. Toni Antonnuci suggests that social support will improve the _____ of older adults.   *health*

  2. Indicate evidence that social support improves the health of older adults.

  3 Indicate the emerging concerns for caregivers to the elderly.

Self Test A: Key Terms and Key Persons

Write the appropriate key term or key person in the space to the right of the definition or description.

  1. The theory that activity positively correlates with satisfaction with life.   _____

  2. The physical and emotional caretaking for older members of the family.   _____

  3. One of the three social theories of aging that contends negative societal views and inadequate social services promote aging.   _____

  4. The individual who reworked Erik Erikson's eighth psychosocial stage of development.   _____

  5. A social policy issue that concerns the allocation of resources in a way that favors older members over younger members of the society.   _____

  6. Either of the two psychoanalysts who viewed old age as similar to childhood.   _____

  7. Robert Peck's label for one of the three developmental tasks faced by older adults who must define themselves in terms of something other than their work roles.   _____

  8. A view that successful aging is the result of the three factors of selection, optimization, and compensation.   _____

  9. A widely used index of general well-being, particularly for older adults.   _____

  10. Prejudicial and discriminatory acts against an individual on the basis of their age.   _____

Self Test B: Multiple Choice

1. Those who adopt a disengagement theory of aging believe that
   a. as older adults slow down they gradually withdraw from society.
   b. the more active adults are, the less likely they will age.
   c. the more active adults are, the more satisfied they will be.
   d. negative societal attitudes about aging limit the number and kind of services older adults receive.

2. When Sarah sold her business and retired, she gradually became less active and withdrew from society. This is an example of the _____ theory of aging.
   a. activity
   b. life review
   c. life satisfaction
   d. disengagement

3. As an older retired adult, Bill maintains his interest in friends, golf, and the stock market. He best illustrates the _____ theory of aging.
   a. engagement
   b. disengagement
   c. activity
   d. generational equity

4. According to activity theory, when one of an older person's roles is taken away from him or her, he or she should
   a. withdraw from society.
   b. become self-preoccupied.
   c. lessen emotional ties with others.
   d. find a replacement role.

5. Margaret finds that reaching old age is made more stressful by the general impatience and disregard that society displays toward her. She best illustrates the _____ theory of aging.
   a. social breakdown-reconstruction
   b. disengagement
   c. activity
   d. generational disparity

6. _____ is a term that is defined as negative social stereotyping of older adults.
   a. Scapegoating
   b. Ageism
   c. Generation gap
   d. Senility

7. All but which of the following are examples of ageism?
   a. mandatory retirement ages
   b. when older couples holding hands are labeled as cute
   c. when older adults are asked to serve as "grandparents" for teenage parents
   d. letting employees go because they reach a certain age

8. People over 65 make up about 12 percent of the population and account for _____ percent of the total health-care bill in the United States.
   a. about 12
   b. over 25
   c. over 30
   d. over 50

9. One philosophical concern over the current medical system is that it is
   a. "care"-oriented, while most elderly health problems are chronic.
   b. "care"-oriented, while most elderly health problems are acute.
   c. "cure"-oriented, while most elderly health problems are chronic.
   d. "cure"-oriented, while most elderly health problems are acute.

0. Which group is affected the most by rising medical costs?
   a. parents of newborn children
   b. single-parent families
   c. middle-aged adults who smoke and use alcohol
   d. older adults

11. Problems with eldercare include all but which of the following?
    a. the age of the persons giving the care
    b. the increasing number of women in the job market
    c. the uncooperativeness of the medical profession
    d. the costs

12. A policy issue that focuses upon the greater amount of resources received by the elderly compared to those received by younger adults is referred to as
    a. generational equity.
    b. eldercare.
    c. ageism.
    d. role preoccupation.

13. Sixty-year-old Ann is single and living alone. If she is typical of single, elderly females, it is most likely that Ann is
    a. emotionally depressed.
    b. among the physically disabled population.
    c. poor.
    d. more in control of her life.

14. The poorest population group in America is
    a. Black females over 70.
    b. the so-called "hidden poor."
    c. Hispanic Americans with severe physical disabilities.
    d. ethnic American males who must depend upon churches for assistance.

15. During the 1970s and 1980s, poverty among both elderly and nonelderly adults
    a. rose sharply.
    b. rose slightly.
    c. did not change.
    d. declined.

16. Most elderly adults prefer to live
    a. alone or with spouses.
    b. with an adult child or relatives.
    c. in a retirement community.
    d. in the Sunbelt.

17. Who is the best example of the concept of "triple jeopardy?"
    a. Maximilian, who is 75 years old, poor, White, and male
    b. Mattia, who is 75 years old, poor, Black, and female
    c. Carlos, who is 15 years old, poor, Hispanic, and male
    d. Doua who is 15 years old, poor, Asian, and female

18. All of the following support systems help older American minority women cope with their triple jeopardy except
    a. their husbands.
    b. their churches.
    c. their families.
    d. their neighbors.

19. Traditionally, Americans have associated the ideas of high status for the elderly with _____ cultures.
    a. Australian
    b. Asian
    c. Eastern Europe
    d. South American

20. Which 72-year-old has a characteristic which *is not* typically associated with elevating the status of elderly individuals within a culture?
    a. Melvyn, who, like most people in his country, will live to be about 90
    b. Louis, who controls his family's wealth
    c. Haing, who possess information valuable to the welfare of his country
    d. Walter, who is given promotions and more authority in his company based on performance and time on the job

21. Retirement seems to lead to greatest changes in a
    a. "traditional" family with a working male and homemaking female.
    b. families where both spouses work and retire at the same time.
    c. families in which both parents work, but retire at different times.
    d. single-parent household.

22. The traditional older couple adjust best to retirement when
    a. the husband gets a part-time job.
    b. the wife gets a part-time job.
    c. both members of the couple become more expressive.
    d. both members of the couple become more independent.

23. The key ingredient to the dating relationship for older adults is
    a. the availability of a sexual partner.
    b. companionship.
    c. the availability of a dance partner.
    d. physical attraction.

24. When it comes to falling in love, older adult daters, compared to their younger dating counterparts,
    a. report the same feelings.
    b. are more relaxed.
    c. seldom label their feelings as romantic love.
    d. are more likely to "play the field."

25. Which of the following facts about grandparents is true?
    a. grandfathers are more satisfied with the grandparenting role than grandmothers
    b. younger grandparents are less willing to care for grandchildren than older grandparents
    c. paternal grandparents spend less time with their grandchildren than maternal grandparents
    d. about 50 percent of grandparents say they are happy with their relationship with their grandchildren

26. Regarding their relationship with grandchildren, most grandparents report that
    a. grandchildren these days show little respect for their elders.
    b. grandfathers are more satisfied than grandmothers.
    c. grandparenting is less difficult than parenting.
    d. older grandparents, compared to younger grandparents, are more likely to be stricter with grandchildren.

27. In the _____ style, according to Neugarten and Weinstein, grandparents were a source of leisure activity who emphasized mutual satisfaction.
    a. formal
    b. fun-seeking
    c. distant
    d. nurturant

28. Which of the following grandparents is most likely to display a formal style of interaction?
    a. one under 65 who lives near grandchildren
    b. one over 65 who lives near grandchildren
    c. one over 65 who lives far away from grandchildren
    d. one under 65 who lives far away from grandchildren

29. Erik Erikson believed that which final life-cycle stage characterizes late adulthood?
    a. integrity versus despair
    b. trust versus mistrust
    c. identity versus role confusion
    d. autonomy versus inferiority

30. Which of the following developmental tasks, according to Robert Peck, requires older adults to face and accept the reality of death and the value of their lives?
    a. life review versus life satisfaction
    b. differentiation versus role preoccupation
    c. body transcendence versus body preoccupation
    d. ego transcendence versus ego preoccupation

31. Older adults who have derived part of their identity from their physical appearance are going to have the most difficult time with Peck's _____ developmental stage.
    a. differentiation versus role preoccupation
    b. ego transcendence versus ego preoccupation
    c. keeping the meaning versus rigidity
    d. body transcendence versus body preoccupation

32. Life review can produce all but which of the following?
    a. increased fear of death
    b. the discovery of the meaning of one's life
    c. a new sense of self
    d. an opportunity to share insights with significant others

33. The concept of self-esteem in adolescence is analogous to the concept of _____ in late adulthood.
    a. self-efficacy
    b. life satisfaction
    c. self-definition
    d. life orientation

34. According to the optimization component of the selective optimization with compensation model, a 70-year-old secretary who complains about her poor eyesight interfering with her proofreading skills should
    a. buy a computer with a built-in grammar and spell checker.
    b. just accept the fact that she cannot perform the way she used to.
    c. practice grammar and spell checking during her off-time.
    d. quit her job.

35. Traditionally, elderly _____ females have actually improved their social status.
    a. Asian
    b. Black
    c. Hispanic
    d. All of the answers are correct.

Answers for Self Test A

1. activity theory
2. eldercare
3. social breakdown-reconstruction theory
4. Robert Peck
5. generational inequity
6. Sigmund Freud or Carl Jung
7. body transcendence versus body preoccupation
8. selective optimization with compensation model
9. life satisfaction
10. ageism

Answers for Self Test B

1.	a	LO 1.1
2.	d	LO 1.1
3.	c	LO 1.2
4.	d	LO 1.2
5.	a	LO 1.3
6.	b	LO 1.4
7.	c	LO 1.4
8.	c	LO 1.7
9.	c	LO 1.8
10.	d	LO 1.9
11.	c	LO 1.9
12.	a	LO 1.10
13.	c	LO 1.11
14.	a	LO 1.11
15.	d	LO 1.11
16.	c	LO 1.13
17.	b	LO 2.3
18.	a	LO 2.4
19.	b	LO 2.6
20.	a	LO 2.7
21.	a	LO 3.1
22.	c	LO 3.2
23.	b	LO 3.3
24.	a	LO 3.3
25.	c	LO 3.4
26.	c	LO 3.4
27.	b	LO 3.5
28.	c	LO 3.5
29.	a	LO 4.2
30.	d	LO 4.3
31.	d	LO 4.3
32.	a	LO 4.5
33.	b	LO 4.6
34.	a	LO 4.9
35.	b	LO 5.1

Chapter 21   Death and Dying

Learning Objectives with Key Terms in Boldface

1.0 Defining Death and Life/Death Issues

  A. *Issues in Determining Death*

    1.1   Indicate how death was defined 25 years ago.

    1.2   Define **brain death** and indicate controversies concerning its definition.

  B. *Decisions Regarding Life, Death, and Health Care*

    1.3   Define and distinguish between **living wills** and **durable powers of attorney**.

    1.4   Define **euthanasia** and distinguish between **active euthanasia** and **passive euthanasia**.

    1.5   Indicate the legal and ethical issues each type of euthanasia raises.

2.0 Death and Sociohistorical, Cultural Contexts

  A. *Changing Historical Circumstances*

    2.1   Indicate historical changes in the incidence of death.

  B. *Death in Different Cultures*

    2.2   Compare and contrast the meaning and experience of death in several past and present cultures.

    2.3   List ways that we deny death in the United States.

3.0 A Developmental Perspective on Death

  A. *Causes of Death and Expectations About Death*

    3.1   Define **sudden infant death syndrome (SIDS)**.

    3.2   Indicate the typical causes of death during the major life periods.

  B. *Attitudes Toward Death at Different Points in the Life Span*

    3.3   Describe and compare attitudes toward death typical of children, adolescents, and adults.

4.0 Facing One's Own Death

    4.1   Discuss how knowledge of one's own death influences younger and older adults.

  A. *Kübler-Ross's Stages of Dying*

    4.2   Define and distinguish among Elisabeth Kübler-Ross's **denial and isolation, anger, bargaining, depression**, and **acceptance** stages of dying.

    4.3   Evaluate Kübler-Ross's claims about the sequence and adaptive value of her stages of death.

  B. *Perceived Control and Denial*

    4.4   Compare and contrast the benefits and drawbacks of perceived control and denial approaches to death.

  C. *The Contexts in Which People Die*

    4.5   Compare and contrast hospitals, homes, and **hospices** as places in which people die.

    4.6   Discuss current issues in and concerns about hospice care for the dying.

5.0 Coping with the Death of Someone Else

  A. *Communicating with a Dying Person*

    5.1   Explain why dying people should know they are dying.

    5.2   List recommendations about how to converse with a dying individual.

  B. *Stages and Dimensions of Grief*

    5.3   Define **grief**, and distinguish among the shock, despair, and recovery stages of grief as applied to the death of another.

    5.4   Compare the stages of grief to Kübler-Ross's stages of dying.

Guided Review and Study

1.0 Defining Death and Life/Death Issues

A. *Issues in Determining Death*

  1. Twenty-five years ago the end of certain biological functions and the rigidity of the body were clear signs of _____ .   *death*

  2. A neurological definition of death is called _____ death.   *brain*

  3. A person is _____ dead when all electrical activity of the brain has ceased for a specified period of time.   *brain*

  4. A flat _____ recording for a specified period of time is one criterion of brain dead.   *EEG*

  5. Summarize the controversy regarding the definition of brain death.

B. *Decisions Regarding Life, Death, and Health Care*

  1. Express the concept of *living will* in your own words.

  2. Explain the concept of *durable power of attorney* in your own words.

3. _____ refers to the act of painlessly putting a person to death who is suffering from an incurable disease.

Euthanasia

4. Euthanasia is sometimes called _____ killing.

mercy

5. Define and provide an example of:

active euthanasia

passive euthanasia

6. Issues of _____ of life arise from the technological advances in life-support devices.

quality

7. Explain why some say that dying has become medicalized and distorted.

2.0 Death and Sociohistorical, Cultural Contexts

A. Changing Historical Circumstances

1. Three _____ changes regarding death include the complexity of determining when a person is dead, an _____ likelihood that death will not occur until late adulthood, and an _____ likelihood that a person will die away from his or her family.

historical
increased
increased

B. Death in Different Cultures

1. The prevailing goal of the _____ was to live a full life and die in glory.

Greeks

2. In contrast, _____ learn to live as though they were never going to die.

Americans

3. Most societies have a death _____ .

ritual

4. Most societies _____ view death as the end of existence.

do not

5. Perceptions about death vary and reflect the diverse values of different _____ .

cultures

6. Explain what it means to say that the citizens of the United States are predominantly death avoiders and deniers.

3.0 A Developmental Perspective on Death

A. Causes of Death and Expectations about Death

1. Individuals _____ at different ages for different reasons

die

2. Sudden infant death syndrome, or _____ , refers to the sudden death of an apparently healthy infant that usually occurs between 2 to 4 months of age for no apparent reason.

SIDS

3. Indicate the major causes of death during childhood.

4. Compared with childhood, death in _____ is more likely to result from suicide, automobile accidents, and homicide.

adolescence

5. _____ adults are more likely to die from chronic diseases, whereas _____ adults are more likely to die from accidents.

Older
younger

B. Attitudes Toward Death at Different Points in the Life Span

1. A _____ conception of death includes an understanding of the finality of death, the irreversible nature of death, that death represents the end of life, and that all living things die.

mature

2. Children, adolescents, and adults have different _____ toward death.

attitudes

3. In infancy, the loss of a _____ can negatively affect the infant's health.

parent

4. Children between the ages of 3 and 5 may confuse death with _____ .

sleep

5. Young children may blame _____ for the death of someone close to them.

themselves

6. Research indicates that that children _____ years of age and older begin to recognize the finality and universality of death.   *9*

7. Describe the strategy that most psychologists believe is best for discussing death with children.

8. In _____ the subject of death may be avoided, glossed over, joked about, and otherwise neutralized.   *adolescence*

9. Adolescents develop more _____ conceptions of death than children do.   *abstract*

10. Indicate the orientations toward death in early adulthood, middle adulthood, and late adulthood.

11. Adults who fear death the most are usually in the _____ adulthood period of development.   *middle*

12. Indicate why older adult may be more accepting of death than individuals in other phases of the life span.

4.0 Facing One's Own Death

1. When asked how they would spend the last six months of their lives, _____ adults said they would travel and complete unfinished projects, whereas _____ adults said they would spend time in thought and meditation.   *younger* *older*

A. Kübler-Ross's Stages of Dying

1. Elisabeth Kübler-Ross divided the behavior of dying people into _____ stages: denial, anger, bargaining, depression, and acceptance.   *5*

2. Characterize the following five Kübler-Ross stage of dying:

    denial and isolation

    anger

    bargaining

    depression

    acceptance

3. Although Kübler-Ross never intended the stages to be an _____ sequence of steps toward death, she did argue that those who go through the five stages _____ their ability to face death.   *invariant* *optimize*

B. Perceived Control and Denial

1. Perceived control and _____ may work together to help some older adults face death.   *denial*

2. Explain what it means to say that denial may be a fruitful way for some individuals to approach death.

3. There are _____ forms of denial. For example, individuals who deny their death may deny _____ , the implications of the disease or circumstances, or the finality of death.

3
facts

4. The potential _____ and _____ consequences of denial must be evaluated on an individual basis.

positive
negative

C. The Contexts in Which People Die

1. Most people die in one of _____ contexts: either in a hospital or other type of institution, at home, or in a hospice.

three

2. Dying in a _____ offers the advantages of readily available professional staff members and life-prolonging medical advances.

hospital

3. Most individuals prefer to die at _____ , but also worry about the lack of space, the burden they place on others, and the availability of professional help.

home

4. Describe the methods and conclusions of a study of 9,000 acutely ill patients in a hospital.

5. An institution committed to making the end of life as free from pain and anxiety as possible is called a _____ .

hospice

6. The _____ movement began in London in the early 1960s with the primary goals bringing pain under control and in helping individuals face death in a psychologically healthy way.

hospice

7. The dying member's _____ is frequently included in the care given by the hospice

family

8. Portray the hospice movement in the United States.

5.0 Coping with the Death of Someone Else

A. Communicating with a Dying Person

1. Most psychologists believe that it is best for _____ individuals to know they are _____ .

dying
dying

2. Indicate several advantages of knowing you are dying.

3. Conversations with a dying individual should focus on the dying person's _____ growth.

internal

4. Review Table 21.1 for some effective strategies for communicating with a dying person.

B. Stage and Dimensions of Grief

1. The emotional numbness, disbelief, anxiety, despair, sadness, and loneliness that accompany the loss of a loved one is called _____ .

grief

2. Averill indicates that we undergo the three stages of _____ : shock, despair, and recovery, whereas Parkes proposes that the four stages of grief are numbness, pining, _____ , and recovery.

grief
depression

3. According to Averill, the shock stage of grief usually lasts about _____ to _____ days.

1; 3

4. The painful longing for the dead, memories of the deceased, and sadness, insomnia, and restlessness characterize the second or _____ stage of grief.

despair

5. When a grieving person resumes ordinary activities and begins to recall pleasant memories of the dead individual he or she is in the _____ stage of grief.

recovery

5. Like Kübler-Ross's stages of dying, the stages of grief _____ invariant.

are not

7. As an alternative to _____ of grief, one might consider the _____ of grief such as pining, separation anxiety, emotional blunting, despair and sadness, and recovery.

stages
dimensions

C. Making Sense of the World

1. A benefit of _____ is that it stimulates many individuals to make sense of their world.

grieving

2. Each _____ individual may contribute something to this process.

bereaved

D. Losing a Life Partner

 1. Usually the most difficult death is the death of an _____ partner.   *intimate*

 2. There are _____ times as many widows as widowers.   *5*

 3. Indicate factors that promote optimal adjustment after a death of a life partner.

 4. _____ support helps widows or widowers adjust to the death of a spouse.   *Social*

E. Forms of Mourning and the Funeral

 1. _____ refers to the Hindu practice of burning a dead man's widow to increase the family's   *Suttee*
    prestige.

 2. The _____ is an important aspect of mourning and provides a form of closure to the   *funeral*
    relationship with the deceased in many cultures.

 3. About 1 in _____ bodies in the United States is cremated.   *11*

 4. Indicate the controversy regarding the funeral industry.

 5. Although individuals can make _____ arrangements in advance to avoid exploitation at the *funeral*
    time of death, only about _____ percent of the individuals over 60 have made funeral   *24*
    arrangements.

6.0 Death Education

 1. People who study death and dying are called _____ .   *thanatologists*

 2. Thanatologists believe that death _____ provides a positive preparation for both the dying *education*
    and living.

 3. In many ways the United States remains a death-_____ society.   *avoiding*

7.0 Chapter Boxes

A. *Sociocultural Worlds of Development: The Family and Community in Mourning —The Amish and Traditional Judaism*

 1. Compare and contrast the roles of family and community in mourning among the Amish and
    traditional Jews.

B. *Critical Thinking About Life-Span Development: Exploring Your Own Death and Dying*

 1. Answer the various questions about your own death and dying and indicate what you can learn
    from this endeavor.

C. *Critical Thinking About Life-Span Development: Talking with Individuals Who Interact on a Regular Basis with People Who Are Dying*

 1. Indicate what you would learn by talking with and identifying the perspectives of people who
    interact on a regular basis with people who are dying.

D. *Life-Span Health and Well-Being: Diversity in Healthy Grieving*

 1. Contemporary orientations on grieving emphasize the importance of breaking _____ with   *bonds*
    the deceased and the return of survivors to _____ lifestyles.   *autonomous*

 2. Non-western cultures demonstrate varied beliefs about continuing bonds with the _____ . *deceased*

 3. Describe the methods and conclusions of three studies about maintaining contact with the
    deceased.

4. Although different peoples _____ in various ways, healthy grieving entails growth, flexibility, and appropriateness within a _____ context.

grieve
cultural

Self Test A: Key Terms and Key Persons

Write the appropriate key term or key person in the space to the right of the definition or description.

1. A neurological definition of death that specifies electrical brain activity must be absent for a specified period of time. _____

2. A document that ensures an individual's rights to choose whether to accept heroic measures to sustain his or her life. _____

3. A stage of dying according to Elisabeth Kübler-Ross in which the person hopes death can be delayed somehow. _____

4. Individuals who study the phenomena of death and dying. _____

5. The individual known as the "suicide doctor." _____

6. A context for dying in which the emphasis is placed on minimizing pain, anxiety, and depression rather than on curing illness and prolonging life. _____

7. The unusual death of an apparently healthy infant who stops breathing, which often occurs between 2 and 4 months of age; the cause is unknown. _____

8. The individual who proposed a five stage theory of dying. _____

9. The act of painlessly putting a person to death deliberately by such means as injecting a lethal dose of a drug in contrast to simply withholding available treatment. _____

10. The emotional numbness that result from the loss of someone we love. _____

Self Test B: Multiple Choice

1. Twenty-five years ago all but which of the following were clear signs of death?
   a. lack of breathing
   b. rigor mortis
   c. brain death
   d. nonexistent blood pressure

2. Although the actual nature of "death" remains under debate, it appears that if 20-year-old Britt were in an accident and suffered cellular death to all areas above the lower brain stem, doctors would most likely agree that Britt is _____ dead.
   a. psychologically
   b. physiologically
   c. philosophically
   d. clinically

3. Active euthanasia is
   a. allowing the patients, if they so choose, to self-administer a lethal dose of drug.
   b. letting the person die naturally.
   c. the intentional administration of a lethal drug dose by medical personnel to the dying patient.
   d. allowing the dying patient to decide when painkilling drugs should be administered.

4. Most people tend to find fewer ethical problems with _____ euthanasia, especially when it involves older, terminally ill individuals.
   a. involuntary
   b. active
   c. intentional
   d. passive

5. In the United States about _____ percent of all deaths occur in institutions or hospitals.
   a. 20
   b. 50
   c. 80
   d. 90

6. Which of the following represents the predominant attitude to death in the United States?
   a. general acceptance of the aged in our communities
   b. the medical community's general interest in reducing human suffering
   c. acceptance
   d. searching for a fountain of youth

7. Denial of death in the United States takes all but which of the following forms?
   a. the use of phrases like passing on
   b. the never-ending search for a fountain of youth
   c. the emphasis on human suffering rather than on prolonging life
   d. the rejection of the elderly

8. One day Jennifer gets a call from her sister who informs Jennifer that her niece has died from sudden infant death syndrome (SIDS). As a physician, Jennifer realizes that while the cause of SIDS remains unknown, her niece actually died because
   a. she had a heart attack.
   b. she stopped breathing.
   c. she had a massive cerebrovascular accident.
   d. her immune system failed.

9. Older adults are more likely to die of _____ ; younger adults more often die of _____ .
   a. suicide; homicide
   b. accidents; chronic disease
   c. chronic disease; accidents
   d. homicide; suicide

10. Death in childhood is most often the result of
    a. childhood diseases.
    b. SIDS.
    c. accidents or illness.
    d. cancer.

11. Most preschool-aged children are not upset by seeing a dead animal. The most likely reason is that
    a. the dead animal is not a pet and they, therefore, have not become attached to it.
    b. they have often seen dead animals and heard of death in stories and on TV.
    c. they have had little experience with death and, therefore, have not learned to fear it.
    d. they believe that the dead can be made alive again.

12. An individual who believes that people die because they were bad or because they wanted to die is most likely in the _____ period of development.
    a. infancy
    b. early childhood
    c. middle or late childhood
    d. adolescence

13. The individual who glosses over death and kids about it but can also describe it in terms of darkness and nothingness is most likely in the _____ period of development.
    a. middle childhood
    b. late childhood
    c. adolescent
    d. early adulthood

14. The advantages of knowing that you are dying include all but which of the following?
    a. being able to finish unfinished projects
    b. dying the way you want to die
    c. having the opportunity to reminisce
    d. the stress of knowing that you are dying may speed up the process

15. When asked how they would spend the next six months of their lives if they knew they were going to die, older adults are more likely than younger adults to want to
    a. travel.
    b. be alone.
    c. finish a project around the house.
    d. read all of the books they never had time to read.

16. The order of the stages of dying as proposed by Elisabeth Kübler-Ross are
    a. denial, anger, bargaining, acceptance, depression.
    b. anger, denial, bargaining, depression, acceptance.
    c. denial, anger, bargaining, depression, acceptance.
    d. anger, bargaining, acceptance, depression, denial.

17. During which stage of death is a person most likely to request to be alone?
    a. denial
    b. bargaining
    c. depression
    d. acceptance

18. The biggest complaint against Elisabeth Kübler-Ross's stages of dying is that they
    a. don't actually form an invariant sequence.
    b. only apply to females.
    c. last much longer than she thought.
    d. only explain the pattern found in older adults.

19. Denial of death comes in all but which of the following forms?
    a. denying the facts
    b. denying the implications of disease
    c. denying the finality of death
    d. denying the inevitability of death

20. Which idea is in direct contrast to the underlying goals of a hospice?
    a. morphine for pain
    b. family for support
    c. cure for a disorder
    d. no intensive-care unit

21. When the terminally ill patient becomes depressed, others should
    a. attempt to cheer up the patient.
    b. talk about anything other than death.
    c. accept the depression as normal.
    d. tell the medical staff about this turn of events.

22. A person who has just lost a parent and is having trouble sleeping, is restless, and thinks of the dead parent often is most likely in the _____ stage of grief.
    a. shock
    b. numbness
    c. despair
    d. recovery

23. Grief work for a spouse is coming to an end when the mourner
    a. begins to date again.
    b. recalls the good times shared with the person who died.
    c. sells the house and moves away.
    d. stops crying and returns to work.

24. During Averill's _____ stage of grief, the survivors remember and long for the deceased, as well as experience sleeplessness and general irritability.
    a. shock
    b. recovery
    c. despair
    d. pining

25. Which of Averill's stages of grief is similar to Kübler-Ross's acceptance stage for the dying person?
    a. despair
    b. shock
    c. recovery
    d. pining

26. Which family is engaging in the most common postdeath group experience concerning the loss of a family member?
    a. The Cleavers, who each blame themselves for Jerry's death
    b. The Conners, who refuse to discuss anything about Melissa's recent death
    c. The Cartwrights, who seem to be reliving and recalling more about the last few weeks of Loren's life
    d. The Mitchells, who are thinking about only positive interactions that occurred with Jay before his death

27. Which of the following life stresses requires the most adjustment, according to your textbook?
    a. death of an infant
    b. death of a beloved pet
    c. death of a spouse
    d. death of a sibling

28. _____ is an outlawed Hindu practice in which widows of deceased men were burned.
    a. Hara-kiri
    b. Mortali
    c. Suttee
    d. Mensa

29. Recently the common U.S. funeral practice of _____ has come under fire as being simply a money-making scheme.
    a. putting bodies in a casket
    b. open caskets
    c. underground burial
    d. prefuneral wakes

30. Which practice is *not* commonly associated with Amish mourning?
    a. holding the funeral ceremony in a barn
    b. a horse and buggy "hearse"
    c. a deceased body dressed in black
    d. support for bereaved family members

Answers for Self Test A

1. brain death
2. living will
3. bargaining
4. thanatologist
5. Jack Kevorkian
6. hospice
7. sudden infant death syndrome (SIDS)
8. Elisabeth Kübler-Ross
9. active euthanasia
10. grief

Answers for Self Test B

1. c   LO 1.1
2. a   LO 1.2
3. c   LO 1.4
4. d   LO 1.5
5. c   LO 2.1
6. d   LO 2.2
7. c   LO 2.3
8. b   LO 3.1
9. c   LO 3.2
10. c   LO 3.2
11. d   LO 3.3
12. b   LO 3.3
13. c   LO 3.3
14. d   LO 4.1
15. b   LO 4.1
16. c   LO 4.2
17. c   LO 4.2
18. a   LO 4.3
19. c   LO 4.4
20. c   LO 4.5
21. c   LO 5.2
22. c   LO 5.3
23. b   LO 5.3
24. c   LO 5.3
25. c   LO 5.4
26 c   LO 5.6
27. c   LO 5.7
28. c   LO 5.10
29. b   LO 5.12
30. c   LO 7.1